THE MYTHOLOGY OF CRIME AND CRIMINAL JUSTICE

Second Edition

THE MYTHOLOGY OF CRIME AND CRIMINAL JUSTICE

Second Edition

Victor E. Kappeler
Eastern Kentucky University

Mark Blumberg
Central Missouri State University

Gary W. Potter
Eastern Kentucky University

WAVELAND
PRESS, INC.

Prospect Heights, Illinois

For information about this book, write or call:
Waveland Press, Inc.
P.O. Box 400
Prospect Heights, Illinois 60070
(847) 634-0081

Chapter Opener Photo Credits

Chapter 3, Jan Weissman; Chapter 4, Milwaukee Sentinel Photo; Chapter 8, UPI/Bettman News Photos; Chapter 9, *Chicago Tribune* Photo by Chris Walker; Chapter 10, *Chicago Tribune* Photo by Carl Wagner; Chapter 11, AP/Wide World Photos; Chapter 12, AP/Wide World Photos; Chapter 13, *Chicago Tribune* Photo by Chris Walker; Chapter 15, *Chicago Tribune* Photo by Jim Prisching.

Acknowledgments

Our book made its way into print through the vision of many people who directly contributed to the work or contributed to the authors' development. Not the least of these people are Carol and Neil Rowe of Waveland Press, Inc. They either took a risk or just became tired of reading traditional criminal justice textbooks. We openly acknowledge their vision and contribution to our work and the field of criminal justice. We also note the special contribution of Dr. Philip Jenkins for allowing us to include his excellent chapter on serial murder.

One of the demands of "scholarly" writing is to credit the source of information and ideas. We have attempted to meet this demand but have found it a difficult task since ideas are often the product of past conversations, education, and misplaced readings that tend to fold into one another. We gratefully acknowledge the contributions of the following persons to our development: Dorothy Bracey, Dennis Longmire, Frank Williams, Victor G. Strecher, Peter B. Kraska, Larry K. Gaines, Stephen Mastrofski, William Chambliss, Donald Wallace, James J. Fyfe, Lawrence W. Sherman, Douglas Heckathorn, Robert Antonio, Roger C. Barnes, Geoffrey Alpert, and the late Donald J. Newman. Writing this book was a collaborative effort — three authors plus the contributions acknowledged above, aided by all the influences whose origins cannot be clearly delineated.

While it may be difficult to trace the evolution of the ideas which helped shape this book, it is easy to identify the people who helped guide the manuscript through the publishing process. We thank Kathleen Horn, Jeni Ogilvie, and Stephen Dungan of Waveland Press for their attention to detail and for smoothing the process for us.

About the Authors

Victor E. Kappeler is Associate Professor of Police Studies at Eastern Kentucky University in Richmond, Kentucky. He received undergraduate degrees in Police Administration and Juvenile Corrections as well as a master's degree in Criminal Justice from Eastern Kentucky University. His doctoral degree in Criminal Justice is from Sam Houston State University in Huntsville, Texas. Dr. Kappeler has written articles on issues related to police deviance, law and civil liability which have been published in *Justice Quarterly*, the *American Journal of Criminal Law*, the *American Journal of Police*, the *Journal of Police Science and Administration*, the *American Journal of Criminal Justice*, *Criminal Law Bulletin*, the *Journal of Criminal Justice*, and *Police Chief*, among others. He is co-author of *Policing in America*, and *Forces of Deviance: Understanding the Dark Side of Policing*. He is the author of *Critical Issues in Police Civil Liability* and editor of *Police and Society: Touchstone Readings*. Dr. Kappeler is the editor of *Justice Quarterly* and the founding editor of *Police Liability Review* and *Police Forum*.

Mark Blumberg is Professor of Criminal Justice at Central Missouri State University in Warrensburg, Missouri. He received his undergraduate and master's degrees in Sociology from the University of Kansas, Lawrence. He received an additional master's and doctoral degree in Criminal Justice from the State University of New York, Albany. Dr. Blumberg has written extensively on both police use of deadly force and on the impact of AIDS on various criminal justice issues. Dr. Blumberg has authored numerous book chapters and journal articles. His work has appeared in *Crime and Delinquency*, the *Criminal Law Bulletin*, *Justice Professional*, the *Prison Journal*, *Journal of Criminal Justice*, the *American Journal of Police* as well as in other publications. He is the author of an edited book entitled, *AIDS: The Impact on the Criminal Justice System*.

Gary W. Potter is Professor of Police Studies at Eastern Kentucky University in Richmond, Kentucky. He received his doctorate in Community Systems Planning and Development from Pennsylvania State University. Dr. Potter has co-authored *Drugs in Society* with Michael Lyman and *The City and the Syndicate* with Philip Jenkins. He is the author of *Criminal Organizations* and *The Porn Merchants*. He has written articles on issues related to organized crime which have been published in the *American Journal of Police*, *Corruption and Reform*, the *American Journal of Criminal Justice*, *Deviant Behavior*, *Criminal Justice History*, *Police Forum*, *Criminal Justice Policy Review*, *Policy Studies Review* and the *Journal of Criminal Justice*, among others.

Preface

In some respects, *The Mythology of Crime and Criminal Justice* may seem an improbable book. In a humorous vein, it is somewhat unlikely that graduates from the Pennsylvania State University, State University of New York, and Sam Houston State University would collaborate on anything more than professional conferences or occasional forays for field research purposes. It is said that these institutions of higher education approach issues of crime and justice from very divergent perspectives and produce very different scholars of justice. Perhaps this too is a myth of criminal justice. Admittedly, we do have very diverse backgrounds and interests; thus, perhaps it was unusual that we would collectively produce a book that addresses "myths" in criminal justice given the broad range of possible topics. That is, however, one of the wonders of academia and one of the strengths of the social sciences. Divergent people, ideas, and approaches to understanding contribute to an environment where varying perspectives, interests, and backgrounds can blend to create unique works.

On a more serious note, the most unlikely part of this collaboration is that a publisher would agree to expend the resources and energies required to produce and market this work. It is not that each author has not published books in the past or made scholarly contributions to the literature (or so we would like to think). Rather, this book does not fit neatly into any specific academic category. The book is not pure sociology, criminology, or criminal justice. It is certainly not a work that would fall under any single recognized ideological or theoretical framework. It is neither a radical nor a traditional approach to criminology, conflict or functionalist sociology. It is also not a traditional systems or empirical approach to criminal justice.

What we have tried to create is a work that focuses on very popular issues of criminal justice — issues that have captured the attention of the public as well as the scholarly community. Our hope is that the work challenges many popular notions of crime, criminals, and crime control. Unlike many other texts available, this book offers students of crime and justice an alternative to traditional criminal justice texts. Each chapter of this book questions our most basic assumptions of crime and justice and traces the development of a crime problem from its creation to society's integration of a myth into popular thinking and eventually social policy.

At the risk of characterizing the work as everything to everybody, we feel that it has broad application. The issues selected challenge habitual perspectives. Although the book was written for the undergraduate student, it could also stimulate discussion in the graduate classroom. It can be used as an alternative to standard introductory treatments of criminal justice or as a supplement to criminology or issues-orientated classes. Even though we feel the work has broad application, it was not intended to be the last word in myths of crime or justice. Rather, we hope that the text will serve as a very good starting point for understanding the realities of criminal justice and as an alternative to reinforcing crime myths in the classroom.

Victor E. Kappeler
Eastern Kentucky University

Mark Blumberg
Central Missouri State University

Gary W. Potter
Eastern Kentucky University

Contents

4   Myth and Murder
The Serial Killer Panic

5   Of Stalkers and Murder
Spreading Myth to Common Crime

6   Blue Smoke and Mirrors
The "War" on Organized Crime

11   Order in the Courts   235
The Myth of Equal Justice

12   Cons and Country Clubs   257
The Mythical Utility of Punishment

13   The Myth of a Lenient Criminal Justice System 287

14   Debunking the Death Penalty   307
Myths of Crime Control and Capital Punishment

15 Merging Myths and Misconceptions of Crime and Justice   331

THE SOCIAL CONSTRUCTION OF CRIME MYTHS

1

People study social problems for a variety of reasons. The most obvious is to find solutions to society's concerns. Sometimes the solution must be sought not only in the content of the issue itself but in why a particular problem becomes more prominent than another. Many scholars in many disciplines look at the origins, diffusion, and consequences of social issues which capture the public's attention. Two very different perspectives can be used to explain the existence of a social problem. One perspective would be taken by people who have been characterized as "claims-makers," "moral entrepreneurs," "political activists," "social pathologists," and "issue energizers" (Schoenfeld, Meier and Griffin, 1979). These individuals have vested interests in the problem they bring to the public's attention. They usually advocate formal social policy to address the new problem, which they feel is real, unique in its characteristics, and grave in its consequences.

The other perspective is taken by people who study social problems and how those problems are constructed. These people often see social problems as being constructed from collective definitions rather than from individual views and perceptions. Since social problems are composite constructions based on accumulated perceptions and presentations of information, they can never truly exist in this collective, socially distorted form. People from this perspective often speak of social problems in terms of their origins and attribute the conception and definition of the problems to the mass media (Fishman, 1976), urban legend (Best and Horiuchi, 1985), group hysteria (Medalia and Larsen, 1958), ideology (Ryan, 1976), political power (Quinney, 1970), or some other often latent social force that directs public attention and shapes the nature and characteristics of emerging social problems. We will use this viewpoint to examine several myths of crime and justice.

We have chosen the term "myth" to describe some of the collective definitions society applies to certain crime problems and their solutions. The word myth seems most appropriate to the social definition of many different kinds of criminal behavior brought to the public's attention. One common meaning of myth is a traditional story of unknown authorship, with a historical basis, serving to explain some event. The events of myth are based on exaggeration or heightening of "ordinary" events in life. Other uses of the term carry the connotation of nonscientific, spoken or written fiction used as if it were a true account of some event.

The phrase "crime myth" does not stray too far from these accepted definitions. Crime myths are usually created in nonscientific forums through the telling of crime-related fictions or sensational stories. These crime fictions often take on new meanings as they are told and retold—and at some point evolve into truth for many people.

The fiction in crime myth comes not only from fabrication of events but from the transformation and distortion of events into social and political problems. Many of our contemporary issues of crime and justice are the product of some real event or social concern. Whether or not these events are based on "truth" is largely irrelevant because they "gain their persuasiveness and motivating power from their larger-than-life quality" (Bromley et al., 1979:44). As crime-related issues are debated and redebated, shaped and reshaped in public forums, they become distorted. Once transformed and repeatedly played out in public arenas, the mythical social problems are incorporated into the public consciousness.

This book focuses on the processes by which criminal events and issues of criminal justice become distorted and are given unprecedented social consideration. Single authors of short, crime-related fictions are given scant attention. Instead, we attempt to illustrate the range of social processes by which popular thought concerning a crime issue transforms the original concern into a crime problem taking on the characteristics of myth. This distortion of the reality of crime and criminal justice issues into myths emerges from a "collective," sometimes "unconscious," enterprise (Mannheim, 1936). Our inquiry concentrates on current issues in crime and justice that have reached or are near their mythic potential plus the costs of myth production to society.

The Function of Crime Myths

The study of myths in crime is not a novel or merely academic undertaking. Crime myths are real in the minds of their believers and have definite social consequences. Crime myths have numerous effects on our perceptions; we may not even be conscious that they are at work. Myths tend to organize our views of crime, criminals, and the proper operation of the criminal justice system. They provide us with a conceptual framework from which to identify certain social issues as crime-related, to develop our personal opinions on issues of justice, and to apply ready-made solutions to social problems. The organization of views through crime myths contributes to the cataloging of social actors into artificial distinctions between law-abiding citizens, criminals, crime fighters, and victims. Casting certain segments of society into the category of "criminal" offers others a reassuring self-conception. "For many people, it is comforting to conceive of themselves as law abiding citizens. . . . No doubt there are a few paragons of virtue, but not many. Most people manifest common human frailties. For example, evidence suggests that over 90 percent of all Americans have committed some crime for which they could be incarcerated" [citations omitted] (Bohm, 1986:200–1).

Myths also support and maintain prevailing views of crime, criminals, and the criminal justice system, strengthening the tendency to rely on established conceptions of crime and justice. Myths reinforce the current designation of conduct as criminal, support existing practices of crime control, and provide the background assumptions for future designation of conduct as criminal. Once a crime myth has been generated and accepted by the public, it provides the necessary pre-understandings to generate other myths of crime and justice. In a sense, society becomes intellectually blinded by the mythology of crime and justice. The established conceptual framework may not enable us to define issues accurately, to explore new solutions, or to find alternatives to existing socially constructed labels and crime control practices.

Myths tend to provide the necessary information for the construction of a "social reality of crime" (Quinney, 1970). Crime myths become a convenient mortar to fill gaps in knowledge and to provide answers to questions social science either cannot answer or has failed to address. Where science, empirical evidence, and education have failed to provide answers to the public's crime concerns, mythology has stepped in to fill the knowledge void. "One of the major contradictions that confronts American society is that one of the wealthiest and most technologically advanced countries in the world contains widespread poverty, unemployment and crime. Historically, a myth that has been perpetrated to resolve this contradiction is that crime is an individual problem. . . . Conceived this way there is no social or structural solution to the problem of crime" (Bohm, 1986:203). This crime myth not only explains a social contradiction but it tells us where in society the crime problem resides; where we should look to find solutions; and what solutions are acceptable. Because of the manner in which the myth is framed, acceptable solutions are usually those that do not disrupt existing social arrangements regardless of the extent to which they contribute to understanding or control. Collectively, myths create our social reality of crime and justice.

Finally, crime myths provide an outlet for emotionalism and channel emotion into action. Myth "imperatively guides action and establishes patterns of behavior" (Fitzpatrick, 1992:20). Myths not only allow for interpretation of general social emotions and sentiment but direct those emotions to designated targets. Crime myths condone social action based on emotionalism while providing justification for established views of behavior, social practice, and institutional responses to crime.

Criminal Mythmakers

The social construction of myths of crime and criminal justice seems to follow a series of recurrent patterns. These patterns allow a disproportionate amount of social attention to be focused on a few isolated criminal events or issues. This attention is promoted by concentrated, but often brief, mass media coverage of a chosen problem. Intense social concern with an issue is achieved by a variety of means. The mass media, government, law enforcement officials, interpersonal communications, and the interests of reform groups all play a major role in focusing the public's attention on select social problems. There is, if you will, a myth-producing enterprise in our society. The largest and most powerful myth-makers in this enterprise are the mass media.

Modern mass communication has virtually replaced traditional vehicles of communicating myth. Mass communication is a formalized and institutionalized system of conveying messages. It consists of sending messages by way of technology to large groups of people. The traditional process of communication and myth distribution, once based solely on word of mouth and later extended by the written word, has been replaced by rapid electronic-based communication. This modern mass communication system has enabled myths to spread in unprecedented numbers and with frightening speed. Over forty-five years ago, Edwin H. Sutherland (1950:143) noted that, "Fear is produced more readily in the modern community than it was earlier in our history because of increased publicity. . . ." Technology has enhanced our ability to generate, refine, distribute, and reinforce myths. What were once stories restricted in dissemination to small interactive social groups are now instantly projected to millions of people internationally by the mass media. This increased ability to project myth has been coupled with an ever-decreasing circle of people who control the means and mediums of myth production. This restricted number of mythmakers has given the modern media, reform groups, and government almost a monopoly on the myth industry. Today, the media and government select our crime problems for us and focus our attention on social issues. The roles of the individual and small social groups no longer predominate in the dissemination of modern crime mythology.

Media as Mythmaker

The media choose and present unique crime problems for public consumption. The selection of crime problems is often limited to the most bizarre or gruesome act a journalist or investigator can uncover. Incident and problem selection are driven by the competitive nature of modern media. By culling unique and fascinating issues for public exhibition, the media ensure the marketability and success (viewers and advertising dollars) of a given media production. Once an incident has been selected, it is then presented as evidence of a common, more general, and representative crime problem. The practice of using sensational stories to attract readers and increase profit is sometimes referred to as "yellow" journalism. Television news has not escaped the economic lure of sensationalism. Local stations learned "late in the 1960s, that news could make money—lots of money. By the end of the 1970s, news was frequently producing 60 percent of a station's profits . . . and a heavily entertainment-oriented form of programming began to evolve" (Hallin, 1990:2). Economic lure coupled with sensationalism has caused one researcher to refer to the practice as the "commodification of crime." Kenneth Tunnell (1992:300) remarks that "crime news, as well as the content of the new breed of crime fascination programs, represents the selection and construction of stories that further contribute to news and entertainment corporations' profit maximization as much as to the objective dissemination of news." Like any for-profit organization the media merely respond to the dynamics of the economy by marketing their crime products "to attract a large viewing audience which, in turn, sells advertising" (Bohm, 1986:205).

Prompted by the nature of the media industry, television and newspaper reporters focus on "hot topics" of entertainment value. In the early stages of myth development, a media frenzy develops which allows for expanded coverage of isolated and unique events. Typically, the appearance of an uncritical newspaper or magazine article exploring a unique social problem starts the chain of events. The journalist has uncovered a "new" social evil. Other journalists, not wanting to be left out, jump on the bandwagon. The accounts which follow may eventually blossom into highly publicized quasi-documentaries or even movies that graphically portray the problem. Social problems reach their media-built myth potential when sensationalism reaches its height and when they are reported by tabloid-television investigators. Isolated incidents thus become social issues and, through politicalization, eventually crime problems.

Media frenzies often start in single newsrooms and later spread across information mediums, giving the false impression of order and magnitude to criminal events. As Mark Fishman (1976:535) points out in his discussion of "crime waves":

> Journalists do not create themes merely to show an audience
> the appearance of order. . . . In particular, editors selecting and
> organizing the day's stories need themes. Each day news editors
> face a glut of "raw materials" out of which they must fashion
> relatively few stories. . . . The chances that an event or incident
> will be reported increase once it has been associated with a
> current theme in the news.

Once a theme has been set by the lone newsroom, selection of
newsworthy stories are based on that theme. Other events that may
or may not be related to the existing news theme are then culled
from an abundance of material and are fashioned to fit within the
crime theme of the day. Themes then spread across communication
mediums giving the impression of a crime epidemic.

Although the media reach enormous audiences instantly, their
advantages in disseminating information are balanced by disadvantages in other areas. As Mortimer Zuckerman (1994:64) warns:

> Public events . . . require context, an understanding of the past,
> explanations of complexities. . . . Television, in particular, is so
> focused on pictures and so limited by time that in the normal
> run of reporting it cannot begin to provide the context that gives
> meaning and perspective.

He continues the discussion by pointing out that incidents of
violence are collected and then condensed into 120 seconds of
compelling footage—often "graphic images of pain and outrage
beamed into our homes," increasing pressure for immediate
commitment to a plan—any plan—to stop the wanton violence
(Zuckerman, 1994:64). The editorial quotes Walter Lippmann on
the process, "the public will arrive in the middle of the third act
and will leave before the last curtain, having stayed just long
enough perhaps to decide who is the hero and who the villain"
(Zuckerman, 1994:64).

While the media play an important role in the identification and
construction of crime myth, they are not the sole participants in
the enterprise. Journalistic freedom of topic selection is often guided
by events and influences external to the media. While the media
may be guilty of not reporting an incident in the proper perspective,
the media are not solely to blame for sensational reporting.
Unfortunately, repugnant crimes do occur. Some events which are
blown out of proportion still warrant public attention. Each myth
considered in this book also contains legitimate cause for public
concern. Yet, social policy cannot be developed based on distortion,
sensationalism, or a few newsworthy events. We will return to the
media's role in constructing crime myths later.

Government as Mythmaker

There are other methods beyond the naturally occurring bizarre and unusual crimes captured by the media that begin the myth construction process. These sometimes contrived or directed government events help alert the media to a new "hot topic." In some cases, the directed information helps refocus a media frenzy. Harold Pepinsky and Paul Jesilow (1985:10) opened their book *Myths that Cause Crime* with a powerful statement: "The sooner we recognize that criminal justice is a state protected racket, the better." In the context of crime myth, this means that the government has a vested interest in maintaining the existing social definition of crime and extending this definition to groups and behaviors that are perceived to be a threat to the existing social order. Similarly, the government has an interest in seeing that the existing criminal justice system's response to crime is not significantly altered in purpose or function. While some "system tinkering" (Kraska, 1985) is permissible, major change in the system's response to crime is never implemented because it serves the interests of government, crime control agencies, and social elites. We build more prisons, mete out longer prison terms, reinstate the death penalty, and move more offenders through the criminal justice system at faster speeds, but all these changes are intellectually bonded by a myth-based philosophy of punishment and crime control that reflects the interests of government and the criminal justice system.

The government secures its interest in identifying crime and criminals and maintaining the established criminal justice system by promoting crime myths. Since the government can control, direct, and mold messages, it is one of the most powerful myth-makers in the crime production enterprise. "The public is far more likely to accept the pronouncements of a federal department than a voluntary private organization. There is the element of propaganda development. Due to its public nature, a federal department is more skilled in dealing with the public and in preparing propaganda for public consumption" (Dickson, 1968:147). The government can suppress information for national security reasons; it can punish "obscenity"; it can reward the media for presenting official versions of crime myths; and it can "bring a wide range of pressures to bear on its critics" (Dickson, 1968:147). Shaping the content of messages and rewarding the media for myth presentation are frequently done under the guise of "public service announce-ments" and controlled press briefings.

The government functions not only as a controller and director of the mass media—it is a form of media. The government controls extensive print publication resources, commissions and funds research, operates radio stations, and exposes the television viewing audience to government-sponsored messages. Additionally, the government tunes the media in to certain crime myths by directing their attention and holding controlled press briefings. "Reporters' dependence on authorities makes them—and by extension media consumers—particularly vulnerable to deliberate attempts to mislead by governments and agencies" (Hynds, 1990:6).

The "war on drugs" is an excellent illustration of the govern-ment's role as a media starter in the myth construction enterprise. While drug scares in the United States can be traced back over two hundred years, the government's role has been most evident in the last forty years (Reinarman, 1996). The highest offices in govern-ment have been used as stages for constructing the public's conception of crime. In the 1970s, President Nixon was careful to call drug abuse "public enemy number one" and characterized it as "the worst threat the country ever faced." Hinting at a solution, he employed the war metaphor equating drug abuse to "foreign troops on our shores" (see Dumont, 1973:534). Nixon's call for a war on drugs was sounded against a backdrop of drug hysteria that began at least forty years earlier when the Bureau of Narcotics attempted to expand its organizational power.

The Bureau of Narcotics' 1937 campaign against marijuana under the leadership of Harry Anslinger is a classic example of the media's dissemination of government-sponsored crime myths. The Bureau of Narcotics, wanting to expand its bureaucratic domain by adding marijuana to the list of controlled substances it was responsible for monitoring, put together a series of mythological and outrageous stories about atrocities allegedly committed by people under the influence of marijuana. These stories included the murder of a Florida family and their pet dog by a wayward son who had taken one toke of marijuana. Newspapers printed this story and others like it. Thus, the myth of the "dope fiend" was born out of the minds of law enforcement officials. The media involvement with the Bureau of Narcotics disinformation campaign continued with editorial calls for the suppression of the dangerous drug. In fact, such hysteria resulted that the Bureau's own legal counsel recom-mended discontinuation of the propaganda campaign. During the height of the media frenzy and while the Marijuana Tax Act of 1937 was being debated in Washington, news stories covering the testimony of leading medical experts about the relative safety of the drug and objections by the scientific community to the criminalization of marijuana were lost in the coverage of the government-created crime wave (see Galliher and Walker, 1977; Dickson, 1968).

In the 1980s President Reagan rekindled the drug hysteria and further solidified the war solution in the minds of many citizens by abandoning the treatment orientation of President Carter's administration. "Almost immediately after his election, Reagan outlined a seven-step plan to eradicate drugs from society. This included a diversion of $708.8 million from education, treatment, and research programs to law enforcement programs. An additional $127.5 million were appropriated for increasing prison space, and to increase the personnel of the Drug Enforcement Administration. . . ." (Kraska, 1990:117). Municipal law enforcement agencies revitalized their narcotics units, created drug task forces, and organized multi-jurisdictional strike teams because of an influx of new federal funding generated by the government's proliferation of drug propaganda and the attendant public hysteria. Once again law enforcement was revitalized to wage yet another war on drugs.

In 1990 President Bush's administration arranged for the Drug Enforcement Administration (DEA) to conduct a high-profile drug arrest. Since public focus on the "drug war" was waning due to concern over other social problems, the administration needed an "event" to refocus public and political attention on the "drug war." Following a DEA drug bust just outside the White House, the president made a national television address concerning the drug issue. It was later learned that the DEA had to go to considerable means to persuade the drug dealer to meet the agents at the desired location—just outside the White House. Following the arrest, then-President Bush went on national television holding a baggie of white powder and instructing the nation that drugs had encroached to the steps of the White House. Public attention was once again directed to the drug issue.

President Clinton managed to avoid the drug hysteria of his predecessors, but was less successful in depoliticizing crime. Clinton actively contributed to an unprecedented level of fear of violent crime in America. Appearing in public service announcements with his arms around children, answering questions in town meetings, and making speeches across the nation, he warned citizens about the rise of violent crime and its dreadful effect on children. Similarly, Attorney General Janet Reno emphasized America's growing problem of child abuse and exploitation. Yet with presidential approval, Reno ordered the Federal Bureau of

Investigation (FBI) to storm the Branch Davidians' home in Waco, Texas. The raid resulted in the death of at least seventy-nine people—many were children. Ironically, the siege at Waco triggered the rage that resulted in the bombing of the Alfred P. Murah federal building in Oklahoma City—two years to the date after the FBI raid. Stories about "Terror in the Heartland" filled the airwaves in 1995. Fears of such massive, random violence prompted calls for fewer restrictions on government surveillance. The Clinton administration furthered in the public's mind simplistic solutions to complex crime problems, advocating the deployment of thousands of additional police officers, broadening the powers of the police to conduct warrantless searches of housing projects, adopting a "three strikes and you're out" correctional policy, and expanding the use of the death penalty. By the mid-1990s, the Clinton administration had effectively shifted public attention away from the drug war and focused social concern on a violent and predatory urban America.

Suffice it to say that whether self-initiated or governmentally generated, the media and government focus public attention on unique social problems. They establish the seriousness of the problem and inform the public of viable solutions; crime myths thus begin to take shape. As we will discuss later, these events comprise all the necessary ingredients for creating crime myths.

Merging Mythmakers

During the latter part of the 1980s, a new form of television programming began to emerge. Following the format of information-commercials (programs appearing as fact-based presentations of information but designed to sell products), television crime programs began to blend entertainment and government-sponsored messages. These shows used government officials, well-known relatives of crime victims, and law enforcement officers to inform the public about crime. As Kenneth Tunnell (1992) instructs, these television programs, broadcast from local stations across the nation under various names like *Crime Solvers*, *Secret Witness*, and *Crime Line*, increased from forty-eight shows in 1980 to at least five hundred in 1984. The programs encourage viewers to report crime and criminals in exchange for monetary rewards. They were predecessors of the government's national media campaign, *Taking a Bite Out of Crime*, which mustered citizen participation in support of crime prevention, citizen self-protection, and neighborhood cooperation (Tunnell, 1992).

The growth of this new form of crime-news entertainment did more than just advocate crime prevention and citizen cooperation— and support these efforts with monetary rewards. Using government officials as spokespersons gave viewers the impression of official credibility. Television shows like *Unsolved Mysteries*, *Rescue 911*, *48 Hours*, *America's Most Wanted*, *Cops*, and *Top Cops* reenacted crimes accompanied by narratives from law enforcement officials. As the name *Unsolved Mysteries* suggests, often the facts of the particular crime had yet to be uncovered. Still, these and other programs filled fact voids by reconstructions born out of the minds of law enforcement officials. In 1989, *Unsolved Mysteries* added a new segment to the show called *FBI Alert*. The segment was hosted by FBI director William Sessions and spent its time describing American fugitives (Tunnell, 1992). *Bad Girls* and *Gangs, Cops, and Drugs*, both broadcast by the National Broadcasting Company (NBC), featured drug czar William Bennett who "eschewed any social-structural explanation for drug-related crime . . . As mindless as these depictions were, *Gangs, Cops, and Drugs* aired two nights during prime time, evidently cashing in on a recent crime fad" (Tunnell, 1992:299). These shows and their spin-offs contributed to an unprecedented level of fear of crime in American society (Cavender and Bond-Maupin, 1993) and draw upon the believability of government officials.

As mentioned earlier, TV creates its own graphic images of reality. Producers massage the message, which is further affected by hot lights and microphones. Members of the Police Executive Research Forum commented on the merits of reality programs like *Cops*. They noted that the presence of television encourages more aggressive behavior from police officers. "They don't doctor the tapes but they only depict a portion of policing . . ." (Goode, 1994:53). Viewers who rely on such information may end up with a distorted view of the world as more dangerous than it really is.

Despite the often contrived nature of these crime presentations, their use of government officials to lend credibility to their claims, and their selective presentations of atypical, serious and violent crime, did these shows really have any effect on the viewing public? The following incident serves as an illustration of one destructive consequence of merging mythmakers.

One evening Rudell Combs and several other employees of a tool manufacturing company watched *America's Most Wanted*. On this particular evening, the show was featuring fugitive Don Moore, a former teacher from Los Angeles who was wanted by the police for twenty-one counts of fondling, masturbation, oral copulation, and sexual intercourse with several fifth-grade students. While watching the program Combs and his fellow employees became convinced that one of their coworkers, Richard Maxwell, was the fugitive. The following day they called *America's Most Wanted* and explained that Maxwell's age, appearance, and a missing fingertip, matched the description of Don Moore. Compounding their suspicion, Maxwell failed to show up at work the day after the episode aired.

Staff from *America's Most Wanted* contacted a detective from the Los Angeles Police Department, and he faxed the *America's Most Wanted* information sheet to local police officers. The bulletin contained a photograph, a fingerprint classification, and specific identifiers which described Moore as a male Caucasian, 5'11", 175 pounds, with gray hair, green eyes, a fair complexion, a gray mustache, a goatee and missing the tip of his left index finger. Local police officers went to the manufacturing company and summoned Maxwell. During the course of their interview with Maxwell they learned that he was a male Caucasian 6'5", 270 pounds, with gray hair, green eyes, a gray mustache and missing the tip of his left middle finger. Over his protests, Maxwell was arrested and taken to the local police department for fingerprinting. The fingerprints established conclusively that Maxwell was not Moore, and he was returned to work—to the company of coworkers who had willingly suspended any personal knowledge of him in favor of a televised image and characterization and whose suspicions had been momentarily "confirmed" by his handcuffing and arrest.

His recourse for this embarrassing, reputation-destroying incident was to sue the city whose police officers had compounded the process initiated by the "reality" programming. A court reviewing the case made the following observations concerning the reliability of the television description of Moore and the acceptability of the police officers' actions:

> Presumably, a T.V. show such as *America's Most Wanted*, undoubtedly viewed by millions, would broadcast descriptions that have a high degree of reliability. Otherwise, one risks people fingering neighbors—co-workers—who loosely fit the description of one or another fugitive. . . . Maxwell is a full six inches taller than Moore and weighs almost one hundred pounds more. While weight is a mutable characteristic, the size of the difference here should have given the police officers pause. In the same vein, Maxwell was missing the tip of his left middle finger, not his left index finger. Certainly a missing fingertip in an industrial plant

cannot be so unusual that the officers would not have scrutinized more closely which particular fingertip was damaged. Furthermore, . . . neither the officers' affidavits nor their report indicate that any of them asked Maxwell about his work record or work history. And curiously, it appears that none of the officers asked him for an alibi, or even whether he would consent to fingerprinting. . . . No other factors in this instance can be construed as circumstances warranting an arrest. . . . the officers had no grounds for suspecting Maxwell was engaging in any of the conduct Moore was charged with (*Maxwell v. City of Indianapolis*, 1993:432–33).

If *America's Most Wanted* was aware of Maxwell's anguish and the findings of the court, it seemingly did not find it necessary to implement safeguards against future occurrences. As it celebrated its 300th criminal capture in 1994, it also publicly apologized for inadvertently placing an innocent citizen's photograph on television accompanied by a story of criminal acts the citizen had not committed. Whether a televised apology is sufficient to recover one's reputation is surely debatable.

These and other media depictions of crime and justice in America have consequences that reach far beyond the individual miscarriage of justice described above. As Tunnell (1992:299–300) argues, "the very nature of crime programs further alienates the underclass because the majority of crimes depicted on those programs and, hence in the forefront of Americans' minds, are street crimes committed by poor, inner-city, young men. The programs further alienate social relationships as viewers are transfixed into hounds and underclass criminals into foxes." He goes on to note that, "The driving logic of these crime depictions is that individual deviants are at fault, which ignores social arrangements. As a result, humans become further alienated and segregated from and suspicious of others . . . these crime programs not only contribute to an increased and unrealistic fear of crime but, more important, further legitimate political decisions (e.g., fiscal and legislative) to combat crime, all while the American public contentedly reassures itself there is nothing wrong with the social world but a few 'rotten apples'" (Tunnell, 1992:299–300).

Creating Crime Myths

Public attention and media focus alone cannot create a crime myth. Generally, public concerns are related in some measure to social or economic conditions. Erich Goode and Nachman Ben-Yehuda (1994:49) point out the "Fear and concern *do*, for the most part, grow out of very real conditions of social life. But no, they need *not* be commensurate with the concrete threat posed specifically by that which is feared." In order for a myth to develop to the point where it becomes more than a social concern for a majority of citizens, it must be properly packaged and marketed. A requirement for myth production often repeated throughout this work is that the crime problem must be reported to occur in "epidemic" propor- tions. A quantum leap must occur from uncovering an incident to depicting it as pervasive. Only by exaggerating the magnitude of the problem can public attention be sustained for prolonged periods, fear be instilled, calls for institutional control be made, and public support be mustered to institute formal sanctions—all the ingredients required for a myth to reach its full potential.

Exaggeration of the magnitude of a problem and the manufac- turing of a crime myth are accomplished by several means. First, the media can suddenly focus on crimes that they had previously ignored (Fishman, 1976). The media can collect and selectively choose crimes to present to the public. The organization of these presentations can create the image of a crime problem when they are taken out of their geographical, temporal, or social contexts. Crime myths are also created when the media fail to pursue stories beyond their initial reporting. Crimes reported to constitute a pattern may later be found unrelated or even conceptually distinct. There is, however, no requirement that the media or government correct their mistakes or recall their myths. Joel Best and Gerald Horiuchi's (1985:490) study of Halloween sadists' attacks against children found that the media greatly exaggerated their occurrence.

> There simply was no basis for *Newsweek*'s (1975) claim that "several children had died." The newspapers attributed only two deaths to Halloween sadists, and neither case fit the image of a maniacal killer randomly attacking children. In 1970, five- year-old Kevin Toston died after eating heroin supposedly hidden in his Halloween candy. While this story received considerable publicity, newspapers gave less coverage to the follow-up report that Kevin had found the heroin in his uncle's home, not his treats. . . . In 1974, eight-year-old Timothy O'Bryan died after eating Halloween candy contaminated with cyanide. Investigators concluded that his father had contami- nated the treat. . . . Thus, both boys' deaths were caused by family members, rather than by anonymous sadists.

The fear generated from exaggerating Halloween sadism not only affected the general public but also organizations and individuals who are expected to have valid information regarding the reality of crime. In 1982 the International Association of Chiefs of Police (IACP) and the confectionery industry established, through sponsorship, a "Halloween Candy Hotline." The hotline was devised to give police departments technical assistance with suspected candy tampering cases. According to a news item by the IACP, the hotline received sixty-eight calls in 1990, but the article failed to note if any of these calls were actual tamperings (Editorial Staff, 1991). By 1994, a journalist's interview with IACP's Charles Higginbotham revealed that "he's one of the few who ever dials the number anymore; he calls each year to make sure it's working" (Dunn, 1994:25). Although the Halloween hotline does serve as an example of a possible positive effect of exaggerating crime, it raises questions as to whether the nation's leading police executives are able to discern between actual crime problems and media-generated myths of crime.

How often does the media distort or exaggerate the crime problem in our society? Harry Marsh (1991:67–68) reviewed the research devoted to the study of the content of newspapers. His examination of literature found the following patterns:

- The vast majority of newspaper crime coverage pertains to violent or sensational crimes.
- The high percentages of violent crimes reported in the newspapers are not representative of the percentages reflected in official crime data.
- The over-emphasis of violent crimes and failure to address personal risk and prevention techniques often lead to exaggerated fears of victimization in certain segments of society.
- Newspaper coverage tends to support police views and values about crime and criminals. . . .

Robert Bohm's (1986:205) review of the research perhaps best captured the essence of the type of crime information consumed by the public:

> Crime-related television programs have been estimated to account for about one-third of all television entertainment shows. Information that the public receives from these shows is anything but accurate. Studies have indicated that 1) the least committed crimes, such as murder and assault, appear more frequently than those crimes committed more often, such as burglary and larceny; 2) violent crimes are portrayed as caused by greed or attempts to avoid detection rather than by passion

accompanying arguments as is more typical; 3) the necessary use of violence in police work is exaggerated; 4) the use of illegal police tactics is seemingly sanctioned; 5) police officers are unfettered by procedural law; and 6) the police nearly always capture the "bad guys," usually in violent confrontations [citations omitted].

To what extent does the public rely on the media to make judgments about crime, and what effects do these distortions have on the public's view of crime? Kenneth Tunnell (1992:295) addressed these issues, "96 percent of the respondents [in a National Crime Survey] reported relying on the news media to learn about crime and criminals, and 49 percent of those surveyed believed the media gave the right amount of attention to stories about crime." Tunnell goes on to report that, "At that time, more than 50 percent of the news stories were of violent crime, whereas only 6 percent of the actual crimes involved some form of violence. Not surprising, 88 percent of those surveyed overestimated the number of crimes they believed involved violence" [citations omitted]. Melissa Barlow, David Barlow, and Theodore Chiricos (1995a; 1995b) also studied crime news and found that the media escalates the threat of violent crime and plays down property crimes. Clearly, the media's distortion of crime and justice has an impact on the public's conception of crime.

Misuse of statistics promotes crime myths. The misuse of statistical information can range from limiting public access to information to deliberate attempts to mislead the public by presenting false information or using deceptive formats to present information. Consider Tunnell's (1992:300) discussion of the relationship between the public's fear of crime and the presentation of statistical information.

> Americans' fear of crime results, in part, from their limited access to official crime data. When they are informed of crime trends, it is nearly always by the media, who present them in such inane methods as time capsules (e.g., a crime of violence occurs every 24 seconds, a property crime every 3 seconds) rather than annual population-based rates, which is a more representative measure of crime levels. Because of the public's lack of access to crime data, the media have the ability, indirectly at least, to manipulate the fear of crime.

Vested interests can manipulate "facts" when they have control of information, choose the mode of presentation, and control access to channels of dissemination (see Orcutt and Turner, 1993). As we shall see in later chapters, debates on organized crime are particularly susceptible to misuse and control of information, as are discussions of missing children and rising crime rates. Statistics presented for public consumption are often clouded by broad definitions of crime that tend to group distinct behaviors, offenders, and victims into single categories giving the impression of an epidemic. In a study of the social reaction to sex crimes, Sutherland (1950:144) wrote, "Fear is seldom or never related to statistical trends in sex crimes. . . . Ordinarily, from two to four spectacular sex crimes in a few weeks are sufficient to evoke the phrase 'sex crime wave.'" Statistics and information often mislead the public when they are stripped from their original context and inferences are made between research studies. Causal links are often inferred or claimed between the crime myth under construction and some other more pervasive social concern. For example, in recent years the use of drugs has been linked to other crimes, high school dropouts, decreased employee productivity, the rise of youth gangs, the corruption of the police, the spread of AIDS, and a multitude of other social maladies. The incidence of drug use in society may or may not have been perceived as a major social threat; when coupled with other spin-off social problems, the perception of epidemic is ensured. In later chapters we will explore the myth-built links between drug use and other social problems.

Characterizations of Crime Myths

In order for the momentum of a crime myth to be prolonged and public support for institutionalized controls to be generated, myths must be accompanied by certain characterizations. Momentum is achieved if the crime problem has traits that either instill fear or threaten the vast majority of society in some appreciable way. Not unlike Greek mythology, modern crime myths must follow certain themes for success. There must be "virtuous" heroes, "innocent" victims, and "evil" villains who pose a clear and certain threat to the audience. Only then can a crime myth reach its potential. Characterizations common among myths in crime and criminal justice include: 1) the identification and targeting of a distinct deviant population; 2) the presence of an "innocent" or "helpless" victim population; 3) the emergence of brave and virtuous heroes; and 4) the existence of a substantial threat to established norms, values, or traditional lifestyles.

Crime myths are often built around unpopular groups in society. This targeting helps to ensure sustained support for a myth. Unpopular groups are particularly vulnerable as possible targets of mythical fears. Groups most vulnerable to myth targeting are those that are easily distinguishable from the dominant social group. Distinctions are often as crude as race, color, or national origin, but need not be limited to visual appearance. Minorities and immigrants have had their share of myth targeting. Differences in religious beliefs, political views, or even sexual preferences are attractive targets for mythmakers. This characterization in the construction of crime myth has been used by hate groups, pro-slavery advocates, supporters of prohibition, and advocates of the death penalty. The distinction has been used to develop crime control policy, enact criminal laws, and even bring nations to war.

The importance of this characterization of "difference" cannot be overstated. Scholars have observed the targeting of groups labelled as different. In his insightful book, *Blaming the Victim*, William Ryan (1976:10) states:

> This is a critical and essential step in the process, for difference is in itself hampering and maladaptive. The Different Ones are seen as less competent, less skilled, less knowing—in short less human. The ancient Greeks deduced from a single character-istic, a different language, that the barbarians—that is, the "babblers" who spoke a strange tongue—were wild, uncivilized, dangerous, rapacious, uneducated, lawless, and, indeed scarcely more than animals. [Such characterization] not infrequently justifies mistreatment, enslavement, or even extermination of the Different Ones.

Fear of minorities, foreigners, and differences in cultural or religious values has led to the creation of some shocking myths of organized crime. The birth of the Mafia myth in America is based on the created fear of cultural differences. The murder of New Orleans police chief David Hennessey in 1890 provides an excellent example. New Orleans was one of the cities that experienced a large influx of Italian immigrants during the end of the nineteenth century. Chief Hennessey was gunned down on a New Orleans street one night. As he was dying, the chief was said to have uttered the words "Dagos, Dagos." Officers later rounded up a large number of petty criminals of Italian descent and presented them before a grand jury that indicted them for the chief's murder. Since evidence of their involvement was lacking, the jury acquitted them of the charges. Acquittal did not deter the citizens of New Orleans who marched to the jail, seized the defendants (and others who were not even on trial) and killed eleven of them. This lynching and subsequent trials and acquittals of "different ones" is said to be the genesis of the American Mafia myth (Smith, 1975).

The difference requirement of the myth construction process is built into issues surrounding crime and justice. There is a convenient supply of unpopular people—those whom society labels criminal. Criminals are probably the most unpopular minority in any society, although they are difficult to identify visually aside from the undesirable conduct.

Another requirement for myth development is that "helpless" or "innocent" victims (people like ourselves) must be depicted as suffering the brunt of the newly found social evil. The more "innocents" perceived as being affected by the myth, the greater the likelihood of public attention and support for the creation of crime myths targeting unpopular groups. Women, children, law enforcement officers killed in the line of duty, prison officials who contract AIDS from criminals, or unwitting business people who become the victims of "organized" crime are often used as the "virtuous" victim who suffers at the hands of the unpopular deviant. Sutherland (1950:144) observed, "The hysteria produced by child murders is due in part to the fact that the ordinary citizen cannot understand a sex attack on a child. The ordinary citizen . . . concludes that sexual attack on an infant or girl of six years must be the act of a fiend or maniac. Fear is the greater because the behavior is so incomprehensible."

Casting victims as "innocents" authorizes the implementation of stiff criminal sanctions against the deviants—accompanied by feelings of moral superiority and satisfaction over retribution. It is common for the media to dwell on the virtues of the innocent victim to the exclusion of the offender (see Drechsel, Netteburg and Aborisade, 1980; Karmen, 1978). After all, what parents do not feel their child is either a "good student," a "likable person," or "a good boy or girl." This is not to say that innocents do not become the targets of violent crime, but rather to illustrate that media coverage of crime stories often focuses extensively on the innocent person victimized by the evil stranger. The irony here is that "good" and "evil," "deviants" and "conformists" are creatures of the same culture, inventions of the same imagination (Messner and Rosenfeld, 1994:2; citing Erikson, 1966:21). As we shall see in later chapters on child abduction and abuse, strangers are not the greatest threat to our nation's children. In the construction of crime mythology, there are no "ordinary" victims or criminals.

The subjects of myths are characterized as constituting a major threat to middle-class values, norms, or lifestyles. Myths of crime and justice when blended with threats to religious beliefs, economic systems, sexual attitudes or orientation, the traditional family, or political preference become a volatile mix. These characterizations of crime myths serve to fuel emotionalism. The fear generated by this mixture of the unpopular offender, the innocent victim, and the perceived threat to traditional lifestyles can produce a formal and even violent social response. The argument is simple; a growing menace is plaguing society. Not only is the conduct the preference of a deviant group, it is affecting innocents and endangering tradition.

The idea that "normal" life might break down adds to the value of a crime myth and provides for its continued existence long after media attraction has vanished. These characterizations ensure that major social institutions become involved in the reform process, since the conduct is perceived as not only a physical threat but a substantial threat to existing social arrangements and institutions. Crime myths in this guise are similar to moral panics; they clarify the moral boundaries of society and demonstrate that there are limits to how much diversity will be tolerated. Erich Goode and Nachman Ben-Yehuda (1994:31) assert that moral panics are "characterized by the feeling . . . that evildoers pose a threat to the society and to the moral order as a consequence of their behavior and, therefore, 'something should be done' about them and their behavior." The "something" usually means strengthening social controls, according to Goode and Ben-Yehuda (1994:31): "more laws, longer sentences, more police, more arrests, and more prison cells. If society has become morally lax, a revival of traditional values may be necessary; if innocent people are victimized by crime, a crackdown on offenders will do the trick. . . ."

The hysteria over child abduction in the 1980s led some parents to return to traditional parenting roles instead of child care. Such a focus reinforces traditional values and allows blame to be placed on parents rather than the absence of positive alternatives to traditional child rearing practices. "If only she had not worked outside the home," instead of "if only the government supported and monitored alternative child-care industries." The child-care issue was so entrenched in the public's mind that it became part of the 1992 presidential campaign with then-President Bush coming under fire for vetoing the parental leave bill and President Clinton signing the bill as one of his first official acts.

Mythmaking and the characterization of crime problems as major threats to traditional values and society serve important political functions for law enforcement. Consider organized crime and vice.

Leaders in the law enforcement community testifying before Congress and state legislators can present the issue in one of two ways. They can present a relatively safe myth which suggests that organized crime is a foreign conspiracy (Italians, Colombians, Jamaicans, etc.) which has invaded America and threatens the peace and security of a homogeneous and righteous society. Organized crime brings with it numerous evils. It corrupts otherwise incorruptible politicians and police; it makes people gamble away their life savings; it introduces drugs into the schools; it uses prostitutes to seduce family men. Even worse, organized crime is an intricate, highly structured foreign conspiracy which can only be eliminated with more money, more justice personnel, and more enforcement power. The myth is safe and convenient. It points to the different ones as the source of a problem, so we do not have to change our lifestyle or take responsibility for the problem. Finally, it explains why law enforcement has yet to win the war against organized crime in America. The alternative would be to expose the myth. Organized crime is an integral part of American society. It could not exist if the citizenry did not wish to have ready access to drugs, pornography, prostitution, gambling, no-questions-asked loans, or stolen goods. Many of the "crimes" of organized crime would not be important or profitable if the business community did not collaborate in money laundering, the illegal disposal of toxic wastes, and the fencing of stolen goods. Organized crime would find itself quite harried if an array of politicians, law enforcers, and others were not willing to "grease the skids" of organized crime. To uncover the myth of crime and vice, however, carries no bureaucratic rewards for law enforcement or government; it would offend people and end law enforcement and political careers. A rational bureaucrat or politician will find characterizing crime in terms of different ones and threats to traditional values more useful than fact.

Techniques of Myth Characterization

Mythmakers do not simply uncover crime and transmit information; they serve to structure reality by selecting and characterizing events—thereby cultivating images of crime (Schoenfeld et al., 1979; Gerbner, 1972; Lang and Lang, 1969). The characterization of criminal events into myth is largely a process of bias and distortion. This distortion is often an unintended consequence of the process by which information is collected, processed, and prepared for dissemination by mass media, government, and interest groups. Research on the media, the news particularly, concludes that misrepresentation and distortion are not uncommon practices (see Tunnell, 1992; Marsh, 1991; Bohm, 1986).

The collection of crime events for public presentation is often shaped by reporters' perceptions. Journalistic accounts are rarely the product of actual observation. When they are, they are often conducted by reporters largely untrained in field research. More often than not, reporting of crime is based on secondhand information a reporter gleans from witnesses or public officials. The process of listening and interviewing witnesses and crime victims invites bias. Frequently, the wrong questions are asked, essential questions are omitted, and sensationalism becomes the reporter's focus. After all, journalists are in competition when creating a product for audience consumption. The untrained observer or journalist who is driven by the competitive nature of the modern mass media may selectively observe or interview with the end product in mind. Outcome and conclusion may already have been drawn before the investigator begins collecting information.

Following a journalist's selection of a topic and initial investigation of a potential media story, the reporter's observations must make a transformation to communicable material. It must be written for dissemination or presentation. In this process of moving from observation to presentation, several problems arise. First, there is the possibility of selective memory or even the injection of personal preference by the reporter. Forgotten statements or observations may later be recalled by the journalist in the process of constructing a crime story. As information is recalled, initially insignificant observations may take on new meaning as the story unfolds. Second, after initial drafts of the presentation are constructed, they must be edited. In this editorial process a story can change considerably. Reports are often edited by a series of people who are guided by numerous constraints. Editorial constraints often include the time available to present a story, the page space available, and the marketability of the final product. The audience and editorial ideology also influence decisions. This process requires persons often unassociated with the initial crime to make judgments about what should be said or what should be shown. Editorial decisions are not always made in conjunction with the advice of the original observer.

The selection of which stories eventually appear in the news is based on the ordering of stories into media themes, as mentioned earlier. Mark Fishman (1976:536) notes that:

> The selection of news on the basis of themes is one ideological production of crime news. . . . This procedure requires that an incident be stripped of the actual context of its occurrence so that it may be relocated in a new, symbolic context: the news theme. Because newsworthiness is based on themes, the attention devoted to an event may exceed its importance, relevance, or timelessness were these qualities determined with reference to some theory of society. . . . Thus, something becomes a "serious type of crime" on the basis of what is going on inside newsrooms, not outside them.

Finally, after the presentation of a story there is the possibility of selective observation and retention on the part of the audience. Many will only remember the bizarre or hideous part of a communication to the exclusion of other information. While media focus on crime myth is often short-lived, visceral images created may linger with the audience long after the media have moved on to a different topic.

There are, however, other techniques used in the manipulation of information and the construction of crime myths. There is a rich history of research and literature on the use of propaganda by the media and government. Propaganda is a technique for influencing social action based on intentional distortions and manipulation of communications. While not all media and government presentation, or even a majority of it, is a conscious attempt at propaganda, many crime myths are the product of propaganda techniques. "One important point to remember is that objective reporting is a myth. Every reporter brings to the story his/her own biases and world view. Each reporter has to make choices in writing the story: what to include, what to leave out, what sources to use. A few well-placed adjectives, a few uses of 'alleged' or 'so-called' can cast a definite ideological twist" (Hynds, 1990:5). These techniques tend to shape the presentation of a crime, create images for the uncritical audience, and promote social reaction. Some of the most common techniques employed by the media, government, government officials, and interest groups for characterizing crime myths include:

- *Creating criminal stereotypes.* This practice amounts to presenting crime as a unidimensional and non-changing event. Certain phrases such as "crime against the elderly," "child abduction," "street crime," and "organized crime" group wide varieties of behavior into single categories that have been previously characterized by the media. The use of stereotyped phrases links broad and popular conceptions of crime to diverse criminal behavior. For example, "organized crime" often creates the image of large "well-structured" groups of foreign-born individuals who engage solely in criminal enterprise.

- ***Presentation of opinion as fact.*** This practice involves injecting personal opinion into media presentations without factual basis. Phrases that present opinions as fact might include: "the police are doing all they can to prevent this crime" or the "community is in a state of panic."

- ***Masking opinions through sources.*** This activity involves collecting opinions of others that closely match the proponent's viewpoint on a given issue. A reporter may select people to interview on the basis of how well their opinions fit the theme of the story.

- ***Value-loaded terminology.*** Biased language is used to characterize and label crime, criminals, or victims. A serial murderer may "stalk" the victim; a group of individuals may be referred to as a "crime family"; or a group of youths may become a "gang" that "preys" on "unsuspecting" victims.

- ***Selective presentation of fact.*** Presenting certain facts to the exclusion of others strengthens a biased argument. To emphasize the issue of child abduction, a proponent could cite that thousands of children are missing each year without presenting the fact that the vast majority of missing children are runaways.

- ***Information-management.*** The editorial process by which a particular news story is shaped and selected for presentation to the exclusion of other stories is one way to manage information. Presenting stories about sensational crimes like serial murder, stalkers, crack babies, and child abduction to the exclusion of stories on corporate crime, securities fraud, and other more common crimes are examples of the results of such management.

- ***Undocumented sources of authority.*** Vague references including statements like "many police officials feel" or "many people are saying" without specific reference to who is saying what and what constitutes "many" is a misleading reference to authority.

- ***Stripping fact from its context.*** A variation of the characteristic above is using facts or statements of authorities appropriate in one context and transferring them to another to support a particular position or injecting facts that are unrelated to the issue. A media presentation on drug abuse that focuses on statistics about the high school drop-out rate without addressing whether or not there is an empirical link between the two is stripping fact from its original context.

• **Selective interviewing.** A final method of portraying a position as more solid than the facts indicate is interviewing one or two authorities on a topic and presenting their remarks as the generalized expert opinion on a given topic. For example, interviewing one or two criminologists and giving the audience the impression that those views are reflective of the criminological community.

In the chapters that follow, we will address specific myths of crime and criminal justice. Each myth or series of myths presented in this text differ in the fashion in which they rely on these practices and other characterizations to create a crime myth.

On Analyzing Crime Myths

There are no traditional or standard crime myths. Myths have at their origin unique events that may or may not be noticed by particular mythmakers in society. A criminal event or series of events cannot become a myth unless a sufficient number of people contribute to its transformation. The story that is conceived but never told does not become an issue or a crime myth. Crime myths are unique in that they are a product of the social, political and economic atmosphere of a time. That is to say, the audience must be ready or made ready to accept a crime myth. A criminal event that has the potential for becoming a crime myth at one given moment may not be a viable myth at another point in time. Myths are constructed within a given context and that context includes existing myths of crime and justice.

Mythmakers are varied and their roles are dynamic. Sometimes the government is the mythmaker, and the media respond to the official myth. Other times the government responds to the myths created by the media or special interest groups. These varied mythmakers and shifting roles all make crime myths unique. Crime myths also differ in their purposes and consequences. Some myths result in the criminalization of behavior while others die quietly without social or political response. Some myths serve the interests of powerful groups in society or serve a needed social function, while others serve no useful social purpose.

The uniqueness of the origins, detection, construction, and consequence of crime myths does not lend itself well to traditional criminological analysis. There are no master keys or magic statistical bullets to understanding and solving all crime myths. There is no blanket sociological theory that explains the development and purpose of all crime myths. Each crime myth requires individualized treatment and analysis. Such a situation is an invitation for criticism. It is, however, also a strength. Wedding oneself to a particular theory, perspective, or method of knowing is like relying on a single sense to describe a garden of flowers. This work is grounded in a variety of perspectives and supports its numerous contentions with varying means of understanding. We shall leave it to the reader to judge whether we have described a rose or merely wandered into the bramble bush.

Sources

Barlow, M., Barlow, D., Chiricos, T. (1995a). Mobilizing Support for Social Control in a Declining Economy: Exploring Ideologies of Crime within Crime News. *Crime & Delinquency* 41(2): 191–204.

———. (1995b). Economic Conditions and Ideologies of Crime in the Media: A Content Analysis of Crime News. *Crime & Delinquency* 41(1): 3–19.

Best, J. and Horiuchi, G. (1985). The Razor and the Apple: The Social Construction of Urban Legends. *Social Problems* 32:488–99.

Bohm, R. (1986). Crime, Criminal and Crime Control Policy Myths. *Justice Quarterly* 3(2): 193–214.

Bromley, D., Shupe, A. and Ventimiglia, J. (1979). Atrocity Tales, the Unification Church, and the Social Construction of Evil. *Journal of Communication* 29(3): 42–53.

Cavender, G. and Bond-Maupin, L. (1993). Fear and Loathing on Reality Television: An Analysis of "America's Most Wanted" and "Unsolved Mysteries." *Sociological Inquiry* 63(3): 305–17.

Dickson, D. (1968). Bureaucracy and Morality: An Organizational Perspective on a Moral Crusade. *Social Problems* 16:143–56.

Drechsel, R., Netteburg, K. and Aborisade, B. (1980). Community Size and Newspaper Reporting of Local Courts. *Journal Quarterly* 57:71–78.

Dumont, M. (1973). The Junkie as Political Enemy. *American Journal of Orthopsychiatry* 42(4): 533–40.

Dunn, K. (1994). Crime and Embellishment. *Los Angeles Times Magazine*, (April, 10): 24–25, 36–39.

Editorial Staff (1991). Halloween Candy Hotline. *Police Chief* (September): 70.

Fishman, M. (1976). Crime Waves as Ideology. *Social Problems* 25:531–43.

Fitzpatrick, P. (1992). *The Mythology of Modern Law*. London: Routledge.

Galliher, J. and Walker, A. (1977). The Puzzle of the Social Origins of the Marijuana Tax Act of 1937. *Social Problems* 24:371–73.

Gerbner, G. (1972). Communication and Social Environment. *Scientific American* 227:153–60.

Goode, E. (1994). The Selling of Reality. *U.S. News & World Report*, (July 25).

Goode, E. and Ben-Yehuda, N. (1994). *Moral Panics: The Social Construction of Deviance*. Cambridge: Blackwell.

Hallin, D. (1990). Whatever Happened to the News? *Media & Values* 50:2–4.

Hynds. P. (1990). Balance Bias with Critical Questions. *Media & Values* 50:5–7.

Jenkins, P. and Katkin, D. (1988). Protecting Victims of Child Sexual Abuse: A Case for Caution. *Prison Journal* 58(2): 25–35.

Karmen, A. (1978). How Much Heat? How Much Light: Coverage of New York City's Blackout and Looting in the Print Media. In *Deviance and Mass Media*, C. Winick (ed.). Beverly Hills: Sage Publications.

Kraska, P. (1990). The Unmentionable Alternative: The Need for, and the Argument Against, the Decriminalization of Drug Laws. In *Drugs, Crime and the Criminal Justice System*, R. Weisheit (ed.). Cincinnati, OH: Anderson Publishing Company.

_____ (1985). Personal Communication. Huntsville, TX: Sam Houston State University.

Lang, K. and Lang, G. (1969). *Television and Politics*. Chicago: Quadrangle Books.

Mannheim, K. (1936). *Ideology and Utopia*. New York: Harcourt, Brace and World.

Marsh, H. (1991). A Comparative Analysis of Crime Coverage in Newspapers in the United States and Other Countries From 1960–1989: A Review of the Literature. *Journal of Criminal Justice* 19(4): 67–79.

Maxwell v. City of Indianapolis, 998 F.2d 431 (7th Cir. 1993).

Medalia, N. and Larsen, O. (1958). Diffusion and Belief in a Collective Delusion: The Seattle Windshield Pitting Epidemic. *American Sociological Review* 23:180–86.

Messner, S. and Rosenfeld, R. (1994). *Crime and the American Dream*. Belmont, CA: Wadsworth.

Orcutt, J. and Turner, J. (1993). Shocking Numbers and Graphic Accounts: Quantified Images of Drug Problems in the Print Media. *Social Problems* 40(2): 190–205.

Pepinsky, H. and Jesilow, P. (1985). *Myths that Cause Crime*, 2nd ed. Cabin John, MD: Seven Locks Press.

Pfohl, S. (1977). The Discovery of Child Abuse. *Social Problems* 24:310–23.

Quinney, R. (1970). *The Social Reality of Crime*. Boston: Little, Brown.

Reinarman, C. (1996). The Social Construction of Drug Scares. In *Social Deviance*, E. Goode (ed.). Boston: Allyn and Bacon.

Ryan, W. (1976). *Blaming the Victim.* New York: Vintage Books.

Schoenfeld, A., Meier. R. and Griffin, R. (1979). Constructing a Social Problem: The Press and the Environment. *Social Problems* 27:38–61.

Smith, D. (1975). *The Mafia Mystique.* New York: Basic Books.

Sutherland, E. (1950). The Diffusion of Sexual Psychopath Laws. *American Journal of Sociology* 56:142–48.

Tunnell, K. (1992). Film at Eleven: Recent Developments in the Commodification of Crime. *Sociological Spectrum* 12:293–313.

Zuckerman, M. (1994). The Limits of the TV Lens. *U.S. News & World Report,* (July 25): 64.

CRIME WAVES AND CRIME FEARS
The Myth of an American Crisis

2

The people of this country are fed up with crime. The media report it. Statistics reflect it. Polls prove it.
> —FBI Director Louis J. Freeh

When Federal Bureau of Investigation Director Freeh made the remark above to the National Press Club, in 1994 he was echoing the popular mood in America. That same year, a national news magazine published the following quotation and analysis:

> What are we going to do about these kids (monsters) who kill with guns??? Line them up against the wall and get a firing squad and pull, pull, pull. I am volunteering to pull, pull, pull.

> That's not a rap lyric. It's from an anonymous letter to a judge in Dade County Florida—part of the shared unconscious talking.

And suddenly we're all ears. In one of the most startling spikes in the history of polling, large numbers of Americans are abruptly calling crime their greatest concern. Confronted by clear evidence of a big issue, politicians everywhere, including the one in the White House, are reaching for their loudest guns: prisons, boot camps, mandatory sentences. Months before the start of baseball season, the air is full of shouts of "Three strikes and you're out" (Lacayo, 1994:51).

A *Time* public opinion poll reported that 19 percent of all Americans regard crime as the country's most serious problem, up from only 4 percent one year earlier (Lacayo, 1994). The poll showed that twice as many Americans were more worried about crime than the economy or unemployment and four times as many were more concerned with crime than with the budget deficit. And, on the face of it, it's no wonder that they are so worried about crime in America. As Director Freeh (1994:5) went on to say in his speech: "In the past 30 years, homicides have nearly tripled, robberies and forcible rapes each are up over 500 percent, and aggravated assaults have increased more than 600 percent. According to the most recent National Crime Victimization Survey, nearly 37 million people have been injured by criminals in this country in the past 20 years. It is estimated that crime has cost America $19 billion since 1991."

Director Freeh's ominous report included seemingly irrefutable data from the National Crime Victimization Survey (NCVS). Another passage from that survey revealed:

Persons age 12 or older, living in the United States, experienced 34.7 million crimes in 1991 according to the National Crime Victimization Survey (NCVS). Approximately 6.4 million of these victimizations consisted of violent crimes such as rape, robbery, and aggravated and simple assaults. Another 12.5 million victimizations were crimes of theft—larcenies both with and without contact between the victim and offender. Finally there were 15.8 million household crimes in 1991 (Bastian, 1992:1).

These are truly horrifying numbers that clearly suggest Americans are being attacked, killed, and maimed by criminals in such numbers and at such an alarming rate that drastic measures must be taken to deal with this national crisis. If these reports are correct, we are somewhere between three and six times more likely to be attacked by a violent criminal than in the past, and about one in four Americans are in dire danger of criminal victimization each and every year.

Not only are the crime trends as presented by Department of Justice officials very menacing, but our perception of the individual who will inflict this harm is equally menacing. Jeffrey Reiman (1990:42) details our view of the typical criminal as: "He is, first of all a he. Second, he is a youth—most likely under the age of twenty. Third, he is predominantly urban—although increasingly suburban. Fourth, he is disproportionately black—blacks are arrested for Index crimes at a rate three time that of their percentage in the national population. Finally he is poor." Reiman (1995:52–53) goes on to comment:

> This, then, is the Typical Criminal, the one whose portrait President Reagan described as "that of a stark, staring face, a face that belongs to a frightening reality of our time—the face of a human predator, the face of the habitual criminal. Nothing in nature is more cruel and more dangerous" . . . This is the Typical Criminal feared by most law-abiding Americans. His crime, according to former Attorney General John Mitchell (who was by no means a typical criminal), is forcing us "to change the fabric of our society, . . . forcing us, a free people, to alter our pattern of life, . . . to withdraw from our neighbors, to fear all strangers and to limit our activities to 'safe' areas."

Just as we have images of the typical criminal, we also have mental images of the typical crime. Once again, Reiman (1995: 59–60) describes the mental image most people have of a "crime":

> Think of a crime, any crime. Picture the first "crime" that comes into your mind. What do you see? The odds are you are not imagining a mining company executive sitting at his desk calculating the costs of proper safety precautions and deciding not to invest in them. Probably what you see in your mind's eye is one person physically attacking or robbing something from another on the threat of physical attack.

Not only is crime rampant, dangerous, and threatening to explode in America, but it is the worst kind of crime. It is the kind of crime portrayed by George Bush's infamous "Willie Horton" commercials during the 1988 presidential campaign. The Bush campaign took a single case where one convicted violent offender participating in a highly successful prison furlough program in Massachusetts committed a violent crime while on furlough. The ad campaign had a devastating effect on the governor of the state, Michael Dukakis, in his presidential election bid. It also played to the worst fears and prejudices Americans harbor about crime. It portrayed a violent crime, with a weapon, committed by a stranger, who was sent to prey on society by a "soft" criminal justice system. Perhaps even more important was the fact that Willie Horton was an African-American male whose predations were directed at white females.

The Bush campaign exploited our worst images of crime—violent crime, committed by sociopathic strangers, preying upon otherwise sober, cautious, ascetic, industrious and righteous citizens. Is it any wonder that 81 percent of the public favors life imprisonment for anyone convicted of three serious crimes or that 65 percent of the public favors the imposition of a 10 P.M. curfew for citizens under the age of 18? (Lacayo, 1994). Is it any wonder that politicians clamor for more police, more prisons, and more severe sentences to combat an ever-increasing panoply of crimes? The mood of the American public is becoming increasingly ugly toward these violent predators, leading to an attitude of "Line them up and pull, pull, pull."

Before we "line them up," perhaps a moment of sober reflection is necessary—sober reflection isolated from the ritualistic wailing of politicians for more police and prisons; sober reflection detached from the hysterical reports of the tabloid media; sober reflection disconnected from the self-serving warnings of law enforcement executives seeking to enhance their powers, personnel, and budgets. As this chapter will suggest, a period of sober reflection results in very different conclusions about this wave of crime allegedly gripping America and threatening the innocent. Facts have been curiously missing from the debate about crime in America, and the facts, once uncovered, are startling:

- There is no crime wave in the United States. Criminal victimization has been steadily and drastically declining for the past two decades. The American crime wave is a myth.
- Of those crimes that do occur, the overwhelming majority are the result of minor incidents involving neither serious economic loss nor extensive physical injury. Most crimes are not the serious, violent, dangerous crimes which compose the public stereotype of America as a predatory jungle.
- Of those violent crimes which do threaten our well-being, most are committed by relatives, intimate friends and acquaintances—those we trust the most—not by psychopathic, predatory strangers lurking in urban shadows.
- Most crimes, even violent crimes, do not involve the use of a weapon.
- Most crimes, particularly violent crimes, are intraracial, thereby contradicting the subtle and not so subtle appeals to racism by our crime fighters.

How Much Crime Is There?

Crime statistics must be treated with great caution and not an inconsiderable amount of skepticism. When numbers are bandied about purporting to reflect the danger of crime in society, two primary questions must be asked before accepting their validity. The first is, are they measuring what they claim to measure? And the second is, where do these numbers come from? Do they emanate from a source which has something to gain from the way crime is presented to the public?

The Official Crime Rate

The most commonly recognized measures of crime in America are to be found in the Federal Bureau of Investigation's (FBI) *Uniform Crime Reports (UCR)*. Despite its popularity since its inception in 1930 (Thompson, 1968), the *UCR* has drawn strong criticism (see, Wolfgang, 1963). These reports are issued annually and are compilations of "crimes known to the police." Crimes known to the police is a relatively ambiguous category, for the most part composed of complaints from citizens indicating that a crime has occurred (Chambliss, 1988). This does not mean that a crime has actually occurred. In reporting "crimes known to the police," the FBI does not insist that a suspect be arrested, or, for that matter, that the crime even be investigated and "founded" (Chambliss, 1988:29). The only requirement is that someone, somewhere, for some reason, believed that a crime may have been committed.

In addition, the crime categories and definitions used by the FBI are designed in such a way as to maximize both the severity of the crime and the number of crimes that are reported by local police departments. As Chambliss (1988:29–30) points out:

> The crime categories used in the *UCR* are often ambiguous. For example, burglary requires the use of force for breaking and entering in many states, but the FBI tells local police departments to report the crime as burglary simply if there is unlawful entry. Merging these two types of offenses makes statistics on "burglary" ambiguous. More important is the way police departments are instructed to fill out the forms. In every instance, the instructions are designed to show the highest incidence of crime possible. The *Uniform Crime Reporting Handbook* states: "If a number of persons are involved in a dispute or disturbance and police investigation cannot establish aggressors from the

victims, count the number of persons assaulted as the number of offenses."

In reporting homicides, the instructions to the police are equally misleading from the point of view of gathering scientifically valid information. The instructions tell police departments that they should report a death as a homicide regardless of whether other objective evidence indicates otherwise: ". . . the findings of coroner, court, jury or prosecutor do not unfound [change the report of] offenses or attempts which your [police] investigations establish to be legitimate."

In addition, studies of the police reporting of crime by social scientists have demonstrated with regularity that these statistics are subject to political manipulation. For example, Richard Nixon, while president, instituted a crime control experiment in Washington, D.C., to demonstrate the effectiveness of his crime control proposals for the nation. The Nixon administration wanted the crime rate to go down to claim success. The crime rate did indeed go down—not because of any diminution in crime but because of bureaucratic manipulation in the reporting of crime by the police. The District of Columbia police simply began listing the value of stolen property at less than $50, thereby removing a vast number of crimes from the felony category and thus "reducing" the crime rate (Seidman and Couzens, 1974).

Selke and Pepinsky (1984) in a study of crime reporting practices over a thirty-year period in Indianapolis found that local police officials could make the crime rate rise or fall, depending upon political exigencies, virtually at will. Other studies have also demonstrated the ease with which crime rates can be manipulated (Mcleary, Nienstedt and Erven, 1982).

Finally, *UCR* data are presented in ways which are far from scientific. The FBI creates "Crime Clocks" and other highly visual gimmicks designed to exaggerate the incidence of crime and the threat it poses to the public (see also, Tunnell, 1992). For example, the 1993 *UCR* tell us that one criminal offense occurs every two seconds; one violent crime occurs every sixteen seconds; one forcible rape occurs every five minutes; one burglary occurs every eleven seconds. These presentations of *UCR* data are designed to exaggerate the amount of crime in society and to leave the impression that violent victimization is imminent. Chambliss (1988:31) commented on the use of such gimmicks: "This makes good newspaper copy and serves to give the law enforcement agencies considerable political clout, which is translated into ever-increasing budgets, pay raises, and more technologically sophisticated 'crime-fighting' equipment. It does not, however, provide policy makers or social scientists with reliable data."

Further indication of the suspect nature of *UCR* data comes from an article in the *Wall Street Journal* which begins "This is the tale of crime in two cities" and goes on to use the most recent *UCR* data to show New York City's rate of serious crime is 56 percent lower than Tallahassee's. The FBI includes seven crimes—murder, rape, robbery, aggravated assault, burglary, larceny and motor-vehicle theft in its index. In 1993, New York City had 600,346 reported index crimes for a population of 7.3 million. Its crime rate is therefore 82 crimes per 1,000 people. Tallahassee reported 19,426 crimes and has a population of 132,252. Its rate was 147 crimes per 1,000 (Bennett, 1995). According to the FBI, Tallahassee residents were almost 60 percent more likely to be assaulted and almost three times more likely to be raped (Bennett, 1995). Clearly, the "facts" represented by the FBI figures need additional explanation. The first clarification is to note, again, that these figures are based on *reported* crime. If New Yorkers have been conditioned to accept some crimes as inevitable and not worth reporting, that skews the rate. If crimes must be reported in person at the precinct station versus a squad car being dispatched to take a report, that's another significant factor. If residents of both cities do not take the same precautions (locked car doors, valuables hidden, windows secured in houses), the rates will differ. Tallahassee has a large number of college students, which can affect the likelihood of certain crimes. There are a number of essential details that need to be addressed before numbers tell us anything.

Crime rates tell us virtually nothing about crime. "Crimes known to the police" is an ambiguous category, subject to political manipulation, and easily adjusted to the bureaucratic requirements of law enforcement agencies. They may tell us a little about police department practices and policies, but they tell us absolutely nothing useful about crime. Nonetheless, it is on the basis of "crime rates" that both criminal justice officialdom and the media inform us about the ever-increasing threat from crime and criminals. It is, in part, based on these very questionable statistics that FBI Director Freeh warns us about massive increases in violent crime in the past thirty years.

Having said all of this, it may be startling to note that the FBI has reported a 3 percent decline in violent crime and 4 percent decline in crime overall for the first six months of 1993 based on their aggregation of "crimes known to the police" (Lacayo, 1994:51). At the close of 1994, the *UCR* showed that serious crime reported to the police had declined for the third consecutive year (BJS, 1995). The first quarter of 1995 shows a continuation of that decline (Staff, 1995). Even more startling is the fact that any decline in "crimes reported to the police" is remarkable for two reasons having nothing to do with the actual incidence of crime. First, there are many more police on the streets today than in the past. The number of police officers has increased about 20 percent in the last two decades; there are about 800,000 police on the streets today (BJS, 1994). More police, patrolling a greater area with greater frequency, should be reporting a greater amount of crime. If the number of police officers increased by 20 percent, we would expect reported crime to increase about the same amount. Instead we find a significant decline. Second, citizen reporting of crime is up markedly in the past two decades (see table 1). Every single category of crime shows an increase in the percentage of victims reporting crimes to the police. This means that the decrease in reported crime rates is even greater than it appears at first glance because people are reporting much more crime.

As we shall see, this reported decline in the crime rate is not a result of greater care in the culling of data or a sudden change in the direction of the political manipulation of crime rate statistics. It is, in fact, a vast understatement of just how much decline in the amount of crime in society there really has been.

Table 1

Percentage of Victimizations Reported to the Police in 1973 and 1991

Crime	Percent of Victimizations Reported	
	1973	**1991**
Rape	49%	59%
Robbery	52%	55%
Aggravated Assault	52%	58%
Simple Assault	38%	42%
Larceny with Contact	33%	38%
Larceny without Contact	22%	28%
Household Burglary	47%	50%
Household Larceny	25%	28%
Motor Vehicle Theft	68%	74%

Source: Bastian, L. D. (1992). *Criminal Victimization 1991*. Washington, D.C.: Bureau of Justice Statistics, p. 5.

Victimization Rates

Another, and a far better, source of crime data is the National Crime Victimization Survey (NCVS). Since 1972, the Department of Justice has conducted an annual survey of 100,000 households across the country, asking respondents if they or any member of their households had been a victim of crime in the past year. The victimization surveys are clearly superior to *UCR* data in that they measure both reported and unreported crime, and they are unaffected by technological changes in police record keeping, levels of reporting by victims to the police, and the other factors that call into question the validity of *UCR* data (Bureau of Justice Statistics, 1993). The NCVS data comes from questionnaires (carefully designed for validity and reliability by social scientists) administered to a very large, demographically representative sample of the U.S. population. While no survey is perfect, the NCVS represents the best available source of data on crime victimization in the United States. While the way the data are reported and presented is subject to political manipulation, the data themselves are scientifically valid.

The NCVS data speaks volumes about crime in America. Most importantly, it tells us that crime has been decreasing in America for the past two decades—and that the decrease has been precipitous. From 1973 to 1991 personal crimes (rape, robbery, assault, and personal larceny) have decreased by 25.3 percent and household crimes (burglary, household larceny and motor vehicle theft) have decreased by 25.2 percent. The victimization rate for rape is down 11.6 percent; for robbery 17.2 percent, for aggravated assault 22.2 percent, and for burglary the victimization rate has declined 42.1 percent (see table 2). Only simple assault, a relatively minor crime which will be discussed later, and motor vehicle theft have shown increases. The simple, indisputable fact is that crime in the United States is down 25 percent. It appears that a massive decrease in the incidence of crime has somehow sparked a massive increase in concern about crime. As Samuel Walker (1994:5) succinctly puts it: "This is one of the longest and most significant declines in the crime rate in American history. Much of the public hysteria about crime is misplaced."

Let us be very clear about this. The only reliable, scientific data we have on crime in America tell us that crime is decreasing, has been decreasing, and continues to decrease. Furthermore, those decreases are not small or marginal, they are consistent decreases which have resulted in a 25 percent diminution in the amount of

Table 2

Victimization Rates Per 1,000 Households in 1973 and 1991

Crime	Victimization Rates		Percent Change
	1973	1991	
Rape	1.0	0.8	− 11.6
Robbery	6.7	5.6	− 17.2
Aggravated Assault	10.1	7.8	− 22.2
Simple Assault	14.8	17.0	+ 15.1
Larceny with Contact	3.1	2.3	− 23.5
Larceny without Contact	88.0	58.7	− 33.3
Household Burglary	91.7	53.1	− 42.1
Household Larceny	107.0	88.0	− 17.7
Motor Vehicle Theft	19.1	21.8	+ 14.3

Source: Bastian, L. D. (1992). *Criminal Victimization 1991*. Washington, DC: Bureau of Justice Statistics, p. 4.

crime in America. The irony of this prolonged and significant decrease in crime resulting in so much public hysteria should not be lost on us.

The decrease in crime over the past eighteen years is only a part of the story. The victimization survey also tells us that 90.8 percent of the American population was *not* the victim of any kind of personal crime. In addition, the vast bulk of crime that does occur is not the heinous, violent predatory crime that we imagine. By the victims' own accounts, most crime is of relatively little impact and importance.

The Reality of Crime

For 1991, the NCVS victimization rate for crimes of violence was 31.3 per 1,000 households. Roughly, this victimization rate suggests that about 3 percent of the population aged 12 and older was the victim of a violent crime. As defined by the NCVS, these crimes of violence include rape, robbery, and aggravated and simple assault (see table 3). When the victimization rates for rape, robbery,

Table 3

Victimization Rates for Personal and Household Crimes, 1991

Crime	Victimizations per 1,000 persons age 12 or older or per 1,000 households
Personal Crimes	92.3
Crimes of Violence	31.2
Rape	.8
Robbery	5.6
Assault	24.8
Aggravated	7.8
Simple	17.0
Crimes of Theft	61.0
Personal Larceny with Contact	2.3
Personal Larceny without Contact	58.7
Household Crimes	62.9
Household Burglary	53.1
Household Larceny	88.0
Motor Vehicle Theft	21.8

Source: Bastian, L. D. (1992). *Criminal Victimization 1991*. Washington, DC: Bureau of Justice Statistics, p. 6.

and aggravated assault are totaled independent of simple assault, we arrive at a figure of 14.2 victimizations per 1,000 households. Thus, the majority of violent crime victimizations are the result of simple assault (17.0 per 1,000 households).

While simple assault is a crime, and no argument is made that it should be ignored or condoned, it is not the kind of violent crime emphasized by the media or law enforcement officials—nor is it the type of violent crime consistent with the public stereotype. What is simple assault and how threatening is it to public safety? As William Chambliss (1984:169) has pointed out in analyzing victimization survey data: "The most likely crime of violence that one will experience is 'simple assault,' an attack without a weapon resulting either in minor injury (e.g., bruises, black eye, cuts, scratches, swelling) or an undetermined injury requiring less than

2 days of hospitalization. Also includes attempted assault without a weapon."

Unlike the public image of a typical crime, simple assault involves no weapon and only minor injury. Furthermore, unlike our image of the typical crime, the offender in a simple assault is usually a friend, relative, or acquaintance, and the crime takes place in the course of normal social interaction, not in a dark alley:

> Almost half the "simple assaults" were altercations between people who were "not strangers" . . . As other research has shown, there is an interaction process characteristic of assaults which always lays open the question of who is the victim and who is the offender. Since only the viewpoint of the victim is being surveyed, these figures on assault . . . , while not very high, are nonetheless probably an overstatement of the stereotyped picture of an "assault" in which someone who is "doing nothing" is suddenly and maliciously attacked by a stranger. Further details on the circumstances may reveal that many of the so-called assaults were (a) arguments where one person started swinging . . . first or (b) trivial pushing and shoving. This interpretation is also supported by the fact that two-thirds of the assaults were not reported to the police, and the reasons for not reporting most often given were that the incident was unimportant or that "nothing could be done" because of "lack of proof" (Chambliss, 1984:169–70).

So, while simple assault is a crime, it is often a private matter, between friends, relatives, and acquaintances, involving no serious injuries, but comprising a majority of all violent victimizations.

Turning to crimes of theft we find a similar situation. The NCVS data tell us that in 1991 the victimization rate for crimes of theft was 61.0 per 1,000 households, or roughly 6 percent of the population over age twelve. Once again, however, considerable ambiguity exists over these victimizations. Crimes of theft are made up of personal larceny with contact and personal larceny without contact. Ninety-six percent of all crimes of theft victimizations are personal larcenies without contact (see table 3). Again, we must ask, what constitutes a personal larceny without contact?

> We do not know what the actual event was that led people to say that they had had something stolen. But given the fact that these incidents consist of the taking of personal property without personal contact when the property was away from home, it is probable that the vast majority of these "crimes" consists of property being taken after the victim left it in a subway station and which was gone when he or she returned to retrieve it, or having small amounts of money or personal property that had

been left in an unlocked desk, locker or office removed. Certainly bicycle theft would account for a large share of these "personal crimes without contact" (Chambliss, 1984:168).

There is no doubt that the stealing of bicycle or the removal of a gym bag from a locker or a briefcase from a subway stop is a crime. But, once again, it is not the kind of serious, life-threatening, dangerous crime perpetrated by a weapon-wielding offender which is so prominent in the public mind. The crimes of simple assault and personal larceny without contact make up 75.7 percent of all personal crime victimizations.

In addition, victims often regard the crimes they report as not being very important. In 1990, those respondents to the NCVS who did not report crimes to the police indicated in 6.2 percent of the cases that the crime was "not important enough." In 20 percent of the cases, they did not report the crime because it was a "private or personal matter." And in 4.4 percent of the cases, they reported that these crimes, classified as violent by the NCVS, were so unimportant that they didn't want to take the time or incur the inconvenience of reporting them (*Sourcebook*, 1992:268–69). Once again, this does not mean that a crime was not committed, nor does it mean that the crime should be ignored, but it does mean that the nature of the crime differs greatly from the popular perception of crime. "Making rough estimates from the data presented, we could conservatively conclude that over half of the victimizations were on the borderline of criminal behavior and consisted of acts that in no way pose a serious threat to the 'life and property' of the nation's people" (Chambliss, 1984:169).

In 1992 the National Crime Victimization Survey was redesigned (Department of Justice, 1994). Categories of crime were changed. For example, rape was aggregated with sexual assault to create a new crime classification; aggravated and simple assault were combined with "attempted assault with weapon" and "attempted assault without weapon," thereby creating a new category of crime. This redesign may have simply been part of the ongoing methodological review of the NCVS which attempts annually to increase the reliability and validity of the data. On the other hand, this redesign may have had more sinister and diabolical implications. As we have seen, the NCVS has demonstrated clearly that contrary to politicians' proclamations and public impressions, serious crime has been declining precipitously in America for the past two decades. Those are hardly data which justify new expenditures on law enforcement and prisons; expansion of the criminal law; the extension of the death penalty to a plethora of new offenses; and a "crime crisis" mentality in policy making. The reclassification of criminal acts in the redesigned survey makes it inevitable that the victimization rates and frequencies will be higher than in the surveys of the previous twenty years. Perhaps the survey redesign was a bit of methodological legerdemain intended to give the appearance that the incidence of victimizations was increasing. Perhaps the intent was simpler. By changing the survey and the classification of crimes in that survey the Justice Department has made it impossible to continue a longitudinal comparison of data into the future. It is therefore not possible to determine if the clear trends of declining victimization have continued through 1992 and 1993. The Department of Justice has, intentionally or otherwise, made continuing analysis of a trend which negates the official position impossible.

While the data for 1992 and 1993 are no longer comparable with earlier data, they do provide clues which indicate that even a change in survey design cannot obfuscate the continuing drastic decrease in serious crime. Based on the NCVS data for those two years it is clear that serious crime is still declining and still declining markedly. For example, the new category of "Rape/Sexual Assault" showed a decrease of 20.9 percent in the two-year period of the new survey. "Completed Rape" showed a decline of 9.2 percent; "Attempted Rape" declined by 24.5 percent; "Sexual Assault" declined by 26.6 percent (Department of Justice, 1994). In other crime categories victimization declines have also continued and are also steep: "Completed Robbery" declined by 5.2 percent; "Simple Assault Completed With Injury" declined by 6.9 percent; "Theft" declined by 2.2 percent; and all "Property Crimes" declined by 0.9 percent (BJS, 1995; Department of Justice, 1994).

The newly designed survey can no longer be compared directly with previous years, but it still demonstrates the simple fact that criminal victimizations continue to decline year after year. The justification for crime-war hysteria is clearly absent in both old and new victimization studies.

Strangers and Crime

There are other strong indicators that tell us that crime is less of a threat than the popular stereotype would have us believe. For example, at least half of all homicides in the United States take place among people who know each other. One out of five homicides (19.7 percent) where the victim-offender relationship can be determined occur in situations in which the offender and victim are members of the same family, and over half of the homicides (57.4 percent) occur among people who are friends or acquaintances (Prothrow-Stith, 1994). The popular image of a homicide as being related to burglary, youth gangs, drug trafficking, stalkers, and serial killers accounts for less than 25 percent of all homicides.

In other crimes the picture is similar. For example, about half of all rapes of females were perpetrated by someone known to the victim, not by a stranger lurking in an alley or hiding behind bushes (Bureau of Justice Statistics, 1993). If we look at the victimization rate for violent crimes we find that males are more likely than females to be victimized by a stranger, but that both males and females are more likely to be victimized by someone they know (see table 4). Women, in particular, have considerably more reason to fear those close to them than they have to fear predatory strangers. Overall, we are about 60 percent more likely to be victimized by someone known to us. Clearly, it is not the lurking stranger whom we must fear; those closest to us pose the greatest danger.

Weapons, Injury, and Crime

Our images of crime are also filled with weapons, wielded by violent strangers, causing great physical harm. Once again, however, the

Table 4
Violent Crime Rates and Victim/Offender Relationships

Victim/offender Relationship	Violent crime rate per 1,000	
	Females	Males
Strangers	5.4	12.2
Relatives and Acquaintances	11.9	13.4
Intimates	5.4	.5
Other Relatives	1.1	.7
Acquaintance	5.4	12.2

Source: Bureau of Justice Statistics (1993). *Highlights from 20 Years of Surveying Crime Victims.* Washington, DC: U.S. Government Printing Office.

data indicate that such crimes are the exception not the rule. Only one out of three violent crimes involve the use of a weapon (Bureau of Justice Statistics, 1993). Of all violent crimes 32 percent involved a weapon; in 9 percent of those cases a handgun was used, in 7 percent a knife, and in 6 percent a blunt object of some type. The typical violent crime does not involve a weapon of any type.

Not only do violent victimizations typically not involve weapons, but they typically do not involve injuries. When they do, the injuries are minor. In all violent victimizations less than 33 percent of the victims are injured, and only 4 percent suffer serious injury. Of those who are injured, 84 percent received bruises, cuts, or scratches; 1 percent received gunshot wounds; 4 percent received knife wounds, and 7 percent either suffered a broken bone or had teeth knocked out (Bureau of Justice Statistics, 1993). In summary, less than about 3 out of every 1,000 violent crime victims are shot, about 12 are wounded by a knife, and about 20 or so have broken bones or teeth knocked out. In addition, only 9 percent of all victims of violent crimes lost any time at all from work, and only 10 percent incurred medical expenses as a result of the crime (Bureau of Justice Statistics, 1993). By 1993 less than 1 in 4 violent crimes resulted in an injury and 70 percent of all violent crimes were attempted but not completed (BJS, 1995). Unlike the picture of crime presented by the media, politicians, and the police, the truth is that even in "violent" crimes very few people are injured—and even fewer are seriously injured.

Race and Crime

Finally, we turn to the issue of race and crime. Both crime reporting by the media and anti-crime railing by politicians and law-enforcement executives have played callously and cynically on a deeply ingrained racism in American culture. George Bush's Willie Horton ad was designed not just to raise the issue of crime but to link it with the offender most feared by white middle-class America. Similarly, tabloid media coverage of shootings of white tourists by young African American men at rest stops, gang attacks on innocent passersby in our cities, or acts of vigilantism by the Bernard Goetzes of the world against minority youth appeal to the same racist fears. The fact is, however, that interracial crime is very rare and interracial crime images can be dismissed as blatant and insidious appeals to the darkest parts of the American soul. Seventy-five percent of white crime victims are victimized by whites, and 85 percent of African-American crime victims are victimized by

African Americans. In 80 percent of all violent crimes, the victims and offenders are of the same race (Bureau of Justice Statistics, 1993). Furthermore, in 1993 African Americans were almost twice as likely to become the victims of violent crime; persons living in households with income below $7,500 were over twice as likely to be victimized than those with incomes over $75,000 (BJS, 1995). Once again, lack of knowledge about crime statistics leave the public vulnerable to the most divisive myth. Attempts to link crime and race play to the audience's worst impulses.

Crime and Perception

Since crime, particularly serious crime, is and has been declining significantly, why is the fear of crime—accompanied by feelings of public punitiveness—increasing so dramatically? At least three factors appear to be responsible for the lack of congruence between the facts and public perception: the media and their reporting of crime; alarms raised by the law enforcement establishment; and the politicalization of crime.

The media seriously distort our view of crime and its dangers through their presentation of both news and entertainment programming. Tabloid television shows such as *Hard Copy* and *A Current Affair* present almost daily reports on some type of crime. The crimes they choose to feature are hardly the mundane, relatively unimportant crimes that make up the bulk of actual crime committed. After all, few viewers would stay tuned to watch a special segment on the theft of little Tommy's bicycle or the picking of Mr. Jones' pocket during his lunch break. But viewers will tune in for sensational murders, like those of Nicole Brown Simpson, Ronald Goldman, and the Menendez killings in California; for lurid details on the serial murders of Ted Bundy or Jeffery Dahmer; or for a segment on the murder of a tourist at a Florida highway rest stop. Despite the fact that patricide among the privileged, serial murder, and rest stop killings of tourists are relatively rare events, they are emphasized and highlighted by these programs.

The exaggeration of the violent and the weird can be seen in both "straight" news programming and entertainment programming. The local 6 P.M. evening news predictably leads with a story about a murder committed in the course of a robbery—or even a robbery without a murder, as long as violence was threatened. The hundreds or thousands of normal, mundane crimes that occur daily in every city are scarcely mentioned. Entertainment shows such as *NYPD Blue, Matlock, Law and Order*, and even the somewhat more refined *Murder She Wrote* feature crimes of violence. Few people want to see Matlock vigorously defend a case of "personal larceny without contact" or Jessica Fletcher solve a troublesome case of misplaced luggage in Cabot Cove. A study by Ericson, Baranek and Chan (1989) discovered that crime takes up 20 percent of all local television news shows, 13 percent of all national news shows, and 25 percent of the column inches in newspapers. Beirne and Messerschmidt (1991) suggest that the media distort our images of crime in three primary ways. First, the intense coverage of crime in the media conveys the incorrect image that we are a society suffering an epidemic of violent crime. As they point out, murder constitutes only 0.2 percent of all crimes reported to the police, yet it occupies 25 percent of newspaper reports about crime. Second, the media create the impression, with the help of law enforcement agencies, that crime rates are continually increasing. Finally, the media downplay the amount of nonviolent crime, creating the false image that crime means acts of predatory violence. Simply put, the media, in an attempt to attract viewers and advertising dollars, play up the most atypical, violent, heinous crimes and downplay the recurrent dull crimes which make up the overwhelming majority of crimes committed in the United States.

The law enforcement establishment also has a pecuniary interest in portraying crime as a serious and growing threat. At the state and local level in the United States, there are about 17,500 police agencies, with 800,000 employees—and annual budgets in excess of $28 billion (Cole, 1995). Add to these the approximately 50 to 60 federal agencies employing almost 69,000 officers (BJS, 1994) with budgets in excess of $12 billion and you will find a large interest group for crime control issues. This interest group is even more impressive in size when the 13,000–15,000 courts in the United States are added and the $37 billion spent in the past two decades on prison construction is considered (Smolowe, 1994).

It is in the interests of police administrators, prison officials, judges and prosecutors to keep crime in the forefront of public debate. Enormous sums of money, millions of jobs, and bureaucratic survival depend on permanent concerns about crime. Year after year official statistics have been presented to increase public fear and downplay any decrease in criminal activity. Policy decisions and jurisdictional issues are also concerns for the criminal justice system in presenting crime as a major threat. For example, the "war on drugs" expanded the jurisdiction and police powers of many federal law enforcement agencies. The FBI, the keeper of crime statistics, was the primary beneficiary. Attempts to remove due process protections and to expand the scope of the legal code also depend on an active public interest in crime matters.

Finally, both the media and the criminal justice system find ready allies among those officeholders and office seekers who must court the public. Crime is a relatively easy issue. No one is for it; therefore being against it is a safe political issue. Exaggerating and distorting the amount and shape of the crime threat is standard fare for politicians. Democrats and conservative Republicans both compete to see who can spend the most money and appear the most punitive in putting together crime control legislation. Imagine justifying costly crime control packages by explaining that crime is less of a threat today than in 1973. It is not scientific proof which persuades, it is appeals to fear about serial killings, stalkers, child abductions, drive-by shootings, car-jackings, and violent predators. Supporting such measures will no doubt curry favor with the voting public; telling the truth could lead to premature retirement.

It appears that we have a warped and distorted view of crime in America. Whether it is the media, politicians, police—or a combination of all three—who are responsible, we have created a popular image of crime that is a myth. The American crime wave does not exist. Crime is decreasing and decreasing substantially. The prominent image fixed in the public mind, the "Typical Criminal," does not exist. Crime is committed primarily in social settings by unarmed people who are relatives, friends and acquaintances of their victims. The prototypical crime is also a myth. Most crime is minor in nature and content, and very little crime results in serious injury. We have either been duped or have duped ourselves.

The distortion of the image of crime does not stop with myths of crime waves, archetypical criminals and prototypical crimes. As you will find in the chapters that follow, we have refined the mythology of crime in America. Not only is crime presented as dangerous and rampant, it is depicted in the most frightening and stark manner. Images of serial killers, stalkers, child kidnappers, and cop killers hyperbolize an already exaggerated phenomenon. We will return repeatedly to the same questions. How do such outrageous myths become ingrained in our social fabric—and whose interests do the divisive exaggerations serve?

Sources

Bastian, L. (1992). *Criminal Victimization 1991*. Washington, D.C.: Bureau of Justice Statistics.

Beirne, P. and Messerschmidt, J. (1991). *Criminology*. New York: Harcourt Brace Jovanovich.

Bennett, A. (1995) Apples and Oranges: Is Tallahassee Really as Plagued by Crime as New York City? *Wall Street Journal*, (January 5): A1, A8.

Bureau of Justice Statistics (1995). *Criminal Victimization 1993*. Washington, DC: U.S. Government Printing Office.

_____ (1994). *Federal Law Enforcement Officers, 1993*. Washington, DC: U.S. Government Printing Office.

_____ (1993). *Highlights from 20 Years of Surveying Crime Victims*. Washington, DC: U.S. Government Printing Office.

_____ (1992). *Sourcebook, 1991*. Washington, DC: U.S. Department of Justice.

Chambliss, W. (1988). *Exploring Criminology*. New York: Macmillan.

_____ (1984). *Criminal Law in Action*. New York: John Wiley.

Cole, G. (1995). *The American System of Criminal Justice*, 7th ed. Belmont, CA: Wadsworth.

Department of Justice (1994). *Crime Rate Essentially Unchanged Last Year*. Washington, DC: Bureau of Justice Statistics.

Ericson, R., Baranek, P. and Chan, J. (1989). *Negotiating Control: A Study of News Sources*. Toronto: Toronto University Press.

Freeh, L. (1994). Responding to Violent Crime in America. *FBI Law Enforcement Bulletin*, (April). Washington, D.C.: U.S. Government Printing Office.

Lacayo, R. (1994). Lock 'em Up. *Time*, (February 7): 51–53.

Mcleary, R., Nienstedt, B. and Erven, J. (1982). Uniform Crime Reports as Organizational Outcomes: Three Time Series Quasi-experiments. *Social Problems* 29:361–72.

Prothrow-Stith, D. (1994). Stop Violence Before it Begins. *USA Today*, (February 24): 11A.

Reiman, J. (1995). *The Rich Get Richer and the Poor Get Prison*, 4th ed. Boston: Allyn & Bacon.

_____ (1990). *The Rich Get Richer and the Poor Get Prison*, 3rd ed. New York: Macmillan.

Seidman, D. and Couzens, M. (1974). Getting the Crime Rate Down: Political Pressure and Crime Reporting. *Law and Society Review* 8:457–93.

Selke, W. and Pepinsky, H. (1984). The Politics of Police Reporting in Indianapolis, 1948–78. In Chambliss, W. (ed.), *Criminal Law in Action*. New York: John Wiley.

Smolowe, J. (1994). . . . And Throw Away the Key. *Time*, (February, 28).

Staff (1995). Going Down for the Third Time. *Law Enforcement News* 21:1, 6.

Thompson, J. (1968). Uniform Crime Reporting: Historical IACP Landmark. *Police Chief* (February): 22–34.

Tunnell, K. (1992). Film at Eleven: Recent Developments in the Commodification of Crime. *Sociological Spectrum* 12:293–313.

Walker, S. (1994). *Sense and Nonsense About Crime and Drugs*, 3rd ed. Belmont, CA: Wadsworth.

Wolfgang, M. (1963). Uniform Crime Reports: A Critical Appraisal. *University of Pennsylvania Law Review* 3:708–38.

The Myth and Fear of Child Abduction

3

To be unaware of the issue of missing children in America is to be totally isolated from newspapers, television, mail, or other forms of communication. Beginning in the early 1980s, barely a week went by when the public was not exposed to photographs, stories, and debates on the issue of missing and abducted children. Virtually every form of media was used to circulate the faces and stories of missing children. From milk cartons to flyers in utility bills to television documentaries, Americans were made aware of the child abduction "epidemic" (Kappeler and Vaughn, 1988). "Toy stores and fast-food restaurants distributed abduction-prevention tips for both parents and children. Parents could have their children finger-printed or videotaped to make identification easier; some dentists even proposed attaching identification disks to children's teeth" (Best, 1987:102). By 1991 a study in *Clinical Pediatrics* showed that parents were more frequently worried about abduction than about anything else, even car accidents.

In 1995, the Family Protection Network took out full-page advertisements in major newspapers and magazines across the country. "If your child were missing, you'd think about it every minute." The copy describes how the service will put a photograph of the child and other information into a database reaching numerous sources including the police, media and private investigators to help avert "the terrifying problem of child abduction." At the end of the advertisement, the $250 annual fee is mentioned followed by "But think what you might get in return." The general manager denies that his company is preying on paranoia and says, "This is a prudent way for parents to prepare for their child's safety. No one has the dedicated massive resources we do, the private investigators, the technology, the commitment (Zorn, 1995:1)."

The image of missing and exploited children commands public attention and causes emotional response in even the most callous individuals. One cannot be exposed to the stories and images of these victims and not feel some emotion. Shedding the issue of emotionalism, however, produces serious questions concerning the true magnitude of the missing children problem and the necessity of drastic social changes aimed at its prevention. Several factors have culminated in the creation of an unprecedented level of fear and concern about the possibility of child abduction in America. Combining the concepts of missing children and exploited children precipitates increased emotionalism and concern. The thought of a child being abducted conjures images of strangers hiding under cover of darkness, waiting to whisk away someone's child, intent on committing some unspeakable crime.

Indisputably, there are hideous acts committed against children. These incidents often receive great media attention and remain embedded in the public's mind for extended periods of time. The media have and continue to focus extensively on sensational cases like the abductions and murders of Polly Klaas, Megan Kanka and Adam Walsh and the serial murders of children in both Atlanta and Texas. Recently the media focused on the abduction and abuse of ten-year-old Katie Beers from her home in Bay Shore, New York. Katie was abducted and held for seventeen days by John Esposito, a friend of Katie's family, in an underground room. Newspapers across the county reported the incident, focusing almost exclusively on the attempted sexual abuse and the "hidden dungeon," "secret room," and "coffin of confinement" where the child was held. The horror of such examples becomes the key ingredient in the public's perception of the child abduction problem. As one group of researchers remarked, the popular stereotype of kidnapping "draws its imagery from nationally notorious and tragic cases of abduction . . ." (Finkelhor, Hotaling and Sedlak, 1992:226).

Besides drawing on the imagery of notorious cases, the media and politicians alike have linked child abduction with sexual exploitation. In 1981 when the issue of missing children was first taking shape, Senator Hawkins remarked that "once they [missing children] are on the street they are fair game for child molestation, prostitution, and other exploitation (Hawkins, 1991:2, as quoted in Best, 1987:105). Little has changed in the 1990s. In November of 1992 and again in May of 1993, the television show *America's Most Wanted* aired specials devoted to child abduction. To promote the first show, the producers ran advertisements in *TV Guide* stating that "over one million children are reported missing every year" (*TV Guide*, 1992:123). The 1992 special spent considerable time forging the imagery of child abduction with talk of "serial child molesters" and "child predators," vowing to get "the people who hunt our children" (*America's Most Wanted*, 11/20/92).

Media imagery aside, children can be missing without being the victims of sexual exploitation or abuse. Conversely, exploitation and abuse can occur in the child's own home; unfortunately, these acts are not limited to strangers. The media did attract enormous public attention in 1994 when Susan Smith's two young sons were allegedly kidnapped in a car-jacking. The nation watched in horror as it was later revealed that Susan Smith had released the parking brake on her car and let it roll into a lake with her sons strapped in their car seats (Gibbs, 1994). "However bone-chilling the idea of stranger-danger, more children are murdered by parents than kidnapped by strangers. Susan Smith is more the norm than Richard Allen Davis [on trial in 1995 for the murder of Polly Klaas]. Yet every magazine has had its cover stories on stranger-danger; every television show its scare segments; every school its lessons. In every home, parents wrestle with their terrors and with how to warn their children away from the unfamiliar" (Goodman, 1995:11). Countless other cases do not receive national attention. Consider a few incidents of "missing" and abused children that were given only passing mention by the media:

- Alice Brown of Leavenworth, Kansas, pleaded guilty to involuntary manslaughter in the death of her four-year-old son, Steven. His body was found encased in concrete on the family's back porch (*USA Today*, 5/18/93:3A).

- Tanisha Nobles of Dayton, Ohio, who reported her son, Erick age two, missing from a shopping mall was charged with murder after she admitted to police that she had drowned her child because he "got on her nerves" (*USA Today*, 1/14/93:6A).

- Reenee Lloyd and Bertha Toombs, the aunt and grandmother of five-year-old Marquisha Candler, were charged with murder after police uncovered the child's remains in a California desert. The two women had made public pleas for help in locating the missing child (*USA Today*, 9/30/92:10A).

The issue of child abduction is further complicated by the lack of a clear criterion for defining the term "missing children." While this may seem to be a trivial point, an analysis of the issue illustrates that the ambiguity of the definition "missing" distorts the public's perception of the "reality" and "extent" of the missing children problem. Joel Best (1987:105) insightfully captured the context in which the definition of missing children was constructed when he contended that reforms advocating new laws to address the missing children problem "preferred an inclusive definition of missing children." Under their definition a child would have included people as old as twenty and people missing for a few hours, and the events surrounding the child's disappearance would include most "misadventures which might befall children" (Best, 1987:105).

Eventually because of the political pressure generated by individuals, reform groups, and the media, Congress took action to address the problem of missing children in America. The Missing Children's Assistance Act (MCAA) of 1983 defined "missing child" as:

1) any missing person thirteen years of age or younger, or;

2) any missing person under the age of eighteen if the circumstances surrounding such person's disappearance indicate that such person is likely to have been abducted (Sec. 272).

The Missing Children's Assistance Act passed in 1984 created the National Center for Missing and Exploited Children (NCMEC) and defined "missing" in the following language:

1) . . . "missing child" means any individual less than eighteen years of age whose whereabouts are unknown to such individual's legal custodian if—

(A) the circumstances surrounding such individual's disappearance indicate that such individual may possibly have been removed by another from the control of such individual's legal custodian without such custodian's consent; or

(B) the circumstances of the case strongly indicate that such individual is likely to be abused or sexually exploited. . . . (Sec. 5772).

The text of the new law clearly forged a linkage between sexual exploitation and child abduction. Persons encompassed by these definitions may be missing for a variety of reasons unrelated to stranger abductions. Children can be abducted by a parent who does not have legal custody, an act commonly termed "child stealing" (McCoy, 1978). They may be missing because they ran away from home; or they may be suffering from some form of illness such as amnesia; or in some cases they may have committed suicide. Clearly, not all children counted as missing are lost as a result of some stranger's criminality. It is with these broad definitions of missing children that the reality of the problem becomes distorted.

The failure to formulate clear typologies of missing children combined with law enforcement's merging the two categories—exploited and missing—contribute to the public's perception of the extent and context of the problem. Taken together, these factors produce a situation conducive to imprecise reporting of statistics to the public, often in such a fashion as to exaggerate the potential danger of a child being abducted by strangers.

For the purposes of clarity, the terms child stealing, child snatching and parental abduction (often used interchangeably) are defined as the taking of a child by a parent in violation of a court's custody order. Child kidnapping is defined as a stranger's abduction of a child in violation of criminal law. With these distinctions in mind, let's begin considering how the "reality" of missing children is created and how the problem has become defined in American society.

Creating Reality and Defining the Problem

The public is exposed to statistics on missing children published by sources varying from newspaper articles and private organizations to governmental reports. These reports generally indicate that anywhere between 1.5 and 2.5 million children are missing from their homes each year (Regnery, 1986; Treanor, 1986; *Congressional Record—Senate*, 1983; Dee Scofield Awareness Program, 1983a). Of those reported missing, it is predicted that as many as fifty thousand children will never be heard from again (Schoenberger and Thomas, 1985; Thornton, 1983). It is also estimated that as many as five thousand of these missing children will be found dead (*Congressional Record—Senate*, 1983).

These are the statistics distributed by various sources for public consumption. A more critical examination of these statistics finds that within some jurisdictions between 66 and 98 percent of those children listed as missing are in reality runaways and were not abducted at all (Treanor, 1986; Schoenberger and Thomas, 1985). Police departments receive many more reports of missing runaways than other types of missing cases. Regnery (1986) estimates that nearly 1 million of the reportedly 1.5 million missing children are runaways. As many as 15 percent of the missing children may be parental abductions (Schoenberger and Thomas, 1985). In fact one author has maintained that about one out of twenty-two divorces ends in child theft (Agopian, 1981). Others estimate that between twenty-five thousand and one hundred thousand incidents of missing children are parental abductions (*Congressional Record— Senate*, 1983; Foreman, 1980).

In a Michigan study (Schoenberger and Thomas, 1985), the researchers found that 76 percent of the 428 entries examined in Michigan's lost children files should have been removed because the persons entered as missing had been located. These 325 children had been found but were not removed from the active files. The vast majority of children listed as missing in law enforcement records are found within twenty-four hours. Similarly, the Massachusetts State Police Missing Persons Unit estimates that 40 percent of their computer listings on missing persons are in reality solved cases that have not been removed from the data base (*Crime Control Digest*, 1985). These files along with data from other states are used to support contentions about the scope of the missing children problem. The presence of inaccurate data in many law enforcement record systems has contributed to dramatically overestimating the number of children missing.

Bill Treanor (1986:BI), Director of the American Youth Center, presents even more conservative figures:

> Up to 98 percent of so-called missing children are in fact runaway teenagers. . . . Of the remaining 2 percent to 3 percent, virtually all are wrongfully abducted by a parent. That leaves fewer than two hundred to three hundred children abducted by strangers annually. The merchants of fear would have you believe that five thousand unidentifiable bodies of children are buried each year. In truth, it's less than two hundred dead from all causes, such as drowning, fire and exposure, not just murder.

To compound the problem, statistics are presented regarding the number of children murdered each year. It is maintained that approximately twenty-five hundred children are murdered yearly including homicides committed by ". . . psychopathic serial murderers, pedophiles, child prostitution exploiters and child abusers" (Regnery, 1986:42). However, of these twenty-five hundred children murdered, the number reported missing prior to their victimization was not determined. Additionally, it is not reported how many of these victims were killed by their parents or other family members.

By 1992 researchers had determined that out of 63 million children living in the United States, each year only two hundred to three hundred cases of missing children met the imagery of the stereotypic kidnapping (Finkelhor, Hotaling and Sedlak, 1992). The odds of having a child abducted by a stranger are about 1 in 25,200. In fact, the missing children on the milk cartons have most likely been taken by a non-custodial parent. These distinctions are easily blurred in the public's eyes. Statistics, often without qualification, are distributed to the public from official governmental sources. Such findings raise serious doubts as to the accuracy of the statistics presented to the public concerning the number, nature, and ultimate fate of missing children in America. Growing public awareness and concern over the missing children issue has been promoted through the use of inconsistent and inaccurate statistics. Such statistics and the effect they have on the public and its perception of the extent of the missing children problem have both obvious and unintended consequences.

Latent Functions of Prevention

The primary obvious function of increased awareness of the problem of child abduction is prevention. Public preoccupation with child safety has become evident in the proliferation of children's literature addressing safety and the prevention of abduction. With increasing frequency, books and other forms of literature are becoming available to children illustrating the dangers of social contact with persons who are not considered a member of the family or extended family unit. These texts often inform children of the danger of speaking or having contact with strangers.

Children's books of this nature can have at least three negative latent functions. First, through children's literature the feelings of danger are equated with social contacts outside the family unit. This perception can result in increased social isolation and alienation of children from the community. As both parents and children begin to equate social contact outside the family with danger and impending harm, community interaction may decrease. The fear of child abduction, while limiting social interaction, may reduce the family's dependence on third parties for child care. Parents may begin to rely less and less on day-care facilities, in-house sitters, and other third-party child care sources. As parents take greater responsibility for the care of their children, the contact within the family unit may increase and greater dependence may be placed on the interactions of family members. The family unit may gain greater solidarity as social interaction with community decreases, but the cost may be increased fear and stunted social development.

Second, these texts often give questionable information to children. A specific case in point is a children's book entitled *Never Talk to Strangers* (Joyce, 1967), which advises children through the use of animal characters that they should never talk to strangers, but that it is acceptable to become friendly with acquaintances of the family. This notion is reinforced by a government program sponsored by the National Child Safety Council (NCSC). According to H. R. Wilkins of the Michigan based NCSC, millions of milk cartons were printed utilizing animal characters to instruct children of the dangers of contact with strangers (*Juvenile Justice Digest*, 1985a). Yet, the literature and research on both sexual abuse of children and child abduction indicates that children are more often victimized by acquaintances rather than strangers. Consider these statistics:

- A study of three states found that 96 percent of female rape victims under the age of twelve knew their attackers (BJS, 1994b:2).
- A study of murder found that 63 percent of the children murdered under the age of twelve were killed by family members. In 57 percent of these cases children were murdered by a parent (BJS, 1994a:5).

As children are taught to run from unfamiliar persons, they are also being taught to run into the arms of those most often engaged in child abuse. These media also promote the notion that if properly educated, children can distinguish between those individuals who are "safe" and those persons to avoid, a distinction even criminologists are reluctant to make. The fear invoked by the spread of prevention literature and the indoctrination of children with safety tips like avoiding strangers may be a zero sum game. Such prevention measures only replace the unfounded fear of child abduction with a new and equally unfounded fear of strangers. These approaches to prevention may confuse children and promote paranoia and insecurity. "We must also begin to acknowledge the risks of protectiveness. Risks that come to a diverse society when kids grow up suspicious of others. Without even knowing it and with the best of intentions, we can stunt our children with our deep longing to keep them safe" (Goodman, 1995:11). Where would a child abused by a family member turn given such mixed messages—to a stranger?

Third, the proliferation of literature on child safety stresses that it is the duty of the parents to educate their children. This responsibility in itself is not damaging and may very well contribute to prevention. However, placing blame on parents for failing to educate their children allows the responsibility for child safety to be shifted from social control agencies such as the police and society as a whole to individual family members. In effect, what these texts suggest is that if parents fail to educate their children and if children fail to heed their warnings, they will be abused or abducted and the responsibility rests on them alone—rather than on the offender or society as a whole. We in effect begin to "blame the victim" and shift focus from the offender and crime control agencies to the child and the nonvigilant parent.

The link between literature and the behavior of adolescents has been well illustrated by the works of David McClelland (1961). He found that the economic performance of a culture varied with the degrees of achievement portrayed in literature. Parallels were drawn between the declines and increases in achievement, and the decline and increase of literature depicting economic success. This research shows that literature has an effect on behavior. Whether it is motivation to excel economically or motivation to withdraw socially, the effect is profound. By depicting strangers as the persons to fear and avoid due to the possibility of abduction and exploitation, we circumvent serious consideration of the extent to which relatives, friends, and family members are involved in child abuse and abduction. We also divert attention away from the fact that most missing children are runaways.

Concern for child safety and fear of child abduction have not been limited to children's literature. The fear of child abduction is beginning to motivate legal reform designed to criminalize a vast scope of behavior involving children. Society is turning to solutions to a problem which has been defined based on fear and inaccurate information.

Legal Reform: Creating Crime and Criminals

The emotional furor and fear of child abduction has created an atmosphere conducive to the creation of a new crime and class of criminals. In California, prior to 1976, if a parent took his or her child in violation of a custody order, it was not considered a criminal offense. Since October 1, 1977, legislation in California has been enacted making it a criminal offense for parents to take custody of their own children in violation of a court custody order (Agopian, 1980; 1981).

The state of New York has enacted similar legislation, making parental child abduction a felony offense. In February of 1985, the National Governors' Association called for all states to adopt legislation making child snatching a felony offense, regardless of whether the violator was a parent or stranger to the child. As of 1983, forty-eight states had adopted the Uniform Child Custody Jurisdiction Act and forty-two states had classified child snatching as a felony (Silverman, 1983). The legal response to this behavior has also been addressed at the federal level.

Prior to 1983, the United States Department of Justice restricted the issuance of warrants for the arrest of parents who took illegal custody of their children and subsequently crossed state lines. Since December 23, 1982, federal and local law enforcement officials can seek federal arrest warrants for child snatching even if there is no evidence to suggest the child is in physical danger (*United States Attorneys Bulletin*, 1983). In the Sixth Report to Congress on the implementation of the Parental Kidnapping Prevention Act of 1980, the Department of Justice indicated that during 1982, thirty-two "fugitive parents" were arrested by the Federal Bureau of Investigation (FBI). These arrests took place prior to removal of the warrant restrictions imposed by the Department of Justice. During the first nine months of 1983, after the removal of restrictions, the number of parents arrested by the FBI doubled to sixty-four (U.S. Department of Justice, 1983). With these reforms at both the state and federal levels, we have created the crime of child stealing and the criminal classifications of "fugitive parents" and "custody criminals."

While in some circles this easing of restrictions on the FBI and the criminalization of custody violations may be viewed as a positive step in solving the problem of child abduction by parents, there are certainly negative effects associated with the increased arrests of fugitive parents. An undetermined number of these children are physically and emotionally better off with the parent who committed the illegal act. This point was illustrated in the case of a Long Island girl who was abducted by her mother after the father was awarded custody. After lengthy consideration of the case, New York Justice Alexander Vitale ordered that the mother should retain custody of the child, having decided that this was in the best interest of the child's welfare. The best interests of the child are not always paramount in the court's decision-making process; jurisdictional concerns are often given equal importance in deciding custody cases after an abduction has occurred (*In re Nehra v. Uhlar*, 1977).

The second problem arises out of labeling as criminal the parent who removes his or her child from an abusive atmosphere. While not all parents who abduct their children do so with such noble intentions, these parents often have little recourse. They must decide either to comply with the law and allow their children to endure further abuse or to violate the law in the best interest of the child. Legal avenues are often closed to parents. Fees associated with custody battles often restrict a parent's ability to obtain legal redress in these matters. Regardless of the individual's ability to access the courts, child abduction is often seen as the last alternative to maintaining a full-time parental relationship (Agopian, 1980). While some degree of formal social control may be required to prevent parental abductions, better screening and investigation by the courts before awarding custody could reduce the incidents of well-meaning child abduction. We can only speculate as to the motivations of a parent who would abduct a child or children from an apparently stable family, but the abducting party must (at a minimum) feel that an inadequate custody arrangement was made in the judicial process. More equitable custody arrangements may be one way of reducing child abduction by parents.

A more pragmatic consideration is the utility of fugitive warrants. A fugitive warrant does not allow the FBI to take a child into custody or even to return the child to the parent with legal custody. These children are often kept in foster homes or other community shelters while courts review the custody arrangements. In some cases these environments may be more damaging than staying with the abducting parent. Arrests on fugitive warrants do not reflect the number of children who are actually returned to their legal guardians as a result of arrest. Furthermore, the warrant does not allow agents to effect arrests of persons other than those named on the warrant, who may have materially participated in the abduction or currently have physical custody of the child.

The emotional atmosphere created by increased publicity of the dangers of child abduction has been used as a political tool to advocate stiffer punishments for offenders. In the cases of true stranger abductions, this may be a desirable prevention measure. It is, however, questionable whether stiffer sanctions would prevent hideous crimes against children. The desire to control and sanction stranger abduction often becomes politicized with calls for stiffer penalties for all offenders who commit crimes against children. Calling for legislative "reform," Congressman Henry J. Hyde advocated mandatory life sentences for persons who kidnap a child and the death penalty for child abduction that results in death. The congressman stated, "I do not feel it is too harsh to say that one who kidnaps or murders a child has forfeited his right to freedom forever" (*Juvenile Justice Digest*, 1985b:4). A call for the death penalty for child snatchers has not been limited to the political arena. Private organizations devoted to the location of missing children have also called for legislative "reform." Dee Scofield Awareness Program (1983b), a private organization located in Tampa, Florida, recommends that child abduction be elevated to a federal offense punishable by either death or life imprisonment. The most disturbing point here is that the proposed reform fails to make a clear distinction between parental custody violations and stranger abductions.

Conclusion

McClintock and Haden (1970) have pointed out that the manner in which a problem is defined is related to the type of social control systems available to address that problem. The problem of missing children in America is no exception to their contention. It becomes clear from the analysis of the missing children problem that the issue has been defined as epidemic in proportion and criminal in nature. Given this definition and perception of the issue, the current course of action—the criminalization of this behavior—is clearly a logical consequence. As a society, we have defined the problem as an abnormal behavior on the part of a select group of individuals we have chosen to call criminal. We have chosen social control agencies and criminal sanctions as the solutions for this epidemic. In an attempt to prevent this behavior, we have subsequently created a new classification of crime and criminals without distinguishing the motives and reasoning behind this behavior. In short, we have defined missing children in America as a legal problem with legal solutions.

As long as this definition and solution dominate the missing children problem, a solution is not forthcoming. The legal "solution" is merely a reaction to an undesirable behavior. However, if we define the scope of the problem more accurately and develop a clear understanding of the various types of incidents that collectively compose the problem, an alternative solution may yet emerge.

As previously mentioned, the missing children problem includes runaways, parental abductions, and stranger abductions. Incorporating runaways into missing children statistics produces the perception of an epidemic. The inclusion of stranger abduction in the composite figures permits the problem to be defined as criminal. Linking sexual abuse and exploitation provokes emotionalism. Incorporating parental abductions and then criminalizing all abductions promotes conceptualization of the issue as both epidemic and criminal.

In order to begin to address the problem of missing children in America, we must first understand the problem in a social rather than a legal context. Only then can we begin to take preventive rather than reactive measures. The nature of family relationships must be explored in order to begin to understand why 1.5 million children flee their homes each year. We must also begin to realize that our legal system, both criminal and civil, is not a panacea for all social problems. One of the most preposterous illustrations of using the legal system to address a social problem took place in Will County, Illinois in 1995. Associate Judge Ludwig Kahar sentenced two sisters aged twelve and eight to spend the night in a foster home for refusing to visit their father in North Carolina, as mandated by a court-ordered visitation schedule. The following week, he sentenced the older girl to the county juvenile detention center. "Visit your father or go to jail" seems counterproductive to promoting familial relationships!

We must begin to separate the missing children problem into its parts—social and legal. The fact that thousands of children each year are abducted by their parents raises serious questions about our legal system's ability to define family relations equitably through divorce and child custody orders.

Our adversarial trial system, so often alluded to in the criminal process, is omnipresent in civil courts as well. The adversarial process creates what amounts to custody battles. These events can only be seen as creating conflict, setting the stage for continued discord between the winners (those awarded custody) and the losers (those denied custody). Unless a more equitable process is developed—one void of the conflicts resulting from the current system—child stealing will remain a result of custody battles. If we cannot adequately understand the behavior of runaway children and the reaction of parents who are denied the custody of their children, or develop workable solutions to custody arrangements, how can we hope to understand or prevent child abductions by strangers?

While this chapter has attempted to address some of the latent and manifest functions of the fear of child abduction, the true effects of increased awareness, fear, and use of prevention programs may not become evident for some time. It is too early to speculate on the possible effects the promotion of these fears will have on future generations of parents, children, and legal reforms.

The preliminary indications are that we will continue to attempt to handle the issue through increased legislation and stiffer penalties for offenders. However, it is evident that the campaign against missing children, while well intended, will have negative effects socially. It would appear prudent to consider the social effects of prescribing criminalization and prevention in mass dosages. It is readily apparent that critical research designed to reflect accurately the scope of the problem of missing children in America is desperately needed. Furthermore, we can no longer afford to implement prevention programs without first giving critical thought to both the manifest and latent social functions of these policies.

Sources

Agopian, M. (1981). *Parental Child Stealing*. Lexington, MA: Lexington Books.

_____ (1980). Parental Child Stealing: Participants and the Victimization Process. *Victimology: An International Journal* 5:263–73.

Best, J. (1987). Rhetoric in Claims-Making: Constructing the Missing Children Problem. *Social Problems* 34(2): 101–21.

Bureau of Justice Statistics (1994a). *Murder in Families*. Washington, DC: U.S. Department of Justice.

Bureau of Justice Statistics (1994b). *Child Rape Victims, 1992*. Washington, DC: U.S. Department of Justice.

Congressional Record—Senate (1983). Statements on Introduced Bills and Joint Resolutions, (October 27): S14787.

Crime Control Digest (1985). Massachusetts' New Missing Children Law Requires Immediate Reports. Investigations, (January 14): 10.

Dee Scofield Awareness Program (1983a). Federal Legislation: The First Steps Tampa, Florida. (Educational Report No. 5).

_____ (1983b). Estimated Annual-Missing Children (Educational Report, November). Tampa, Florida.

Finkelhor, D., Hotaling, G. and Sedlak, A. (1992). The Abduction of Children by Strangers and Non-Family Members: Estimating the Incidence Using Multiple Methods. *Journal of Interpersonal Violence* 7(2): 226–43.

Foreman, J. (1980). Kidnapped! Parental Child-Snatching, A World Problem. *Boston Globe*, (March 16): B1.

In re Nehra v. Uhlar, 43 N.Y. 2d 242 (1977).

Gibbs, N. (1994). Death and Deceit. *Time*, (November 14): 43–48.

Goodman, E. (1995). Our Problem with Strangers. *Chicago Tribune*, (July 18), sec. 1: 11.

Joyce, I. (1967). *Never Talk to Strangers: A Book About Personal Safety.* Racine, WI: Western Publishing Company.

Juvenile Justice Digest (1985a). National Campaign to Locate Abducted Children Enters Phase II. (February 25): 2.

_____ (1985b). Kidnapping and Abuse: Rep. Hyde Seeks Life in Prison or Mandatory Death Sentence for Crimes Against Children. *Juvenile Justice Digest* (July 1): 4.

Kappeler, V. and Vaughn, J. (1988). The Myth and Fear of Child Abduction: Defining the Problem and Solutions. *The Justice Professional* 3(1): 56–69.

McClelland, D. (1961). *The Achieving Society.* New York: Free Press.

McClintock, F. and Haden, T. (1970). Law and Social Control Systems: A Functional Analysis. In *The Division and Classification of the Law*, Jolowicz, J. (ed.). London: Butterworth.

McCoy, M. (1978). *Parental Kidnapping: Issues Brief No. ID 77117.* Washington, DC: Congressional Research Service.

Missing Children's Assistance Act of 1983, 28 U.S.C. 534.

Missing Children's Assistance Act of 1984, 42 U.S.C 5772.

National Governors' Association (1985). Policy on Missing and Exploited Children. National Governors' Association.

Regnery, A. (1986). A Federal Perspective on Juvenile Justice Reform. *Crime and Delinquency* 32:39–51.

Schoenberger, R. and Thomas, W. (1985). Missing Children in Michigan: Facts, Problems, Recommendations. *Juvenile Justice Digest* 31:7–8.

Silverman, B. (1983). The Search for a Solution to Child Snatching. *Hofstra Law Review* 11:1073–1117.

Thornton, J. (1983). The Tragedy of America's Missing Children. *U.S. News and World Report*, (October 24): 63–64.

Treanor, B. (1986). Picture Our Missing Children: The Problem Is Blown Far Out of Proportion. *The Houston Chronicle*, (February 1).

United States Attorneys Bulletin (1983). (April 29): 31.

U.S. Department of Justice (1983). *Sixth Report to Congress on Implementation of the Parental Kidnapping Prevention Act of 1980.* Washington, DC: U.S. Department of Justice.

Zorn, E. (1995). Fear of Abductions Is Bad for Parents Good for Business. *Chicago Tribune* (May 25), sec. 2:1.

Myth and Murder
The Serial Killer Panic
Philip Jenkins*

4

I f we relied solely on the evidence of the mass media, we might well believe that every few years a particular form of immoral or criminal behavior becomes so dangerous as to threaten the foundations of society. Some of these media scares or moral panics have been analyzed by social scientists, including the "dope-fiend" in his or her many guises (most recently, the crack enthusiast); the "sex-fiend" of the 1940s; and the white slavers of the Progressive Era (Duster, 1970; Becker, 1963; Tappan, 1955).

These panics are important in their own right for what they reveal about social concerns and prejudices—often based on xenophobia

---

* Pages 69–78 were excerpted from "Myth and Murder: The Serial Killer Panic of 1983–85," *Criminal Justice Research Bulletin*, 3(11): 1–7,1988. The additional material was adapted from *Using Murder: The Social Construction of Serial Homicide*, Aldine de Gruyter, 1994 with the permission of the publisher.

and anti-immigrant prejudice (Gusfield, 1981). Also, bureaucratic factors sometimes play a part when an agency promotes a panic in order to enhance its own power and prestige. An example often quoted in support of this theory is the view that Harry Anslinger and the Federal Bureau of Narcotics promoted a marijuana scare in the mid-1930s for just these ends. . . .

Describing such issues as panics does not imply that they are without some real foundation. There were and are rapists and pimps, and drugs can cause immense damage to individuals and communities. However, such a "scare" period immensely inflates the perceived scale and prevalence of the original problem. . . . Severe legislation is proposed which in turn fuels . . . the original issue and compounds the process.

The 1980s were a particularly fruitful period for such media panics over crack, child sexual abuse, juvenile satanism, sex and violence in rock lyrics, and (in a rather different category) AIDS (Jenkins and Katkin, 1987). Each of these concerns had its particular stages of origin and growth and deserves study. Here, the focus will be on the source of another modern panic—serial murder. This is a topic at least as old as Jack the Ripper and his contemporaries.[1] However, between 1983 and 1985, serial murder suddenly attained a major place in media attention [and has retained that position] because of a number of specific incidents that we will examine.

It will be argued that the serial murder panic illustrates the way in which the media discover and publicize certain forms of criminality, but it also suggests certain important directions in contemporary views of the origins and causation of crime and deviancy.

Creating a Myth

Between late 1983 and mid-1985, serial murder was the topic of numerous stories in magazines and newspapers, as well as television programs. Most of these stressed the same group of themes, which can be conveniently summarized from a front-page *New York Times* article of January 1984 (Lindsey, 1984). The key concepts were that serial murder was an "epidemic" in contemporary America; that there were a great many such offenders active at any given time . . . ; and that the new wave was qualitatively different from earlier occurrences, with more savage torture and mutilation of victims. Serial killers accounted for perhaps 20 percent of American murder victims, or some 4,000 a year, according to the accounts. It was also strongly implied that this appalling "disease" was largely a distinctive American problem.

According to Lindsey (1984:1), "the officials [quoted] assert that history offers nothing to compare with the spate of such murders that has occurred in the United States since the beginning of the 1970s." He quotes Robert O. Heck of the Justice Department for the view "that as many as 4,000 Americans a year, at least half of them under the age of eighteen, are murdered this way. He said he believes at least thirty-five such killers are now roaming the country." Many of their victims were to be found among the thousands of bodies that turned up each year unidentified and unexplained. As for the explanation of the new phenomenon, Lindsey quoted favorably the view that exposure to sexually explicit and sado-masochistic material tended to arouse the violent instincts of individuals already prone to extreme acts by an abusive upbringing.

The essentials of Lindsey's story were repeated extensively during 1984 and 1985, especially the estimate of 4,000 serial victims each year (Berger, 1984; Kagan, 1984). This was cited in a *Life* article, which placed particular emphasis on serial murder as an almost uniquely American problem, and in many leading newspapers and magazines (Darrach and Norris, 1984). In *Newsweek*, it was stated that "Law-enforcement experts say as many as two-thirds of the estimated 5,000 unsolved homicides in the nation each year may be committed by serial murderers" ("Random Killers," 1984). . . .

The "unsolved" category from the Uniform Crime Reports would be frequently quoted in this context. Sometimes, a story about the importance of serial murder would cite the number of "unsolved" killings (roughly 5,400) and then go on to estimate how many of these might be serial victims—anywhere from 10 percent to two-thirds, as here. Some stories, however, would simply state the number of "unsolved" homicides without comment. This left the reader with the impression that this *was* the serial victim category.

The visual media strongly reinforced the concept of a new and appalling menace, with each story—almost without fail—beginning with the estimate of 4,000 victims a year. Each of the major news magazines of the *60 Minutes* format had at least one story of this type, while an *HBO America Undercover* episode was a documentary focusing on three well-known serial killers of the last decade: Ted Bundy, Edmund Kemper, and Henry Lee Lucas. Interviews with all three were featured, as were harrowing (and controversial) reconstructions, using actors.

The Lucas Case

Lucas was the most frequent vehicle for a news story on this topic, which customarily referred to FBI sources for background on the scale of the murder wave. Lucas was a convicted murderer and arsonist, who began confessing numerous murders in the fall of 1983. By the end of the year, his alleged "kill" had exceeded three hundred, and he did much to shape the stereotype of the multiple murderer.

Lucas gave plausibility to the estimate of thousands of victims each year. His case also placed emphasis on the serial killer as a wanderer, a drifter who travelled between many states and regions. The roaming killer was much cited in 1983–85, especially when media attention was focused on the nationwide murder spree of Christopher Wilder in the spring of 1984 (eleven victims in six states). This suggested the need for new federal or interstate agencies to combat the menace, for which local agencies were clearly inadequate. Finally, Lucas and his partner Otis Toole claimed responsibility for the murder of a number of child victims including Adam Walsh, a notorious case that gave rise to national concern about missing children. This helped ensure publicity and linked the murder issue with other contemporary panics in which unsubstantiated figures were being severely misused. . . .

During 1985, the Lucas case effectively collapsed under investigation from a number of journalists. The estimate of three hundred murders had fallen to about ten, spread over several states. The basis of at least part of the panic had disappeared. It should be noted incidentally that the credence given to Lucas had never been universally shared, and the *New York Times* had published a very critical article as early as November 1983 (Joyce, 1983). However, the case continued to be a media event well into the following year.

To return to the substance of the issue: how accurate were the claims made by writers on serial murder in these years? The Lucas affair does not discredit the existence of a real phenomenon, and the media were drawing very heavily on the opinions of major official agencies, above all in the Justice Department. The figure of 4,000 seems to have been orthodox opinion, but none of these reports recognized how far such a view departed from established views on the nature of murder. That in itself certainly would not disprove the idea, but it is a statistic with remarkable consequences. Each year (it appears), one American murder in five is committed by a serial killer like Ted Bundy or John Wayne Gacy—perhaps

40,000 victims between 1976 and 1986. If this is correct, then clearly our views of violent crime need to be radically reformed. So would our policies and funding priorities in law enforcement. This was also an important argument for a growing federal role in law enforcement, as only national coordination could prevent the depredations of a Wilder or a Lucas.

The Reality of Serial Murder

There are a number of questions about this "murder wave" that must be handled separately. That this type of crime had become much more common is not in dispute. However, its numerical impact on the murder statistics may be challenged. Finally, how may this sudden concern about serial murder be explained, especially when reports of notorious multiple murder cases were no more frequent in 1983 than five or ten years previously?

In studying the reality of serial murder, there are a number of important problems. There is a sizeable literature on multiple murder, but it has important gaps and discontinuities. We have a distinguished psychiatric literature on the causation of this type of offense, and there is a superb and accessible synthesis of theories and typologies (see Nettler, 1982; Lunde, 1976; Abrahamsen, 1973, 1960, 1945; Toch, 1969). We have many case-studies of killers, some of the "True Crime" type, but many rising above it to real insight; but the real lack is in systematic or "epidemiological" studies of the phenomenon. Without such a broad survey, changes in the frequency or distribution of serial murder are not possible. Only in 1985 did a really scholarly work of this nature appear (Fox and Levin, 1985) and even it made no attempt to compare the frequency of serial murder reports in the period studied (1974–79) with earlier periods (for the growing academic interest in the topic, see Egger, 1986, 1984; Hickey, 1986; Leyton, 1986; Vetter and Rieber, 1986).

The present study is based on media publications about serial killers, including a search of the *New York Times* since 1960. Only serial murder cases are noted, rather than mass murderers, and killing for profit or political motive has been excluded—a decision that would by no means be accepted by all students of the topic. This exclusion is sometimes difficult, as in the case of Joseph Paul Franklin, reported in 1984 as a suspect in fifteen murders in eight states between 1977 and 1980. This would appear to be a "serial" case, but there is strong evidence that Franklin acted out of his political beliefs as a white supremacist who used violence against biracial couples. He was thus excluded from the present study, as were black racists Mark Essex and the "Zebra" gang. (For works consulted, see footnote 2. Other books used include Keyes, 1986; Abrahamsen, 1985; Olson, 1983; Wilson and Seaman, 1983; Nettler, 1982; Klausner, 1981; Caute and Odell, 1979; Godwin, 1978; Lunde, 1976; Wilson, 1972).

There are obvious problems in using news media as sources for determining the frequency or scale of serial murder. The nature and quality of reporting is likely to change over the years, while newspapers concentrate on what is likely to interest a local readership. From its prominence in the media, one might well think that the "Son of Sam" case of 1976–77 was uniquely serious or remarkable. In fact, the affair received so much attention chiefly because it occurred in the New York area, and thus near the headquarters of so many news organizations. This geographical bias might lead to the under-representation of offenses occurring in areas of the country that would be considered remote by the important news media, and our knowledge of serial murder would be slanted.

On the other hand, it is possible to defend the view that a media search is likely to produce a reasonably accurate list, at least of extreme serial offenders who killed (say) ten or more victims. Throughout the century, there has been intense media attention on any such case, suggesting that public interest is steady, if not precisely constant from decade to decade. In the 1920s and 1930s, massive publicity was devoted to the cases of American serial killers like Albert Fish, Earle Nelson, Joe Ball, Carl Panzram, and Gordon Stewart Northcott. In fact, coverage was more intense than for any comparable modern case because of the greater rarity of the offense in that era. It is not claimed that the present study can be truly comprehensive, but it is also unlikely that many cases have been omitted. The combination of newspaper records and secondary accounts is likely to yield a sizeable majority of the serial murder cases that actually occurred.

Assessing the scale of the problem and calculating a figure for the victims of serial murder are also real problems. In part, this is because serial offenders remain such a tiny proportion of the population that statistical comparisons are of little use. We are often dependent on the offenders themselves for estimates of their "kill" (the number of victims). False confessions sometimes appear to be part of the psychological make-up of such criminals.

Law enforcement agencies themselves play a vital part in shaping our perceptions here, and this may work in different cases either to swell or to diminish the alleged total of victims. In the late 1960s, for example, the still-anonymous "Zodiac" killed several people in northern California. Recently, a journalist published a well-argued case for believing that the "Zodiac" attacks have continued into the present decade, with the consequence of almost fifty deaths (Graysmith, 1987). If this view is correct, the case would be a classic example of "linkage blindness"—the failure of law enforcement to perceive connections between incidents. On the other hand, bureaucratic self-interest might have the opposite effect, as there is so much pressure to avoid having uncleared cases—especially such glaring and publicized crimes. Law enforcement agencies wish to clear as many murders as possible as "solved," even if this means rather tenuous attributions of the crimes to currently notorious figures.

We are rarely in as reliable a position to estimate the number of victims as in the John Wayne Gacy case, where almost thirty bodies were found in his crawl space. However, even similar evidence can be disputed. In 1985, extensive remains were found at the California home of Leonard Lake, but the conclusions of the forensic investigation were variously interpreted. Lake appeared to be connected with the murders of somewhere between six and thirty people—hardly precise figures. . . .

Despite these problems of assessing scale, there is strong evidence for a dramatic increase in the prevalence of serial murder in the United States from the end of the 1960s. This can be seen if we compare cases between 1950 and 1970 with those since 1971. Between 1950 and 1970, there were only two cases in the United States where a serial murderer was definitely associated with over ten victims (these were Charlie Starkweather in 1958 and the "Boston Strangler" case of 1962–64). There were other celebrated serial cases, but these tended to involve at most eight or nine victims. . . . This is in sharp contrast with the years between 1971 and 1987. There have been at least nine cases where offenders were generally credited with over twenty victims in this period (see footnote 2). . . . There were also twenty-eight cases where people are believed to have killed between ten and twenty victims in the same period. We therefore have a total of thirty-seven cases, involving thirty-nine individuals (in at least two cases, the crimes were committed by pairs of killers).

The Justice Department appears to have somewhat underestimated the number of active serial killers. A 1983 study claimed that since 1973, there had been at least 30 individuals who had killed six or more victims serially. The present author would put the figure at well over 40 for that same decade. However, while understating the number of killers, the same study appears to have grossly exaggerated their victims. A subsequent Justice Department estimate gives a figure of 35 serial murderers active at any one time. Let us assume that this is correct. It is rare for such an offender to kill more than six victims in any particular year, which suggests that the real annual total for serial victims is unlikely to exceed 300, and may well be under 200. Even that may be far too many. In the present study, 71 cases were found where six or more people were killed serially between 1971 and 1987. Certainly, cases have escaped attention, but these 71 cases account for only 950–1000 victims in all—or about 50 to 60 each year.

There are occasional cases where a killer engages in a rampage— Paul Knowles in 1974, Christopher Wilder in 1984—but these usually attract major law enforcement attention and are soon stopped. In other words, someone who kills more than ten or so people in a single year is unlikely to continue his career for more than that one year.

Even if our estimate for the number of active killers is too small, as it may be, then serial murder might account for at most three or four hundred victims each year. This is a terrible figure, but it is far short of the much-quoted "four thousand." In other words, even during a wave of serial murder like the seventeen years between 1971 and 1987, this type of crime accounts for perhaps 2 or 3 percent of American homicides, rather than the 20 percent suggested in 1984. Multiple murder remains an extreme fringe of American crime. . . .

Multiple murderers—those credited with at least ten victims— generally do not "roam." Fox and Levin correctly note that such killers tend to act fairly close to home, often in or around one city, and this view can be confirmed from the cases listed here. Ted Bundy killed in four states, but this was unusual. Of the 39 killers in our sample, only ten killed in more than one state. Two (Wilder and Knowles) went on short-lived "murder sprees," and three were active in neighboring states. The stereotype of "roaming killer" applies best to the case of William Christensen, who was accused in 1985 of 15 murders in the northeastern United States and in Canada. A much more common pattern is the killer who finds and kills most of his victims in one city, or even a small area of that city—from East London in the 1880s to the Sunset Strip in the 1970s. . . .

Explaining a Panic

Serial murder thus must be placed into context. It may have been a growing menace, and steps to curb it should have been vigorously encouraged. However, the official view of the problem was badly flawed. The reasons for misinterpretation were complex and include an element of pure accident. Lucas's confessions tended to cause both media and law enforcement agencies to lose proportion in examining the topic. But the way in which a "murder epidemic" was created is an illuminating example of the relationship between media and official agencies. Also required is an explanation of why Lucas's statements met with the credulity they did.

One consistent theme in the media coverage of 1983–85 was the misuse of UCR murder data, by both experts and lay people alike. Put simply, the argument suggests that motiveless murders had risen dramatically. The UCR stated that in 1966, there were eleven thousand murders in the United States. Of those, 644 (5.9 percent) involved no apparent motive. In 1982, there were twenty-three thousand murders, but the number of "motiveless" killings was now 4,118 (17.8 percent), the figure quoted by Lindsey. By 1984, this "motiveless" category had risen to 22 percent. It was suggested that the increase represented "serial" activity and that serial killers were claiming thousands of lives every year in the United States alone. The figure for recorded murders (some twenty thousand a year) could have actually understated the total, as many victims are not proven to have been murdered until many years later. The total of four thousand serial victims annually therefore seemed plausible. Other sources simply took the "unsolved" figure from UCR statistics. In 1983, 28 percent of murders fell into this category.

Both categories—unsolved and motiveless—require serious qualification, based on an understanding of how UCR data are compiled by individual police departments. When a murder occurs, the police will file a UCR report, with the deadline being the first five days of the month after the crime is reported. They also submit a supplementary homicide report, addressing topics like characteristics of the victim and offender; weapon; relationship of victim to offender; circumstances surrounding death; and so on. "Offenders" can be single, multiple, or unknown. At this early stage, the police might well know neither the offender, a motive, nor the exact circumstances of the death. All these would thus be recorded as unknown.

Weeks or months later, the situation might well change, and the correct procedure would be for the department to submit a new report to amend the first. Here, though, there is enormous room for cutting corners. The death has been reported, and whether a further correction is submitted depends on many factors. A conscientious officer in a professional department with an efficient record system would very probably notify the reporting center that the murder was no longer "unsolved" or "motiveless," especially in an area where murder was a rare crime. Other officers in other departments might well feel that they have more important things to do than to submit a revised version of a form they have already completed. This would in fact represent a third form on a single case.

The chance of follow-up information being supplied will depend on a number of factors: the frequency of murder in the community; the importance given to record keeping by a particular chief or supervisor; the organizational structure of the department (for instance, whether records and data are the responsibility of a full-time unit or of an individual); and the professional standards of the department. The vast majority of departments are likely to record the simple fact of a murder being committed. Only some will provide the results of subsequent investigations—although these are crucial to developing any kind of national statistical profile of American homicide.

Murders depicted in the UCR as having a suspect and motive are likely to be those where there is a very clear-cut situation with the offender immediately identified. Any delay, and it is likely to fall into the limbo of "motiveless" crimes. If a suspect is not found within the same month as the murder, then the case is likely to be entered as "no suspect" and to remain so despite subsequent events. In this case, it is even likely that the later in the month a particular murder takes place, the more likely it is to be described as "motiveless" or lacking a suspect.

Even when no suspect is ever found, it does not necessarily mean that a serial killer is to blame. . . . The remarkable fact about the UCR is the number of murders with an immediate motive and suspect. As to the sharp rise in the number of murders lacking this information, a variety of explanations is possible. These include an increase in homicides arising from narcotics trafficking and gang activities and perhaps deaths resulting from an increase in violent robberies. Although some of the murders indeed indicated serial activity, this was far less than was reported. . . .

To equate either "motiveless" or "unsolved" crimes with the number of serial victims is wholly to misunderstand the nature and composition of that much criticized set of data. It is remarkable that some (by no means all) of the Justice Department sources so frequently quoted tended to continue this confusion, with the results we have witnessed.

As the Justice Department was the source of so much of the information and interpretation about serial murder during 1983–85, it is necessary to ask exactly what was the nature of their interest in the topic. In order to understand the context, it should be recalled that the 1983 work on serial murder became a justification for a new center for the study of violent crime at the FBI Academy in Quantico, Virginia, with a new Violent Criminal Apprehension Program (VICAP). In the previous two years, attempts to expand FBI databanks had met serious challenges, both from civil libertarians and from local law enforcement agencies. Similar opposition might well have been expected to the new federal interest in violent criminals.

In practice, the serial killer panic helped to justify the new proposals, and the creation of a National Center for the Analysis of Violent Crime (NCAVC) was announced by President Reagan in June 1984, with an explicit focus on "repeat killers" (Michaud, 1986). Early NCAVC publicity emphasized how frequently serial crimes "transcend jurisdictional boundaries," while serial murderers were characteristically "highly transient criminals" (NCAVC, 1986). However, it was mentioned that in the future, the new databank would expand its attention—to "rape, child molestation, arson and bombing" (NCAVC, 1986). Serial murder thus provided a wedge for an expansion of the federal role in law enforcement intelligence.

It would be the worst sort of conspiracy theory to claim that the Justice Department created or promoted the post-Lucas murder panic. This is especially true when some FBI officials placed the estimated number of serial victims at several hundred rather than several thousand, contradicting what was quickly becoming orthodoxy. But it was in the interests of the agencies and spokesmen concerned to emphasize certain themes that did in fact emerge strongly in media coverage: the sudden and extreme danger posed by a murder wave—and above all, the national and interstate character of the "new" serial killers. Henry Lee Lucas—at least as he portrayed himself—was tailor-made for such a campaign.

Apart from the bureaucratic interests involved, the new emphasis on serial murder also suggested a shift in popular attitudes toward crime and criminals. The serial killer represented an extreme image of the newer and more conservative stereotype of the offender. The central element in the new concepts can perhaps be described as a quest for evil, a need to understand crime in terms of objective evil. Relativist ethics and environmental theories of causation were both discounted.

In the 1960s, environmental theories were widely held among the educated, though by no means universally. An understanding of the sociology of crime and justice did much to condition the attitudes of the Warren and early Burger Supreme Courts on issues such as capital punishment or defendants' rights. Environmental determinism undermined concepts of absolute responsibility, while rehabilitation was seen as an appropriate response for deviancy. "Evil" fitted poorly with such an intellectual climate.

By the late 1970s, ideas had changed considerably, although it is always a temptation to regard the writings of a few experts as indicating universal trends. Broadly, though, scholars of criminality tended to place more emphasis on the offender as a rational, responsible creature who could be deterred by the certainty and scale of punishment (Wilson and Herrnstein, 1985). Retribution was therefore more suitable than rehabilitation, which was seen as a failed goal. In the new political agenda, criminals were less victims of society than ruthless predators upon it. Solutions to crime were to be found in the justice system, rather than in social or family policy. In the more conservative tone of the 1980s, there was a series of cases where offenders appeared to be not only predators but creatures of extreme, pathological evil. Apart from the serial killers, there was concern about the mass sexual abuse of children, and even suggestions that some such offenses might be connected to devil-worship (Eberle and Eberle, 1986). A book entitled *The Ultimate Evil* suggested that a satanic cult was responsible for numerous serial murders, including those of the Manson family and "Son of Sam" (Terry, 1987).

If ever a moral panic was personified in one individual, then the concerns of the Reagan era were focused in the case of Richard Ramirez. In September 1985, he was arrested as a suspect in 68 offenses, including 14 murders attributed to the "Night Stalker" over the previous year. The allegations were those of a classic serial murder case, while Ramirez himself seemed to be an archetypal "external enemy"—a drifter accused of brutal sexual violence against women. In court, he made apparently satanic references—a horned hand, and a cry of "Hail Satan!" The attention paid to this case—and the Green River case in Seattle—did much to prevent any public doubt that might have arisen as the Lucas case fell apart in the following month or two.

Public fears of the horrors of such atrocious crimes erased public opposition to the expansion of FBI powers. Federal officials stood to gain substantially by establishing serial murder as a growing menace. The Behavioral Sciences Unit (BSU) had been established in the early 1970s at the FBI National Academy. It needed validation for its efforts in profiling criminals (including interviews with convicted mass and serial killers) through extensive crime scene analysis. The profiles are not limited to how the crime was committed; behavioral analysis looks at possible interactions leading to the crime and at what the offender might do after the crime. The behavioral scientists at BSU use this process to construct detailed portraits of the offender—a process which has been labelled "mind-hunting" by some (Jenkins, 1994:70). The FBI experts were extremely skillful in investing the word "serial" with much more significance than a simple definition of "repeated." Serial was linked in the public mind with sinister, irrational, compulsive, extremely violent, and inhuman acts committed by people who crossed state borders to spread their domain of horror (Jenkins, 1994:213).

Extending jurisdiction by promoting their expertise was a common ploy by the FBI. Founded in 1908, it had little impact before the 1930s. At that time, the public was fearful of a perceived increase in kidnapping. The media presented the crime as the work of ruthless, itinerant predators snatching innocent children from the safety of their homes; the official response to the public anxiety created was to declare kidnapping a federal crime. Marijuana, organized crime, and bank robbers were the next areas annexed by the FBI which, in each case, suggested the problem threatened the public on a vast scale and was interjurisdictional in nature, thus requiring federal action. The FBI was portrayed as the appropriate agency because of its superior professionalism and forensic skills. It had enormous resources at its disposal to help support its claims; it had an inside track with Congress; and it cultivated relationships with journalists and other people in the media to help present compatible views of emerging problems (Jenkins, 1994:214).

Serial murder further enhanced the FBI's image as an authoritative source. BSU agents not only offered a systematic overview, but they had actual contact with people who had committed unspeakable crimes. The news media had found a rich vein to mine—sensational stories anchored by the authority of federal law enforcement officials. BSU agent Robert Ressler described how his interaction with a *Chicago Tribune* reporter led to a flattering article in 1980. Immediately thereafter, a number of articles appeared in various publications, including The *New York Times*, *Psychology Today*, and *People*. He was also asked to appear on a number of radio and television programs (Jenkins, 1994:216).

Media depictions reinforced the image of BSU experts as both knowledgeable and heroic and established a closed loop of information. The media reported the Justice Department's statistics without question; the intensity of the coverage helped support the claims of an increasing menace. High public visibility increased the profitability of media reporting of the topic. Any news story or fictional account of serial murder was legitimized by interviews with BSU; those very interviews added to the prestige of the Unit and insured that future stories would also rely on these unquestioned authorities (Jenkins, 1994:217). In addition to interviews with agents, the FBI had the authority to grant or deny interviews with imprisoned killers. Anyone with access to the BSU had the potential for newsworthy stories. Particularly in 1983 and 1984, the FBI skillfully shared the information it was acquiring with accommodating journalists, academics, and filmmakers.

> There was somewhat of a media feeding frenzy, if not a panic, over this issue in the mid-1980s and we at the FBI and other people involved in urging the formation of VICAP did add to the general impression that there was a big problem and that something need be done about it. We didn't exactly go out seeking publicity, but when a reporter called, and we had a choice whether or not to cooperate on a story about violent crime, we gave the reporter good copy. In feeding the frenzy, we were using an old tactic in Washington, playing up the problem as a way of getting Congress and the higher-ups in the executive branch to pay attention to it (Ressler and Schachtman 1992:203, as quoted in Jenkins, 1994).

Serial murder offers an excellent illustration of the complex relationship between law enforcement, the media, and the public. Once public fears had been sufficiently aroused to view the threat as epidemic, the theme of serial killers was established. Innovative variations on that theme could then arise from any of the three segments and find support and acceptance from the other two (Jenkins, 1994:223). The FBI formulated an image which was publicized and adapted to fictional accounts. This image directs public perceptions, and the media publish stories which address the established stereotype. Media images, in turn, affect the behavior of law enforcement officials. Even offenders are affected by the labeling process. Convicted killers often profess to match the prevailing stereotype. Ted Bundy discussed the terrible influence pornography had on him. Henry Lee Lucas claimed far more murders than he had actually committed. While there are numerous explanations for such admissions, their existence further complicates the feedback relationship between officials, the media, and the public (Jenkins, 1994:225).

The FBI was successful in defining serial murder in terms of interjurisdictional cooperation, intelligence gathering, and over-coming linkage blindness. The crime was thus clearly established as a federal law enforcement problem, not a mental health issue or a social dysfunction. Fictional and media depictions had a major impact on the perception of the offenders—an image which dovetailed with that advanced by law enforcement. The serial killer in the 1980s was viewed as a ruthless, inhuman monster who could be stopped only by heroic "mind-hunters" (Jenkins, 1994:16). Thus, the popular view of the extent of serial murder, the nature of the offender, and the only solution all matched the law enforcement image.

While the Justice Department played a significant role in shaping the image of serial murder, the statistics and portrayal they projected would have been irrelevant if the public was unconcerned and ignored the information. The Justice Department found an audience ready and willing to hear and to accept what they had to say. The statistics received instant credibility, with politicians calling for congressional hearings and the public responding. The media would not have maintained their interest in the topic if the public had not been receptive. The Justice model was projected at an opportune time. As mentioned earlier, therapeutic models of crime had been rejected for justice-oriented approaches that emphasized the need to control predatory violence.

Problem construction is a cumulative process; new topics are usually based on predecessors, and the context of the times determines both the constraints and opportunities for new themes. Earlier memories and preconceptions shape current expectations and attitudes.

> Claims-makers must compete for attention. Social problems drop from view when they no longer seem fresh or interesting. New waves of claims-making may depend on the claims-makers' ability to redefine an issue, to focus on a new form of an old threat or to find other wrinkles (Best 1989:140, as quoted in Jenkins, 1994:222).

The serial murder panic followed concerns raised earlier about missing children, child abuse, and the increase in homosexuality and its linkage with a killer disease.

Questionable statistics were readily accepted as credible because they served the purposes of a number of interest groups. Groups with far different agendas could find reasons to elevate the topic of serial murder. African-American groups could use the crime to illustrate a theme of systematic racial exploitation; feminists could find in serial killing another example of violence against women;

children's rights activists linked missing and exploited children with the crime; and religious advocates could find evidence of satanic or ritual murder (Jenkins, 1994:212). John Walsh, whose son Adam was kidnapped and murdered, testified before Senate judiciary hearings in 1982 that the issue of missing children was largely a problem of repeat killers. He alluded to Bundy, Gacy, and others and discussed how widespread the problem was and that linkage blindness made it possible for children to disappear without a trace, until they were located in a mass grave (Jenkins, 1994:59). Conservatives could link sexually motivated multiple homicide with the decline of society's morals, easy access to pornography, media violence, and weakening of family values which allows killers easy access to "disposable" victims (Jenkins, 1994:124).

Many of these interests coalesced around the concern for children. This became the unifying theme, which helps explain how a minor issue—statistically speaking—could achieve such prominence. The linkage of serial murder with the plight of children opened previously closed avenues. In the 1970s, the prevailing moral climate emphasized freedom of consenting adults to determine their private moral conduct. Groups who disapproved of homosexuality or pornography found little support in their attempts to label the behavior immoral. Shifting the focus to children provided a wedge. Children could not give legal consent, therefore the disapproved behavior was neither victimless nor consensual. Undertones of stigmatizing homosexuality could be masked by concerns about children. Serial murder was used to draw attention to the pedophile tendencies of serial killers and to associate homosexuals with violence (Jenkins, 1994:18). Unapproved behavior serves as the basis from which to extrapolate other concerns and, in the process, to denounce a category of people and their lifestyle. Such stereotyping is possible only by exaggerating the prevalence of the offense and the composition of the offender population (Jenkins, 1994:187).

Once a theme captures public attention, myths take hold which are difficult to dislodge. Perhaps inevitably, the accounts of the collapse of many of Lucas's claims in late 1985 received nothing like the national attention of his initial boasts. Probably the American public will long recall the transparent myth that "serial killers account for one-fifth of all murder victims in the United States." The myth is important because it confirms a traditional notion of an overwhelming threat by lethal predators and because it distracts attention away from the reality of most homicide—as an act committed between relatives or acquaintances, often in a domestic setting. Crime is thus transformed from the problem of individuals and groups in a particular environment to a war fought by semi-human monsters against society. The FBI's painstaking efforts to create the impression that only chesslike moves by supremely trained, high technology experts—also well-versed in psychology—could possibly catch diabolically clever criminals outlive documented contradictions.

Most serial killers are caught by police officers performing routine duties. Despite VICAP's existence, the typical case is usually discovered by chance. Joel Rifkin was stopped by Long Island police in 1993 for driving without a license plate. The decomposing remains of one of his victims were found in the car. In California, one suspect was captured when stopped for driving erratically and police discovered a body in the passenger seat. Another offender made an illegal U-turn, was found to be violating parole, and was eventually linked with nineteen unsolved murders. Complaints from neighbors about noise and smell led to the arrests of both Jeffrey Dahmer and John Wayne Gacy (Jenkins, 1994:109). Media stories rarely emphasize such facts. In fact, a BSU agent in his autobiography remarked, "The media have come around to lionizing behavioral science people as supersleuths who put all other police to shame and solve cases where others have failed" (Ressler and Schachtman 1992:241, as quoted in Jenkins, 1994:73). The myth of gladiatorial conflict between worthy heroes and reprehensible villains has much greater appeal to the public than the realities of happenstance.

Similarly, the overwhelming emphasis on sex killers like Ted Bundy leads the media to focus on crimes that most resemble the mythical stereotype. Reinforcing the image of all serial killers as Jack-the-Ripper types can distract attention from other possibilities where opportunities are plentiful and avenues to mask the crimes are available, such as people in the medical or nursing-home professions or women killing children and blaming Sudden Infant Death Syndrome. It seems somehow more comprehensible to attach blame for unthinkable crimes to a conspiracy of organized evil, ritualistic killings, or the work of a sexual sadist. The savagery of such crimes is apparently more "rational" if attached to the accepted stereotype.

Serial killers provide the most graphic illustration of dangerous outsiders. Their behavior is often marked by actions—including cannibalism and mutilation—abhorrent to civilized people. Serial murderers are portrayed in the same terms as those used by Cesare Lombroso in the 1870s in developing his theory of criminality:

> the problem of the nature of the criminal—an atavistic being
> who reproduces in his person the ferocious instincts of primitive
> humanity . . . the irresponsible craving of evil for its own sake,
> the desire not only to extinguish life in the victim, but to mutilate
> the corpse, tear its flesh and drink its blood (Jenkins, 1994:114).

The echoes of this characterization resonate today in calls for
stringent laws against sexual predators:

> Chronic sexual predators have crossed an osmotic membrane.
> They can't step back to the other side—our side. And they don't
> want to. If we don't kill them or release them, we have but one
> choice. Call them monsters and isolate them. . . . I've spoken
> to many predators over the years. They always exhibit amaze-
> ment that we do not hunt them. And that when we capture
> them, we eventually let them go. Our attitude is a deliberate
> interference with Darwinism—an endangerment of our species
> (Andrew Vachss 1993, as quoted in Jenkins, 1994:118).

Once identified, the mere mention of serial killers' names is a
rallying call for public revulsion. Names acquire mythic significance
and evoke powerful images of horror—John Wayne Gacy's crawl
space, Jeffrey Dahmer's apartment, Joel Rifkin's pickup truck
(Jenkins, 1994:222). Names serve as powerful rhetorical tools for
weaving threads of the myth through other themes, as did John
Walsh in his testimony before Congress.

Serial murder played a significant role in the debates over capital
punishment. In states where the death penalty was restored, serial
killers were often the first to be executed. The public could dismiss
previous views that the death penalty was reactionary and racist
when it was applied to monsters for whom rehabilitation was futile
(Jenkins, 1994:131).

After the height of the serial murder panic in 1983–1985, the topic
receded somewhat. In August 1990, five mutilation murders were
reported on the University of Florida campus. Although these
murders were not technically "serial," the fact that the victims were
students at another campus in the same state as Bundy's last
murders created a media stir. Reports speculated on a number of
current and unsolved cases around the country (Jenkins, 1994:75).
The boundaries between fiction and reality were blurred in 1991,
pushing the subject of serial murder to new heights. Thomas Harris'
1988 novel, *The Silence of the Lambs*, was released as a motion
picture (including location shots at Quantico, Virginia) in February
1991. Hannibal Lecter and Buffalo Bill resurrected all the images
of incarnate evil established in the previous decade, while Clarice
Starling and Jack Crawford embodied the fearless heroes using all

their resources to save society. In July 1991, the real-life atrocities of Jeffrey Dahmer magnified the issue. Dahmer's case provided ample evidence for a number of claims.

> [T]hese crimes were hate-motivated. By focusing on Dahmer's alleged homosexuality, [the media] has overlooked the fact that many of his victims were homosexual. Regardless of Dahmer's actual sexual identity, it is clear that he hates homosexuals enough to want to kill them. It is also apparent Dahmer's murders were racially motivated (as quoted in Jenkins, 1994:180).

His trial was carried on *Court TV* and more than four hundred and fifty journalists covered it. Several other cases came to light in the months that followed. Television and the media continued to revisit the topic. Joel Rifkin's crimes and name were even the subtopic of a *Seinfeld* episode in 1994.

The interaction of bureaucratic agencies, the media, and the public create countless permutations of vested interests. The inherent newsworthiness of such crimes intersect with a growth of sensational television and radio programming. Nor does there appear to be any diminution of interest. With VICAP searching for links between unsolved murders, any increase found may be used as proof of a surging serial murder rate—rather than an indication of improvement in investigative technology. Points of similarity between geographically separated cases are bound to be noted, and there will be speculation about links. Unless care is taken, dozens or even hundreds of murders will be blamed on unknown hypothetical killers. The "panic" is likely to be self-sustaining. There were warning signs to this effect from the British experience with that country's equivalent of VICAP, the Home Office Large Major Enquiry System (HOLMES). Use of the system initially produced claims of the existence of hypothetical serial child-murderers, by the linkage of what appear to have been very dissimilar cases. One arrest led to a rapid and embarrassing realization that at least one string of cases was in fact unrelated (Ballantyne, 1987). Demographic changes may result in the perception that the elderly are "new" victims. A future discovery may stir dormant fears of racial or cult conspiracies (Jenkins, 1994:223).

In any given year, serial murder will account for approximately one out of every ten thousand deaths in the United States; 99.99 percent of Americans will die from causes other than multiple homicide (Jenkins, 1994). Despite the minimal threat statistically, the public remains fascinated with the topic and continues to frame it as a major problem. The harm which results from the crime when it occurs cannot be disputed. The reprehensible nature of the crime erases the necessity of establishing harm (as compared to victimless crime, for example). However, that very fact often encourages the use of serial crime as a weapon against other behaviors by linking the two (Jenkins, 1994). If the linkage is not questioned, policy and resources may target more than the indisputable wrong.

Conclusion

This chapter is emphatically not an attempt to trivialize or wish away the problem of serial murder. It is, however, intended as an illustration of the reasons why we should demand the highest standards of accuracy in the portrait of crime that is presented to the public both by law enforcement professionals and by academic researchers in this area—one that is quite literally a matter of life and death. Most clearly, there is the question of resources and the political priorities given to different areas. For example, it might be that a focus on serial murder might have an impact on this type of homicide, here estimated as accounting for perhaps 2 or 3 percent of homicides annually. It might also be that the homicide rate could be reduced still more dramatically by devoting the same resources to other activities. To put the problem in proportion: the total number of victims of serial murder across the United States in a particular year is considerably less than the annual total of homicide victims in Detroit alone. Should resources and activity be directed to a perceived national problem, or might they be better employed in a highly focused way in major metropolitan areas?

The problem of serial murder raises many of the perennial issues of criminal justice: public perceptions of the threat of crime as opposed to the very different reality; the tendency of agencies to direct resources to issues in the public view; and the role of the media in forming public perceptions of the crime problem. Social scientists often find cause to bemoan the myths portrayed by the media, especially in the area of crime and justice. The tendency is to blame sensationalist editors and journalists, but the relationship between the media, government, and the public is much more complex than that. There was sensationalism and also manipulation of the media by official agencies, but the media "panic" also resulted from a more subtle and general shift in public attitudes. The credulity apparent from reactions to the Lucas case is indicative of what has been described here as a "quest of evil," and this attitude forms the context of both public and official responses to a variety of legal and social issues in contemporary America. Understanding this attitude is an essential prerequisite to approaching the political debate over crime, law and order.

Notes

[1] In this article, I have taken what now appears to be the standard United States definition of serial murder, as several killings committed over a period of time. It should be noted that there are problems with this. Opinions differ on how frequently a person must kill to be counted in this category (four and six victims have both been suggested). Also, the "period of time" remains undefined. If someone kills repeatedly over some hours, this is a mass murder. If days elapse, then it might be seen as a "serial" offense, though the exact dividing line is not clear. Finally, there is the problem of an individual committing one murder, and then another mass killing at a later date. Does he become a serial killer?

These points may appear pedantic, but they are important in developing a taxonomy of multiple murderers. It might be suggested that a mass murderer like Richard Speck was no different behaviorally or psychologically from a serial lust-murderer. It merely happened that he found himself with the opportunity to carry out so many of his fantasies at one place and time. Generally, though, there are substantial differences between mass killers like James Huberty and Patrick Sherrill and their serial counterparts, so the distinction is a useful one.

[2] Killers alleged to have claimed twenty or more victims are:

Name	Source
Ted Bundy	(Rule, 1980; Michaud and Aynesworth, 1983)
Dean Corll/Elmer Henley	(Olsen, 1974)
Juan Corona*	(Kidder, 1974)
Bruce Davis	
John Wayne Gacy	(Sullivan and Maiken, 1983; Cahill, 1986)
Donald Harvey	
Patrick Kearney*	(Godwin, 1978)
Gerald Stano	
"Green River Killer"	
Wayne Williams	(Detlinger and Prugh, 1983)

Those associated with between ten and twenty killings are:

Kenneth Bianchi/ Angelo Buono*	(O'Brien, 1985; Schwartz, 1982)
William Bonin*	
William Christensen	
David J. Carpenter*	
Douglas D. Clark*	
Carroll Cole	
Robert Diaz*	
Larry Eyler	
Gerald Gallego	
Robert Hansen	
Frederick Hodge	
Calvin Jackson	(Godwin, 1978)
Edmund Kemper*	(Lunde, 1967; Cheney, 1976)

Paul Knowles	(Fawkes, 1978)
Randy Kraft*	
Leonard Lake*	
Bobby Joe Long*	
Henry Lee Lucas	
Bobby Joe Maxwell*	
Sherman McCrary	
Herbert Mullin*	(Lunde and Morgan, 1974)
Marcus Nisby*	
Richard Ramirez*	
Daniel Lee Siebert	
Coral Watts	
Christopher Wilder	
Randall Woodfield	(Stack, 1984)
"South Side Slayer"*	

(Asterisks denote individuals chiefly active in California)

Sources

Abrahamsen, D. (1985). *Confessions of Son of Sam*. New York: Columbia University Press.

――― (1973). *The Murdering Mind*. New York: Harper & Row.

――― (1960). *The Psychology of Crime*. New York: Columbia University Press.

――― (1945). *Crime and the Human Mind*. New York: Columbia University Press.

Ballantyne, A. (1987). Man Released in Child Deaths Inquiry. *Guardian*, (London) (May 1).

Becker, H. (1963). *Outsiders*. New York: Free Press.

Best, J. (1989). *Images of Issues*. Hawthorne, NY: Aldine de Gruyter.

Berger, J. (1984). Traits Shared by Mass Killers Remain Unknown to Experts. *New York Times*, (August 27).

Cahill, T. (1986). *Buried Dreams: Inside the Mind of a Serial Killer*. New York: Bantam.

Cheney, M. (1976). *The Coed Killer*. New York: Walker.

Caute, J. and Odell, R. (1979). *The Murderers' Who's Who*. London: Pan.

Darrach, B. and Norris, J. (1984). An American Tragedy. *Life*.

Detlinger, C. and Prugh, J. (1983). *The List*. Atlanta: Philmay Enterprise.

Duster, T. (1970). *The Legislation of Morality*. New York: Free Press.

Eberle, P. and Eberle, S. (1986). *The Politics of Child Abuse*. Secaucus, NJ: Lyle Stuart.

Egger, S. (1986). Utility of Case Study Approach to Serial Murder Research. Paper presented to ASC, Atlanta, GA (November).

――― (1984). A Working Definition of Serial Murder. *Journal of Police Science and Administration* 12(3): 348–57.

Fawkes, S. (1978). *Killing Time*. London: Hamlyn.

Fox, J. and Levin, J. (1985). *Mass Murder: America's Growing Menace*. New York: Plenum.

Godwin, J. (1978). *Murder USA*. New York: Ballantine.

Graysmith, R. (1987). *Zodiac*. New York: Berkley.

Gusfield, J. (1981). *The Culture of Public Problems.* Chicago: University of Chicago Press.

Hickey, E. (1986). The Etiology of Victimization in Serial Murder. Paper presented to ASC, Atlanta, GA (November).

Jenkins, P. (1994). *Using Murder.* New York: Aldine de Gruyter.

Jenkins, P. and Katkin, D. (1987). Benefit of Law. Paper presented to ASC, Montreal (November).

Joyce, F. (1983). Two Suspects' Stories of Killings Culled. *New York Times,* (November 4).

Kagan, D. (1984). Serial Murderers. *OMNI.*

Keyes, D. (1986). *Unveiling Claudia.* New York: Bantam.

Kidder, T. (1974). *The Road to Yuba City.* New York: Doubleday.

Klausner, L. (1981). *Son of Sam.* New York: McGraw-Hill.

Leyton, E. (1986). *Compulsive Killers.* New York University Press.

Lindsey, R. (1984). Officials Cite a Rise in Killers Who Roam US for Victims. *New York Times,* (January 22).

Lunde, D. (1976). *Murder and Madness.* New York: W.W. Norton.

Lunde, D. and Morgan, J. (1980). *The Die Song.* New York: W.W. Norton.

Michaud, S. and Aynesworth, H. (1986). The FBI's New Psyche Squad. *New York Times Magazine,* (October 26).

_____ (1983). *The Only Living Witness.* New York: Simon and Schuster.

NCAVC (1986). The National Center for the Analysis of Violent Crime. Behavioral Science Services, FBI Academy, Quantico, VA (revised 4/7/86).

Nettler, G. (1982). *Killing One Another.* Cincinnati: Anderson.

O'Brien, D. (1985). *Two of a Kind.* New York: New American Library.

Olsen, J. (1983). *Son: A Psychopath and His Victims.* New York: Dell.

_____ (1974). *The Man with the Candy.* New York: Simon and Schuster.

The Random Killers (1984). *Newsweek,* (November 26).

Ressler, R. and Schachtman, T. (1992). *Whoever Fights Monsters.* New York: St. Martin's.

Rule, A. (1980). *The Stranger Beside Me.* New York: NAL.

Schwartz, T. (1982). *The Hillside Strangler.* New York: Signet.

Stack, A. (1984). *The 15 Killer.* New York: Signet.

Sullivan, T. and Maiken, P. (1983). *Killer Clown: The John Wayne Gacy Murders.* New York: Grosset and Dunlap.

Tappan, P. (1955). Some Myths About the Sex Offender. *Federal Probation* 19:1–12.

Terry, M. (1987). *The Ultimate Evil.* Garden City, NY: Dolphin.

Thompson, T. (1979). *Serpentine.* New York: Dell.

Toch, H. (1969, revised 1980). *Violent Men.* Chicago: Aldine.

Vachss, A. (1993). Sex Predators Can't Be Saved. *New York Times,* (January 5).

Vetter, H. and Rieber, R. (1986). Dissociative States and Processes. Paper presented to ASC, Atlanta, GA (November).

Wilson, C. (1972). *Order of Assassins.* London: Rubert Hart-Davis.

Wilson, C. and Seaman, D. (1983). *Encyclopaedia of Modern Murder.* New York: Perigee.

Wilson, J. and Herrnstein, E. (1985). *Crime and Human Nature.* New York: Simon and Schuster.

Of Stalkers and Murder
Spreading Myth to Common Crime

5

Were the panics over rising urban crime, child abduction and serial murder merely fads that caught public and government attention for a fleeting moment or will mythmakers continue to advance their misconceptions of crime and justice? Did the panics of the 1980s have an appreciable impact on our perceptions of crime and justice? Is it easier to spread myths and offer simplistic solutions to crime problems today than it was in the past? Events of the 1990s suggest that not only did these panics have lasting effects on our images of crime and justice, but that previously constructed myths are driving our current thoughts about crime. Crime myth is spreading beyond bizarre and unique criminal events into our views of more common crime. Before we consider these events, let's briefly recount some of the necessary techniques used to conjure up mythical crime.

Myths are exaggerations of reality; they form because of an inordinate amount of attention paid to sensational events or because of a sudden government or media fascination with a "newly" discovered behavior. These events or behaviors are presented in social forums that foster fear, accentuate danger, and focus almost exclusively on innocent victims and evil villains. Typically, before adequate definitions of criminal behavior are developed and before clear typologies emerge, dissimilar behaviors are fused to give the appearance of an epidemic. Targeted behaviors are characterized as increasing in frequency and severity. Media depiction of these mythical crimes is accompanied by the language of fear. No one is immune from being preyed upon by the perpetrators of our most recent panic. Strangers "hide" under the cover of darkness to whisk away children; serial murderers "prowl and prey"; and urban street crime is "rampant." "Stalk is another potent word, as in the case of California serial killer Richard Ramirez, the Night Stalker" (Jenkins, 1994:117).

Constructing the Myth of Stalking

The panics of the 1980s served as perfect backdrops for the spread of myth into common forms of crime in the 1990s. "Problem construction is a cumulative or incremental process, in which each issue is to some extent built upon its predecessors, in the context of a steadily developing fund of socially available knowledge" (Jenkins, 1994:220). The rising urban crime, child abduction and serial murder panics provided the "intellectual environment" for the spread of crime myths into other behaviors. The stage had been set, the lines had been well rehearsed, and the public was ready to be incited when the murder of actress Rebecca Schaeffer made the news. Ms. Schaeffer, a star in the television series *My Sister Sam*, was killed by Robert Bardo—a "stalker." The young actress was gunned down at her California apartment. In a very short time, California citizens were informed of the Schaeffer murder as well as the murders of four other women by "stalkers" (Dawsey and Malnic, 1989). Later, other celebrities including David Letterman and Madonna, reported to the nation that they had been the victims of "stalkers" or that they were persistently harassed by obsessive fans (see table 1).

Table 1
Selected Stalkers and Their Victims

Stalkers	Victims
Joni Penn	Sharon Gless, actress
Mark David Chapman	John Lennon, musician
Arthur Jackson	Theresa Saldana, actress
	John F. Kennedy, president
	Tesesa Bergznza, singer
John Hinckley, II	Jodie Foster, actress
Tina Ledbetter	Michael J. Fox, actor
Stephen Stillabower	Madonna, musician
	Sean Penn, actor
Ken Gause	Johnny Carson, TV host
Nathan Trupp	Michael Landon, actor
	Sandra Day O'Connor, Justice
Ralph Nau	Olivia Newton-John, singer
	Marie Osmond, singer
	Cher, singer
	Farah Fawcett, actress
John Smetek	Justine Bateman, actress
Robert Bardo	Rebecca Schaeffer, actress
Billie Jackson	Michael Jackson, singer
Margaret Ray	David Letterman, TV host
Roger Davis	Vanna White, TV star
Brook Hull	Terri Garr, actress
Ruth Steinhagen	Eddie Waitkus, baseball player
Daniel Vega	Donna Mills, actress
Robert Keiling	Anne Murray, singer

Reprinted from: Holmes, R. M. (1993). Stalking in America: Types and Methods of Criminal Stalkers. *Journal of Contemporary Criminal Justice*, 9(4): 319.

Between 1989 and 1993, stalking became a major media issue (Jenkins, 1994). Articles on stalking appeared in a variety of national and local magazines like *U.S. News and World Report, People Weekly, Los Angeles Magazine,* and *Time* (see, Holmes, 1993). Popular media sources invoked the rhetoric of fear with phrases like stalking: the "murderous obsession" and "the terror of stalking" (Beck, 1992; Puente, 1992; Editorial Staff, 1989). While the news media was capitalizing on the sensationalism associated with celebrity stalkings, the entertainment industry was cashing in at the box office. Movies like *Fatal Attraction, Blink* and *The Body Guard* created potent images of stalkers for public consumption. For the news media, the quintessential stalking was a violent predatory act committed by a stranger (Bochove, 1992). An innocent (Hallman, 1992) was hunted and terrorized for months by a fiendish, deranged predator bent on sexually assaulting or killing his victim.

Perhaps the media depiction of Gary Wilensky best captured the fear and sensationalism surrounding stalking. Wilensky was a tennis coach at several exclusive New York City schools. In 1988, he was arrested for "stalking" three children while wearing a black leather "sex" mask and videotaping them at bus stops (Leavitt, 1993). The charges against Wilensky were eventually dropped. According to Jean Arena, one of the victims' mothers: "Its like in the movies: You have to wait for someone to do something really bad before you can get them" (Leavitt, 1993:3A). Years later, according to the police, Wilensky took his own life after attempting to abduct a 17-year-old woman. Police reported that he was intent on kidnapping the woman and taking her to a secluded "hideout" that was equipped with restraints, muzzles, masks, women's wigs, and a police badge (Leavitt, 1993). What the media failed to mention in its reporting of the Wilensky incident was that in 1988 there were no statutes against stalking. The media had effectively redefined Wilensky's behavior and arrest as a stalking five years later. The media was silent as to whether Wilensky "stalked" his last victim. In essence, the media retrospectively labelled his crime to fit our latest crime panic.

Various media characterizations shape the public's conception of stalking. According to most popular accounts, the classic "stalker" is a cunning stranger who has targeted an innocent victim for prey. The stalker's behavior demonstrates an identifiable, systematic and sustained progression that, without official intervention, ultimately culminates in the commission of a hideous crime—typically a sexual assault, child molestation, or a brutal murder. This conception of stalking has crept into some of the academic literature. One academician remarked: "Unbalanced persons send letters and make phone calls to athletes and targeted strangers for purposes of terrorizing and even sexually assaulting and murder. There may be no one truly safe from a predatory stalker" (Holmes, 1993:317). In other academic accounts stalking has been linked, through selective sampling, to serial crimes like sexual assault, rape, and murder.

> Methods within the stalking process become an important and integral part of the act. Norris discusses the process of the stalk as it concerns the sex offender. It appears as a starting point in the selection process of the serial predator. Holmes has also examined the stalking of the sexual predator. He lists 'the stalk' as one of the five steps in the selection and the execution of serial murder. Hazelwood extends a similar discussion with the serial rapist" (citations omitted; Holmes, 1993:318).

The stalking "problem" is constructed to accentuate the helplessness of the innocent victim, the calculated and systematic behavior of the offender, and the inability of our criminal justice system to cope with this new criminality. Others have characterized it as "widespread" and growing (Hoshen et al., 1995:31). Legal scholars have also drawn on the fear-generating and very speculative prey-predator conception of stalking, the innocent victim orientation to the problem, and the unsupported assumption that stalking ultimately culminates in violence. "Victims of stalking must wait and hope the stalker will not actually follow through with threats or go beyond mere pursuit. Many victims live in fear, forced to alter their lives dramatically. Victims may suffer substantial and lasting emotional trauma from such an ordeal" (Sohn, 1994:205; citing Guy, 1993:996). At the heart of the stalking problem is the powerlessness of the police to take action until the ultimate event takes place—an act of violence. The solution is the creation of new criminal laws that allow early formal intervention. "The criminalization of stalking attempts to protect victims by identifying the various stages of stalking and providing for intervention by law enforcement at a time that sufficiently anticipates its culmination in violence" (Sohn, 1994:205; Perez, 1993).

Officializing the Myth

As stalking captured the media's attention, it also captured the attention of legislators across the country. Within two years of the media stories about the Schaeffer murder, almost every state legislative body was circulating proposals for the creation of anti-stalking laws. Some characterized the inordinate amount of state attention to stalking as a "legislative frenzy" (Kolarik, 1992). This characterization may have been chillingly accurate given the speed, scope and lack of thoughtfulness that characterized legislative action.

In 1990, California became the first state to enact an "anti-stalking law." Two years later 29 other states followed suit. By late 1993, 48 states and the District of Columbia had followed California's lead by enacting legislation to prohibit stalking (for lists see, Sohn, 1994; National Criminal Justice Association, 1993; Thomas, 1993). Only two states, Maine and Arizona, had not enacted stalking statutes. The federal government also entered the picture when the Congress directed the National Institute of Justice to develop model anti-stalking legislation. The act mandated that:

> The Attorney General, acting through the Director of the National Institute of Justice, shall: (1) evaluate existing and proposed anti-stalking legislation in the States, (2) develop model anti-stalking legislation that is constitutional and enforceable, (3) prepare and disseminate to State authorities the findings made as a result of such evaluation, and (4) report to the Congress the findings and the need or appropriateness of further action by the Federal Government by September 30, 1993 (U.S. Congress, Pub L. 102–395, Sec. 109b, 1993).

The National Institute of Justice in conjunction with the National Criminal Justice Association undertook the project. Project participants interpreted this Congressional mandate to require the development of "a model anti-stalking code to encourage states to adopt anti-stalking measures and provide them with direction in formulating such laws" (National Criminal Justice Association, 1993:5). The extent to which the legislation was intended to encourage state legislative action is open to debate. The fact remains, however, that stalking had become politicized; governors and state legislators used the issue to attract media attention and personal exposure. Vermont's governor, for example, selected Brattleboro for the signing of that state's new stalking bill because reporter Judith Fournier was stalked and killed there by her former boyfriend (Editorial Staff, 1993a). Similarly and with some ceremony, Nevada's governor signed legislation that allowed police monitoring of telephone conversations to investigate stalkers (Editorial Staff, 1993b). While political grandstanding was clearly evident, the scope of politics was even more obvious in legislative debates surrounding applicability of the statutes to abortion protestors and labor union activists (Editorial Staff, 1993d) as well as provisions that would exempt law enforcement officers from civil liability for failure to notify stalking victims that an arrested suspect had been released (Editorial Staff, 1993e). Clearly, legislators were concerned about both the social position of certain activists and the distribution of responsibility for failure to protect victims.

As state legislators were crafting stalking statutes and allowing the issue of stalking to drive other legislation, questionable statistics concerning stalking were being circulated. There were estimates that some 200,000 people are stalked each year (Guy, 1993), that five percent of women will be stalked at some point in their lives (*Congressional Record*, 1993), and that 90 percent of the women killed by their spouses or former boyfriends were stalked prior to their murder (Beck, 1992). Despite the first two exaggerated claims, the government panic over stalking virtually ignored the claim that 90 percent of stalking victims were women (*Congressional Record*, 1993). The government's project to develop a model code for stalking as well as legal treatises attempted to neutralize the possibility that this crime might be conceptualized as gender based. The following instruction appeared in a prominent location in the government's report and was emphasized in bold: "Stalking is a gender neutral crime, with both male and female defendants and victims" (National Criminal Justice Association, 1993:xi). One legal writer remarked that "there are both female and male stalkers" (Sohn, 1994:n9) and an academician notes that "husbands and wives seek out their former mates to terrorize" (Holmes, 1993:317).

Certainly there are occasional cases of women who stalk men, just as there are male victims of domestic violence and serial murder. This tact, however, served to sever the obvious gender differential and domestic aspects of most of the violence directed at women. Yet in the construction of crime mythology it also served to extend support for proposed legislation by broadening considerably the number of persons who could now view themselves as potential victims. In other words, it established a necessary requirement for myth production that no group is insulated from stalkers. Such a gender obfuscation of the issue also lent political power to the criminalization movement by appealing to those who would ultimately determine whether or not stalking would be criminalized—male legislators. Additionally, constructing stalking as a gender neutral crime detracts from its domestic nature and allows the predatory stranger conceptions to flourish. Reason as well as extrapolation from existing research would suggest that the vast majority of stalkings, like serial murder and domestic violence, are perpetrated by men against women (BJS, 1993).

Whether the project participants were influenced by the stereotypic image of the fiendishly clever stalker who could foil any constraint, or whether they could not specify precisely what behavior defined stalking, the end result was ambiguous, imprecise phrasing. The participants intentionally did not enumerate prohibited acts, rationalizing "that ingenuity on the part of an alleged stalker should not permit him to skirt the law" (National Criminal Justice Association, 1993:44). Of course, failure to specify what particular acts constitute stalking leave the power of interpretation and application to law enforcement officials.

As with missing children and serial murder panics, legislative action was taken before the development of an adequate definition of stalking. Six years after Rebecca Schaeffer's death thrust the term into the nation's conscience, there was "no widely accepted definition of 'stalking.' Although stalking is against the law in almost every state, the term is not defined in *Black's Law Dictionary*, nor is it discussed in major legal treatises such as *American Jurisprudence* or *Corpus Juris Secundum*" (Sohn, 1994:204–5). Similarly, there existed no reliable and empirically-based criminological definition of stalking. "Nevertheless, the term 'stalker' arouses certain common images in most people's minds. . . . The term brings to mind a wide range of harassing behaviors that frighten or terrorize the victim" (Sohn, 1994:204–5). Despite the lack of a clear definition of "stalking" and admitting to the absence of any empirical evidence as to its frequency, severity, or demographic characteristics, the federal government had a model code developed and encouraged states to adopt it.

States either followed California's model or heeded the encouragement of the federal government by enacting statutes that prohibited everything from being "present" (5 states) to "approaching" (4 states), "following" (43 states), "pursuing" (43 states) through "non-consensual communications" (20 states), surveillance (3 states) and "lying in wait" (3 states)—all designed to allow the police to take enforcement action before the ultimate crime (National Criminal Justice Association, 1993).

Consider the breadth of antistalking statutes. California's stalking law, for example, prohibits any "willful course of conduct directed at a specific person which seriously alarms, annoys, or harasses the person, and which serves no legitimate purpose" (Cal. Penal Code, 1990:646). At least 14 states do not require intent to cause fear on the part of a suspect. In 18 states an explicit threat or act is not required to satisfy the elements of the crime of stalking. The California statute defines a course of conduct as "a pattern of conduct composed of a series of acts over a period of time, however short, evidencing a continuity of purpose" (Cal. Penal Code, 1990:646). Most state statues, however, only require two incidents to satisfy the "course of conduct" requirement. In 1993, Iowa amended its stalking statute to allow police to intervene after a single incident (Editorial Staff, 1993c). After enactment of the stalking statute, following a person is criminal in California, although "following" is left undefined in the statute as well as in the laws of other states (see, Thomas, 1993). In some states, Florida for example, following someone even without an accompanying threat is considered a misdemeanor (Fla. Stat. Ann., 1992).

What is interesting about such a rapid and widespread adoption of so many broad and vague statutes is that almost every state already had laws on the books that prohibited the acts most frequently described as stalking (for list see, Sohn, 1994). Admittedly, following someone was not criminal before the stalking panic, but trespass, vandalism, terroristic threatening, harassment, assault and battery or variants of these behaviors were, of course, illegal in almost every state. More specifically, 46 states had criminal trespass laws, 28 had harassment statutes, 19 prohibited terroristic threatening (National Criminal Justice Association, 1993) and, needless to say, every state had a prohibition against assault.

The existence of these statutes coupled with the availability of civil protections undermines the claim that existing laws were inadequate to handle this newly discovered criminality. Recourses of a noncriminal nature available to victims of stalkings include civil protection orders, restraining orders, civil contempt, mental heath commitments, emergency detentions and tort actions. In short, the characterization of existing laws as inadequate was a myth. Likewise, portrayal of the police and victims as powerless against stalkers was pure fabrication. The more plausible explanation of any ineffectiveness of existing law was a lack of willingness by law enforcement officers to expend the energies necessary to educate and to assist domestic victims of stalking with existing legal remedies. As one commentator put it: "The suspicion is that in some quarters when the police hear the word 'domestic,' they still roll their eyes and want to venture off in pursuit of 'real' crime" (*Tribune*, 1993:4). Despite easily identifiable legal restrictions on behaviors identified with stalking, the official position on stalking closely matched the expression of one writer: "*lax or non-existent laws* give stalkers of women (and of men) repeated opportunities to *play with their prey*—to follow or harass, terrorize or beat them—to make them afraid to live their lives" (our emphasis, as cited in Sohn, 1994:203).

Consequences of Criminalization

Given the range of existing criminal and civil laws available to both police and stalking victims, what motivated law enforcement to support the enactment of these new statutes? The results of the National Criminal Justice Association's (1993) survey of police shed light on the utility of statutory change as well as law enforcement's motivation. Their survey of police found that, "Intervention options available to police with or without stalking laws are many and varied. Survey respondents' answers indicate that departments in states with anti-stalking laws depend on alternative responses as much as states without such laws" (National Criminal Justice Association, 1993:40). This finding raises questions as to whether the stalking statutes were necessary, since law enforcement officers in jurisdictions with the new statutes use them in conjunction with existing laws. In other words, stalking is a reconstituted crime used by law enforcement officers as an add-on charge. More specifically, the survey found that in states with stalking laws, "81 percent charge offenders with trespassing, while 74 percent of agencies without such laws charge offenders with trespassing. Seventy-four percent of agencies enforcing stalking laws charge offenders with assault while 60 percent of states without laws charge offenders with assault" (National Criminal Justice Association, 1993:40).

The utility of these statutes was essentially to increase the punitiveness of the criminal law and to grant law enforcement officers greater powers of arrest. Law enforcement agencies in jurisdictions that did not yet have the statutes wanted them, and law enforcement agencies with the statutes wanted more power. "Eighty-six percent of respondents with anti-stalking laws in place felt that the intervention options available to them were adequate;

only 43 percent of agencies without stalking laws felt their intervention options were adequate. . . . Still others thought that an antistalking law that did not require a third-party witness or police presence at the time of the crime would be helpful" (National Criminal Justice Association, 1993:40). In essence, the police wanted the power to arrest as they saw fit. They sought arrest decisions based solely on police discretion not on judicial review or actual observation of a crime. The power of law enforcement officers to arrest had previously been curtailed to those incidents where they observed a crime or, in the alternative, were forced to seek judicial review of their case and secure a warrant before making an arrest. Now law enforcement officers are no longer hindered by these inconveniences. Antistalking laws were created to give law enforcement an "immediate cause to make an arrest and the state an immediate reason for prosecution" (Comment, 1992:A20).

It is almost impossible to distinguish the difference between the types of behavior addressed by the new statutes and those that have been prohibited in the past. The important distinction, of course, is that the new statutes grant the police extraordinary powers to arrest before a common crime has occurred. The statutes are so broad and vague that violating their provisions will most likely be determined based on victim abilities to convince the police that they were afraid or annoyed and on police willingness to view suspects as those in need of state control.

Another consequence of the new antistalking laws was an increase in the punitiveness of the criminal justice system. Reconstituting common crime as stalking allowed the media-generated characterization of the phenomenon to shape penalty provisions of the statutes. Arguing that a vandal, trespasser or mere harasser should be denied bail and, if convicted, be sentenced to a 10-year prison term could meet strong objections. A "stalker," however, is another matter entirely. These statutes impose a greater penalty on the same types of behaviors that their counterpart statutes prohibited. While the typical stalking statute defined the crime as a misdemeanor subject to a one-year incarceration, at least nine states allowed felony charges. Some states that classify stalking as a felony permit terms of imprisonment of 10 to 20 years, and all states have penalty enhancement provisions. In some states, felony charges mean the accused may be ineligible for bail. For example, the Illinois stalking statute allows courts to hold a stalking suspect without bail while facing a felony sentence that may be punishable by three years of incarceration. Several of the new stalking statutes specifically prescribe the denial of bail. Other statutes allow the courts to qualify pre-trial release; for instance they may require suspects to be placed on electronic monitoring.

Finally, the effects of being labeled by the criminal justice system a "stalker" rather than a trespasser, harasser or vandal carries the stigmatization associated with the media depiction of the classic stalker. The full range of consequences associated with this label has yet to become apparent. The label is already infused with negative connotations which could affect family, friends and business associates. A conviction for stalking would undoubtedly color any subsequent arrest. One can only speculate on the full range of social consequences of being labeled as a stalker.

How these statutes will be enforced in the future remains to be seen, but two of the first cases prosecuted in Florida following enactment of its stalking statute offer grim warnings of the consequences of laws passed in haste. A 12-year-old boy who had left a threatening note in the locker of one of his seventh grade classmates (Editorial Staff, 1992) was arrested and detained. A 66-year-old man was arrested, despite the "victim's" own assertion that he never threatened her but merely called on several occasions and showed up at her home without an invitation (Friedberg, 1992). One hopes these cases are just as much aberrations as the mythical strangers who stalk innocent victims for months—always eluding the police and always killing their victims.

Conclusion

Faulty premises are more likely to be accepted if the audience is fearful and if the premises coincide with a familiar worldview: "no one should be fearful in their own home." Public attention is produced by a crisis—particularly one which disturbs the expected routine. How the public defines the situation after their attention has been focused determines the response. False premises or expectations, such as "existing laws are inadequate for enforcement" or "the police can control or prevent random violence" prompt inappropriate responses. As Robert Merton (1949:80) has pointed out: "To seek social change, without due recognition of the manifest and latent functions performed by the social organizations undergoing changes is to indulge in social ritual." Ancient fears about humanity, fear of the dark, fear of strangers, fear of the unknown all contribute to our social construction of crime problems. The strength of such fears is a sobering warning about attempts to point out contradictions in the "evidence" of a particular crime. "For all the science and quantification used to substantiate a new problem, its true momentum will be located in its appeal to deep-rooted anxieties that respond poorly to rational inquiry, still less rebuttal" (Jenkins, 1994:229).

The media construct a reality of epidemic violence in which victims are selected at random. In an age of control, the lack of prediction is terrifying. Giving irrational behavior a name, like stalking, offers the illusion of control; it allows us to fill the frightening, unexplainable void with words and hollow action. The relentless push for legislation against every possible attack presents a soothing fiction that the problem is understood and has been addressed. The action of passing laws against predatory strangers belies society's helplessness in the face of that threat. Draconian punishments theoretically balance the terror inspired by random violence. One irony is that the very randomness of the behavior limits the possibility that perpetrators will be caught and controlled. Another irony is that catapulting certain behaviors into a new category will not eliminate irrational acts but instead results in equally irrational fears and expectations. Turning tragic misfortunes into the potential for injustice raises unrealistic expectations about our ability to control violence.

Sources

Beck, A. (1992). Murderous Obsession. *Newsweek*, (July 13): 60.

Bochove, D. (1992). Living in Fear. *Calgary Herald*, (July 26): A10

Bureau of Justice Statistics (1993). *Highlights from 20 Years of Surveying Crime Victims*. Washington, DC: U.S. Department of Justice.

California Penal Code (1990). Section 646.9. St. Paul: West.

Comment (1992). Making Stalking a Crime. *Atlantic Journal and Constitution*, (June 16): A20.

Congressional Record, (1993). 139 (October 4): S12901–01.

Dawsey, D. and Malnic, E. (1989). Actress Rebecca Schaeffer Fatally Shot at Apartment. *LA Times*, (July 19): 1.

Editorial Staff (1993a). Across the USA. *USA Today*, (June 16): A9.

_____ (1993b). Across the USA. *USA Today*, (April 15): A9.

_____ (1993c). Across the USA. *USA Today*, (February 4): 10A.

_____ (1993d). Across the USA. *USA Today*, (March 18): 6A.

_____ (1993e). Across the USA. *USA Today*, (March 18): 6A.

_____ (1992). Fla. Stalking Arrest. *USA Today*, (January 13): 9A.

_____ (1989). A Fatal Obsession with the Stars. *Time*, (July 31): 43–44.

Florida Statute Annotated (1992). Sec. 784.048. St. Paul: West.

Friedberg, M. (1992). Elderly Man May Be First Charged Under Florida Stalking Law. *Houston Chronicle*, (July 12): 16.

Geberth, V. (1992). Stalkers. *Law and Order* 40(10): 138–43.

Guy, R. (1993). The Nature and Constitutionality of Stalking Laws. *Vanderbilt Law Review* 46:991.

Hallman, T. (1992). Stalker Robs Girl of Innocence. *The Oregonian*, (March, 9): Al.

Hazelwood, R. (1989). The Serial Rapist: His Characteristics and Victims. *FBI Law Enforcement Bulletin* 58(2): 18–25.

Holmes, R. (1993). Stalking in America: Types and Methods of Criminal Stalkers. *Journal of Contemporary Criminal Justice* 9(4): 317–19.

Holmes, R. and DeBurger, J. (1985). Profiles in Terror: The Serial Murderer. *Federal Probation*, (September): 29–34.

_____ (1988). *Serial Murder*. Newbury Park, CA: Sage Publications.

Hoshen, J., Sennett, J. and Winkler, M. (1995). Keeping Tabs on Criminals. *IEEE Spectrum* 21(2): 26–32.

Jenkins, P. (1994). *Using Murder: The Social Construction of Serial Homicide*. London: Aldine de Gruyter.

Jenkins, P. and Katkin, D. (1988). Protecting Victims of Child Sexual Abuse: A Case for Caution. *Prison Journal* 58(2): 25–35.

Kolarik, G. (1992). Stalking Laws Proliferate. *American Bar Association Journal* (November): 35–36.

Leavitt, P. (1993). Tennis Coach Was Stalking Suspect. *USA Today*, (April 28): 3A

Merton, R. (1949). *Social Theory and Social Structure*. Glencoe, IL: The Free Press.

National Criminal Justice Association (1993). *Project to Develop a Model Anti-Stalking Code for States.* Washington, DC: National Institute of Justice.

Perez, C. (1993). Stalking: When Does Obsession Become a Crime? *American Journal of Criminal Law* 20:263.

Puente, D. (1992). Legislators Tackling the Terror of Stalking. *USA Today,* (January 21): 9A.

Sohn, E. (1994). Antistalking Statutes: Do They Actually Protect Victims? *Criminal Law Bulletin* 13:203–41.

Thomas, K. (1993). How to Stop the Stalker: State Antistalking Laws. *Criminal Law Bulletin* 12:124–36.

Tribune (1993). October 29: Section 4.

United States Congress (1993). United States Departments of Commerce, Justice, and State, and Senate Judiciary and Related Agencies. *Appropriations Act for Fiscal Year 1993.* Pub. L. 102–395, Section 109(b).

Blue Smoke and Mirrors

The "War" on Organized Crime

6

There are few social phenomena that attract as much public attention as organized crime. It has been the subject of countless novels, magazine articles, movies, newspaper reports, criminal investigations, congressional hearings, and public inquiries by criminal justice agencies. The American fascination with the covert world of organized crime has created a popular view of this phenomenon that has elevated it to legend. But, if federal law enforcement officials are to be believed, the glamour of organized crime and those things of which legends are made are undergoing drastic change.

After years of frustration, the tide of the battle has turned, according to Justice Department officials. New York Mayor Rudolph Giuliani, the former state's attorney reported: "This has been the Mafia's worst year . . . eventually they [will] become just another street gang" (McFadden, 1987). The official in charge of the Justice

Department's organized crime section added: "Their standing as a powerful and untouchable entity in the United States is in serious trouble and may well be a thing of the past in terms of their power" (Kahler, 1986). Philadelphia's District Attorney was ready to claim victory. According to him, recent indictments against southeastern Pennsylvania Mafiosi, ". . . will bring an end to organized crime in the Philadelphia-South Jersey area as we know it" (Linder, 1987). More recently, the conviction of John Gotti was heralded as bringing chaos to the Cosa Nostra.

As optimistic as these claims may sound, they are quite misleading. For more than half a century, law enforcement agencies have pursued, prosecuted, imprisoned and even executed organized criminals. Professional, well-funded agencies have been established to investigate organized crime and expose its many intricate conspiracies. Billions of dollars have been spent on "closing the borders" to the drug trade, on "stinging" labor racketeers, and on auditing the tax returns of gamblers. And still organized crime continues to conduct business-as-usual. There is little or no evidence to show that organized crime activities have been or are being significantly disrupted. In fact, most of the available evidence points to the contrary. With all of the time, effort, and money that has been expended in this area, we are still confronted with the basic questions of what can be done about organized crime and how will we know if we have been successful?

The answers to these questions are contingent upon a more basic question: what is organized crime? For the most part, policymakers have answered this question by pointing to a myth of organized crime in America.

The Official Myth of Organized Crime

What do we know about organized crime in America? How much empirically verified information do we have and how much data is simply based on myth and misconceived belief? How dependent is criminal justice policy on dubious facts presented as "proof" of a criminal conspiracy? As Charles McCaghy and Stephen Cernkovich (1987:265) comment:

> During the medieval ages Christian theologians pondered the question, How many angels can dance on the point of a needle without jostling one another? Although we might argue the subject's importance, we must at least marvel at any attempt

to solve such a problem. After all, there is little evidence on angels' width and dancing abilities. The modern-day equivalent of angel counting is "syndicate structuring." Today's Mafia watchers have about as much data as the angel counters did as they debate the nature of organized crime's organization.

Many federal law enforcement officials and some scholars think they know how many angels are dancing on the point of organized crime's needle. For them the answer is simple. Organized crime in the United States is a conspiracy of outsiders ". . . a group of men motivated by criminality and a sense of loyalty foreign to an open, democratic society" (Smith, 1978:168). Organized crime was imported to the United States during the late nineteenth and early twentieth centuries in the wave of Italian immigration. With these foreign immigrants came secret, outlaw, feudal societies such as the Mafia and the Camorra, the seedlings planted on American soil from which organized crime sprouted (Bequai, 1979). In 1931, these secret, feudal societies went through a catharsis, the Castellamarese War, which successfully wiped out the last vestiges of feudal Sicilian rule in the mob, removed illiterates from power and placed Americanized, business-oriented, Italian gangsters in charge of organized crime. By 1932 organized crime, years ahead of the business world, had become a sleek, modern, bureaucratized Italian crime corporation, made up of 24 (or 25, or 27) "families" based on Italian lineage and extended family relationships, governed by a national commission.

This massive, alien conspiracy was first called to our attention in a systematized manner by the Federal Bureau of Narcotics in 1946 (Smith, 1976). In later years, Senator Kefauver's Committee on interstate gambling (1951), Senator McClellan's Committee on labor racketeering (1957), investigations of the "Apalachin Meeting," and the testimony of Joe Valachi (1963) formed the cornerstones of the alien conspiracy theory. Following the lead of the law enforcement community, ambitious politicians, presidential commissions, journalists, academics, and writers of novels and screenplays eagerly advanced the theory. The President's Crime Commission (Task Force on Organized Crime, 1967) and Donald Cressey's *Theft of the Nation* (1967) gave the theory scholarly credibility and presented it in terms useful to policymakers. Since then, virtually every journalistic account and a host of academic treatises have championed the myth of an alien conspiracy (see, for example: Demaris, 1981; Chandler, 1975; Pace and Styles, 1975; Cook, 1973, among many others).

The myth of alien conspiracy is relatively simple. First, organized crime groups are viewed as criminal equivalents of legitimate corporate sector enterprises—exhibiting similar structural features and bureaucratic organization. Instead of president, vice-president, chairman of the board, general managers, personnel directors and the like, we have "bosses," "underbosses," "counselors," "captains," and "soldiers" (Salerno and Tompkins, 1969:84–85). Authority and discipline in the organization are based on violence, bribery, and a clan-based feudal hierarchy. Second, organized crime "families" exhibit an inexorable tendency toward monopoly and the formation of massive international cartels to dominate illicit goods and services (Task Force on Organized Crime, 1967). Third, group membership is determined by ethnic identity. As the Task Force Report on Organized Crime tells us (1967:6), "their membership is exclusively men of Italian descent." If anyone else, unlucky enough not to have been born Italian, wishes to engage in the provision of illicit goods and services, they do so only at the sufferance of the Mafia. And finally, organized crime groups attack the very foundations of democracy by their corrupting of otherwise upstanding and loyal public servants. They are an alien force perverting sound economic and political institutions (Pace and Styles, 1975; Salerno and Tompkins, 1969).

Of course times change, and myths must be adjusted to new realities. In the case of the alien conspiracy theory, drug trafficking by non-Italian groups presented a particularly thorny problem. So, in the last decade, the official depiction of organized crime in the United States underwent a pluralist revision. Federal, state, and local law enforcement organizations began noticing a growing number of new organized crime groups. The "traditional" Mafia was joined by "forceful new competition from Asian and Latin American underworld groups that specialize in heroin, cocaine, and marijuana" (Rowan, 1986:26). By the end of 1986, various law enforcement agencies had added to the list: Jamaicans, Colombians, Cubans, Japanese, Canadians, Irish, Vietnamese, Mexicans, African Americans, Russians, the pornography syndicate, and outlaw motorcycle gangs (*Organized Crime Digest*, 1986a; Pennsylvania Crime Commission, 1986; President's Commission on Organized Crime, 1984).

What is most intriguing about this shift in the official myth of organized crime is not how much it has changed but how steadfastly it clings to the fundamental assertions of the alien conspiracy myth. First, the pluralist revision is true to the conspiracy myth in that all of the new groups are defined as racially, ethnically, or culturally homogenous. They have "alien" origins and are inevitably described in terms of some kind of culturally delineated "family" structure that resembles a corporate bureaucracy, but which is rooted in the foreign customs of their homelands. They are all rabidly expansionist in their marketing strategies and inevitably are described as "more violent," "more secretive," and "more closely knit" than the traditional Mafia. In fact, the primary explanation used for the decline of Mafia power is that it has been Americanized. That is, younger Italians have adopted mainstream American values—presumably making them less violent, less secretive, and less closely-knit (Ianni, 1974; 1972). According to this view, the Mafia has lost its edge because of declining interest in high-risk ventures by new leadership and moderation in the use of violence.

> The leadership is old, and the next generation of managers seems to lack spirit, dedication, and discipline. "Today you got guys in here who have never broken an egg," a New Jersey Mafia leader complained in a conversation bugged by the FBI (Rowan, 1986:24).

So, in the tradition of corporate America, at least as interpreted by law enforcement officials, Italian organized criminals have elected to make deals in lieu of using intimidation. And, of course, these same law enforcement officials point with pride to their role in debilitating the Mafia through intense surveillance and prosecution under the Racketeer Influenced and Corrupt Organization (RICO) Act (Rowan, 1986).

This is the federal law enforcement version of Darwin's theory of natural selection. Old groups give way to new and better adapted ones. The new groups assume the old Mafia functions, and the Mafia moves on into new enterprises such as the disposal of toxic wastes, securities fencing, and fraud. Essentially, the same alien conspiracies remain; the only difference is that occasionally they involve new aliens.

It is interesting to note that as federal law enforcement agencies scramble to account for new forces in illicit markets without seriously impairing their myth of organized crime, they have not only relied on the tenets of an old myth, but they have also relied on old tactics. In the early twentieth century the same kind of alien conspiracy was touted as being responsible for America's drug problems. The temperance movement, for example, was a part of a nativist panic over the diminution of traditional rural, middle-class, white Protestant, native lifestyles in America. As Joseph Gusfield (1963:122–23, 124) comments:

The power of the Protestant, rural, native Americans was greater than that of the Eastern upper classes, the Catholic and Jewish immigrants, and the urbanized middle class. This was the lineup of the electoral struggle. In this struggle the champions of drinking represented cultural enemies and they had lost . . .

Increasingly the problem of liquor control became the central issue around which was posed the conflict between new and old cultural forces in American society. On the one side were the Wets—a union of cultural sophistication and secularism with Catholic lower-class traditionalism. These represented the new additions to the American population that made up the increasingly powerful political force of urban politics. On the other were the defenders of fundamental religion, or old moral values, of the ascetic, cautious, and sober middle class that had been the ideal of Americans in the nineteenth century.

So, like organized crime in the 1990s, liquor in the 1890s was a foreign, alien impingement upon an otherwise righteous society.

The same fear of alien influence can be seen in discussions surrounding early narcotics legislation. Despite the fact that the 250,000 addicts in the United States at the turn of the century were predominantly middle-aged, middle-class, white women (Brecher, 1972), the problem of drugs was laid squarely at the feet of aliens.

In the nineteenth century addicts were identified with foreign groups and internal minorities who were already actively feared and the objects of elaborate and massive social and legal restraints. Two repressed groups which were associated with the use of certain drugs were the Chinese and the Negroes. The Chinese and their custom of opium smoking were closely watched after their entry into the United States about 1870. At first, the Chinese represented only one more group brought in to help build the railroads, but, particularly after economic depressions made them a labor surplus and a threat to American citizens, many forms of antagonism arose to drive them out, or at least to isolate them. Along with the prejudice came a fear of opium smoking as one of the ways in which the Chinese were supposed to undermine American society.

Cocaine was especially feared in the South by 1900 because of its euphoric and stimulating properties. The South feared that Negro cocaine users might become oblivious of their prescribed bounds and attack white society. . . .

Evidence does not suggest that cocaine caused a crime wave but rather that anticipation of black rebellion inspired white alarm. Anecdotes often told of superhuman strength, cunning, and efficiency resulting from cocaine. One of the most terrifying beliefs about cocaine was that it actually improved pistol marksmanship. Another myth, that cocaine made blacks almost unaffected by mere .32 caliber bullets, is said to have caused southern police departments to switch to .38 caliber revolvers. These fantasies characterized white fear, not the reality of cocaine's effects and gave one more reason for the repression of blacks.

By 1914 prominent newspapers, physicians, pharmacists, and congressmen believed opiates and cocaine predisposed habitués toward insanity and crime. They were widely seen as substances associated with foreigners or alien subgroups. Cocaine raised the specter of the wild Negro, opium the devious Chinese, morphine the tramps in the slums, it was feared that use of all these drugs was spreading into the "higher classes" (Musto, 1973:5–7, 65; cited in McCaghy and Cernkovich, 1987).

Musto (1973) links similar fears toward Mexicans with the passage of the Marijuana Tax Act of 1937.

The fear of immigrants and repressed racial and ethnic groups in the United States was used to construct a conspiracy myth of drug use, just as it was used to construct a conspiracy myth of organized crime. The argument has always been the same: forces outside of mainstream American culture are at work which seek to pervert an otherwise morally sound, industrious, and democratic people. It is a convenient and easily understood argument. It is, in fact, the only depiction of organized crime that could gain widespread popular appeal. To suggest that righteous citizens are being perverted, intimidated, and forced into vice by alien forces is far more palatable than suggesting that "native" demands for illicit drugs, sex, and gambling invite the creation of organized crime groups. So, despite the minor alterations in the alien conspiracy myth, we can clearly discern that its revisionist form is neither new, clever, nor very different from the Mafia myth.

Historical Myths of Organized Crime

The "constructed proofs" used to justify the alien conspiracy myth range from the dubious to the preposterous. First, the assertion that the Sicilian Mafia was transplanted to America in the waves of Italian immigration is open to question. Research on the Mafia in Sicily indicates that it was never a highly structured criminal conspiracy; rather, it was an intermediary and fragmented force of mercenaries providing local control of the peasantry for absentee landlords (Blok, 1971). In addition, it is more than a little curious that other nations which received waves of Italian immigrants at the same time as the United States failed to develop anything even close to the American version of the Mafia (Potter and Jenkins, 1985). The importation myth derives from a combination of press sensationalism and nativist sentiments in the United States (Smith, 1976; 1975).

The great revolution in organized crime, the Castellamarese War, never happened. Rather than the forty assassinations credited to the "young turks" led by Lucky Luciano, only four possibly related murders have been identified after extensive research efforts. In addition, serious questions have been raised about the logistical improbabilities of such an uprising (Block, 1978; Nelli, 1976). The Kefauver Committee heard a great deal of testimony about organized crime and its role in gambling. However, it failed to produce a single knowledgeable witness who even mentioned the Mafia (Smith, 1975). The investigation of the Apalachin conclave was so tangled in New York state politics that no one really knows what happened there, who was there, or what they were doing. The sparse information which is available is amenable to many more credible explanations than that of an international Mafia conclave (Albini, 1971). Finally, the 1963 testimony of Joe Valachi and subsequent statements by alleged Mafia turncoat, Jimmy "the Weasel" Fratianno, have been shown to be riddled with contradictions, factual errors and uncorroborated assertions. In addition, neither of these informers was in any position to provide the insights credited to them (Albanese, 1985; Morris and Hawkins, 1970). As another "informer" commented:

> I remember when Joe [Valachi] was testifying before that Senate committee [McClellan] back in 1963. I was sitting in Raymond Patriarca's office [New England mob boss] . . . and we were watching Joe on television. I remember Raymond saying: "This bastard's crazy. Who the hell is he? . . . What the hell's the Cosa Nostra?" Henry asked, "Is he a soldier or a button man? . . . I'm a zipper." "I'm a flipper." . . . It was a big joke to them (Teresa, 1973:24–25, 28).

Rather than substance, the alien conspiracy myth is supported by the testimony of a few government-sponsored informants and public release of heavily edited and carefully selected police files and surveillance transcripts—all tied together by official speculation. Peter Reuter (1983), in his meticulous research on organized crime, has questioned both the knowledgeability of the government (pointing to problems and inaccuracies in the monitoring of legal, open, and public industries) and the inherent bias in the data collection process utilized by law enforcement agencies which seek only evidence to support their own assumptions about organized crime. If other groups had been subjected to the same level of wire-tapping, surveillance, interrogation, arrest and comprehensive investigation as groups of aged Italians, federal officials would no doubt have been startled to learn that "new" organized crime groups were not new at all — some have been active for the past century.

Empirical Evidence and Organized Crime

Quite apart from the historical problems with the alien conspiracy myth are problems revealed by the current body of empirical research on organized crime. Virtually every empirical study of organized crime conducted in the past twenty years has reached conclusions diametrically opposed to those in the official myth. Studies have demonstrated that rather than being a tightly structured, clearly defined, stable entity, organized crime operates in a loosely structured, informal, open system. Organized crime is made up of a series of highly adaptive, flexible networks that readily take into account changes in the law and regulatory practices, the growth or decline of market demand for a particular good or service, and the availability of new sources of supply and new opportunities for distribution. It is this ability to adapt that allows organized crime to persist and flourish. The inflexible, clan-based corporate entities described by law enforcement agencies could not survive in this turbulent environment.

It makes far more sense to conceive of organized crime as a partnership arrangement, or a patron-client arrangement, rather than as an immutable bureaucratic structure with a clearly defined hierarchy. Mark Haller's (1987) research reveals that organizations such as those surrounding the Capone gang and Meyer Lansky's extensive operations were in reality a series of small-scale business partnerships, usually involving several senior "partners" (Capone, Nitti, Lansky) and many junior partners who sometimes conducted business in concert with one another and often conducted business separately. Organized crime was not directed by Lansky or Capone in any bureaucratic sense but was merely a series of investment and joint business ventures. Joseph Albini (1971), as a result of his study of organized crime in Detroit, concluded that organized crime was made up of certain criminal patrons who traded information, connections with government officials, and access to a network of operatives in exchange for the clients' economic and political support. The roles of client and patron fluctuated depending on the enterprise; combinations were formed, dissolved and reformed with new actors. William Chambliss' (1978) study of organized crime in Seattle depicts an overlapping series of crime networks with shifting memberships highly adaptive to the economic, political and social exigencies of the community—without a centralized system of control. Alan Block's (1979b:94–95) study of the cocaine trade in New York concluded that the drug trade was operated by "small, flexible organizations of criminals which arise due to opportunity and environmental factors." John Gardiner's (1970) study of corruption and vice in "Wincanton," Ianni's (1974, 1972) two studies of organized crime in New York, and a study of organized crime in Philadelphia (Potter and Jenkins, 1985) reach similar conclusions. Peter Reuter's (1983) study of Italian organized crime in New York found that no group exercises control over entrepreneurs in gambling and loansharking. Reuter concludes that rather than the officially depicted view of organized crime as a monolithic conspiracy, it is in fact characterized by conflict and fragmentation.

The empirical research clearly reveals that organized crime is made up of small, fragmented, and ephemeral enterprises. There are very practical reasons for this. First, small size and segmentation reduce the chances of getting caught and prosecuted. Since employees in illicit industries are the greatest threat to those operations, and make the best witnesses against them, it is an organizational necessity for organized crime groups to limit the number of people who have knowledge about the group's operations. This is achieved by small size and segmentation so that employees only know about their own jobs and their own level of activity in the enterprise. Such arrangements are clear in the gambling and drug industries. In gambling, runners and collectors are distanced from the bank itself (Potter, 1994). In drug trafficking, production, importation, distribution, and retail activities are kept as discrete functions, often performed by completely different organized crime groups, most of which are both temporary and small (Wisotsky, 1986; Hellman, 1980).

For the same reasons that organized crime groups choose to limit the number of employees, they also tend to limit the geographic areas they serve. The larger the geographic area, the more tenuous communication becomes, requiring either the use of the telephone (and the threat of electronic surveillance) or long trips to pass on routine information in person, a most inefficient means of managing a business. In addition, the larger the geographic area served, the greater the number of law enforcement agencies involved and the higher the costs of corruption (Wisotsky, 1986). In his study of New York, Reuter (1983) found no evidence of centralization in gambling and loansharking, and he argues persuasively that in drug trafficking even less permanence and centralization is found.

The evidence also calls into question the assumption in the official myth that organized criminals act as the corrupters of public officials. Available evidence indicates that a more accurate perspective is that organized criminals, legitimate businessmen, and government officials are all equal players in a marketplace of corruption. Each brings to the market things wanted by the others, and routine series of exchanges occur. The purveyors of illicit goods and services wish to exchange their products, money, and influence for protection, selective enforcement against competitors, and favorable policy decisions by government authorities. Public officials put their policy-making and enforcement powers on the market. Who initiates such a deal depends upon circumstances, and the initiator is as likely to be the "legitimate" actor as the "criminal."

It is not uncommon for a series of exchanges between the under- and upperworlds to develop into a long-term corrupt relationship. Studies have shown that in some cases those who occupy positions of public trust are the organizers of crime (Block and Scarpitti, 1985; Potter and Jenkins, 1985; Chambliss, 1978; Gardiner and Lyman, 1978; Gardiner, 1970). Investigations of police corruption in Philadelphia and New York have demonstrated how thoroughly institutionalized corruption can be among public servants. In the private sector, respected institutions such as Shearson/American Express, Merrill Lynch, the Miami National Bank, Citibank, and others have eagerly participated in illicit ventures (*Organized Crime Digest*, 1987a; 1987b; 1986a; 1986b; Moldea, 1986; Lernoux, 1984; President's Commission on Organized Crime, 1984). For example, a study of the savings and loan "scandals" found that "these conspiracies more closely approximate organized crime than corporate crime" (Calavita and Pontell, 1993:519). Public officials are not the pawns of organized crime; they are part of its fabric — the part found in America's respected institutions.

The investigations of the Bank of Credit and Commerce International (BCCI) and its illegal activities around the world provide ample confirmation of the cozy relationship between drug traffickers, white collar criminals, the intelligence community, and leading politicians in the United States. BCCI was the seventh-largest privately owned financial institution in the world. It operated in seventy-three countries and had over four hundred branch offices (Schmaltz, 1988). According to Jack Blum, the former chief investigator of the Senate Subcommittee on Terrorism, Narcotics and International Operations, BCCI was, in the truest sense of the word, a "full-service bank."

> It offered full banking services to facilitate transactions that no one else would touch. It was the bank for drug dealers, arms dealers, money launderers—indeed whoever had an illegal project and money to hide . . . [BCCI was] a kind of Federal Express for illicit goods . . . ready to move currency, gold, weapons, drugs for anyone who wanted them moved (Meddis, 1991:9A).

BCCI's illegal activities have covered the full gamut of organized crime, white collar crime and political crime, including:

- laundering at least $14 million in narcotic profits for the Colombian cocaine cartels, shifting money to banks in the Bahamas, Britain, France, Uruguay, and Luxembourg to avoid detection (Schmaltz, 1988).
- playing a major role in the Iran-Contra scandal by acting as a conduit for weapons deals involving international arms merchant Adnan Khashoggi and drug deals (which funded the arms purchases) involving Panamanian president Manuel Noriega (Waldman et al., 1991). It is alleged that BCCI also served as a conduit for CIA funds destined for the Contras to support illegal arms deals and Contra-backed cocaine trafficking (Cauchon, 1991).
- helping Philippine president Ferdinand Marcos to transfer his personal fortune, accrued through corruption and graft, out of the Philippines before his ouster (Waldman et al., 1991).

While the full extent of its criminal activities may never be known, BCCI was a major criminal enterprise operating within the corporate sector with cooperation from other "legitimate" financiers and businesses and with, at the very least, the acquiescence of those government agencies charged with ferreting out drug trafficking, terrorism, and business corruption. BCCI had powerful political allies including Clark Clifford (former Secretary of Defense and close adviser to Presidents Truman, Kennedy, Johnson, and Carter), Edwin Meese (former Attorney General during the Reagan presidency) and Black, Manafort and Stone (the advertising consultants to the Republican Party). There were also political connections with Senator Alfonse D'Amato of New York; former President Jimmy Carter; and former President George Bush (Waldman et al., 1991).

The Justice Department is still investigating allegations that BCCI directly bribed United States government officials. How thorough that investigation will be is open to considerable question. Indications are, however, that this type of criminal conduct will not be treated with the same sense of panic or retribution as are other forms of crime. It is doubtful that the FBI or the Justice Department will establish international programs to analyze violent political crime and corporate criminals. There have been no public calls for enhanced funding to track, apprehend, and convict politically well-connected white collar criminals, nor are new prisons or the death penalty being proposed as the solutions to corporate and political crime networks.

The BCCI investigation leaves a vague sense of *deja vu*. Conspiracies involving banking institutions (i.e., the Nugan Hand Bank), the United States intelligence community, powerful politicians, arms merchants and drug lords have been commonplace since the Vietnam War.

In fact organized corruption can become so entangled with the normal operations of government that it creates organized crime activities of its own, activities labelled as state-organized crime. State-organized crime consists of acts described by law as criminal and committed by state officials in pursuit of their jobs as representatives of the state (Chambliss, 1989).

James Mills in *The Underground Empire: Where Crime and Governments Embrace* (1986) charges that the United States government is a major player in international drug crime networks. Mills (1986:1160) says: "The largest narcotics conspirator in the world is the government of the United States whose intelligence agencies conspire with or ignore the complicity of officials at the highest levels in at least 33 countries." Presenting evidence which clearly contradicts the idea of an underground criminal conspiracy and strongly supports Chambliss' model of "state-organized crime," Mills (1986:1140–41) describes organized crime in the drug trade this way:

> The international narcotics industry could not exist without the cooperation of corrupt governments. Our own government leans over backward to conceal this from the public—to recognize it would cripple foreign relations . . . The highly connected, tuxedo-

clad criminal is left in place to provide intelligence to the United States—and drugs to its citizens. . . . To assuage the public, politicians will continue to wage a civil war, one above-ground sector of the government attacking the drug traffic on front pages and the seven o'clock news, another underground sector secretly permitting the traffic, at times promoting it.

As Mills suggests, the reason why some drug traffickers prosper and grow powerful while others are caught and incarcerated may depend more on their political protection than on their ruthlessness. Since World War II, one of the most critical sources of institutional protection for the drug trade has been the Central Intelligence Agency (CIA) (Marshall, 1991).

Finally, the role of ethnicity in determining the structure of organized crime is misinterpreted and overstated by the alien conspiracy myth. There is ample evidence that many organized crime groups are made up of individuals of varied ethnic backgrounds or those who cooperate on a regular basis with individuals of various ethnic backgrounds (Pennsylvania Crime Commission, 1986; Abadinsky, 1985; Potter and Jenkins, 1985; Block, 1979b). As Haller's (1987) study of Lansky's and Capone's enterprises makes clear, organized criminals who wish to survive and prosper quickly learn the limits of kinship, ethnicity and violence, and proceed to form lucrative business partnerships on the basis of rational business decisions and common needs.

In those cases where organized crime networks do demonstrate ethnic homogeneity, it is merely a reflection of the exigencies of urban social life, not the machinations of a secret, ethnic conspiracy. It makes sense that vice in an African-American neighborhood is going to be primarily delivered by an African-American crime network. Similarly, illicit goods and services in an Italian neighborhood will probably be delivered by entrepreneurs of Italian lineage. This is not an organizational design but merely a reflection of the constituency of small, geographically compact, organized crime networks.

Headhunting

The alien conspiracy myth has dictated an enforcement strategy based on its precepts. Since Prohibition, the federal effort against organized crime has involved identifying and prosecuting group members for *any* available offense. Many times, these offenses are unrelated to illicit entrepreneurship and are often comparatively minor infractions. This strategy is predicated on the assumption that the actual conspiracy is too complex and well organized to be proved in court. As we shall see, this rationale is also part of the myth; the actual structure of organized crime operations is not as complex as the myth asserts. The myth of conspiracy actually becomes an excuse for a lack of success in controlling organized crime. In the headhunting strategy, success is calculated in the form of a body count. Arrests, indictments and convictions are used to justify budgets and ask for new enforcement powers. Because the conspiracy myth places a high premium on position in the hierarchy, the assumption has been that the farther up that hierarchy an arrest goes, the more disruptive it is to the business of organized crime. The most prized catch is the "boss" of a Mafia family. If the alien conspiracy myth is correct, and these groups are tightly structured and disciplined, the incapacitation of a "boss" should be debilitating to the organization.

Of course, because of the myth of an insulated hierarchy, the culture of violence, the code of silence, and the fidelity of clannish conspirators, successful headhunting requires a massive arsenal of law enforcement powers, powers that must be continually augmented and expanded. In addition, new laws, creating new criminal categories (i.e., "drug kingpin," "racketeer") must be created so that heavy sentences and fines can be imposed on those convicted. Simply convicting them of the crimes with which they are charged would not be a sufficient deterrent; additional penalties must be included. All of this and more was provided by the Racketeer Influenced Corrupt Organization Act in 1970. RICO provided for special grand juries to look for evidence, created a more potent immunity law, eased requirements for proving perjury, provided for protective custody of government witnesses, weakened the defense's capacity to cross-examine and exclude illegally obtained evidence, expanded federal jurisdiction to cover conspiracy to obstruct *state* law, and increased prison sentences (Chambliss and Block, 1981). It is a curious, but seldom noted fact, that the Nixon administration, which was responsible for the passage of RICO, chose to ignore organized crime and used the provisions of the act to prosecute anti-Vietnam war protesters (Chambliss and Block, 1981). In addition, RICO has civil provisions that allow the government to pursue what the Justice Department has called a "scorched earth" approach to organized crime — seizing assets and "leaving the mobster with nothing but a return address in federal prison" (Kahler, 1986).

As is the case with many law enforcement programs, rigorous assessments of the headhunting strategy are not available. When organized criminals are successfully prosecuted, this is used as evidence that the strategy is working. When convictions are not forthcoming or when the penalties imposed seem mild, law enforcement complains that "its hands are tied"—that it lacks sufficient resources or legal authority to implement the head-hunting strategy.

Despite the fact that comprehensive statistics are not kept on how many organized criminals have been put away, some fragmentary data is available to suggest the scope of the headhunting effort. A 1986 *Fortune* magazine article listed the "top 50" Mafia bosses (based on interviews with law enforcement officials). The article showed that fifteen of the fifty were in jail, ten were indicted or on trial, and one was a fugitive (Rowan, 1986). This included eight of the top ten. Since the publication of that article twenty-four of the remaining "free" crime leaders have been indicted or jailed. If we look specifically at the fabled five families of New York, we find that all of the top leaders of the Colombo, Bonnano, and Lucchese groups have been incapacitated, along with half of the Genovese group's leaders. From 1981–1985, seventeen of the twenty-four alleged Mafia bosses across the country were indicted or convicted (President's Commission on Organized Crime, 1984). In 1984 alone, organized crime indictments totaled 2,194, almost exclusively alleged Mafia group members.

In addition, conviction rates and sentences have also been going up. The General Accounting Office (GAO) estimated that the conviction rate rose from 56 percent to 76 percent in the period from 1972 to 1980 (Albanese, 1985). The GAO also noted a concomitant increase in jail terms handed down for convictions.

The problem with all of this is that the government has failed to produce any evidence that these prosecutions have resulted in a diminution of organized crime's illicit ventures. The federal government simply has no means to measure the impact of its efforts against organized crime (Potter, 1994). They are, however, indicators which suggest that organized crime is alive and quite healthy despite the prosecutorial efforts.

For example, prosecutions of one major gambling syndicate in Philadelphia in the early 1980s spawned at least two dozen other criminal networks in the same neighborhood to replace the targeted group (Pennsylvania Crime Commission, 1986). Major enforcement efforts directed at "syndicate heads" in Seattle and "Wincanton" resulted in minimal restructuring of street-level operations and no discernible impact on the provision of illicit goods and services (Chambliss, 1978; Gardiner, 1970). Major prosecutions in New York directed at labor racketeering and drug trafficking have had the effect of weeding out inefficient and highly visible operators, leaving more viable organized crime groups in their wake (Chambliss and Block, 1981). Recent prosecutions aimed at the pornography syndicate have resulted in the creation of at least six new groups and the revival of another that had been closed down ten years earlier by successful prosecution (Potter, 1986). Studies of the organization of vice have demonstrated consistently that prosecutions have only negligible impact on the provision of illicit goods and services and the operation of organized crime groups (Reuter et al., 1983; Albini, 1971).

The reason that no impact on organized crime can be demonstrated as a result of the headhunting approach is that it is based on myth. Organized crime groups learned long ago that to be successful in a threatening legal environment they must be prepared to adapt their structures and practices. The irony of the situation is that the more successful federal prosecutors become in incarcerating organized crime leaders, the more the industry responds by decentralizing and maintaining temporary and ephemeral working relationships. Because the headhunting approach never disables more than a small proportion of the total number of organized crime entrepreneurs at any given time, it actually strengthens and rewards some organized crime groups by weeding out their inefficient competitors.

It should also be pointed out that headhunting often involves targeting the easiest cases. Public prosecutions of highly visible (not necessarily highly skilled) crime figures is good press, but has very little impact. The selection of "Little Nicky" Scarfo, for federal prosecution has left the field open for far more powerful and dangerous crime figures. While Scarfo has been designated as the head of organized crime in Philadelphia by federal investigators and the press, his actual role and influence are highly suspect. The differences between Scarfo and his associates who were prosecuted (with mixed success) and those who have been left more or less alone illustrate the failure of the federal enforcement effort. Scarfo is a small-time hood who lacks political influence and has a minuscule share of the illicit market (considerably less than the 25 percent of the gambling market which was credited to his vastly more competent predecessor Angelo Bruno) (Potter and Jenkins, 1985). In addition, Scarfo's vision of criminal enterprise (among other things) is decidedly limited, highlighted by such capers as an extortion scheme directed at hot dog vendors in Atlantic City

(Demaris, 1986). However, also active in Philadelphia during the same time as "Mafia Boss" Scarfo were individuals identified by a variety of sources as controlling a great deal of political clout and a large share of the illicit market. At least one gambler had run a $35 million a year numbers bank virtually unmolested for three decades. A major attorney, identified several times in print as the emissary of Meyer Lansky and later of Alvin Malnik continued to grant favors from his plush offices, allegedly as the sole license-granting authority for illicit activities in Atlantic City (Demaris, 1986). A local realtor whose cocktail parties for judicial candidates are among the premier events of the political season continued to be the primary landlord for the pornography syndicate (Potter, 1986). Not to belabor the point, there are at least two dozen other operatives of similar stature who operated with relative immunity, while the federal government pursued "Little Nicky" with a vengeance far in excess of his importance or his capacity for future importance (Potter, 1994; Demaris, 1986). It is the relative immunity of major figures in organized crime, such as money launderers, corrupt public officials, and other individuals who serve as bridges between the underworld and the upperworld, that so clearly demonstrates the deficiencies in the myth of organized crime on which headhunting strategies are based.

A relatively recent case which captured headlines was the conviction of John Gotti on murder and racketeering charges. Federal prosecutors were quick to capitalize on the Gotti conviction by calling him "the most powerful criminal in America" and predicting that his conviction would bring chaos to the well-structured world of the Cosa Nostra. A quick review of the facts of the Gotti case as revealed in testimony from the trials and the transcripts of wiretaps presented at those trials offers a very different picture.

No one will quarrel with John Gotti's involvement with criminal activities. He has a "rap sheet" that includes hijacking, public intoxication, drug charges, assault, theft, burglary, gambling, and murder. Gotti is heard on the wiretaps alternately threatening, boasting, bragging and whining about the state of his criminal career. It is precisely this view of John Gotti, however, that is most troubling. For a man being touted as "the most powerful criminal in America," he has had a conspicuously troubled career, marked by a series of arrests and a string of unsuccessful criminal acts. John Gotti's career as an organized criminal has been somewhat limited. It is true that he ran a very large dice game in Manhattan. On the other hand, the wiretaps reveal that he was a notoriously bad gambler, frequently losing $60,000 to $70,000 a day. At one point on the tapes he complains that his luck was so bad he would "have to go on welfare." It is also true that Gotti provided leadership to a den of thieves operating out of the "Bergin Hunt and Fish Club." It is equally true that the members of his "crew" frequently complained about his inability to come up with targets for scores and his inability to create income-producing opportunities in other illicit ventures.

While in past trials prosecutors have alleged that Gotti had connections to several drug operations, most of the schemes hatched by his associates failed and resulted in the loss of money. While the wiretaps show Gotti to be a man who thought nothing of using intimidation or threats, they also clearly demonstrate that he was frequently out of control in this regard. He threatened to kill people with regularity—a very dangerous and costly action for a criminal entrepreneur to engage in repeatedly. He also pursued a series of personal, non-business-related vendettas, allegedly including the disappearance of a neighbor. His bail was once revoked because of an incident resulting from a fight over a parking space. While prosecutors have been successful in portraying Gotti as a dangerous sociopath, they have not been successful in portraying him as a major organized crime figure.

Simply put, John Gotti is no Meyer Lansky, no Sidney Korshak, no Alvin Malnik. It is simply inconceivable that someone in Lansky's position would have resorted to physical violence over a parking space. It is equally inconceivable that Lansky would be arrested with shocking regularity for nearly every venture he undertook. And, of course, it is inconceivable that Lansky would be tape recorded threatening to "whack" every other punk with whom he came in contact. The evidence presented against John Gotti portrays him as a hood and a criminal. A hoodlum with a long criminal record and frequent press notices does not qualify one as the head of organized crime. It does, however, make one an excellent target for a headhunting campaign. John Gotti is another in a long list of careless, boastful, somewhat unsuccessful pretenders who are easy prey for public prosecution. The simple fact is that there are hundreds of John Gottis out there.

Men like John Berkery of Philadelphia's K&A gang, Buster Riggins of Washington, D.C.'s sex rings, Jimmy Lambert of Kentucky's cocaine trade, and Jose Battle of the "Cuban Mafia" are every bit as formidable, powerful, and dangerous as Gotti. Every one of them, if we used John Gotti as a model, is a model candidate for "the most powerful criminal in America." To single Gotti out for a leadership role is to misunderstand organized crime and to confuse real power with notoriety. Gotti's alleged heroin operation, for example, was really headed by Mark Reiter and Angelo Ruggerio. They engaged in a series of opportunistic (and unsuccessful) drug deals involving amounts of drugs and money minute in comparison to the activities of dozens of other drug merchants. There is no indication of a monopoly or even dominance in the New York drug market by these actors; in fact, there is considerable evidence that they were fairly small operators. The "Bergin crew" was just that. It was not an offshoot of a powerful syndicate; it was an informal, social network of hoods. The "Members" came together to run a dice game, to do some "muscle work" for a loanshark, or to rob a drug dealer. They never formed a cohesive criminal organization. They were a group of individuals forming and reforming a series of criminal partnerships, some of which involved John Gotti. Even Gotti's most successful criminal venture, his crap game, involved a constantly changing series of participants from a number of crime networks.

While the evidence may have been strong enough for federal prosecutors to allege a criminal organization for RICO purposes, it was not strong enough to suggest anything beyond an informal, loosely structured, ephemeral criminal network. Evidence presented in the case suggested that almost all of New York City was bugged by one agency or another. Literally thousands of hours of conversations were recorded, most of which were irrelevant to the carefully edited versions presented as evidence of a criminal conspiracy. Testimony in the Gotti case described in detail the careers of the informers the government used against Gotti, men like James Cardinale, "Willie Boy" Johnson, Matthew Traynor, and "Crazy Sally" Polisi. It is not a pretty picture. Stories of drugs being supplied in prisons, sexual impropriety by informers and pro-secutors, and outright deals allowing the continuation and further-ance of criminal activity by government witnesses were repeated in detail. The impression left is that the government authorized some organized crime figures to continue dealing drugs, stealing and gambling to trap some other crime figures who were doing precisely the same thing.

One other issue needs to be discussed before moving on — headhunting does not always result in successful prosecutions. For example, charges against Jack Nardi, Jr., a Teamsters Union official, were dismissed on October 9, 1985. In May 1986, all six defendants in the celebrated trial of "Matty the Horse" Ianniello were acquitted in a RICO prosecution in New York. The defendants had been charged with trying to defraud Con Edison. The jury found that charge either laudable or impossible and acquitted the defendants. It took the government five very expensive tries to convict Gotti. In the previous four trials, he was acquitted because, as prosecutors admitted, the jury simply refused to believe turncoat criminals who had been given very lenient sentences in return for testimony. And on December 12, 1987, "Little Nicky" Scarfo and four of his alleged "family" members were acquitted in a drug case. The summation from the jury was simple: "the jury looked at this case that they put on and it stunk" (*Organized Crime Digest*, 1987a). The point of this litany of defeats is not to suggest that federal prosecutors are incompetent but merely to demonstrate that the credibility of the alien conspiracy myth is weakening with juries around the country.

The idea that vigorous prosecution and stiff criminal penalties will win the war against organized crime is at variance not only with current research on organized crime but with historic precedent as well. Literally thousands of cases in which organized crime figures have been arrested, convicted, and imprisoned in the last fifty years could be cited here. The fundamental question remains— so what? There is no evidence that these successful prosecutions have in any way negatively impacted or altered the activities of organized entrepreneurial groups in illicit markets.

Controlling Organized Crime

Our efforts to control and eradicate organized crime have failed. They have failed for two basic reasons: the headhunting strategy is predicated on false assumptions about the importance of "bosses" and the alien conspiracy myth which dictates organized crime policy is bankrupt in its understanding of illicit enterprises. Organized crime groups operate in a complex web of interrelated and tangled environments. They are impacted by the opportunities and constraints of the market, the legal system, politics, "upperworld" commerce, and the community in which they operate. Most attempts to analyze organized crime focus almost exclusively on *criminal* actions. Traditionally, analyses of organized crime have concentrated attention on the deviant aspects of organized crime rather than on its institutionalized and normative aspects. In Chambliss' (1978:6) words this emphasis has "obscured perception of the degree to which the structure of America's law and politics creates and perpetuates syndicates that supply the vices in our major cities."

Empirical research on organized crime suggests that in order to understand it, we must understand its social context. That social context is defined by two consistent threads running through the organization of crime: official corruption and the exigencies of the political economy. The evidence is compelling that organized crime should not be conceptualized as a dysfunction in society, nor as an alien force impinging upon society. Rather, organized crime is part and parcel of the political economic system. Once again, Chambliss (1978:6), in commenting on the organization of vice in Seattle, makes the degree of integration clear:

> Working for, and with, this cabal of respectable community members is a staff which coordinates the daily activities of prostitution, gambling, bookmaking, the sale and distribution of drugs, and other vices. Representatives from each of these groups, comprising the political and economic power centers of the community, meet regularly to distribute profits, discuss problems, and make the necessary organizational and policy decisions essential to the maintenance of a profitable, trouble-free business.

This point of view has compelling implications for policy. The argument advanced here suggests that policymakers have been attacking the wrong targets in their battle against organized crime.

Dwight Smith (1978:162) observes that law enforcement strategy traditionally "has rested on the belief that acts of crime are the sole responsibility of the perpetrator, and that as a consequence of removing him from society, the criminal acts would disappear." However, the evidence suggests that the existence of illicit drug dealers, loansharks, gamblers, and other illegal entrepreneurs is due to the fact that the legitimate marketplace leaves a number of potential customers for these services unserved. The control of organized crime can be achieved only with a greater understanding of organizational and market behavior, by "learning how to reduce the domain of the illicit [entrepreneur] . . . and a wider appreciation of the entire market spectrum, and a deeper analysis of the dynamics that nurture its illicit aspects" (Smith, 1978:175–76). Smith argues that an understanding of the "task environment" of particular enterprises will promote a better and more comprehensive understanding of how such illicit enterprises emerge, survive, and make a profit from crime.

In rethinking strategies to control organized crime, we must begin by conceptualizing organized crime as a business, not an alien conspiracy. Doing so will direct us to efforts that will improve our understanding of the causes of organized criminal behavior and the means used to organize illicit enterprises. In addition, this view directs our attention toward the elimination of arbitrary distinctions between legal and illegal goods and services (particularly in gambling, lending, drug distribution and sexual services) and the importance of corruption in the ability of organized crime to prosper. Chambliss (1978:1–2) supports this view in his study of organized crime in Seattle.

> Money is the oil of our present-day machinery, and elected public officials are the pistons that keep the machine operating. Those who come up with the oil, whatever its source, are in a position to make the machinery run the way they want it to. Crime is an excellent producer of capitalism's oil. Those who want to affect the direction of the machine's output find that the money produced by crime is as effective in helping them get where they can go as is the money produced in any other way. Those who produce the money from crime thus become the people most likely to control the effectively working political economy. Crime is, in fact, a cornerstone on which the political and economic relations of democratic-capitalistic societies are constructed.

> In every city of the United States, and in many other countries as well, criminal organizations sell sex and drugs, provide an opportunity to gamble, to watch pornographic films, or to obtain a loan, an abortion or a special favor. Their profits are a mainstay of the electoral process of America and their business is an important (if unrecorded) part of the gross national product. The business of organized crime in the United States may gross as much as one hundred billion dollars annually . . . the profits are immense, and the proportion of the gross national product represented by money flowing from crime cannot be gainsaid. Few nations in the world have economies that compare with the economic output of criminal activities in the United States.

So, rather than directing control efforts in an enforcement direction aimed at specific individuals or groups, a realistic view of organized crime points to the importance of the market and the political arrangements which sustain organized crime.

The way we conceptualize and understand organized crime dictates the means selected to control it. While detailed policy alternatives are beyond the scope of this discussion, several thematic departures from present policy are dictated by what we know about organized crime. The most important of those policy departures may well be consideration of steps necessary to shrink and control the market for the goods and services of organized crime.

Reducing Market Demand

The largest and most profitable organized crime enterprises are those that provide illicit goods and services to a significant segment of the public eager to obtain them. Among the most important services are drug trafficking, gambling, prostitution, and loansharking. One approach to limiting the demand for these goods is to punish the consumer. In addition to being practically and politically unpalatable, we have also seen that historically (especially with regard to drugs) such tactics have had precisely the opposite effect of the one intended.

Another approach is available, however. The first objective of control policies aimed at organized crime should be reducing the size of the illicit market and the profits emanating from that market — in other words, decriminalization. Laws against consensual crimes create remarkable opportunities for criminal entrepreneurs. The laws against vice are almost unenforceable. All of these behaviors require cooperation between buyer and seller. There is no victim to call the police, there is no complainant to instigate an investigation. As a direct result, these laws are enforced in a highly selective and discriminatory manner. Individuals who are unlucky enough to be arrested under the gambling, drug, and prostitution statutes are almost always the most visible and the easiest to catch. Enforcement of the laws fills the prisons with junkies and streetwalkers. Ironically, the enforcement of these laws serves to strengthen organized crime rather than to control it. Those who will be apprehended are the smallest operators — those with the least organization, the least power, and the least expertise. Organized crime groups find that the law weeds out the inefficient and small operators. Enforcing the law leaves the entire illicit market open to exploitation by better organized, more successful criminal enterprises. The law helps organized crime in a number of other ways as well. Since these types of goods and services are in demand but illegal, organized crime groups can charge dearly for their services. The profits reaped in the heroin and cocaine markets alone are staggering, and it is only the illegality of the drug which makes these profits possible. The immense sums of money realized from entrepreneurship in the illicit market facilitate the purchase of a web of police and political protection.

In view of the fact that the laws are dysfunctional and the markets enormous, it makes sense to end arbitrary distinctions between legal and illegal activities. Organized crime scholars have long argued that decriminalization or legalization is one way to reduce the market domain of organized crime (Albanese, 1985; Luksetich and White, 1982; Anderson, 1979; Albini, 1971). Merely removing the criminal label from gambling, loansharking, prostitution, and drug trafficking—and even legalizing and regulating them— would not eliminate organized crime's involvement entirely. Legalized off-track betting in New York did not drive bookmakers out of business. It did, however, constrain their activity. They must offer odds within the limits of those being offered by the state. They must be restrained in their collection methods. Most importantly, bookmaking profits appear to have stabilized at between 5 and 10 percent (Reuter, 1983). Decriminalization would similarly constrain commerce in the most profitable enterprises in organized crime's portfolio. As long as the profits are high and the risks diffuse, criminal entrepreneurs will continue to engage in these activities. It simply makes sense to take some of the profit out of these markets.

Decriminalization of the illicit goods and services which are at the core of the business of organized crime may be difficult to achieve. The same forces that gave rise to the alien conspiracy myth make decriminalization a difficult option for policymakers to exercise. Americans have historically been unwilling to acknowledge their own role in creating a market for prostitution, gambling, loansharking, drugs, and the like—preferring to label certain acts deviant and criminal rather than accepting them as social constants in society. Decriminalizing, or even legalizing, such activities might be viewed as condoning them or as catering to moral "defects" in the "weaker" members of society. If the political reality remains such that the laws cannot be changed to shrink organized crime's market, then the focus of current law enforcement efforts must be changed to address the problem of organized crime more effectively. Specific policies should be formulated to address the "laundering" of illicit funds, corruption of officials, and improved intelligence and surveillance to target those in control of illegal operations.

Fighting Corruption

It is axiomatic to organized crime that it cannot flourish without a favorable political environment—meaning systematic abuses of the public trust. While there is no reason to believe that the customers of organized crime can be deterred from seeking illicit goods and services, there is every reason to believe that corruption can be deterred. Instead of wasting valuable resources on surveillance of criminals with a "bad reputation," government should focus attention on finding individuals who serve as links between the underworld and the upperworld. Bribery, campaign contributions, delivery of votes, and other favors are used to influence legislators, city council members, mayors, judges, district attorneys, and others (Potter, 1994). It is not possible to place organized crime in a social context without exploring its relationships with the political system. Politicians can guarantee that organized crime is able to continue uninterrupted operations with a minimum of official governmental interference. At a minimum, increased and more comprehensive reporting of assets and sources of income should be required of public officials in key decision-making positions. Closer supervision of public officials and strengthening of conflict of interest laws are required. Obviously, greater restrictions on contributions to political candidates could be enacted—for example, limiting private contributions to $100 or adopting public financing of political campaigns.

Cleaning Up the Money Laundries

The recent increase in drug-trafficking profits has focused attention on the critical role of financial institutions in laundering illicit incomes. Organized crime groups have become dependent on bankers, stockbrokers, lawyers, realtors, and others close to the financial community (Demaris, 1986; Moldea, 1986; Lernoux, 1984). As a first step, there should be a standardized federal requirement for corporate reporting in order to avoid the great variance in state regulations. At a minimum, sufficient information should be required so that investigators will be able to follow money trails with greater ease. Second, the enforcement of existing reporting regulations should be increased in areas involving large sums of money transferred between and among banks. Interbank transfers and wire transfers to foreign banks and corporations should be reported. Foreign currency transactions should be subjected to reporting requirements detailing where the money is going and why. Certainly crimes committed by financial institutions and corporations as part of organized crime operations should be treated with the same severity as crimes committed by the organized criminals themselves. Surely, if the federal government can justify putting labor union locals into receivership based on the criminal records of their officers, the same should hold for brokerage houses. Federal prosecutors should recognize that a corrupt organization is a corrupt organization whether it is the Mafia or Merrill Lynch. The seizure of corporate assets under the RICO statute should become as common as the confiscation of a drug dealer's Cadillac.

Improving Intelligence

Following the money, rather than the perpetrator, should be the hallmark of effective organized crime investigations. By tracing the path of illicit profits, law enforcement agencies would gain valuable information on cash deposits, property transactions, fund purchases, real estate ownership, and foreign currency transfers. It is a reality of organized crime that the point at which illicit wealth accumulates is also the point closest to the most powerful underworld operators.

At the moment, the focus of law enforcement intelligence gathering is primarily limited to preparing a "rogue's gallery" of ethnics with bad reputations. Obtaining useful intelligence on organized crime is admittedly difficult, but law enforcement agencies can vastly improve their understanding of organized crime by focusing on the development of an accurate picture of organized crime markets. Intelligence operations should follow the processes of distribution, supply, manufacturing and financing — regardless of who is involved—or whether they reside in the under- or upper-worlds. This approach to intelligence means that analysts should be more concerned with assessing market, production, and social conditions that shape the patterns of organized criminals' interactions.

In addition, intelligence-gathering operations must be separated from operations designed to produce arrests and convictions. Intelligence gathering, when done correctly, is unlikely to result in quick arrests and certain convictions. Agencies under pressure to show results calculated by numbers of arrests tend to choose the easiest cases and to arrest the most obvious (and usually the least important) criminal operatives. These arrests inflate statistics and contribute little to our knowledge about organized crime. Intelligence gathering must be recognized as important on its own merits, and success must be measured by the quality of data produced, not prosecutors' batting averages. Reactive intelligence-gathering strategies must be replaced by intelligence operations sensitive to shifts in law, enforcement patterns, technology, markets and social trends.

None of these suggestions for changes in policy are new, nor are they likely to be embraced by policymakers. Attacking white collar criminals is not as politically satisfying, nor as easy, as jailing highly visible and reasonably unimportant purveyors of vice on the street. The very fact that law enforcement agencies continue to base their control strategies on mythological characterization and continue to reject a comprehensive attack on organized crime clearly demonstrates the poverty of present policies of control.

Sources

Abadinsky, H. (1985). *Organized Crime*. Chicago: Nelson-Hall.

Albanese, J. (1985). *Organized Crime in America*. Cincinnati: Anderson.

Albini, J. (1971). *The American Mafia: Genesis of a Legend*. New York: Appleton-Century-Crofts.

Anderson, A. (1979). *The Business of Organized Crime: A Cosa Nostra Family*. Stanford, CA: Hoover Institution Press.

Bequai, A. (1979). *Organized Crime: The Fifth Estate*. Lexington, MA: Heath.

Block, A. (1979a). *East Side-West Side: Organizing Crime in New York, 1939–1959*. Swansea, United Kingdom: Christopher Davis, Publishers.

———— (1979b). The Snowman Cometh: Coke in Progressive New York. *Criminology* 17:75–99.

———— (1978). History and the Study of Organized Crime. *Urban Life* (January 6): 455–74.

Block, A. and Scarpitti, F. (1985). *Poisoning for Profit: The Mafia and Toxic Waste*. New York: William Morrow.

Blok, A. (1971). *The Mafia of a Sicilian Village, 1860–1960*. Prospect Heights, IL: Waveland Press.

Brecher, E. (1972). *Licit and Illicit Drugs*. Mount Vernon, NY: Consumers Union.

Calavita, K. and Pontell, H. (1993). Savings and Loan Fraud as Organized Crime: Toward a Conceptual Typology of Corporate Illegality. *Criminology* 31(4): 519–48.

Cauchon, D. (1991). Head of BCCI-linked Bank Quits. *USA Today*, (August 15): 8A.

Chambliss, W. (1989). State-organized Crime. *Criminology* 27(2): 183–208.

_____ (1978). *On the Take: From Petty Crooks to Presidents.* Bloomington: Indiana University Press.

Chambliss, W. and Block, A. (1981). *Organizing Crime.* New York: Elsevier.

Chandler, D. (1975). *Brothers in Blood: The Rise of the Criminal Brotherhoods.* New York: Dutton.

Cook, F. (1973). *Mafia!* Greenwich, CT: Fawcett.

Cressey, D. (1967). *The Theft of the Nation.* New York: Harper & Row.

Demaris, O. (1986). *The Boardwalk Jungle.* New York: Bantam.

_____ (1981). *The Last Mafioso.* New York: Bantam.

Gardiner, J. (1970). *The Politics of Corruption: Organized Crime in an American City.* New York: Russell Sage Foundation.

Gardiner, J. and Lyman, T. (1978). *Decisions for Sale: Corruption and Reform in Land-Use and Building Regulations.* New York: Praeger.

Gusfield, J. (1963). *Symbolic Crusade: Status Politics and the American Temperance Movement.* Urbana: University of Illinois Press.

Haller, M. (1987). Business Partnerships in the Coordination of Illegal Enterprise. Paper presented at the annual meetings of the American Society of Criminology, Montreal, (November).

Hellman, D. (1980). *The Economics of Crime.* New York: St. Martin's Press.

Ianni, F. (1974). *Black Mafia: Ethnic Succession in Organized Crime.* New York: Simon and Schuster.

_____ (1972). *A Family Business: Kinship and Social Control in Organized Crime.* New York: Russell Sage Foundation.

Kahler, K. (1986). The Mob is Winning: Organized Crime in the United States is Richer than Ever. *Gannett Westchester Newspapers,* (May 25): B1, B6.

Knapp Commission (1972). *Report of the Commission to Investigate Alleged Police Corruption.* New York: Braziller.

Koepp, S. (1985). Dirty Cash and Tarnished Vaults. *Time,* (February 25): 65.

Laswell, H. and McKenna, J. (1971). *The Impact of Organized Crime on an Inner-City Community.* New York: Policy Sciences Center.

Lernoux, P. (1984). *In Banks We Trust.* Garden City: Anchor/Doubleday.

Linder, L. (1987). Scarfo Charged with 2nd Murder. *Associated Press,* (April 11).

Luksetich, W. and White, M. (1982). *Crime and Public Policy: An Economic Approach.* Boston: Little, Brown.

Marshall, J. (1991). CIA Assets and the Rise of the Guadalajara Connection. *Crime, Law and Social Change* 16(1): 85–96.

McCaghy, C. and Cernkovich, S. (1987). *Crime in American Society.* New York: Macmillan.

McFadden, R. (1987). The Mafia of the 1980s: Divided and Under Siege. *New York Times,* (March 11): A1.

Meddis, S. (1991). U.S. Role in Bank Probe Criticized. *USA Today,* (July 30): 9A.

Mills, J. (1986). *The Underground Empire: Where Crime and Governments Embrace*. New York: Doubleday.

Moldea, J. (1986). *Dark Victory: Ronald Reagan, MCA, and the Mob*. New York: Viking.

Morris, N. and Hawkins, G. (1970). *The Honest Politician's Guide to Crime Control*. Chicago: University of Chicago Press.

Musto, D. (1973). *The American Disease: Origins of Narcotics Control*. New Haven: Yale University Press.

Nelli, H. (1976). *The Business of Crime*. New York: Oxford University Press.

Organized Crime Digest (1987a). March 25.

_____ (1987b), December 23.

_____ (1986a), May.

_____ (1986b), August.

_____ (1985), November.

Pace, D. and Styles, J. (1975). *Organized Crime: Concepts and Control*. Englewood Cliffs, NJ: Prentice-Hall.

Pennsylvania Crime Commission. (1986). *Report*. Conshohocken, PA: Commonwealth of Pennsylvania.

_____ (1985). *Report*. Conshohocken: Commonwealth of Pennsylvania.

Potter, G. (1994). *Criminal Organizations: Vice, Racketeering, and Politics in an American City*. Prospect Heights, IL: Waveland Press.

_____ (1986). *The Porn Merchants*. Dubuque, IA: Kendall Hunt.

Potter, G. and Jenkins, P. (1985). *The City and the Syndicate: Organizing Crime in Philadelphia*. Lexington, MA: Ginn Press.

President's Commission on Organized Crime (1984). *The Impact: Organized Crime Today*. Washington, DC: U.S. Government Printing Office.

Reuter, P. (1983). *Disorganized Crime*. Cambridge: MIT Press.

Reuter, P., Rubinstein, J., and Wynn, S. (1983). *Racketeering in Legitimate Industries: Two Case Studies*. Washington, DC: National Institute of Justice.

Rowan, R. (1986). The 50 Biggest Mafia Bosses. *Fortune*, (November 10): 24–38.

Salerno, R. and Tompkins, J. (1969). *The Crime Confederation*. Garden City, NY: Doubleday.

Schmaltz, J. (1988). Banks Indicted by U.S. for Money Laundering Case. *New York Times*, (October 12): A56.

Scott, P. (1991). Cocaine, the Contras, and the United States: How the U.S. Government Has Augmented America's Drug Crisis. *Crime, Law and Social Change* 16(1): 97–131.

Smith, D. (1980). Paragons, Pariahs, and Pirates: A Spectrum-Base Theory of Enterprise. *Crime and Delinquency* 26:358–86.

_____ (1978). Organized Crime and Entrepreneurship. *International Journal of Criminology and Penology* 6:161–77.

_____ (1976). Mafia: The Prototypical Alien Conspiracy. *The Annals of the American Academy of Political and Social Science* 423:75–88.

_____ (1975). *The Mafia Mystique*. New York: Basic Books.

Task Force on Organized Crime. (1967). *Task Force Report: Organized Crime*. Washington, DC: U.S. Government Printing Office.

Teresa, V. (1973). A Mafioso Cases the Mafia Craze. *Saturday Review*, (February): 23–29.

Waldman, S., Mabry, M., Bingham, C. and Levinson, M. (1991). The Unified Scandal Theory. *Newsweek*, (September 23): 22–23.

Wisotsky, S. (1986). *Breaking the Impasse in the War on Drugs*. New York: Greenwood Press.

Myths that Justify Crime

A Look at White Collar Criminality

7

Myths of crime and criminal justice, for the most part, revolve around two central themes. First, there is a criminal act or behavior. That behavior is seized upon by the media, law enforcement bureaucracies, and politicians as a way of attracting public attention and raising policy issues related to crime in general. In the ensuing discussion of the behavior, exaggerations, political rhetoric and often outright misconceptions and misunderstandings combine to create a distorted view of the threat to society and to individuals in that society. The burgeoning myths frequently target minority population groups or groups with unpopular beliefs. Thus, we have had crime scares about women and witchcraft, homosexuals and molested children, satanists and ritual murders, Italians and organized crime, people of color and drugs, and immigrants and political subversion. The second recurring theme which we find in exploring myths of crime and criminal justice is a massive law

141

enforcement response to the behavior in question. New laws are passed outlawing certain aspects of the behavior, prison sentences are increased, new powers are granted to investigating agencies, and a proactive campaign of enforcement is launched in an attempt to control the perceived danger. In taking these steps we frequently overreact and make the problem we are trying to solve much worse than it was originally.

In this chapter, however, we will explore a myth of a different kind. This is a myth designed to downplay the importance of criminal behavior and justify a policy of lax enforcement. This is a myth which seeks to mitigate responsibility and excuse misconduct. This is a myth which argues for less enforcement, fewer laws, and less stringent punishment. This is a myth which protects those with political and economic power. In this chapter, we will explore the issue of white collar crime. We will address a series of neutralizations and explanations which have been used to justify political and criminal justice policies which some suggest go so far as to encourage criminality. The first of these myths is that white collar crimes cause less damage, both economic and physical than traditional "street crimes." Government officials have tried to present the issue of white collar crime in terms of embezzlement, or employee fraud, ignoring the more pervasive and dangerous criminality of corporations. The second myth is that white collar crimes are accidents or oversights—that they are unintended crimes lacking the criminal intent found in crimes of violence and theft (see Benson, 1996). The third myth used to explain away white collar crime is that present laws and enforcement efforts are more than sufficient to deal with the problem. This argument is frequently carried a step further to suggest that present laws are too stringent and severe and out of proportion to the danger of the behavior. We will explore the actual patterns of enforcement and the punishments actually meted out to white collar criminals.

"Real" Crime and White Collar Crime

When most people think of crime they think of acts of interpersonal violence or property crimes. In the popular imagination, a crime is an act committed against an innocent victim by an uncaring perpetrator. A crime occurs when someone breaks into your house and steals your television set and stereo. A crime occurs when an anonymous mugger knocks you to the ground and steals your wallet and watch. A crime occurs when a serial killer goes on a rampage and slaughters innocent victims.

These images of crime are perpetuated by the media and by the law enforcement establishment. News reports carry nightly features on robberies at convenience stores, assaults, drug crimes, and murders. Television movies and police shows emphasize crimes of violence, with a particular bent toward the sensational (but rather rare) crime of murder. Police departments, the FBI, and other law enforcement agencies monitor the amount of street crime and gauge the threat of crime in society in that context. When politicians talk about crime, engaging in their ritualistic calls for law and order, they are careful to stress crimes of violence and theft. When George Bush raised the crime issue in the 1988 presidential election, he was careful to portray it in the personage of Willie Horton, an African-American criminal convicted of a violent offense. We spend billions of dollars a year, we employ over 800,000 police and thousands of other government officials and prosecutors in the battle against street crime (BJS, 1994).

Of course, we are all appalled by murder, rape, robbery, and the other violent crimes in society. But our emphasis on these crimes is fundamentally misleading. It conceals two fundamental truths about crime in the United States. The first is that while we may worry about street crimes, there is very little the criminal justice system can do to control them and next to nothing the criminal justice system can do to prevent them. The second basic truth is that all the violent crime, all the property crime, all the crime we concentrate our energy and resources on combating is less of a threat, less of a danger, and less of a burden to society than the crime committed by corporations and crime "committed by a person of respectability and high social status in the course of his occupation" (Sutherland, 1940)—that is, white collar crime. As Bertram Gross (1980:110, 113–15) has commented, these are society's "dirty secrets":

> We are not letting the public in on our era's dirty little secret: that those who commit the crime which worries citizens most — violent street crime — are, for the most part, products of poverty, unemployment, broken homes, rotten education, drug addiction, alcoholism, and other social and economic ills about which the police can do little if anything. . . . But, all the dirty little secrets fade into insignificance in comparison with one dirty big secret: Law enforcement officials, judges as well as prosecutors and investigators, are soft on corporate crime. . . . The corporation's "mouthpieces" and "fixers" include lawyers, accountants, public relations experts and public

officials who negotiate loopholes and special procedures in the laws, prevent most illegal activities from ever being disclosed and undermine or sidetrack "over zealous" law enforcers. In the few cases ever brought to court, they usually negotiate penalties amounting to "gentle taps on the wrist" (cited in Hagan, 1986:111).

The Costs of White Collar Crime

In simple dollar terms, there is no question that white collar crime does significantly more damage to society than all street crimes put together. The economic losses resulting from street crimes are generally estimated to be between $10 and $13.5 billion a year (Coleman, 1994). The total monetary damage from white collar crimes is somewhere between $174 billion and $231 billion annually (Clinard and Yeager, 1980). The savings and loan collapse, largely a product of both organized and white collar crime, alone cost $500 billion.

Some commentators are quick to point out that these economic losses are spread across millions of victims, the damages are diffuse, and the trauma to the victim less than in the case of street crimes. They are also quick to point out that crimes of violence entail losses that far exceed monetary damages in terms of injury and even death. The fact is that they are too quick to point to death and injury as an index of the seriousness of street crimes. White collar crimes kill and maim as well, and in staggering numbers. Consider the following:

- Every year approximately 14,000 workers in the United States are killed on the job.

- Annually 100,000 workers die from diseases contracted in the course of their occupations (Coleman, 1994).

- About 2,000,000 workers a year are injured on the job because of dangerous working conditions maintained by their employers in violation of prevailing safety standards.

- It is estimated that 140,000 people die each year from air pollution alone, most of which is the result of a violation of governmental regulations by corporations.

- Unsafe and defective merchandise produced by corporations and sold to consumers results in an additional 30,000 deaths and 20,000,000 serious injuries a year (Coleman, 1994).

Compare this record of corporate carnage to the approximately 20,000 murders and 850,000 assaults a year committed in the United States; you can then begin to appreciate the extent of victimization from white collar crimes.

White Collar Crime and Criminal Intent

Despite the damage to society resulting from white collar crimes, government officials, corporate executives, and even some law enforcement experts argue that these crimes differ from street crimes in several important respects. They attempt to mitigate the impact of white collar crime by pointing to a lack of *mens rea* (criminal intent) (Clinard and Yeager, 1980). They say that unlike muggers, rapists, and murderers, corporate violators do not set out to commit crime. Violations simply happen in the context of occupational environments. They result from oversights, occasionally from negligence, and from the pressures inherent in the business world. These crimes and violations are not the result of a conscious decision to do harm or to inflict injury.

The argument that corporate offenders lack criminal intent is one of a series of neutralizing myths employed by white collar criminals to excuse their conduct. Unfortunately, the facts simply belie the myth. Studies have shown clearly that injuries and deaths caused by corporate violations are not simply a matter of carelessness or neglect, many are the direct result of willful violations of the law. For example, James Messerschmidt (1986), in a comprehensive review of research studies on job-related accidents, determined that somewhere between 35 and 57 percent of those accidents occurred because of direct safety violations by the employer. Laura Shill Schraeger and James Short, Jr. (1978) found that 30 percent of industrial accidents resulted from safety violations and another 20 percent resulted from unsafe working conditions. Chrysler Corporation was fined $1.5 million for over 800 health and safety violations—including knowingly exposing its workers to poisons such as lead and arsenic (Eitzen and Zinn, 1992). The Environmental Protection Agency estimates that of the 88 billion pounds of toxic waste produced annually by American companies, 90 percent of it is disposed of improperly and in violation of the law (Coleman, 1989).

Anecdotal evidence, while often hard to come by in considering white collar crime, further supports the contention that many of these crimes are willful and deliberate. Consider the case of the asbestos industry in the United States. Major asbestos manufacturers were aware as long ago as 1934, as a result of company-funded research, that asbestos-related diseases (commonly referred to as "white lung") were a distinct threat to their workers (Carlson, 1979). Two of the largest asbestos manufacturers, Johns-Manville and Raybestos-Manhattan, not only knew of the danger but covered up their own research findings. Researchers hired by the asbestos industry were prevented from publishing their findings about the dangers of asbestos, and the Philip Carey Company even went so far as to fire its own medical consultant when he warned of the dangers of asbestos-related diseases. Rather than taking steps to protect workers in the asbestos plants, the companies engaged in a policy of quietly settling death claims from workers who died. Even more shocking is the fact that Johns-Manville did not notify employees when their medical checkups revealed the presence of asbestosis ("white lung"), despite the fact that this is a progressive disease which can be treated successfully in its early stages but is fatal if left untreated.

The Ford Pinto case provides a similar and equally chilling example of a corporate decision to commit an act of violence against consumers. It is estimated that nine hundred people were incinerated due to the engineering of the Pinto gas tank which tended to burst into flames in rear end collisions (Cullen, 1984; Dowie, 1977). The decision to market a potentially deadly product was a calculated one based entirely on profit motivations. Ford had rushed the Pinto into production in the 1960s in an attempt to compete with cheaper, smaller, more efficient, Japanese imports. The company had made a substantial investment in modifying its assembly line to produce this new model when it learned, as a result of its own crash tests, that the gas tank would explode in rear-end collisions. Ford was faced with a dilemma: it could stop production and lose the money it invested in the Pinto, it could make a modification to the gas tank which would cost roughly eleven dollars per car and would correct the problem, or it could say nothing and allow a deadly automobile to be manufactured and sold. They chose the latter. Ford calculated that it would save about eighty-seven million dollars by settling death and injury claims rather than by making the modification in the gas tank. It was not until 1978 that the Department of Transportation finally got around to recalling the Ford Pinto.

Of course, Ford is not the only auto manufacturer who can be held accountable for producing unsafe automobiles. General Motors (GM) had a similar experience in the 1980s (Hills, 1987). GM began production of a new line of cars in 1980, known as X-cars. Its own tests indicated clearly that these X-cars had a tendency for the rear-wheel brakes to lock prematurely, causing the car to spin out of control. Even after fifteen people died in X-cars and at least seventy-one were injured, GM continued to fight government attempts to recall the X-cars for needed repairs.

GM did not limit its production of defective vehicles to cars. They also produced school buses with dangerous defects and delayed as long as possible in making the necessary repairs. When Ralph Nader, the well-known consumer advocate, raised the issue of dangerous school buses with GM, the company responded by hiring private detectives to investigate Nader's personal life in an attempt to blackmail him into silence (Heilbroner, 1973).

As if it were not bad enough that United States corporations produce unsafe cars and school buses, they also produce unsafe tires to put on those vehicles. Firestone produced a series of steel-belted radials in the 1970s known as the "500" series. The company received complaints from consumers about sudden blowouts occurring in these tires. Even after forty-one deaths related to the defective product, Firestone was still fighting to keep the tire on the market and was engaged in a "concerted campaign to keep the truth from the public" (Coleman, 1989:42).

While the highways are acknowledged to be a dangerous place, particularly if you have a Ford Pinto with Firestone steel-belted radials on it, the air is not much better. General Dynamics was warned by one of its engineers in the early 1970s that the cargo doors in its DC-10 aircraft were defective. The warning was ignored and 346 people were killed in a plane crash in France when the cargo door on their plane opened during flight (Nader et al., 1976). In another case, B.F. Goodrich falsified test records and laboratory reports in an attempt to sell defective air brakes to the United States Air Force, a product which would have endangered the lives of thousands of fighter pilots (Heilbroner, 1973).

Other industries provide similar examples of deliberate criminal conduct by corporations. Utah Power and Light Company was cited for 34 safety violations in one of its company-owned coal mines. An underground fire in that mine killed 27 miners, and the subsequent investigation determined that 9 of those violations were directly linked to the start of that fire and its spread throughout the mine shaft (Eitzen and Zinn, 1992). The Beech-Nut Nutrition Corporation mislabeled its baby food, claiming that a substance which was primarily colored sugar water was apple juice for babies. The company entered guilty pleas to 215 criminal counts charging that it had intentionally defrauded and misled the public (Eitzen and Zinn, 1992). Hormel, one of the nation's largest meat-packing companies bribed a Department of Agriculture inspector to ignore violations in their production and packaging of meat (McCaghy, 1976). In fact, Hormel not only produced unsafe food products for original consumption, but the company recycled spoiled meat and sent it back to the market.

> When the original customers returned the meat to Hormel, they used the following terms to describe it: "moldy liverloaf, sour party hams, leaking bologna, discolored bacon, off-condition hams, and slick and slimy spareribs." Hormel renewed these products with cosmetic measures (reconditioning, trimming, and washing). Spareribs returned for sliminess, discoloration, and stickiness were rejuvenated through curing and smoking, renamed Windsor Loins and sold in ghetto stores for more than fresh pork chops (Wellford, 1972:69).

Other examples abound in virtually every industry. Consider the following examples from the pharmaceutical industry (Coleman, 1994, 1989; Braithwaite, 1984):

- William S. Merrell Company submitted false test results and records to the Food and Drug Administration (FDA) in order to avoid losing the money they had invested in developing what turned out to be a dangerous and defective drug.
- Eli Lilly and Company failed to report illnesses and at least fifty deaths associated with their arthritis medication Oraflex.
- The Richardson-Merrell Company, during testing for a cholesterol inhibitor called MER/29, noted serious vision problems caused by the drug and the deaths of laboratory animals. The company not only lied to the FDA about these findings but told the researchers to falsify their data to make the drug look safe and effective.

Not all white collar and corporate crime endangers our health and our lives. Some of it merely endangers our finances. There can be little doubt that when corporations engage in price fixing and restraint of trade, they are engaged in deliberate and premeditated criminality. Estimates on the overall cost to the public from restraint of trade are difficult to calculate, but there is a general consensus that the price we pay for this corporate misconduct is around $20 billion a year (Bequai, 1978). When we consider individual cases, it becomes clear that each violation places an enormous economic burden on society. For example, the Federal Trade Commission has estimated that the public pays $128 million a year in higher prices because of an agreement among four cereal companies to minimize competition, a conspiracy that has been in effect for over thirty years (Mayer and Bishop, 1976). The impact is even more pronounced in the automobile industry where consumers pay $1.6 billion in higher prices because of collusion to limit competition among the major automobile manufacturers (Green et al., 1972). Chrysler Corporation was charged by the federal government with selling thousands of vehicles as new cars even though they had been driven by company employees. They simply disconnected the odometer so consumers would be unaware of the real mileage on the vehicles (Eitzen and Zinn, 1992). Even local conspiracies to fix prices and limit competition are enormously costly. In Seattle and Tacoma, a local price-fixing conspiracy among bakers added four cents to the price of every loaf of bread, resulting in consumer losses of $35 million over the ten-year period the conspiracy was active. Price-fixing conspiracies have even impacted the most basic aspects of life. For example, in 1975 the Justice Department filed an antitrust suit against three of the largest plumbing fixture producers in the United States (Borg Warner, American Standard, and Kohler) for conspiring to fix prices in the amount of $1 billion on bathroom fixtures (Hagan, 1986). Everest and Jennings engaged in an illegal price-rigging conspiracy which raised the price of wheelchairs four times over the market value (McCaghy and Cernkovich, 1987). Southland Corporation and Borden, Inc. rigged bids on contracts on milk to school children in Florida (Hagan, 1994). Of course, the most celebrated example of a price-fixing conspiracy involved twenty-nine corporations in the heavy electrical equipment industry, who conspired to fix prices on government contracts, costing consumers $1.75 billion per year over a seven-year period (Green et al., 1972; Hills, 1971).

Sometimes the devastating effects of white collar crime are harder to quantify and even more difficult to see. Consider the current crisis with regard to environmental pollution. Almost everyone is aware of the Three Mile Island incident in Pennsylvania which involved a nuclear accident that released radioactivity into the atmosphere and required the evacuation of children and pregnant women from the area around the plant. The company involved, Metropolitan Edison, pleaded guilty to using inaccurate testing methods and pleaded no contest to charges of destroying records and five other criminal counts (Hagan, 1986). Other environmental disasters have included the dumping of toxic chemicals at Love Canal, New York [where Hooker Chemical dumped twenty-one thousand tons of chemicals resulting in birth defects and cancer] and Times Beach, Missouri [where all the residents of the town had to move out because of dioxin levels one hundred times above those considered safe for humans] (Beirne and Messerschmidt, 1991). In fact, the Environmental Protection Agency (EPA) estimates that there are thirty-four thousand dump sites with "significant problems" where toxic wastes have been buried in the United States (Brown, 1982). Other cases of environmental crime by corporations abound:

- Olin Corporation illegally dumped thirty-eight tons of mercury, a chemical which causes damage to the human reproductive system and nervous disorders, into the municipal sewage system of Niagara Falls, New York, between 1970 and 1977 (McCaghy and Cernkovich, 1987).

- Kentucky Liquid Recycling, Inc. forced the shutdown of the entire Louisville sewage system in 1977 by dumping toxic chemicals into that system (McCaghy and Cernkovich, 1987).

- Allied Chemical Company dumped Kepone in Virginia's James River and in 1976 pleaded *nolo contendere* to 153 criminal charges (Hagan, 1986).

- The Adolph Coors Co., a major beer producer, claims its products come from pure Rocky Mountain Spring water. But Coors had to pay over $600,000 to settle criminal charges that carcinogenic pollutants were illegally dumped by the company into Clear Creek in Colorado (Eitzen and Zinn, 1992).

Occasionally, corporations actually commit crimes against the state. Once again, in the case of crimes such as defense contract fraud and trading with the enemy, there can be little doubt of the criminal intent of the actors involved. Corporate fraud committed in relation to defense contracts is almost legendary and the cases are too numerous to recount in detail, but a few examples are instructive. Swift and Company, one of America's largest meat packers, sold hams contaminated with rat manure to the Walter Reed Army Medical Center. General Electric pleaded guilty in 1985 to overcharging the Air Force $800,000 on a $47 million contract. General Dynamics corporation charged the Air Force $9,609 for a twelve-cent wrench. In other cases, the Pentagon was charged $659 for an ashtray, $425 for a hammer, $7,622 for a coffee maker, $400 for a socket wrench, and $640.09 for toilet seats (McCaghy and Cernkovich, 1987).

While these overcharges in defense contracts are outrageous and clearly deliberate examples of attempts to defraud the government by major corporations, they pale in comparison to charges of collaboration by United States corporations with the enemy during World War II. Charles Higham (1982), in his study of corporate misconduct during World War II charges that executives of Ford

Motor Company authorized the production of trucks for German troops occupying France; that Chase Manhattan Bank continued to do business with the Nazis throughout the war; and that while gasoline and oil was stringently rationed in the United States to support the war, Standard Oil of New Jersey was shipping fuel to the Nazis through Switzerland.

The Criminogenic Corporation

As shocking as these cases may be, it is important to understand they are not aberrations — they are not merely a collection of apocryphal stories that deviate from the norm. Everything we know about corporate and white collar crime leads us to believe that crime is a way of life for many corporations. While it may be fashionable for government officials and corporate executives to claim that corporations behave responsibly and that these tragic cases are simply isolated incidents, the data conclusively indicate otherwise.

Consider Edwin Sutherland's (1949) findings in his ground-breaking research on white collar crime conducted over fifty years ago. Sutherland searched the records of regulatory agencies and commissions, and federal, state, and local courts looking for adverse decisions handed down against the seventy largest corporations in America over a twenty-year period. His findings were revealing:

> Each of the 70 large corporations has 1 or more decisions against it, with a maximum of 50. The total number of decisions is 980, and the average per corporation is 14.0. Sixty corporations have decisions against them for restraint of trade, 53 for infringement, 44 for unfair labor practices, 43 for miscellaneous offenses, 28 for misrepresentation in advertising, and 26 for rebates (Sutherland, 1949:15).

Sutherland found that major corporations engage in widespread violations and that these corporations are recidivists, committing their crimes both frequently and on a continual basis (97.1 percent of the corporations in his study were recidivists). These numbers are even more compelling when one considers that little effort is put into discovering and prosecuting corporate violations; therefore, adverse decisions represent only a tiny portion of the actual crime committed. Later studies have confirmed Sutherland's conclusions.

In 1980, Marshall Clinard and Peter Yeager published their findings with regard to crimes committed by the 477 largest manu-facturing corporations and the 105 largest wholesale, retail, and service corporations in the United States in 1975 and 1976. In that two-year period, these 582 corporations were the subjects of 1,553 federal cases initiated against them. Because these numbers include only cases brought against the corporations, they once again represent a major underestimate of the total amount of crime committed by these corporations. Clinard and Yeager (1980:111) suggest they had uncovered only "the tip of the iceberg of total violations." They found that in just two years, 60 percent of the corporations had at least 1 action initiated against them, 42 percent of the corporations had 2 or more actions initiated against them, and the most frequent violators were averaging 23.5 violations per corporation (Clinard and Yeager, 1980). In the face of these numbers, it is extremely difficult to argue that corporate criminality is random, isolated, and lacking intent.

An investigation of white collar crime by *U.S. News & World Report* (1982) found that during the decade of the 1970s almost 2,700 corporations were convicted of federal criminal charges. The cost to the public from price fixing, pollution, corruption of public officials, and tax evasion was $200 billion a year.

What these findings also suggest is that there is a double standard of justice operating in the United States. Consider the outrage that would be expressed by the public, politicians, and law enforcement officials if they identified a community of people in which 60 percent of the residents were convicted of a crime, 40 percent were repeat offenders, and a substantial number were committing almost a dozen crimes a year. There would be calls for preventive detention (lock them up before they commit more crimes), automatic add-on sentences for being career criminals (keep them in jail so they can't commit crime), as well as for stepped-up law enforcement efforts (increased patrols, sting operations, career criminal profiling). But does this happen when the criminal justice system confronts white collar crime? Are there calls for a massive crackdown on corporate violence? Do the police break down the front doors of Ford and General Motors in midnight raids? The answer is no. We make little effort to enforce the law against these criminals. When we do manage to catch them at their nefarious deeds, we tap them on the wrist, make them say they are sorry and send them about their criminal business. As Bertram Gross pointed out, the "big, dirty secret" about crime in America is that judges, prosecutors, police, and "law and order" politicians are soft on corporate crime.

Law Enforcement and White Collar Crime

What has the Federal government's "attack" on corporate crime consisted of? The response to the thousands of deaths and injuries and the billions of dollars in damage caused by white collar crime has been, effectively, to give official sanction to continued criminality. Instead of stepped-up law enforcement, more money for investigations and harsher penalties, the government has responded with precisely the opposite. (Isaacson and Gorey, 1981).

- The Consumer Product Safety Commission's budget has been slashed by 30 percent, imperiling consumers more than ever;
- The number of inspectors in the Occupational Safety and Health Administration (OSHA) has been cut by 11 percent. OSHA has less than three thousand inspectors to "regulate" four million workplaces;
- The Federal Trade Commission's antitrust division had its funding, manpower, and enforcement powers cut, making restraint of trade easier than ever;
- The federal government repealed requirements that companies tell workers about dangerous chemicals they are exposed to on the job;
- The requirement that pharmaceutical manufacturers list the possible risks of their medicines to consumers was canceled by the Reagan administration as unnecessary interference with business;
- The requirement that auto manufacturers produce cars that were safe at 5 miles per hour was changed to a requirement that they demonstrate safety at 2.5 miles per hour, making us much safer in an automobile as long as it is not moving.

As Frank Hagan (1986:110) notes, "The enforcement divisions of many regulatory agencies are critically understaffed and can be cut back, as in the Reagan administration's plans for the EPA and other agencies, to inoperable levels." The official response to corporate crime enforcement has roughly been the equivalent of a city experiencing a wave of homicides and pulling the police off the streets to prevent interference with the exercise of free will.

While there are fewer regulators and enforcers available to combat corporate crime, it is even more disturbing to learn who those regulators are and how the laws which govern corporate crime are written. One of the most frequently repeated canards associated with white collar crime is that business is overregulated, and that laws designed to control pollution, the quality of consumer products and worker health and safety are unwarranted interferences in the free enterprise system. Corporate officials and government officials are unrelenting in their claims that laws designed to prevent corporate crime adversely impact profits and, by implication, jobs. They charge that environmentalists, consumer advocates and other "do-gooders" conspire to regulate the free enterprise system out of existence. But the facts suggest otherwise. So powerful is the myth that the Clinton administration had to argue that both the environment and jobs could be reconciled.

The simple fact is that business has no objection to regulation and government interference when it benefits corporate objectives. The history of government regulation of business in the United States is one of business regulating itself for its own benefit. The earliest controls on corporate crime were the antitrust acts of the late 1800s. These early controls were in fact initiated and supported by the very businesses they ostensibly regulated (Pearce, 1976; Weinstein, 1968). Government regulations were used by the robber barons to stabilize the market and to make the economy more predictable. At the same time, they were useful for driving smaller competitors out of business by denying them the use of the same unsavory and illegal tactics that the large corporations had used with such skill in creating their dominant economic positions. The 1906 Meat Inspection Act is a classic case in point. Ostensibly, the act was passed to protect consumers from spoiled, contaminated meat products. In fact, this "government interference" had full support from the large meat-packing companies because it kept imported meat off the United States market at government expense, and the new regulations hindered smaller meat-packing companies by making it hard for them to survive and to compete with the major corporations (Kolko, 1963). The situation in contemporary America is no different. Industry welcomes governmental meddling with price competition, such as the Interstate Commerce Commission's fixed rates on rail and water freight charges and distance (or "long-haul") charges on highway transportation which keep transportation costs artificially high (McCaghy and Cernkovich, 1987). It is simply impossible to reconcile business complaints of overregulation with demands for more controls on foreign imports, requests for government bailouts, and demands for government assistance to "beleaguered" United States companies.

Corporations in the United States have made the most of the protections provided them by regulatory statutes. They have used government regulations, which they help write and help enforce, to create what Mark Green, Beverly Monroe, and Bruce Wasserstein (1972) have called "shared monopolies"—markets controlled by four or fewer firms. Shared monopolies can now be found in the tire industry, aluminum industry, soap industry, tobacco industry, cereals, bread and flour, milk and dairy products, processed meats, canned goods, sugar, soups, and light bulbs. In 1979, the 450 largest American corporations controlled 79 percent of all manufacturing assets and 72 percent of all profits (Simon and Eitzen, 1982).

The few regulators and enforcers which the government employs to enforce laws against corporate misconduct are hardly in an adversarial relationship with the industries they regulate. Those in charge of many of the regulatory agencies and commissions are people who have come to government service from the same corporations they are supposed to be regulating. Contacts between the regulators and the regulated have been cordial and frequently collaborative. Regulators who have come to the government from private enterprise are often more concerned with the needs of the corporations they are regulating than with the safety or economic health of the public. The reciprocity works both ways. Many agency employees leave government service to work for the companies they regulated—compelling evidence of a very cozy relationship (Hagan, 1986). This conflict of interest has been apparent in several cases, but the most blatant example can be found in the Environmental Protection Agency during the Reagan administration. Rita Lavelle was appointed by the president to oversee the government's "superfund" program, designed to clean up the most threatening cases of corporate pollution resulting from improper disposal of toxic waste. She had previously been employed at Aerojet-General Corporation in California. During her tenure at the EPA, she participated in decisions relating to her former employer (a clear conflict of interest), entered into "sweetheart deals" with major polluters, and used the superfund allocations for political purposes. In 1983, Lavelle was convicted on four felony counts (Hagan, 1986).

Government actions even facilitate corporate and white collar crime on occasion. The classic example is the savings and loan scandal. The Reagan administration deregulated the savings and loan industry in order to stimulate growth in the banking idustry. In addition, they increased insurance protection for depositor's accounts at these institutions from $40,000 to $100,000. The administration argued that deregulation would make S & L's more competitive. What it did was make them more criminal. Following deregulation, S & L executives began using institutional funds for their private expenses, thereby robbing their own banks (Calavita and Pontell, 1993). In addition, the new federal regulations allowed the S & L to engage in such practices as accepting deposits contingent upon loans being made to the depositors. The depositors then defaulted on the loans. Not only did those depositors essentially obtain interest-free money to invest in high risk speculations, but go-betweens were paid very generous "finder's fees" for arranging the loans. The S & L's profited because the deposits artificially inflated the assets of the bank, which resulted in higher dividends being paid to stockholders and extravagent bonuses being paid to S & L executives (Calavita and Pontell, 1990). In the end neither the business people who got the phony loans nor the S & L owners and executives (with a handful of exceptions) were held accountable for the billions in missing cash. The bill was presented to the taxpayers.

Underenforcement and Nonpunitive Justice

"Law and order" advocates in politics are quick to argue that crime can be controlled by "sure, swift, and severe punishment." But in the case of white collar crime the opposite is true.

As we have seen, the lack of staff and resources—along with the pervasive conflicts of interest in those agencies—makes the risk of apprehension for white collar criminals very low. The Federal Trade Commission (FTC) offers an excellent example (Hills, 1971). On an annual basis, the FTC receives about nine thousand complaints. Of those nine thousand complaints, one is referred for criminal prosecution. Of those referred for criminal prosecution, some have been delayed as long as twenty years in going to trial by the corporations involved. The FTC only rarely uses its power to conduct hearings and has been extremely reluctant to use any of the enforcement mechanisms granted to it by law. This laxity in enforcement is not unique to the FTC but has been documented for other agencies as well (Benekos, 1983; Snider, 1982; Hagan et al., 1980; Clinard and Yeager, 1979).

In order to make a successful case against a corporation, defendant cooperation is almost always necessary (Hagan et al., 1980). Unmotivated, understaffed, underfunded agencies are not able to litigate even those few cases of corporate crime that actually come to their attention. The result is one of the most bizarre remedial measures found in law, the consent decree. Under the terms of a consent decree, a defendant corporation negotiates with the government over the violations the corporation has committed. It agrees to alter its pattern of conduct. In return, the government agrees that the company will not have to admit guilt. The company does not have to admit its culpability with regard to a crime, but it does have to promise to stop committing the crime, thereby ending the prosecution. The irony of this "sanction" is made clear by Peter Wickman and Phillip Whitten (1980:367):

> Corporations that have been involved in polluting the environment sign consent decrees with the EPA and announce that they are working on the problem. Imagine the public reaction if a common street criminal were to be dealt with in this fashion. Here's the scene: Joe Thug is apprehended by an alert patrolman after mugging an eighty-five-year-old woman in broad daylight on the streets of Paterson, New Jersey. Brought down to police headquarters, he holds a press conference with the assistant police chief. While not admitting his guilt, he promises not to commit any future muggings and announces that he is working on the problem of crime in the streets.

No matter how serious the crime or how flagrant the violation, the fact is that criminal sanctions are rarely applied in the case of corporate criminals. In their study, Clinard and Yeager (1980) found that the actual sanctions applied to corporate criminals were weak at best. The most common sanction was a warning which was issued in 44 percent of the cases. Following warnings, corporate criminals were assessed fines 23 percent of the time, although those fines were negligible. In 80 percent of the cases, they were for five thousand dollars or less — hardly a significant sanction to corporations earning billions of dollars a year. The Senate Governmental Affairs Subcommittee (1983) noted an even more disturbing fact. Over a thirty month period, thirty-two thousand fines levied against white collar crime offenders had gone uncollected by the government. Not only are the fines minuscule in size, but offenders seem to feel free to ignore them altogether. In only 1.5 percent of the cases was a corporate officer convicted of a crime, and in only 4 percent of those convictions did the offender go to jail. Even so, their terms of incarceration were very light — averaging thirty-seven days (Clinard and Yeager, 1980). This pattern appears to be consistent throughout United States history. Albert McCormick, Jr. (1977) studied antitrust cases brought by the Department of Justice from 1890–1969 and found that only 2 percent of the corporate violators served any prison time at all.

A Dual System of Justice

This survey of white collar and corporate crime is cursory and incomplete at best. There are many other equally troubling patterns of criminality in evidence in corporate America which we will briefly mention.

- *Corporate Bribery.* There has been a pervasive pattern of bribes by corporations to foreign governments in return for preferential treatment and contracts. A similar pattern of bribes through illegal campaign contributions in the United States surfaced during the Watergate investigation. Such activities compromise national security abroad and threaten the foundation of democratic government at home.

- *Crime in the Professions.* Researchers who have studied lawyers, doctors, pharmacists, and others have isolated a long list of offenses committed by these professionals ranging from medicaid and medicare fraud, to overcharging for services, fee-splitting, unnecessary surgery, and many others.

  Investigations of the medical profession have found evidence of widespread fraud costing individual patients, insurance companies and the government billions of dollars. Common fraudulent medical practices include "ping-ponging" (providing patients with referrals to other doctors in the same practice), "gang visits" (billing several family members for services to one patient, or billing one patient for multiple services not really provided), and "steering" (directing patients to specific pharmacies with a pecuniary relationship to the attending physician). Doctors also bill Medicaid and Medicare for excessive amounts, for services not rendered to patients, and for non-existent patients. Researchers estimated that $25 billion a year spent by the government on health care for the elderly and poor is stolen through these fraudulent practices (Jesilow et al., 1985; Pontell et al., 1982).

- *Bank and Financial Institution Fraud.* There is a rich and growing literature on crimes committed by banks, savings and loan institutions, and stock brokerage houses. We have not discussed such common offenses as insider trading, money laundering, or financial fraud. The scandal in the savings and loan industry will keep researchers busy for years to come merely recording the enormous numbers of crimes committed.

• *Tax Fraud.* We have also not been able to explore the massive area of illegal tax fraud and legal but inequitable tax laws that protect corporate wealth, pilfer the public treasury, and add to the tax burdens of private citizens. Fraudulent financial schemes designed both to avoid taxes and to inflate the value of company stock are achieved by fabricating sales reports and profit reports. Such major corporations as MiniScribe, Ashton-Tate, DSC and Datapoint have engaged in these practices (Eitzen and Zinn, 1992).

The available evidence on white collar and corporate crime leads to several clear conclusions. Criminality in the corporate sector is widespread and pervasive; few corporate criminals are ever caught or prosecuted. Corporate criminals are recidivists. They commit crimes over and over again with great frequency. They are truly career criminals. When apprehended, they are treated with kid gloves. They are warned, given small fines, or allowed to bargain out of prosecution altogether. In those very rare cases where they are convicted of a crime and sentenced to prison, they are treated with far more consideration and leniency than traditional offenders.

This evidence leads us inexorably to one more myth about the American criminal justice system. Contrary to popular notions and official pronouncements, in opposition to slogans chiseled in marble on courthouses across the country, we do not have an equal system of justice in the United States. There are two very different justice systems. One is for the poor and defenseless, and the other is for the rich and powerful. As Ralph Nader (1985:F3) has commented:

> The double standard — one for crime in the streets and one for crime in the suites — is well known. A man in Kentucky was sentenced to 10 years in jail in 1983 for stealing a pizza. . . . Dozens of corporations have been caught illegally dumping toxic wastes. Yet, only small fines followed.
>
> The double standard prevails in the Justice Department, which has no corporate-crime equivalent to the Federal Bureau of Investigation's Uniform Crime Reporting System. The Bureau has its updated list of the 10 most wanted criminals, but has no high-visibility listings for the most wanton corporate recidivists.

All other forms of criminal behavior in society do not begin to equal the costs, both in terms of dollars and lives, of white collar crime. Yet our government officials, from the president on down, continue to protect wanton acts of criminality as long as they are committed by "respectable society." Over forty years ago, C. Wright Mills (1952) labeled this condition as "the higher immorality," arguing that there was a peculiar and pathological moral degeneracy among the most powerful in American society. Mills argued that corrupt, unethical, and illegal practices by the wealthy and powerful were institutionalized in American society. Sadly, all the available evidence indicates that Mills was entirely correct, as Clinard and Yeager (1980:21) indicate in a summary of their research findings:

> Corporate crime provides an indication of the degree of hypocrisy in society. It is hypocritical to regard theft and fraud among the lower classes with distaste and to punish such acts while countenancing upper-class deception and calling it "shrewd business practice." A review of corporate violations and how they are prosecuted and punished shows who controls what in law enforcement in American society and the extent to which this control is effective. Even in the broad area of legal proceedings, corporate crime is generally surrounded by an aura of politeness and respectability rarely if ever present in cases of ordinary crime. Corporations are seldom referred to as lawbreakers and rarely as criminals in enforcement proceedings. Even if violations of the criminal law, as well as other laws are involved, enforcement attorneys and corporation counsels often refer to the corporation as "having a problem": one does not speak of the robber or the burglar as having a problem.

The evidence speaks clearly. Our political institutions and our criminal justice system, in helping to perpetuate these myths about white collar crime, have indeed institutionalized this "higher immorality."

Sources

Beirne, P. and Messerschmidt, J. (1991). *Criminology*. New York: Harcourt Brace Jovanovich.

Benekos, P. (1983). Sentencing the White-Collar Offender: Evaluating the Use of Sanctions. Paper presented at the Academy of Criminal Justice Sciences annual meetings, San Antonio, TX, March.

Benson, M. (1996). Denying the Guilty Mind: Accounting for Involvement in White-Collar Crime. In *Social Deviance*, E. Goode (ed). Boston: Allyn and Bacon.

Bequai, A. (1978). *White-Collar Crime: A 20th-Century Crisis*. Lexington, MA: Lexington Books.

Braithwaite, J. (1984). *Corporate Crime in the Pharmaceutical Industry*. Boston: Routledge & Kegan Paul.

Brown, M. (1982). Love Canal and the Poisoning of America. In *Crisis in American Institutions*, 5th ed., J. Skolnick and E. Currie (eds.), pp. 297–316. Boston: Little Brown.

Bureau of Justice Statistics (1994). *Federal Law Enforcement Officers, 1993*. Washington, DC: U.S. Government Printing Office.

Calavita, K. and Pontell, H. (1993). Savings and Loan Fraud as Organized Crime: Toward a Conceptual Typology of Corporate Illegality. *Criminology* 31(4): 519–48.

_____ (1991). Other People's Money Revisited: Collective embezzlement in the Savings and Loan and Insurance Industries. *Social Problems* 38:94–112.

_____ (1990). Heads I Win, Tails You Lose: Deregulation, Crime and Crisis in the Savings and Loan Industry. *Crime and Delinquency* 36:309–41.

Carlson, K. (1979). Statement before the Congressional Committee on Education and Labor, Subcommittee on Compensation, Health and Safety, Hearings on Asbestos-Related Occupational Diseases, 95th Congress, Second Session. Washington, DC: U.S. Government Printing Office, pp. 25–52.

Clinard, M. and Yeager, P. (1980). *Corporate Crime*. New York: Macmillan.

_____ (1979). *Illegal Corporate Behavior*. Washington, DC: Law Enforcement Assistance Administration.

Coleman, J. (1994). *The Criminal Elite*, 3rd ed. New York: St. Martin's Press.

_____ (1989). *The Criminal Elite*. New York: St. Martin's Press.

Cox, E., Fellmuth, R. and Schultz, J. (1969). *Nader's Raiders: Report on the Federal Trade Commission*. New York: Grove Press.

Cullen, F. (1984). The Ford Pinto Case and Beyond. In *Corporations as Criminals*, E. Hochstedler (ed.). Beverly Hills: Sage.

Dowie, M. (1977). Pinto Madness. *Mother Jones*, (September): 18–32.

Eitzen, D. and Zinn, M. (1992). *Social Problems*. Boston: Allyn and Bacon.

Green, M., Monroe, B. and Wasserstein, B. (1972). *The Closed Enterprise System: Ralph Nader's Study Group Report on Anti-Trust Enforcement*. New York: Grossman.

Gross, B. (1980). *Friendly Fascism: The New Face of Power in America.* New York: M. Evans and Co.

Hagan, F. (1994). *Introduction to Criminology.* Chicago: Nelson-Hall.

_____ (1986). *Introduction to Criminology: Theories, Methods and Criminal Behavior.* Chicago: Nelson-Hall.

Hagan, J., Nagel, I. and Albonetti, C. (1980). The Differential Sentencing of White-Collar Offenders in Ten Federal District Courts. *American Sociological Review* 45(September): 802–20.

Heilbroner, R. (1973). *In the Name of Profit: Profiles in Corporate Irresponsibility.* New York: Warner Paperback Library.

Higham, C. (1982). *Trading with the Enemy: An Expose of the Nazi-American Money Plot, 1933–1949.* New York: Delacourte Press.

Hills, S. ed. (1987). *Corporate Violence.* Totowa, NJ: Rowman and Littlefield.

_____ (1971). *Crime, Power, and Morality.* Scranton, PA: Chandler.

Isaacson, W. and Gorey, H. (1981). Let the Buyer Beware: Consumer Advocates Retrench for Hard Times. *Time*, (September 21): 22–23.

Jesilow, P., Pontell, H. and Geis, G. (1985). Medical Criminals: Physicians and White Collar Offenses. *Justice Quarterly* 2:149–58.

Kolko, G. (1963). *The Triumph of Conservatism.* New York: Free Press.

Kramer, R. (1984). Corporate Criminality: The Development of an Idea. In *Corporations as Criminals*, E. Hochstedler (ed.). Beverly Hills: Sage.

Mayer, A. and Bishop, J. (1976). Antitrust: Snap, Crackle and Pop. *Newsweek*, (June 14): 14.

McCaghy, C. (1976). *Deviant Behavior.* New York: Macmillan.

McCaghy, C. and Cernkovich, S. (1987). *Crime in American Society.* New York: Macmillan.

McCormick, A., Jr. (1977). Rule Enforcement and Moral Indignation: Some Observations on the Effects of Criminal Antitrust Convictions upon Societal Reaction Process. *Social Problems*, 25:30–39.

Messerschmidt, J. (1986). *Capitalism, Patriarchy, and Crime: Toward a Socialist Feminist Criminology.* Totowa, NJ: Rowman and Littlefield.

Mills, C. (1952). A Diagnosis of Moral Uneasiness. In *Power, Politics and People*, I. Horowitz (ed.), pp. 330–39. New York: Ballantine.

Nader, R. (1985). America's Crime Without Criminals. *New York Times*, (May 19): F3.

Nader, R., Green, M. and Seligman, J. (1976). *Taming the Giant Corporation.* New York: Norton.

Pearce, F. (1976). *Crimes of the Powerful.* London: Pluto Press.

Pontell, H., Jesilow, P. and Geis, G. (1982). Policing Physicians: Practitioner Fraud and Abuse in a Government Medical Program. *Social Problems* 30:117–35.

Schraeger, L. and Short, J., Jr. (1978). Toward a Sociology of Organizational Crime. *Social Problems* 25: 407–19.

Senate Permanent Subcommittee on Investigations, Committee on Governmental Affairs (1983). 98th Congress, First Session, August 3.

Simon, D. and Eitzen, S. (1982). *Elite Deviance.* Boston: Allyn and Bacon.

Snider, L. (1982). Traditional and Corporate Theft: A Comparison of Sanctions. In *White-Collar and Economic Crime*, P. Wickman and T. Dailey (eds.), pp. 235–58. Lexington, MA: Lexington.

Sutherland, E. (1949). *White Collar Crime*. New York: Holt, Rinehart and Winston.

—— (1940). White Collar Criminality. *American Sociological Review* 5:1–12.

U.S. News & World Report (1982). Corporate Crime: The Untold Story. (September 6): 25.

Webster, W. (1984). *Crime in the United States*. Washington, DC: U.S. Government Printing Office.

Weinstein, J. (1968). *The Corporate Ideal in the Liberal State: 1900–1918*. Boston: Beacon Press.

Wellford, H. (1972). *Sowing the Wind: A Report from Ralph Nader's Center for Study of Responsive Law*. New York: Grossman.

Wickman, P. and Whitten, P. (1980). *Criminology: Perspectives on Crime and Criminality*. Lexington, MA: D.C. Heath.

Drug War Cowboys
Myths of the Drug Crisis in America

8

There is probably no social problem that has so captured the imagination of the American public as the problem of drug abuse. Public opinion polls indicate that Americans think drugs are the number-one problem in the nation. In fact, over half of the public favors the use of the military in incursions into drug-producing countries (Benoit, 1989). This strong public reaction should surprise no one. We are bombarded daily by public service messages on television dramatically portraying the horrors of drug abuse. Television talk shows pander to the most sensational aspects of the drug problem, as Oprah, Geraldo, and Phil interview "crack" mothers, violent members of street gangs, and cocaine-dependent Yuppies whose conspicuous consumption has been imperiled by their expenditures on drugs. The rhetoric from politicians and government officials often borders on hysteria as they call for more prisons, more police, the abolition of constitutional protections, and

165

even the death penalty for drug dealers. The problem of drugs has been elevated to a national crusade by leaders like President Ronald Reagan who said, "In this crusade, let us not forget who we are. Drug abuse is a repudiation of everything America is. The destructiveness and human wreckage mock our heritage" (Lyman and Potter, 1996:23). President Bush leaves no doubt as to his administration's feeling on drugs: "Speak the truth: that drugs are evil, that they ruin and end young lives . . . the drug dealers are murderers and should be treated as such" (Lyman and Potter, 1996:62). In the streets of Washington, D.C., New York City, Panama, and Colombia our leaders have called us to war: a war on drugs.

There is no argument that drug abuse poses a significant problem in America. The cost alone is staggering.

> It costs taxpayers $30 billion a year just to pay the criminal court costs for illicit drug trafficking. . . . hospital treatment for victims of drug-dealer wars costs an estimated $1 billion each year. American business must shoulder additional costs totaling an estimated $60 billion in lost productivity, absenteeism, workplace accidents and crime because of illegal drug use in the workplace. . . . All in all, drug and alcohol abuse costs the nation about $150 billion a year, . . . more than double what it cost to fight the war in Vietnam at its height (Benoit, 1989:33).

The specter of babies being born drug dependent to drug-addicted mothers is horrifying. The idea that inner-city youth are introduced to drugs at an early age and are subsequently unable to perform successfully in school or to obtain and hold jobs is a national disaster. The massive violence associated with drug trafficking turf wars (which is often random and claims innocent victims) is repugnant. The idea that citizens, particularly in our major cities, have lost control of their neighborhoods to drug-dealing gangs is unacceptable.

But the question facing the criminal justice system and society as a whole is how do we best deal with these drug-related horrors? For years a debate has raged in the medical, sociological, and law enforcement communities over whether drug use and abuse was a problem for the criminal justice system or for the public health care system. Despite the rhetoric and sensationalism of today's anti-drug campaigns, that question remains unresolved. As David Musto (1973:244) tells us, this is not a new problem:

> American concern with narcotics is more than a medical or legal problem—it is in the fullest sense a political problem. The energy that has given impetus to drug control and prohibition

came from profound tensions among socioeconomic groups, ethnic minorities, and generations — as well as the psychological attraction of certain drugs. The form of control has been shaped by the gradual evolution of federal police powers. The bad results of drug use and the number of drug users have often been exaggerated for partisan advantage. Public demand for action against drug abuse has led to regulative decisions that lack a true regard for the reality of drug use. Regulations with foreign nations, often the sources of drugs, have been a theme in the domestic scene from the beginning of the American antinarcotic movement. Narcotics addiction has proven to be one of the most intractable medical inquiries ever faced by American clinicians and scientists.

It has, indeed, proved to be an intractable problem. It is a problem fueled by politics (Reinarman, 1996) and the bureaucratic needs of law enforcement. The natural reaction for politicians to the drug problem is to pander to popular fear and frame the issue in the starkest, most unyielding terms. The "safe" political response to the issue of drugs is to call for more law and more order. The law enforcement bureaucracy responds to this by accepting the challenge. After all, there are very few issues on which public opinion and the rhetoric of decision-makers so closely coincide with opportunities for bureaucratic expansion. A "war on drugs" offers the opportunity for more money, more personnel and, most importantly, greater police power. It is a very attractive offer most police executives and others in the criminal justice system find impossible to refuse.

However, despite the public consensus, despite the speeches of presidents, and despite the dire warnings of the press and the law enforcement establishment, serious questions have been raised about the drug war. These questions are so serious that some public figures have broken ranks and have openly criticized the law enforcement approach to drug control (Lyman and Potter, 1996). Political leaders like former Secretary of State George Schultz and the mayor of Baltimore, Kurt Schmoke, have called for a discussion of precisely the opposite approach to drug control, drug legalization. They have been joined by conservative political theoreticians, like economist Milton Friedman and columnist William F. Buckley, as well as by liberals like Dr. Benjamin Spock. Most surprisingly, the legalization issue has been raised by some law enforcement officials, such as organized crime expert Ralph Salerno, former New York City police commissioner and Police Foundation head Patrick Murphy, San Jose police chief Joseph MacNamara, federal judge Rufus King and former Minneapolis police chief Anthony Bouza.

The critics have posed a compelling question: Is the war on drugs having any positive impact on the problems associated with drug abuse? If not, what are the alternatives?

This chapter will explore some of the issues related to this debate. First, we will look at the question of drugs and related harm. What exactly do drugs do? What do we know about the potential of illicit drugs to kill and injure users? We will try to put the discussion of harm in context and separate the harms resulting from the abuse of drugs from the harms resulting from the illegality of drugs. Second, we will look at the connection between drugs and crime. One of the most effective tactics of today's drug warriors has been to create a mythical link between drugs and crimes against innocent citizens. This portrayal of drug users as "drug fiends" plays a key role in the popular conception of the drug problem. But is this view justified? Once again, we will try to put the issue of drugs and crime in context and to separate those dysfunctions caused by drugs from those dysfunctions caused by the illegality of drugs. Third, we will look at the drug war itself, the strategies employed, and their impact on the drug problem. Finally, we will consider the viability and importance of noncriminal justice approaches to the problem of drugs. Let us begin by taking a look at the major drugs of abuse.

Drugs and Harm

Central to the case for drug prohibition (and the rationale for the drug war) is the idea that drugs are dangerous to users. The images presented in the media are stark and frightening. Fried eggs are used to simulate "your brain on drugs," addicts are shown cowering in corners in the throes of withdrawal, earnest actors portray cocaine users who have lost their houses, jobs, and spouses to this chemical seductress. No one will dispute that drugs, all drugs, are dangerous. People die of heroin overdoses and occasionally of cardiac and respiratory failure related to cocaine. People also die from lung cancer as a result of smoking tobacco and of a variety of diseases related to the consumption of alcohol, even though these drugs are quite legal. People can die and suffer injury from any drug, even aspirin and penicillin.

The question is not whether illegal drugs are dangerous, but whether they are dangerous enough to justify legal prohibition and the social outrage associated with their use. As with all other issues in the drug debate, the issue of harm has to be put in context and perspective. In order to do this, let us examine the three drugs which have elicited the strongest reaction from law makers and law enforcers: heroin, cocaine, and marijuana.

In the 1960s, during Richard Nixon's drug war, most public attention was focused on heroin. Heroin is a narcotic, a direct derivative of the opium poppy. Heroin users snort, smoke and inject the drug, although for the best "high" most users inject heroin into a vein ("mainlining"). Mainlining produces an immediate euphoric reaction (a "rush") followed by a period of sedation. The principal problem with heroin is that it is highly addictive. Repeated use of the drug creates a physical need for more of the drug. The drug also has a high tolerance level, which means that the more often it is used, the greater the quantity and frequency of use required to reach a "high." The net effect of this cycle of need and tolerance is addiction. Being a narcotic, heroin also suppresses both respiratory and cardiovascular activity, meaning that an overdose can produce respiratory arrest and shock—sometimes leading to death (Inciardi, 1986). However, if properly used, under supervised conditions, heroin is a relatively benign drug. As Inciardi points out, heroin is responsible for "little direct or permanent physiological damage." The real dangers in the use of heroin are attributable to the potential for overdose and the fact that users on the street do not engage in standard practices of good hygiene, resulting in infection from hepatitis and, more recently, AIDS (Inciardi, 1986).

The Reagan and Bush administrations, while still raising the specter of heroin, shifted public concern to the use of cocaine. Cocaine is the most powerful natural stimulant available. It comes from the leaves of the South American coca plant. Like heroin, it produces a "rush" when used, but unlike heroin it is a stimulant which awakens and enlivens users. Most cocaine users snort cocaine hydrochloride (the white, crystalline powder) into their nasal passages. Snorting cocaine allows for rapid absorption of the drug into the bloodstream creating an intense but rather brief "high."

During the 1970s, it appeared that cocaine would become the new drug of choice for the wealthy. It was an expensive drug, selling for about $100 a gram on the street. Because of its expense, it had a limited market of upper middle-class and upper-class users. Cocaine developed the reputation of being a glamour drug associated with sports figures and Hollywood. However, during 1985–1986 cocaine appeared in a new form, "crack," that made it accessible to everyone, even the poor. Crack is simply cocaine hydrochloride powder mixed with baking soda, ammonia, and water, dried and subsequently smoked. Crack sells for ten to fifteen dollars a "hit," making it far more affordable than cocaine hydrochloride. It was the advent of crack that heralded much of the concern about cocaine. In fact, research on the use of cocaine had indicated that it was a relatively safe drug. Surveys of medical examiners and coroners representing 30 percent of the population of the United States and Canada had revealed only twenty-six cases of drug-induced deaths between 1971 and 1976 where cocaine had been the sole drug found in the body (McCaghy and Cernkovich, 1987). With the advent of crack and the subsequent increase in the smoking of cocaine, the numbers of cocaine-related deaths quadrupled. It is important to note that 92 percent of cocaine-related deaths result from smoking the drug, and only about 10 percent of all cocaine users smoke cocaine rather than snort cocaine (Goode, 1984). It would therefore appear that moderate use of cocaine is relatively safe, although heavy cocaine users, particularly those who smoke crack, exhibit a wide variety of symptoms such as nervousness, fatigue, irritability, and paranoia (Ray, 1983).

Before moving on to a discussion of marijuana, let us put the issue of drug-related deaths into context. If one were to listen to speeches of politicians and the warnings in anti-drug ads on television, it would appear that we are in the midst of a massive epidemic of illicit drug-related deaths. While any death is tragic and certainly should raise concern, there are two points to be made about drug-related deaths. First, they are relatively infrequent, despite popular impressions. Second, when they do occur, they are more directly attributable to drug laws than to the drugs themselves.

About 3,600 people die each year from the consumption of all illegal drugs put together (Nadelmann, 1989). This pales in comparison to the number of deaths on an annual basis from just two legal drugs, alcohol and tobacco. There are 200,000 alcohol-related deaths each year (Nadelmann, 1989). Add to that figure the estimated 320,000 people each year who die from illnesses related to the consumption of tobacco and you arrive at a figure 150 times larger than all the deaths related to illicit drug consumption. Yet the federal government has not declared a war on alcohol and tobacco, nor has it attempted to create the hysterical reaction to these legal drugs which has accompanied its campaign against heroin and cocaine.

While the numbers seem to belie the urgency of the "drug war," or at the very least suggest a degree of hypocrisy in that war, it is even more troubling to realize that most of the 3,600 or so drug-related deaths that occur each year occur not as a result of the drug used but as a result of drug laws. Take the case of heroin. As was pointed out earlier, heroin is a relatively benign drug. As Jeffrey

Reiman (1995:32) tells us, "there is no evidence conclusively establishing a link between heroin and disease or tissue degeneration such as that which has been established for tobacco and alcohol." Why then do people die from using heroin? The answer is that the drug laws make inevitable the unregulated production, sale, and use of dangerous drugs. Consumers of heroin and other illicit drugs produced in clandestine laboratories under unregulated conditions are in constant danger of taking drugs which are mixed with other dangerous substances, mixed with other dangerous drugs, and have potencies far in excess of that which the user expects, leading directly to fatal overdoses and poisonings (Nadelmann, 1989). These are deaths directly attributable to the drug laws which force users to buy their supplies in an unregulated, unsafe market. Most drug overdoses result from the ingestion of adulterated drugs, not from user misuse or abuse. In addition, users engage in unsanitary practices which cause both death and injury—again as a result of the clandestine nature of drug use necessitated by drug prohibition. Heroin addicts share needles, spreading disease and illness. One-quarter of all the AIDS cases in the United States can be directly attributed to the unsafe and unsanitary conditions in which illicit drugs are used (Nadelmann, 1989). Finally, the drug laws encourage misuse of illicit drugs. Consider the case of cocaine. Studies show that about 20 million Americans are cocaine users. Of that number, only about 3 percent are ever going to become problem cocaine abusers (National Institute on Drug Abuse, 1987). The real danger from cocaine is a direct result of the drug laws which encourage users to seek a more intense and cheaper high by smoking the drug rather than snorting it. The drug laws drive the price of cocaine up, and users innovate to compensate for the expense. They freebase and use crack for greater efficiency, and they are far more likely to suffer injury or death smoking the drug than snorting it.

So, it seems that the dangers of heroin and cocaine use, while real enough, are exaggerated by the government and exacerbated by the drug laws themselves. What about marijuana, the most commonly used illegal drug in the United States and the drug for which people are most frequently thrown into prison? Marijuana comes from the flowers and leaves of the *cannabis sativa* plant. The dried leaves and flowers are smoked, like tobacco, in cigarettes ("joints") or pipes. All the available evidence we have on marijuana indicates that it is not addictive, nor does a tolerance to the drug develop. In addition, there has never been a death resulting from marijuana consumption (Goode, 1984; Brecher, 1972). In fact, even the Drug Enforcement Administration (DEA) has trouble making marijuana look like a dangerous drug. In September 1988, Francis L. Young, the chief administrative law judge of the DEA reviewed all the medical and scientific evidence on marijuana and came to some startling conclusions.

- There has never been a single documented *cannabis*-related death.

- About 70 million Americans have used marijuana and there has never been a reported overdose, a striking contrast not just with alcohol but with aspirin.

- Marijuana, in its natural form, is one of the safest therapeutically active substances known to man.

- In strict medical terms, marijuana is far safer than many foods we commonly consume (Trebach, 1989).

The real danger to marijuana smokers comes from marijuana which has been tainted by government drug control programs, such as the spraying of paraquat and other herbicides on marijuana crops. While some problems are associated with marijuana use, such as injury to the mucous membranes and interrupted attention spans (Murray, 1986), the harm, especially when compared to tobacco, alcohol, and aspirin, seems out of proportion to the attention it gets from law enforcement agencies.

The data tell us that the danger from the consumption of illicit drugs, while real, does not justify the panic reaction which the media and government have created. The dangers of illicit drugs appear to pale in comparison to the dangers from drugs which are tolerated, and even endorsed, in everyday life. While certainly not related to the issue of the harmfulness of drugs, it is appropriate that in discussing their effects we take note of the potentially positive contributions that illicit drugs could make if it were not for the legal prohibitions controlling them. The fact is that the drug laws, while making drugs more dangerous, also make it virtually impossible for us to make constructive use of these proscribed substances (Nadelmann, 1989; Trebach 1989). Marijuana, for example, has shown itself to be useful in treating disorders such as multiple sclerosis and glaucoma, and in relieving the side effects of chemotherapy for cancer patients. In fact, the Drug Enforcement Administration itself has argued for the medical legalization of marijuana. Heroin is a particularly useful and very safe pain reliever, as is cocaine, both of which are widely used outside of the United States for medical treatment. It appears that in yet another way, the drug laws make our drug problems even worse.

Drugs and Crime

One of the most compelling questions which has been raised in the debate on drug policy is whether drug use and drug addiction leads to an increase in crime in the United States. Those who favor drug prohibition point to several important research findings as indicators of a relationship between drugs and crime. For example, James Inciardi's study of narcotics users and non-narcotics users in Miami during the period between 1978 and 1981 showed that narcotic users "committed more crimes, engaged in a greater diversity of offenses, and in significantly larger proportions committed the more serious crimes of robbery and burglary" (Inciardi, 1986:129). Other findings have seemingly pointed to similar relationships between drugs and crime. For example, it appears that the degree of drug use is directly related to the degree of criminality. Drug addicts tend to commit substantially fewer crimes prior to the beginning of addiction and after the cessation of addiction than they do during addiction (Gropper, 1985). Among heroin users this effect is pronounced. Daily heroin users seem to commit twice the number of property crimes as regular users (those who use the drug three to five days a week) and five times as many property crimes as irregular (those who use the drug two days a week or less) heroin users. As the level of drug usage decreases, the involvement in crime decreases as well. In addition, research indicates that a history of drug abuse is one of the best predictors of involvement in serious criminal offenses (Gropper, 1985).

These are seemingly damning data. However, in order to be understood and to be relevant to a discussion of drug control policy, they must be put into context. While there is an apparent relationship between the use of drugs and the amount of crime committed by users, it is a myth that drugs *cause* crime. Take the case of heroin. A majority of heroin users have been involved in criminal activity *prior* to their use of heroin (McGlothlin et al., 1978). In fact, heroin addicts engage in criminal activity "proportionally in excess of their numbers in the population before becoming involved with narcotics" (Goode, 1984:256). While it is easy for policymakers to make the emotional claim that drugs cause crime, a more accurate appraisal of the data is that "drugs do not cause criminality, but that addiction to narcotics like heroin clearly escalates criminal involvement" (Beirne and Messerschmidt, 1991:144).

There is a further irony in the drugs-crime connection—the only drug for which a clear causal link with crime has been established is alcohol, a drug which is legal. We know that 54 percent of all inmates convicted of violent crimes used alcohol immediately prior to the commission of the crime (Bureau of Justice Statistics, 1987). In addition, we know that individuals convicted of murder, arson, involuntary manslaughter and rape are far more likely to have committed their crimes under the influence of alcohol than any other drug (Bureau of Justice Statistics, 1988).

So, while there is no evidence that drugs themselves cause crime, the same cannot be said for the drug laws. Drug laws adversely affect the market for drugs and the conditions under which drugs are purchased and consumed. As a result, the drug laws create a great deal of serious crime with very real victims.

Illicit drug users, particularly those who have developed an addiction to a drug such as heroin, commit crimes such as robbery, burglary, prostitution, and drug dealing as a means of raising funds to support their drug habits. This criminal behavior results from laws prohibiting the sale and use of drugs, not from the drugs themselves. Because the illegality of drugs artificially and dramatically inflates their price, the cost of drug use quickly exceeds the income of the drug user and soon exhausts personal resources. A heroin user with a relatively moderate habit will spend about $7500 a year on heroin (McCaghy and Cernkovich, 1987). Individuals who come from poverty-wracked urban areas are simply not going to be able to pay for the necessities of life (food, clothing, shelter) and heroin. Compare the cost of illegal heroin with the cost of alcohol and tobacco, two legal drugs which are heavily taxed and regulated, and it becomes clear that legal drugs are far cheaper. It is the prohibitionary laws which inflate the price of illicit drugs forty to fifty times above market value. Drugs do not cause drug users to commit crime. It is the illegality of drugs — with the subsequent outrageous prices which can be demanded in the illicit market — that causes crime.

But the inflated price for drugs caused by prohibition is not the only criminogenic effect of the drug laws. Because drugs are illegal, purchasers are forced into a criminal underworld to buy drugs, thereby making them potential victims of crime and bringing them into contact with criminal actors with whom they would ordinarily never have contact (Kaplan, 1983). Crimes ancillary to drug use take place because of this relationship, a relationship entirely attributable to the illegality of drugs.

Finally, illegal markets, markets created by the criminal law, breed violence for many reasons. The profits realized from the sales of illegal drugs are so high that competition becomes intense and turf wars result. Illicit drug entrepreneurs have no recourse to legal institutions to resolve disputes over turf, quality of merchandise, and "brand" names. Because drugs are illegal, the law itself makes violence the only dispute resolution mechanism available to drug dealers. The victims of that violence are the poor and law-abiding citizens of urban America who have seen their streets turned into battle zones. The increases in urban murder rates in the past few years can be explained almost entirely by the rise in drug dealer killings of one another and the deaths of innocent bystanders in these turf battles (*Newsweek*, 1989).

Law Enforcement Strategies in the War on Drugs

In his book, *Deviant Behavior*, criminologist Charles McCaghy (1985:298) provides the most concise and direct evaluation of the war on drugs in the criminological literature:

> In baseball a player with three strikes is out. But after three dismal failures in trying to stop the use of alcohol, opiates, and marihuana, the United States government still stands at the plate determined to smash the hell out of the drug problem. Unlike ballplayers, who adjust to the peculiarities of various pitchers and who put past experience to use, United States legislators subscribe to a single-minded philosophy — if you don't hit it, you're not swinging hard enough.

Ever since Ronald Reagan proclaimed yet another war on drugs in 1980, the federal government has been swinging harder and striking out with greater regularity than ever before. The Reagan-Bush war on drugs cost the federal government an average of ten billion dollars a year (National Drug Enforcement Policy Board, 1987). The United States imprisons four times as many people as does West Germany and the United Kingdom, seven times as many as Sweden, and eight times as many as the Netherlands. Between 1980 and 1987, drug arrests in the United States increased 61 percent (Trebach, 1989). Of all the felony arrests made in the United States, 23 percent are for individuals arrested on drug charges (National Institute on Drug Abuse, 1987). Of these 750,000 felony arrests, more than 75 percent are not for drug trafficking, not for selling drugs to innocent school children, but for possession of drugs—most commonly marijuana, the most innocuous of all the legal and illegal drugs. Even so, all of these felony convictions account for only a little more than 1 percent of the Americans who use drugs.

Despite all of this law enforcement activity, all of these arrests and incarcerations, little has changed. During the ten years of the Reagan-Bush drug war, the price of a kilo of cocaine dropped 80 percent and there was ten times as much cocaine on the streets as there was when the drug war started (Benoit, 1989). During the same period, the purity of cocaine on the streets has quintupled, and the profits from the sale of cocaine have climbed to an estimated $50 billion a year (Benoit, 1989). Precisely the same effects have been noted with regard to heroin. As of the end of 1991, seventy-five million Americans, or 37 percent of the population over the age of twelve had used illegal drugs. Six percent of the American population are current users (Walker, 1994). About twenty-two million Americans have used cocaine, and three million Americans have used cocaine in the last 30 days (Eitzen and Zinn, 1992). There are about eighteen to thirty-five million regular heroin users (Trebach and Engelsman, 1989). It is probable that these are gross underestimates of drug use because the instruments utilized to reach these conclusions miss a sizeable segment of society altogether. High school dropouts, the homeless, and inner-city youth simply slip through the researchers' nets, and there is some reason to believe that drug use may be higher among these groups than in the general population.

Why has there been so little progress made after such a huge expenditure of money and after so many arrests and incarcerations? As McCaghy (1985) suggested, it is because present drug enforcement policies do not work and cannot be made to work, even with dramatic increases in resources and personnel. The government's strategy in the war on drugs hinges on three basic policies: eradication, interdiction and street-level drug enforcement.

Let us first consider interdiction as a strategy. Interdiction assumes that with sufficient resources drugs can be stopped from entering the United States by controlling the borders. As the numbers reported above indicate, interdiction has failed with regard to both heroin and cocaine. The only minor success that the interdiction campaign can claim is with marijuana, a bulky commodity which is difficult to transport. Yet the net effect of that success has become an even bigger problem. Marijuana smugglers and growers in other countries have simply moved to cocaine and heroin as substitutes for marijuana, meaning even more of those drugs are being imported to the United States, and marijuana production in the United States has increased dramatically in the last ten years. A Rand Corporation evaluation study of interdiction determined that "even massively stepped-up drug interdiction efforts are not likely to greatly affect the availability of cocaine and heroin in the United States" (Reuter et al., 1988). Consider this simple fact: the criminal justice system cannot keep drugs out of maximum security prisons, much less seal the nation's borders to drug trafficking.

Efforts directed at crop eradication in producing countries have failed miserably. The reasons for this should be obvious. First of all, drugs like heroin, cocaine, and marijuana can be grown and processed in a wide variety of locations, making crop eradication programs impossible to implement. Even if a particular locale is targeted and eradication programs are successfully carried out there, growers in other locations will merely make up for the deficit in supply. If heroin supplies in the Golden Crescent (Afghanistan, Iran, Pakistan) are targeted, opium growers in the Golden Triangle (Thailand, Burma, Laos) or in Mexico will simply grow more and supply the demand. These three regions have had no problem in supplying the demand for heroin for the last century, although the relative importance of each fluctuates with enforcement efforts. The case of cocaine is even more instructive. In theory, cocaine should be the easiest of the illicit crops to subject to an eradication strategy. It grows only in South America and principally in Peru and Bolivia (with Colombia, Ecuador, and Brazil making small contributions to the supply). At the moment, the world's entire cocaine supply is grown on 700 square miles of arable land. Even so it would still be prohibitively costly to eradicate the crop. But the fact is that cocaine, even though it can only be grown in certain areas of South America, can be grown on 2,500,000 square miles of arable land (Nadelmann, 1989). Eradication as a control strategy is doomed to failure by Mother Nature herself.

In addition, crop eradication programs in producer countries are very difficult to arrange and carry out. In those countries there is well-organized political opposition to these programs. Obviously, crop eradication cannot be carried out without the support and active participation of the country involved. The production of cocaine and opium brings in billions of dollars in hard currency to impoverished countries and puts money in the pockets of millions of cultivators, processors, and smugglers. These governments, therefore, are extremely reluctant to give their approval to eradication efforts. Even when they do, they are often unable to provide the logistical support necessary for success. Peru is an example of another problem. The prime cocaine-growing areas are not under government control but rather under the influence of the Sendero Luminoso guerrilla group. The government of Peru, even if it wished to support an eradication program, is in no position to do so. The same could be said of opium-growing areas in the Golden Triangle, most of which are ruled by renegade warlords beyond the reach and control of the government (Lyman and Potter, 1996).

A word needs to be said about domestic crop eradication programs as well. Efforts to eradicate the marijuana crop in the United States have not only failed but have made the marijuana industry stronger and more dangerous than ever before (Potter et al., 1990). In Kentucky, where the state participates in a federally-funded program to find and burn the marijuana crop, the net effect of the eradication program has been to spread marijuana cultivation throughout the state, to increase the quantity of marijuana being produced, and to increase the quality of the marijuana being produced. In addition, the eradication program has taken what was essentially a "Mom and Pop" industry a few years ago and turned it into a highly organized criminal cartel which is not only dangerous but also enjoys a high degree of community support in the marijuana-belt counties.

Street-level drug enforcement efforts in the United States have also shown little hope of success in the drug war. Intensive street-level law enforcement efforts are very expensive. Although they result in the arrests of thousands of low-level drug dealers and users, they have little impact on the other elements involved in illicit drug supply. While some of these enforcement efforts claim "temporary and transitory success," they have not impacted at all on the availability of illegal drugs (Chaiken, 1988). In fact, many illegal drug prices have fallen, purity has increased, the supply has increased, and use levels have increased in jurisdictions where intensive street-level enforcement has been tried. In addition, crimes ancillary to drug trafficking have increased in almost every case where saturation enforcement strategies have been utilized.

The classic case study of draconian law enforcement efforts being employed against drug use and drug trafficking is New York's experience with the infamous "Rockefeller Drug Law." In 1973, New York law was amended as part of an all-out drug war in that state. Individuals caught selling drugs were subjected to mandatory prison terms of fifteen to twenty-five years. In 1977, the New York Bar Association appointed a commission to evaluate New York's "drug war." They found that the state had spent $32 million in implementing the laws, but the net effect of the three years of intensive enforcement was negligible. There was no reduction in drug-related crime or in heroin usage, and there were ample supplies of drugs still on the streets. The commission declared the law an expensive failure (Association of the Bar of the City of New

York, 1978). Despite these findings, New York has tripled its prison capacity since 1982 and spends more per capita on corrections than any state in the country. Sixty percent of the prison population is serving time for nonviolent crimes; 44 percent of new felons each year are for drug offenses. In 1995, George Pataki, despite a conservative reputation decided the state had to choose between fighting violent crime and fighting the drug war. He hopes drug rehabilitation, community service and electronic monitoring offer alternatives to expensive prison sentences. New York's problem mirrors a national problem. In 1982, prisoners serving time for drug convictions were 22 percent of the federal inmate population; mandatory sentences have increased that percentage to 70 percent. One-third of the prisoners are non-violent, low-level offenders with no criminal record. Drug inmates typically serve longer federal sentences than those convicted of sex offenses or manslaughter. In fact, the history of the drug laws is clear. Drug use actually increases during periods in which criminal penalties are harshest and enforcement most vigorous.

In addition, the drug war has been blatantly racist. Forty-eight percent of all arrests for drug offenses are African Americans (Walker, 1994). This, despite the fact that African Americans make up only 14 percent of all drug users and National Institute on Drug Abuse data show the prevalence of drug use is almost identical among whites and African Americans (Walker, 1994). In fact, Randolph Stone, states: "All reports indicate that the percentage of illegal drug use is the same among racial groups. But the drug problem among blacks and Hispanics is dealt with in the criminal justice system. Among whites, it's dealt with largely as a health problem" (Marx, 1995:2). Arthur Lurigio confirms, "African-Americans have borne the brunt of the drug war because drug arrests are easier in socially disadvantaged, inner-city neighborhoods than in middle-class suburban areas. In the inner city, drug dealing is more public and the dealers are more willing to sell to strangers."

As mentioned earlier, crack cocaine is made by combining simple ingredients with cocaine power. A gram of powder cocaine retails for $65 to $100. Rocks of crack cost $5 to $20. Who would receive a stiffer sentence if caught? In the chapter on organized crime, the government attempts to target "kingpins." Here, the supplier can expect about forty-one months; the dealer at least ten years with no parole. Crack is predominately found in the inner city, cocaine in middle- and upper-class suburbs. Three out of five powder offenders are white; 90 percent of crack offenders are African American or Hispanic (Editorial, 1995). As Nkechi Taifa of the

ACLU states, the law "punishes poor people and people of color more heavily" (Smolowe, 1995:45). The U.S. Sentencing Commission affirmed the uneven treatment: 88.3 percent of federal crack distribution convictions were for black defendants; only 27.4 percent of cocaine convictions. The average crack prison sentences are 3 to 8 times longer. The Commission stated, "Issues of fairness or just punishment result when relatively low-level crack retailers receive higher sentences than the wholesale-level cocaine dealer from whom the crack seller originally purchased the powder to make the crack" (Smolowe, 1995:45). The commission's recommendations become law automatically in November 1995, unless Congress acts. Since the disparity in sentencing resulted from the drug panic of 1986 when crack sales spread rapidly through urban areas, that may happen. Janet Reno is among those who oppose the new guidelines: "I strongly oppose measures that fail to reflect the harsh and terrible impact of crack on communities across America" (Smolowe, 1995:45). Perhaps, the Attorney General should look at the harsh and terrible impact of currently mandated sentencing.

As if it were not enough that these drug war strategies have failed, they have also created a number of serious problems that would not exist if it were not for the intensive enforcement efforts against drugs.

First, intensive drug enforcement efforts lead to corruption of law enforcement and other criminal justice personnel. The immense amounts of money generated by the drug trade makes it possible to offer substantial inducements to enforcement personnel to overlook activities by specific traffickers and groups. Political and police corruption in America is certainly nothing new. Official corruption related to liquor and gambling laws has been well documented in virtually every American city during the early years of the century when alcohol prohibition was in effect. The same type of prohibition-style corruption is rampant today in drug enforcement. For example, in 1988, over seventy-five Miami police officers were under investigation for involvement in criminal activities including drug dealing, robbery, theft and murder. One investigation in particular revealed several officers who had ambushed drug dealers bringing cocaine into Miami. This investigation revealed that officers loaded the cocaine into marked police vehicles. Duffel bags full of cocaine were reportedly "stacked to the ceilings of the patrol car." Three of the suspects, in an effort to escape, jumped into the river and drowned (Lyman and Potter, 1996). The Miami case is not atypical. According to a report in the *New York Times*, more than one hundred drug corruption cases involving law enforcement officers are prosecuted in federal and state courts each year (Shenon, 1988). Piers Beirne and James Messerschmidt (1991:247) report other examples of police corruption:

> In several rural Georgia areas certain sheriffs accepted bribes of $50,000 each to allow drug smugglers to land planes on stretches of abandoned highway.
>
> A member of the Justice Department's Organized Crime Strike Force provided drug dealers with the identities of government informants for $210,000.
>
> An FBI agent accumulated over $850,000 in money, real estate, and other property for not only allowing drug dealers to sell cocaine, but selling it himself.
>
> A customs agent was paid $50,000 for each marijuana-packed automobile he allowed to cross from Mexico into the United States without inspection.

While we usually think of corruption in relation to police officers on the street and local prosecutors, the drug war has managed to offer incentives for corruption that reach to the very highest levels of the United States government. It is indeed ironic that the very agencies of government who are beating the drums loudest in the war on drugs have also established an infamous record of accepting assistance from and providing logistical support to some of the largest drug-trafficking syndicates in the world. Consider the following examples (Mills, 1986; Lernoux, 1984; Chambliss and Block, 1981; McCoy, 1972).

- For more than three decades the United States government has directly supported the opium-growing warlords of the Golden Triangle in Southeast Asia. Not only does the government provide them with military assistance and arms under the guise of fighting communism, but it has also protected corrupt governments, such as that of Thailand, which nurture the heroin industry.

- During the Vietnam war and for some time thereafter, CIA-funded Laotian tribesmen were used to refine opium poppies into heroin. A CIA front company, Air America, was used to transport the heroin out of Southeast Asia.

- The CIA has helped to establish money-laundering facilities for the Southeast Asian heroin connection. The Nugan Hand Bank, established in Australia in 1973, laundered funds for both the CIA and the Southeast Asian heroin traffickers.

- CIA associates in the Caribbean, including the paymaster for the ill-fated Bay of Pigs invasion, played key roles in the operations of Castle Bank, a Florida money laundry for organized crime's drug money.

- Another Florida bank with strong intelligence-community connections, the Bank of Perrine, has been used by the Colombian cartels to launder money from their burgeoning cocaine business.

- The CIA and organized crime played a key role in establishing and operating the World Finance Corporation, a Florida-based company involved in laundering drug money and supporting terrorist activities in the early 1970s.

- Mexican heroin magnate Alberto Sicilia-Falcon not only claimed to have been a CIA agent operating on orders from Washington but also had access to classified CIA documents and had a chief enforcer with CIA ties.

- The world's largest opium merchant, Chang Chi-fu, operated as a CIA "client." Another heroin czar, Li Wen-huan, was given direct financial and logistical assistance by the CIA. A third major heroin trafficker, Lu Hus-shui, was protected from a Drug Enforcement Administration investigation on orders from the CIA.

- The CIA effectively blocked a major DEA investigation of drug trafficking and money laundering by Manuel Noriega in Panama. The State Department blocked an investigation targeting the government of the Bahamas after evidence revealed that the government and drug traffickers were making a deal to use the islands as a safe haven for both drugs and money.

These cases represent only the tip of the iceberg. In other cases still under investigation, suspicious trails have been found linking United States government agencies to drug trafficking by the Contras in Nicaragua and by the governments of Guatemala and Chile.

Closely related to the spread of drug-related corruption has been the added impetus the drug war has given to organized crime. Drug laws and intensified enforcement strategies related to the drug war have strengthened organized crime and created a whole new generation of prohibition-conceived organized crime groups (Lyman and Potter, 1996). Drug enforcement is by its very nature highly selective and discriminatory. It targets only those easiest to catch and most visible to the police. Those dealers who are arrested are the least important, smallest operators. The net effect of drug enforcement is to weed out the inefficient drug dealers, giving organized crime an exclusive monopoly in drug trafficking. The mob now makes the most of its monopoly, raking in profits of $78 billion a year from drugs and conducting their business with virtual immunity. Compare that figure with organized crime's profits of about $200 million in the bootlegging of tobacco, a legal drug, and it is easy to understand why organized crime is such a strong supporter of drug prohibition (Nadelmann, 1989). The only reason organized crime can realize such enormous profits in the drug market is the fact that drugs are illegal. The actual cost of growing and producing illegal drugs is modest, but the criminal surcharge that organized crime can add to the cost of drugs, because it competes with no legitimate suppliers, is staggering. The drug laws, in effect, act like a government-sponsored subsidy to organized crime, a subsidy worth billions of dollars a year.

Finally, the war on drugs is beginning to spill out of its inner-city boundaries. The zeal to win the war against drugs has caused the courts to abrogate the Fourth Amendment protections against unreasonable search and seizure. Increasingly, the courts have cast a lenient eye on whether forced-entry, no-knock raids are necessary to protect evidence and to avoid violence. In June 1995, the Supreme Court decided that school administrations should not be bound by the niceties of presumption of innocence if drugs are the issue. A seventh-grader in Vernonia, Oregon refused to sign a form agreeing to submit to random urine tests to detect drug use by members of the football team. "The government may not ransack every house in a neighborhood on the off-chance that it will make a few interesting discoveries. To search a 13-year-old's room, or his pockets, police need probable cause to think he's broken the law. But to inspect his urine, the court now says, school officials need nothing beyond a vague fear of drugs. . . . The policy may not have a great effect on drug abuse among adolescents, but it will teach them that they have no rights of privacy that the government is obliged to respect" (Chapman, 1995:27).

Not only have the strategies designed to control drug use and drug trafficking been unsuccessful, but the very act of vigorously enforcing the drug laws has created social problems far more serious than any caused by drug use alone. Let us be clear on this point. Drug control policy has not failed for lack of resources, funding, legal powers, or adequate manpower. It has failed because the problem is not amenable to a criminal justice solution. As the Pennsylvania Crime Commission concluded in its 1987 report on organized crime, "It should be understood that, short of creating a police state, there is no evidence to suggest that vast expansion of investigative efforts would lead to the eradication of illegal drugs."

In the past decade, expenditures on drug enforcement have tripled; the number of Americans in prison has doubled. Paying for the construction and maintenance of prisons now represents the fastest growing item in state budgets. Yet, despite this dramatic increase in punitiveness, most aspects of the drug problem are getting worse.

Making Peace in the War on Drugs

The list of failures of our present drug control initiatives could go on endlessly. We could talk about the inconsistency in the drug laws. The two most dangerous drugs in America—tobacco and alcohol—are freely available, while less dangerous drugs lead to felony convictions. We could talk about the racist nature of drug enforcement. We could talk about the threats to our basic constitutional rights created by questionable police tactics emanating from the difficulties of drug enforcement. We could talk about the disrespect for the law, in general, bred by drug enforcement. However, the facts are straightforward and relatively simple. Law enforcement efforts directed at the drug problem have failed and will continue to fail.

We have allowed the drug problem to be framed by political leaders and law enforcement officials as strictly a criminal justice system problem. As we have seen, the problem of drugs is far more complex than this simple approach. While it is beyond the purview of this present discussion to fully explore the alternatives to a criminal justice approach to drugs, we can take the time to raise a few issues.

First, there appears to be a much greater chance of success in reducing the incidence of drug use through drug education and drug treatment programs than through the use of the criminal law. Everything we know about rehabilitation and education programs demonstrates that they are exponentially more effective than law enforcement strategies in reducing drug use.

- *Drug Rehabilitation.* Despite the fact that available research points to great successes in drug rehabilitation and drug counseling, the problem is that these programs are simply not available where they are needed (particularly the inner city) nor are they available in sufficient number. Currently, there are more than 100,000 persons on waiting lists for drug treatment in the United States, (National Commission on AIDS, 1991). Available evidence, although sparse, would seem to indicate that the diversion of resources from enforcement to control through educational and medical strategies would result in a net decline in drug use (Trebach, 1989).

• *Drug Education*. Using drug education to deglamorize drugs might be the single most important component of any national drug control strategy. Deglamorization programs combine drug education in schools with useful and realistic portrayals of the problems of drugs in media advertising in an attempt to convince would-be drug users to exercise extreme caution in making their choices. All the available evidence suggests that drug education is the most effective means of drug control. However, such a strategy would require a massive diversion of funds from law enforcement into educational programs in order to be successful. Present drug education efforts are woefully underfunded (Lyman and Potter, 1996).

Second, it is time to revive an idea which showed great promise in dealing with the problems of drug addiction/drug maintenance (Trebach, 1989). Drug maintenance is not a new idea. In the period between 1919 and 1923, after the passage of the Harrison Narcotics Act, there were at least forty clinics operating in the United States which distributed morphine and heroin to thousands of opiate addicts. Later experiments with drug maintenance included a New York City experiment with methadone maintenance in the 1960s. Methadone is a heroin substitute which does not cure addiction, but which does allow addicts to function quite normally in society despite their addiction. Despite the criticisms of how methadone maintenance programs were administered and the moral objection that methadone merely panders to addiction, methadone main-tenance is the most successful approach to American drug control in the history of American drug policy. Drug maintenance experiments have also shown great success in the Liverpool-Mersey area of England, where health professionals have worked with both the police and educators to develop a series of interrelated projects designed to free addicts from both their addiction and the social environment of drug users. The Liverpool-Mersey experiment includes the dispensing of drugs to addicts as part of a regular program of drug maintenance; a needle-exchange program; detoxification counseling; and the provision of general health care to drug abusers (Trebach, 1989).

Finally, it is time to open the debate on the alternative to current law enforcement efforts against drugs. It is time to begin to talk about the legalization of drugs. This is a topic which must be approached with great caution, as Arnold Trebach (1989:4–5) has urged:

> While I do not recommend it at this point in history, I have become convinced in recent years that our societies would be safer and healthier if all of the illegal drugs were fully removed from the control of the criminal law tomorrow morning at the start of business. If that happened, I would be very worried about the possibility of future harm, but less worried than I am now about the reality of present harm being inflicted every day by our current laws and policies.

As difficult as it may be to raise the issue of legalization in the present environment of drug war hysteria, there are some possible benefits which should be subjected to further research and debate.

- Repealing drug prohibition will save us at least $10 billion a year in enforcement costs which could be used to supplement the present inadequate funding for more promising approaches such as education and rehabilitation.
- Repealing the drug laws could result in a reduction of crime, particularly in the inner city where the quality of life might well improve; homicide, burglary and robbery rates would fall.
- We would certainly see some diminution in the dangerous trend toward large-scale, systematic political and law enforcement corruption, which threatens our whole system of criminal justice.
- Organized crime groups, particularly those newer groups dependent on the drug trade which have not yet had the time to expand their enterprises into more traditional areas of vice, would be dealt a severe and potentially terminal setback.
- Certainly the quality of life for hundreds of thousands of drug abusers and millions of drug users would improve significantly if legal controls were removed (Nadelmann, 1989).

Admittedly, legalization is a dangerous policy alternative. No one knows how such a system would operate. No one knows if there would be a subsequent increase in drug use. Certainly we do not want to create a situation in which heroin and cocaine are as prevalent and freely used as tobacco and alcohol. There are, however, some encouraging indicators which should at least stimulate the debate.

In the eleven states which decriminalized marijuana during the 1970s, there was no significant increase in the level of marijuana usage over levels noted prior to decriminalization (Nadelmann, 1989). This would seem to mitigate against concerns that the removal of legal prohibitions would lead to an epidemic of drug use, particularly if educational programs were in place and functioning.

In addition, the experience with drug decriminalization in the Netherlands has been very encouraging. In the Netherlands, the decriminalization of marijuana led to actual declines in the consumption of marijuana from 10 percent of the population in 1976 to 2 percent in 1985. Overall marijuana consumption in the Netherlands is considerably less than in the United States where marijuana possession is still illegal. Fully a third fewer people use marijuana in the Netherlands than use marijuana in the United States. Finally, the decriminalization of cocaine has shown an even more disparate pattern of use. In the Netherlands, decriminalized cocaine is used by 1200 percent fewer people than in the United States (Trebach and Engelsman, 1989). While there are clear differences in the two societies, particularly in the provision of quality health care and social services, the experience of the Netherlands in successfully handling its drug problems is worthy of further study and discussion.

While none of these alternatives promises to solve all aspects of the problem and many of them are highly controversial, they do represent new and innovative ideas. The simple fact is that the many myths which have been fostered about drug use and drug users make constructive policy choices difficult. A realistic drug policy requires that we look beyond these myths. While there may be moral objections to drug policy reform, questions about how best to proceed, and disagreements over the dangers of new initiatives, there are no questions about the law enforcement approach to drug control. It is a failure. A failure which makes a very bad situation much worse. It would be much more dangerous to continue on the present course, knowing the disasters which confront us, than to reconsider the parameters of drug control in America.

Sources

Association of the Bar of the City of New York (1978). *The Nation's Toughest Drug Law: Evaluating the New York Experience*. New York: Association of the Bar of the City of New York.

Beirne, P. and Messerschmidt, J. (1991). *Criminology*. New York: Harcourt Brace Jovanovich.

Benoit, E. (1989). The Case for Legalization. *Financial World*. (October 3): 32–35.

Brecher, E. (1972). *Licit and Illicit Drugs*. Boston: Little, Brown.

Bureau of Justice Statistics (1988). *Sourcebook of Criminal Justice Statistics, 1987*. Washington, DC: U.S. Department of Justice.

_____ (1987). *Sourcebook of Criminal Justice Statistics, 1986*. Washington, DC: U.S. Department of Justice.

Chaiken, M. (1988). *Street-Level Drug Enforcement: Examining the Issues*. Washington, DC: U.S. Department of Justice.

Chambliss, W. and Block, A. (1981). *Organizing Crime*. New York: Elsevier.

Chapman, S. (1995). A Freedom Denied. *Chicago Tribune*, (June 29), sec. 1:27.

_____ (1995). Criminal Behavior. *Chicago Tribune*, (February 9), sec. 1:27.

Editorial (1995). The Elusive Logic of Drug Sentences. *Chicago Tribune*, (March 30), sec. 1:20.

Eitzen, D. and Zinn, M. (1992), *Social Problems*. Boston: Allyn and Bacon.

Goode, E. (1984). *Drugs in American Society*. New York: Alfred A. Knopf.

Gropper, B. (1985). Probing the Links Between Drugs and Crime. *National Institute of Justice: Research in Brief*. Washington, DC: U.S. Government Printing Office.

Inciardi, J. (1986). *The War on Drugs: Heroin, Cocaine, Crime, and Public Policy*. Palo Alto, CA: Mayfield.

Kaplan, J. (1983). *The Hardest Drug: Heroin and Public Policy*. Chicago: University of Chicago Press.

Lernoux, P. (1984). *In Banks We Trust*. New York: Doubleday.

Lyman, M. and Potter, G. (1996). *Drugs in Society*, 2nd ed. Cincinnati, OH: Anderson.

Marx, G. (1995). Swift Justice. *Chicago Tribune*, (April 27), sec. 5:1–2

McCaghy, C. (1985). *Deviant Behavior*. New York: Macmillan.

McCaghy, C. and Cernkovich, S. (1987). *Crime in American Society*. New York: Macmillan.

McCoy, A. (1972). *The Politics of Heroin in Southeast Asia*. New York: Harper & Row.

McGlothlin, W., Anglin, M. and Wilson, B. (1978). Narcotic Addiction and Crime. *Criminology* 16 (November): 293–315.

Mills, J. (1986). *The Underground Empire*. New York: Doubleday.

Murray, J. (1986). Marijuana's Effects on Human Cognitive Functions, Psychomotor Functions, and Personality. *Journal of General Psychology* 113(1): 23–55.

Musto, D. (1973). *The American Disease: Origins of Narcotic Control*. New Haven: Yale University Press.

Nadelmann, E. (1989). Drug Prohibition in the United States: Costs, Consequences, and Alternatives. *Science* 245 (September): 939–47.

National Commission on AIDS (1991). *Report: The Twin Epidemics of Substance Use and HIV*. Washington, DC: U.S. Government Printing Office, July.

National Drug Enforcement Policy Board (1987). *National and International Drug Law Enforcement Strategy*. Washington, DC: Department of Justice.

National Institute on Drug Abuse (1987). *Data from the 1985 National Household Survey on Drug Abuse.* Rockville, MD: National Institute on Drug Abuse.

Newsweek (1989). A Tide of Drug Killing. (January 16): 44.

Pennsylvania Crime Commission (1987). *Annual Report.* Conshocken: Commonwealth of Pennsylvania.

Potter, G., Gaines, L. and Holbrook, B. (1990). Blowing Smoke: Marijuana Eradication in Kentucky. *American Journal of Police* 9.

Ray, O. (1983). *Drugs, Society and Human Behavior.* St. Louis: C.V. Mosby.

Reiman, J. (1995). *The Rich Get Richer and the Poor Get Prison.* Boston: Allyn and Bacon.

Reinarman, C. (1996). The Social Construction of Drug Scares. In *Social Deviance,* E. Goode (ed.). Boston: Allyn and Bacon.

Reuter, P., Crawford, G. and Cace, J. (1988). *Sealing the Borders: the Effects of Increased Military Participation in Drug Interdiction.* Santa Barbara, CA: The Rand Corporation.

Shenon, P. (1988). Enemy Within: Drug Money Is Corrupting the Enforcers. *New York Times,* (Apr. 11): A1, A12.

Smolowe, J. (1995). One Drug, Two Sentences. *Time,* (June 19): 45

Trebach, A. (1989). Drug Policies for the Democracies. Statement before the Public Hearing on Drug Control, Interior Committee of the Deutscher Bundestag, The Parliament of the Federal Republic of Germany (March 13).

Trebach, A. and Engelsman, E. (1989). Why Not Decriminalize? *New Perspectives Quarterly* (Summer): 40–45.

Walker, S. (1994). *Sense and Nonsense About Crime and Drugs,* 2nd ed. Belmont, CA: Wadsworth.

The Transmission of HIV
Exploring Some Misconceptions Related to Criminal Justice

9

According to the Centers for Disease Control and Prevention (1994), a cumulative total of 441,528 persons had been diagnosed with Acquired Immunodeficiency Syndrome (AIDS) in the United States by the end of 1994. In addition, the Public Health Service estimates that at least one million Americans are infected with the Human Immunodeficiency Virus (HIV), the agent that causes AIDS (Hammett et al., 1994). Fortunately, HIV is extremely difficult to contract. Researchers have concluded that the virus is transmitted in only three ways: 1) as a result of sexual activity; 2) through contact with infected blood (most often involving the sharing of infected needles by injection drug users) and; 3) perinatally (from an infected mother to a newborn child). Studies of individuals living in households where persons with AIDS reside indicate that the virus is not transmitted through casual nonintimate contact (Friedland et al., 1986).

Despite these facts, many persons working in the criminal justice system continue to harbor mythical beliefs about the transmission of HIV. An incident in 1995 highlighted the rampant misperceptions about the virus. Fifty gay and lesbian officials were invited to the White House. Four of the seven security guards put on protective gloves before conducting routine examinations of briefcases and other personal belongings. While White House officials were horrified when the guards' behavior was reported, decision making has too often been hindered by precisely such faulty assumptions and misinformation. In many cases, the system has responded in an inappropriate manner to cases involving persons infected with HIV/AIDS. In some states, prison inmates have been denied participation in programs and activities that present no risk of viral transmission (Cauchon, 1995). In other jurisdictions, courts have sometimes sentenced seropositive offenders to extremely harsh sentences for engaging in assaultive behaviors that pose relatively little real danger to others (Hammett et al., 1994). This chapter explores the epidemiology and dynamics of HIV transmission in an attempt to correct a number of myths and misconceptions that have affected policy debate. The following beliefs are challenged:

1) Persons who work in the criminal justice system face a significant risk of HIV infection as a result of the assaultive behavior of seropositive offenders (blood tests of individuals infected with the human immunodeficiency virus register "seropositive").

2) Transmission of HIV by female prostitutes to male customers is an important source of viral infection in the United States.

3) Female rape survivors face a significant risk of being infected with the AIDS virus.

4) HIV is transmitted regularly in the nation's prisons.

5) Intravenous drug users (IVDUs) will not alter their "high-risk" behavior.

Occupational Transmission and Criminal Justice

Many persons who work in the criminal justice system believe that their occupational responsibilities place them at risk of HIV infection (Kinkade and Leone, 1994). There are even several police officers who claim that they were infected through their employment (Bigbee, 1993). Nonetheless, the Centers for Disease Control and

Prevention have not documented a single case of occupational transmission among any person working for a criminal justice agency in the United States since the beginning of the epidemic (Hammett et al., 1994). This does not mean that these individuals face absolutely no risk. However, it does suggest rather strongly that the danger is significantly lower than many other hazards that criminal justice personnel willingly face every day.

The findings from two recent studies support this conclusion. In an analysis of 870 incidents involving possible exposure to HIV, Hammett et al. (1994) note that there were no reports of seroconversion ("seroconversion" refers to a positive HIV antibody status for an individual who was not previously infected). These incidents included many of the things that public safety personnel often worry about (e.g., needlesticks, human bites and exposures to contaminated blood).

Ippolito, Puro and De Carli (1993) examined similar incidents among health care workers (HCWs). These researchers aggregated data from 21 studies of HCWs who were exposed to the virus in the course of their employment. Among the 6,170 individuals in this group, only 10 seroconverted for a rate of 0.16 percent. Clearly, even among persons who come in close contact with AIDS patients and perform invasive procedures, the Human Immunodeficiency Virus is not easy to contract.

The risk to persons working in the criminal justice system is even smaller. After all, police and correctional officers do not perform invasive procedures. Almost all interactions between offenders and criminal justice agency personnel involve the kinds of nonintimate casual contact that present no risk of viral transmission.

However, justice system personnel often express anxiety that certain types of assaultive behavior on the part of offenders falls outside the definition of casual contact and therefore may place them at risk. Specifically, there is anxiety regarding three types of assaults: 1) being spit upon or bitten by a seropositive assailant; 2) being cut by an assailant in the course of a fight; and 3) being stabbed with a needle that is contaminated with the blood of a seropositive offender. The inherent risks of HIV transmission in each of these scenarios are examined below.

Spitting and Biting Incidents

The Human Immunodeficiency Virus has been isolated in the saliva of some infected persons. Nonetheless, there is strong evidence indicating that transmission of the virus through spitting is highly improbable. Laboratory tests have revealed that HIV is present in the saliva of very few infected persons (Ho et al., 1985). When the virus is present, it is in such minute quantity that transmission to another person would be extremely difficult. It has been estimated that one quart of saliva would have to enter the bloodstream of an individual for infection to occur (Hammett, 1988). HIV does not pass through intact skin. Unless a seropositive person spit directly upon an open sore, transmission could not occur even if the virus were present in sufficient quantity (which it is not) in saliva.

Finally, because the risks associated with saliva are so minimal, the Centers for Disease Control (1988) no longer recommend that universal body fluid precautions (i.e., that all such fluid be treated as if it were infectious) be followed when contact with saliva is anticipated unless it contains visible blood.

Biting incidents are another source of anxiety for persons working in the criminal justice system. Because HIV is a blood-borne disease, bites are a special concern in cases where the perpetrator has blood in his/her mouth at the time of the assault. Fortunately, the scientific evidence indicates that the risk of viral transmission under these circumstances is quite minimal. Despite numerous cases of bites by persons infected with HIV/AIDS, there are only two reports in the medical literature where the virus may have been transmitted in this manner (Richman and Richman, 1993).

Richman and Richman (1993) estimate that bites probably result in the transmission of 20 times fewer HIV-infected cells than a needlestick injury. Because the likelihood of becoming infected from the latter is already quite low (0.42 percent), these researchers conclude that "the transmission of HIV through human bites is biologically possible but remains unlikely, epidemiologically insignificant, and as yet, not well documented."

Despite the scientific evidence, some courts continue to treat incidents of this nature as extremely serious. Hammett et al. (1994) report that appellate courts in New Jersey, Georgia, Texas, and Indiana have upheld attempted murder charges against seropositive offenders who bit or spit upon others. In New Jersey, the defendant was given a 25-year prison term. The highest court in the state of Texas affirmed a life sentence for spitting in the face of a corrections officer. This kind of response by the justice system sends the wrong message to both the public and to persons who must interact with seropositive offenders; it incorrectly implies that assaults of this nature present a serious risk of viral transmission. Offenders who assault corrections officers should be punished. However, it should be made clear that this action is being taken in response to the offender's behavior and not because there is a danger of HIV transmission.

Violent Assailants

Law enforcement and corrections officers are often called upon to restrain violent individuals. Sometimes, these offenders are attempting to resist lawful arrest. In other cases, intervention is necessary in order to terminate an altercation between citizens or inmates. As a consequence, some criminal justice personnel remain anxious that these occupational duties could expose them to infection via contaminated blood.

The medical literature notes that transmission has resulted from involvement in a fight (O'Farrell et al., 1992). This apparently occurred when the virus entered the body through an open wound. However, these reports are extremely rare. None of the documented cases involved a person who was employed by a criminal justice agency. Clearly, whatever risk exists is quite minimal. Nonetheless, public safety workers should be certain to follow the various procedures for infection control that have been recommended by the Centers for Disease Control (1989), including keeping all open sores bandaged and wearing gloves when contact with blood or body fluids containing visible blood is anticipated.

Needle Sticks

Another source of concern among persons working in the criminal justice system is that they will suffer accidental or intentional wounds from needles that are contaminated with the blood of seropositive individuals. Needle sticks do present a small risk of HIV infection. Studies of health care workers who have accidentally pricked themselves with needles that were used on seropositive patients indicate that the risk of viral transmission under these circumstances is approximately 0.42 percent (Richman and Richman, 1993). In other words, there will be one seroconversion for every 250 needle sticks that involve exposure to contaminated blood. For this reason, criminal justice agencies must institute operational procedures that minimize the likelihood that this type of injury will occur. Offenders who intentionally assault others with needles should be subject to legal sanctions. In addition, employees who receive such injuries should be counseled regarding the low probability that viral transmission will actually occur and instructed on the proper method by which to apply first aid to the wound.

Female Prostitution

Many female prostitutes in the United States have become infected with HIV. To date, the evidence indicates that this has occurred predominantly as a result of intravenous drug use and not from sexual contact with customers (Luxenburg and Guild, 1993). However, because the AIDS virus is transmitted primarily through sexual activity, concern has been expressed that these individuals could become a conduit for viral transmission into the general population. Often, this anxiety is exacerbated by media stories about infected prostitutes who remain sexually active (*New York Times*, 1987) and by enforcement policies that are based on the assumption that prostitutes are transmitting the virus to clients (Cohen et al., 1988). A number of states have enacted statutes that mandate HIV testing for persons charged with or convicted of prostitution (Luxenburg and Guild, 1993). Other jurisdictions have reclassified prostitution as a felony in situations in which the offender has previously tested seropositive. In Las Vegas, a prostitute was sentenced to twenty years imprisonment under such a statute (Gostin, 1990).

Despite the severe punishments that are occasionally inflicted on infected prostitutes, there is little evidence to indicate that female prostitutes are actually transmitting HIV to their male clients (Luxenburg and Guild, 1993). There are over 56,000 females arrested for prostitution each year in the United States (Maguire and Pastore, 1994). The average female prostitute sees approximately 1,500 male customers per year (Bergman, 1988). It is estimated that there are more than 200,000 female prostitutes who engage in more than 300 million sexual acts each year (AIDS and Civil Liberties Project, 1990). If sexual contact with female prostitutes were an important source of HIV transmission, there should have been thousands of AIDS cases reported among males who had engaged in sexual activity with these individuals (Bergman, 1988).

The following question naturally arises: if HIV is a sexually transmitted disease, why are female prostitutes not infecting their male clients in substantial numbers? Several factors probably help to explain this apparent anomaly. First, the likelihood of viral transmission as a result of a single heterosexual encounter involving vaginal intercourse is quite low (Hearst and Hulley, 1988). Second, many prostitutes have been educated about safer sex and are using condoms to prevent infection (Rosenberg and Weiner, 1988). Third, studies have indicated that oral sex [which presents a low risk of viral transmission (Lyman et al., 1986)] is the most common sexual activity requested of female prostitutes and that anal sex [which presents a high risk (Winkelstein, et al., 1987)] is not commonly performed (Rosenberg and Weiner, 1988). Finally, the AIDS virus is apparently transmitted with less efficiency from females to males than in the opposite direction.

There are other reasons to be confident that female prostitutes are not a significant source of viral transmission in the United States. Early reports which suggested that contact with female prostitutes was a risk factor for AIDS infection among military personnel (Redfield et al., 1985) have turned out to be false. Many servicemen who initially claimed contact with a female prostitute as their only risk factor eventually admitted to having engaged in traditional "high-risk" behaviors (same-sex contact or intravenous drug use) upon being reinterviewed by civilian public health authorities (Potterat et al., 1987). It is not surprising that these military personnel would initially claim contact with a female prostitute as a risk factor and deny having engaged in either homosexual behavior or intravenous drug use. After all, the former is not punishable and the latter are serious breaches of military discipline.

Epidemiological data also lend credence to the belief that female prostitutes are not transmitting HIV to their male clients in substantial numbers. As of December 1994, there have been 376,889 documented adolescent/adult AIDS cases among males in the United States. Ninety-one percent of these have occurred among persons who engaged in homosexual activity and/or intravenous drug use (Centers for Disease Control, 1994). Furthermore, in an earlier study of cases occurring among males who were initially reported to the CDC without any identifiable risk factor, further investigation revealed that only 76 claimed sexual contact with a prostitute as their only risk factor (Centers for Disease Control, 1994).

This finding is bolstered by the fact that among thousands of New York State inmates who were tested for HIV, there was no relationship between being seropositive and a history of sexual contact with prostitutes (Lachance-McCullough et al., n.d.).

Finally, the incidence and distribution of AIDS cases among females also suggest that viral transmission from prostitutes is not a major factor in the spread of this epidemic. If it were, we would expect to come across reports indicating that female partners of men who had patronized prostitutes were becoming infected, since many of these individuals are married or have girlfriends. There would also be cases in which these women were giving birth to seropositive infants. This has not occurred. To date, the overwhelming majority of AIDS cases among females have been diagnosed among individuals who are either intravenous drug users (IVDUs) or the sex partners of IVDUs. Likewise, most pediatric cases are linked to mothers who report these risk factors (Centers for Disease Control and Prevention, 1994). Clearly, there is little evidence that males are contracting HIV from female prostitutes.

Female Rape Survivors

Females who are sexually assaulted may be at risk for a number of sexually transmitted diseases (Glaser et al., 1989). Because HIV is also transmitted through sexual contact, it is plausible to assume that these females face a serious risk of HIV infection as well. However, a close examination of data regarding both the epidemiology and dynamics of HIV transmission in the United States suggests that this is not the case.

In order to assess the risk of HIV transmission for female rape survivors, it is necessary to answer three questions.

1) What types of sexual assaults are committed by rapists?
2) What are the risks of HIV infection associated with various forms of sexual activity?
3) What proportion of rape assailants are infected with HIV?

Holmstrom and Burgess (1980) report that almost all cases of sexual assault directed at females involve forced vaginal intercourse. The risk of viral transmission that is likely to result from a single assault of this nature is quite minimal. Saracco et al. (1993) investigated the seroconversion rate of a group of uninfected women who engaged regularly in unprotected sex with their seropositive male partners. The annual seroconversion rate was 5.7 percent. In other words, approximately 19 out of 20 women in this sample did not become infected despite regular sexual contact with an infected male for an entire year. Because the crime of rape generally involves a single exposure, the risk for survivors is much lower. Hearst and Hulley (1988) calculate that the likelihood of a female seroconverting as a result of a single act of unprotected intercourse with an infected male to be approximately 1 in 500. The risk will be greater for some survivors due to the violent nature of rape. Padian et al. (1990) have noted that bleeding during intercourse is associated with an increased risk of HIV transmission. Since many assailants experience sexual dysfunction during the commission of this crime (Groth and Burgess, 1977), the risk of seroconversion is lessened in such instances.

Females who are sexually assaulted are sometimes the victims of either oral and/or anal sodomy as well. Although oral sex has been linked to the transmission of HIV (Rozenbaum et al., 1988), the risks associated with this practice are believed to be minimal (Lyman et al., 1986). Anal sex is quite risky (Padian et al., 1990). In fact, Kingsley et al. (1990) report that more than 90 percent of new infections among gay males are attributable to anal intercourse. Fortunately, only a small proportion of assaults directed at females (5 percent) involve this type of "high-risk" behavior (Holmstrom and Burgess (1980).

As previously noted, the number of rape survivors who can be expected to seroconvert is also a function of the proportion of offenders who are seropositive. There is reason to believe that this percentage is quite small. First, over 90 percent of the adult/adolescent AIDS cases among males in the United States have been linked to homosexual behavior and intravenous drug use (Centers for Disease Control and Prevention, 1994). Gay males are unlikely to direct sexual assaults at females. Intravenous drug users are also unlikely to engage in this type of behavior. Generally, alcohol is far more likely to be a precipitating factor in the crime of rape than drug addiction.

Second, the preliminary evidence from a number of studies that have tested sex offenders suggests that the rate of HIV infection among this group is quite low. Vlahov et al. (1990) report that among male entrants to the Maryland prison system, seropositive inmates were significantly less likely to have committed a sex offense. In another study, individuals enrolled in a community-based treatment program for certain sex offenders were examined (Giovanni et al., 1991). None of the 77 participants were infected with HIV.

Finally, a Seattle study that tested rape survivors for evidence of sexually transmitted diseases (Jenny et al., 1990) resulted in similar findings. Although the researchers concluded that these individuals had a substantial risk of acquiring other STDs, none became infected with HIV as a result of the assault. However, the findings must be interpreted with caution because the sample size was small and this study was limited to one community.

Unfortunately, statistical data are not available to definitively address the question of how many female rape survivors have seroconverted. Although there are anecdotal reports indicating that this has occurred (Albert et al., 1994; Murphy et al., 1989), the Centers for Disease Control and Prevention do not present any information regarding sexual assault in the very detailed break-down of AIDS cases that is reported in its *HIV/AIDS Surveillance Report.* The tragic fact is that more than 40,000 completed rape victimizations (excluding attempts) take place annually in the United States (Maguire and Pastore, 1994). While that brutality cannot be minimized, the data suggest that risk of HIV transmission as a result of sexual assault is quite low.

HIV Transmission within Correctional Institutions

Another common misconception about HIV transmission is the belief that our correctional institutions have become breeding grounds for the spread of the virus. After all, prisons and jails contain a substantial number of inmates who have a history of intravenous drug use (Vlahov and Polk, 1988), and there is evidence that indicates a substantial proportion of prisoners engage in homosexual behavior during incarceration (Nacci and Kane, 1983; Wooden and Parker, 1982). In an attempt to prevent institutional transmission from occurring, Alabama and Mississippi have adopted policies that are quite controversial such as isolating seropositive inmates from the general prison population (Cauchon, 1995). Despite these fears regarding AIDS, the evidence to date suggests that little HIV transmission is occurring within the nation's prison system.

Several studies have been conducted which seek to determine the extent of institutional viral transmission among correctional populations. The best method to assess the extent of this problem is to employ a longitudinal methodology in which a cohort of inmates is tested for HIV and then retested at a later date. It is noteworthy that in the most comprehensive study of this kind, only 0.3 percent of 2,300 male inmates in Illinois who were initially seronegative became HIV-positive after spending one year in prison (Hammett et al., 1994). Low rates of seroconversion have also been reported in Maryland (Brewer et al., 1988) and Nevada (Horsburgh et al., 1990).

There is other evidence to suggest that the virus is not being transmitted with great frequency in correctional institutions. First, various studies indicate that preincarceration intravenous drug use is the major risk factor for HIV infection among prison inmates in both the United States and Europe (Vlahov et al., 1990). Second, an earlier analysis of prison records in New York and Florida revealed very few cases of AIDS among inmates who had been continuously incarcerated for a substantial period of time (Hammett, 1988). These data suggest that while institutional transmission does occur, it is a relatively infrequent event (Blumberg and Langston, 1995; Hammett et al., 1994; and Vlahov, 1990).

More research is needed on this question. It is known that there are substantial differences between jurisdictions with regard to the rate of seroprevalence among inmates (Hammett et al., 1994). It is quite likely that there are also differences between facilities with respect to the incidence of "high-risk" behavior. However, there is no reason to believe that prisons and jails have become fertile breeding grounds for the spread of HIV/AIDS.

Risk Reduction among Intravenous Drug Users

The final myth to be addressed in this chapter is the "general impression that IVDUs are incapable of (or disinterested in) changing their behavior" (Becker and Joseph, 1988:403) in order to protect themselves from the AIDS virus. The ability and willingness of IVDUs to reduce their level of risk is a very important question from the standpoint of public health. One-third of new AIDS cases in the United States are now associated with intravenous drug use (Des Jarlais and Friedman, 1994). In addition, the majority of cases that involve either heterosexual or perinatal transmission are also linked to intravenous drug use (Centers for Disease Control and Prevention, 1994). Although educational campaigns designed to eliminate "high-risk" behavior have been very effective in reducing the level of new AIDS cases among gay men, many persons remain skeptical of whether such efforts can succeed among IVDUs.

Programs to educate IVDUs about AIDS are more difficult to implement than similar campaigns that have reached out to gay men. First, the gay community already had a well developed organizational structure in place prior to the AIDS crisis (Friedman et al., 1987). Intravenous drug users, on the other hand, lack this organizational structure and are usually socially isolated. Second, many homosexual males are well educated and come from middle-class backgrounds. This contrasts with IVDUs who generally have little education and are often drawn from the ranks of the economically disadvantaged. Third, gay men are often deeply involved in a network of social relationships. IVDUs lack these ties and generally have fragile relationships with family members and friends. Because they are involved in an activity that violates the law, IVDUs frequently are suspicious of public officials and agencies.

Despite these obstacles to behavioral change, a review of various studies suggests that many IVDUs have already taken steps to reduce their risk of HIV infection (Des Jarlais and Friedman, 1990). These measures have included such practices as: no longer sharing injection equipment, reducing the number of persons with whom they share needles, only using sterile needles, cleaning injection equipment prior to use, or reducing their level of drug use.

Additional evidence that IVDUs wish to change their behavior comes from evaluations of needle and syringe exchange (NSE) programs. Despite their success in many European cities, these efforts to provide injection drug users with clean "works" have often been quite controversial in the United States (Raymond, 1988). Opponents have charged that NSE programs send the wrong message and encourage IVDUs to continue their illicit behavior. It is also claimed that addicts will not use sterile injection equipment even when it is made available.

To assess these concerns, researchers have examined NSE programs in a number of different countries (Des Jarlais and Friedman, 1994). Invariably, these evaluations have concluded that IVDUs are very eager to participate in exchange programs. Many individuals receiving sterile needles reported a decrease in the incidence of "high-risk" behavior. Contrary to the fears expressed by opponents, there is no evidence that NSE programs lead to increased drug use (Des Jarlais and Friedman, 1994). In fact, the data suggest that NSE efforts can reduce the level of illicit drug activity by reaching out and encouraging IVDUs to enter treatment programs (Blumberg, 1992). A two-year evaluation of addicts enrolled in the NSE program in New York City found reduced overall rates of HIV-infection (Lee, 1994). In 1992, Connecticut legalized over-the-counter sales of syringes by pharmacies (one of only five states with such laws). Two studies published in *The Journal of Acquired Immune Deficiency Syndrome* reported a 40 percent drop in needle-sharing (Judson, 1995). Since almost one-third of AIDS victims today are either IVDU users, their sex partners or their children, the increased use of clean needles should directly affect the spread of the disease. The director of the AIDS division of the Connecticut health department, Beth Weinstein, pointed out an additional benefit. "This is something that made a dramatic change in behavior at no cost to the public. This is not a big outreach program. It's not a needle exchange that costs the government money. It's a change in the law" (Judson, 1995:A1).

In 1988 Congress prohibited federal funds for needle exchange programs but allowed the policy to be reversed if the surgeon general found such programs to be effective. The National Research Council released a report on September 19, 1995 which stated that exchange programs reduce the spread of AIDS without encouraging the use of illegal drugs (Borg, 1995). The federal government currently spends $6 billion yearly on AIDS; both exchange programs and the experience in Connecticut offer effective solutions restricted by current policy.

In spite of the encouraging findings from almost all the studies undertaken, much remains to be accomplished. Many IVDUs continue to engage in behavior that places both themselves and others at risk of HIV infection. There is evidence that fewer precautions are being taken to avoid sexual transmission than are being taken to safeguard injection practices (Vlahov, 1994). Many IVDUs need to be educated about the dangers of unsafe practices, and the public needs to relinquish myths about the futility of education and the symbolism of needle exchange or sale programs.

Conclusion

In the preceding discussion, it has been observed that: 1) persons who work in the criminal justice system face a minimal risk of HIV infection from assaultive seropositive offenders; 2) female prostitutes rarely transmit the AIDS virus to their male customers; 3) the risk of HIV infection is minimal for most female rape victims; 4) there is evidence that the rate of viral transmission in the prison system is relatively low; and 5) many IVDUs have responded to the threat of AIDS and modified their "high-risk" behavior.

A clearer understanding of these facts—as opposed to relying on mythical impressions—can lead to more informed policy decisions. For example, if the actual risks associated with a biting or spitting incident were more widely known, courts would be unlikely to impose lengthy prison sentences just because the offender is infected with HIV. Likewise, persons who are the victims of such assaults might become less concerned with learning the HIV antibody status of the offender.

Correctional policy could also benefit from dissemination of accurate information. Prison administrators sometimes defend inappropriate restraints placed upon HIV/AIDS infected inmates with the rationale that the public demands these policies. Perhaps, such pressures would diminish if it were recognized that institutional transmission of HIV is not a common occurrence.

Finally, efforts to curb the spread of HIV among IVDUs might be greatly enhanced with greater appreciation of four important facts: 1) many drug injectors wish to change their behavior; 2) a substantial number have already taken steps to reduce their risk of viral infection; 3) needle and syringe exchanges do not encourage drug abuse and; 4) there is a great deal of evidence that these schemes can be an effective tool in the battle against HIV/AIDS. As Des Jarlais and Friedman (1994) note, "the biggest obstacle to reducing the spread of HIV among drug users is neither a lack of resources nor a lack of knowledge but a lack of political resolve to utilize already existing information."

Sources

AIDS and Civil Liberties Project (1990). Mandatory HIV Testing of Prostitutes: Policy Statement of the American Civil Liberties Union. In *AIDS: The Impact on the Criminal Justice System*, M. Blumberg (ed.). Westerville, OH: Merrill Publishing Company.

Albert, J., Wahlberg, J., Leitner, T., Escanilla, D. and Uhlen, M. (1994). Analysis of a Rape Case by Direct Sequencing of the Human Immunodeficiency Virus Type 1 pol and gag Genes. *Journal of Virology* 68(9): 5918–24.

Becker, M. and Joseph, J. (1988). AIDS and Behavior Change to Reduce Risk: A Review. *American Journal of Public Health* 78(4): 394–410.

Bergman, B. (1988). AIDS, Prostitution, and the Use of Historical Stereotypes to Legislate Sexuality. *The John Marshall Law Review* 21:777–830.

Bigbee, D. (1993). Pathogenic Microorganisms: Law Enforcement's Silent Enemies. *FBI Law Enforcement Bulletin* 62(5): 1–5.

Blumberg, M. (1992). Needle and Syringe Exchange Schemes: An Examination of the Empirical Evidence. *Criminal Justice Journal* 14(1): 11–28.

Blumberg, M. and Langston, D. (1995). The Impact of HIV/AIDS and Tuberculosis on Corrections. In *The Dilemmas of Corrections: Contemporary Readings*, 3rd ed., K. Haas and G. Alpert (eds.), pp. 572–84. Prospect Heights, IL: Waveland Press.

Borg, G. (1995). Needle Exchange Programs Reduce Spread of AIDS. *Chicago Tribune*, (September 20), sec. 1:21.

Brewer, T., Vlahov, D., Taylor, E., Hall, D., Munoz, A. and Polk, B. (1988). Transmission of HIV within a Statewide Prison System. *AIDS* 2(5): 363–66.

Cauchon, D. (1995). AIDS in Prison: Locked Up and Locked Out. *USA Today*, (March 31):6A.

Centers for Disease Control and Prevention (1994). *HIV/AIDS Surveillance Report* 6(2).

_____ (1990) *HIV/AIDS Surveillance Report*, (June)

Centers for Disease Control and Prevention (1989). Guidelines for Prevention of Transmission of HIV and Hepatitis B Virus to Health-Care and Public-Safety Workers. *Morbidity and Mortality Weekly Report* 38(S-6).

_____ (1988). Update: Universal Precautions for Prevention of Transmission of Human Immunodeficiency Virus, Hepatitis B. Virus, and Other Bloodborne Pathogens in Health-Care Settings. *Morbidity and Mortality Weekly Report* 37(2): (June 24).

Cohen, J., Alexander, P. and Wofsy, C. (1988). Prostitution and AIDS: Public Policy Issues. *AIDS & Public Policy Journal* 3(2): 16–22.

Des Jarlais, D. and Friedman, S. (1994). AIDS and the Use of Injected Drugs. *Scientific American* (February):82–88.

_____ (1990). Target Groups for Preventing AIDS Among Intravenous Drug Users. In *AIDS: The Impact on the Criminal Justice System*, M. Blumberg (ed). Westerville, OH: Merrill Publishing Company.

_____ (1988). The Psychology of Preventing AIDS Among Intravenous Drug Users. *American Psychologist* 43(11): 865–70.

Editorial Staff (1995). Controlling AIDS with Clean Needles. *Chicago Tribune*, (September 16), sec. 1:16.

Friedland, G., Saltzman, B., Rogers, M., Kahl, P., Lesser, M., Mayers, M. and Klein, R. (1986). Lack of Transmission of HTLV-111/LAV Infection to Household Contacts of Patients with AIDS or AIDS-Related Complex with Oral Candidiasis. *The New England Journal of Medicine* 314(6): 344–49.

Friedman, S., Des Jarlais, D., Sotheran, J., Garber, J., Cohen, H. and Smith, D. (1987). AIDS and Self-Organization Among Intravenous Drug Users. *The International Journal of the Addictions* 22(3): 201–19.

Giovanni, C., Jr., Berlin, F., Casterella, P., Redfield, R., Hiken, M., Falck, A., Malin, H., Gagliano, S., Schaerf, F. and Roberts, C. (1991). Prevalence of HIV Antibody Among a Group of Paraphilic Sex Offenders. *Journal of Acquired Immune Deficiency Syndromes* 4(6): 633–37.

Glaser, J., Hammerschlag, M. and McCormack, W. (1989). Epidemiology of Sexually Transmitted Diseases in Rape Victims. *Review of Infectious Diseases* 11(2): 246–54.

Gostin, L. (1990). The AIDS Litigation Project—A National Review of Court and Human Rights Commission Decisions, Part 1: The Social Impact of AIDS. *Journal of the American Medical Association* 263(14): 1961–70.

Groth, A. and Burgess, A. (1977). Sexual Dysfunction During Rape. *The New England Journal of Medicine* 297(14): 764–66.

Hammett, T. (1988). *AIDS in Correctional Facilities: Issues and Options*, 3rd ed. Washington, DC: National Institute of Justice, (April).

Hammett, T., Harrold, L., Gross, M. and Epstein, J. (1994). *1992 Update: HIV/AIDS in Correctional Facilities*. National Institute of Justice and Centers for Disease Control and Prevention, (January).

Hearst, N. and Hulley, S. (1988). Preventing the Heterosexual Spread of AIDS: Are We Giving Our Patients the Best Advice? *Journal of the American Medical Association* 259(16): 2428–32.

Ho, D., Byington, R., Schooley, R., Flynn, T., Rota, T. and Hirsch, M. (1985). Infrequency of Isolation of HTLV-111 Virus from Saliva in AIDS. *The New England Journal of Medicine* 313(25): 1606.

Holmstrom, L. and Burgess, A. (1980). Sexual Behavior of Assailants During Reported Rapes. *Archives of Sexual Behavior* 9(5): 427–39.

Horsburgh, C., Jarvis, J., McArthur, T., Ignacio, T. and Stock, P. (1990). Seroconversion to Human Immunodeficiency Virus in Prison Inmates. *American Journal of Public Health* 80(2): 209–10.

Ippolito, G., Puro, V. and De Carli, G. (1993). The Risk of Occupational Human Immunodeficiency Virus Infection in Health Care Workers. *Archives of Internal Medicine* 153:1451–58.

Jenny, C., Hooton, T., Bowers, A., Copass, M., Krieger, J., Hillier, S., Kiviat, N., Corey, L., Stamm, W. and Holmes K. (1990). Sexually Transmitted Diseases in Victims of Rape. *New England Journal of Medicine* 322(11): 713–16.

Judson, G. (1995). Study Finds AIDS Risk to Addicts Drops if Sale of Syringes Is Legal. *New York Times*, (August 30): A1 and A12.

Kingsley, L., Rinaldo, C., Lyter, D., Valdiserri, R., Belle, S. and Ho, M. (1990). Sexual Transmission Efficiency of Hepatitis B Virus and Human Immunodeficiency Virus Among Homosexual Men. *Journal of the American Medical Association* 264(2): 230–34.

Kinkade, P. and Leone, M. (1994). To Protect and Serve? Public Perception of Policing Responsibility and the AIDS Patient. *American Journal of Police* 13(4): 135–55.

Lachance-McCullough, M., Tesoriero, J., Sorin, M. and Lee, C. (n.d.). *Correlates of HIV Seroprevalence Among Male New York State Prison Inmates: Results from the New York State AIDS Institute Criminal Justice Initiative.* Albany: New York State Department of Health.

Lee, F. (1994). Data Show Needle Exchange Curbs H.I.V. Among Addicts. *New York Times*, (November 26):1.

Luxenburg, J. and Guild, T. (1993). Women, AIDS, and the Criminal Justice System. In *It's a Crime: Women and Justice*, R. Muraskin and T. Alleman (eds.). Upper Saddle River, NJ: Regents/Prentice Hall.

Lyman, D., Ascher, M. and Levy, J. (1986). Minimal Risk of Transmission of AIDS-Associated Retrovirus Infection by Oral-Genital Contact. *Journal of the American Medical Association* 255(13): 1703.

Maguire, K. and Pastore, A. (1994). *Sourcebook of Criminal Justice Statistics–1993.* Albany, NY: The Hindelang Criminal Justice Research Center.

Murphy, S., Kitchen, V., Harris, J. and Forster, S. (1989). Rape and Subsequent Seroconversion to HIV. *British Medical Journal* 299(16): 718.

Nacci, P. and Kane, T. (1983). The Incidence of Sex and Sexual Aggression in Federal Prisons. *Federal Probation* 47(4): 31–36.

O'Farrell, N., Tovey, S. and Morgan-Capner, P. (1992). Transmission of HIV-1 Infection After a Fight. *Lancet* 339:246.

Padian, N., Shiboski, S. and Jewell, N. (1990). The Effect of Number of Exposures on the Risk of Heterosexual HIV Transmission. *The Journal of Infectious Diseases* 161:883–87.

Potterat, J., Phillips, L. and Muth, J. (1987). Lying to Military Physicians About Risk Factors for HIV Infections. *Journal of the American Medical Association* 257(13): 1727.

Raymond, C. (1988). U.S. Cities Struggle to Implement Needle Exchanges Despite Apparent Success in European Cities. *Journal of the American Medical Association* 260(18): 2620–21.

Redfield, R., Markham, P., Salahuddin, S., Wright, D., Sarngadharan, M. and Gallo, R. (1985). Heterosexually Acquired HTLV-111/LAV Disease (AIDS-Related Complex and AIDS): Epidemiologic Evidence for Female-to-Male Transmission. *Journal of the American Medical Association* 254(15): 2094–96.

Richman, K. and Richman, L. (1993). The Potential for Transmission of Human Immunodeficiency Virus Through Human Bites. *Journal of Acquired Immune Deficiency Syndromes* 6(4): 402–6.

Rosenberg, M. and Weiner, J. (1988). Prostitutes and AIDS: A Health Department Priority? *American Journal of Public Health* 78(4): 418–23.

Rozenbaum, W., Gharakhanian, S., Cardon, B., Duval, E. and Coulaud, J. (1988). HIV Transmission By Oral Sex. *Lancet* 1(8589): 1395.

Saracco, A., Musicco, M., Nicolosi, A., Angarano, G., Arici, C., Gavazzeni, G., Costigliola, S., Gervasoni, C., Luzzati, R., Piccinino, F., Puppo, F., Salassa, B., Sinicco, A., Stellini, R., Tirelli, U., Turbessi, G., Vigevani, G., Visco, G., Zerboni, R. and Lazzarin, A., (1993). Man-To-Woman Sexual Transmission of HIV: Longitudinal Study of 343 Steady Partners of Infected Men. *Journal of Acquired Immune Deficiency Syndromes* 6(5): 496–502.

Vlahov, D. (1994). HIV Seroconversion Studies Among Intravenous Drug Users. *AIDS* 8(2): 263–65.

_____ (1990). HIV-1 Infection in the Correctional Setting. *Criminal Justice Policy Review* 4(4): 306–18.

Vlahov, D., Brewer, T., Castro, K., Narkunas, J., Salive, M., Ullrich, J. and Munoz, A. (1991). Prevalence of Antibody to HIV-1 Among Entrants to U.S. Correctional Facilities. *Journal of the American Medical Association* 265(9): 1129–32.

Vlahov, D., Munoz, A., Brewer, F., Taylor, E., Canner, C. and Polk, B. (1990). Seasonal and Annual Variation of Antibody to HIV-1 Among Male Inmates Entering Maryland Prisons: Update. *AIDS* 4(4): 345–50.

Vlahov, D. and Polk, B. (1988). Intravenous Drug Use and Human Immunodeficiency Virus (HIV) Infection in Prison. *AIDS Public Policy Journal* 3(2): 42–46.

Winkelstein, W., Lyman, D., Padian, N., Grant, R., Samuel, M., Wiley, J., Anderson, R., Lang, W., Riggs, J. and Levy, J. (1987). Sexual Practices and the Risk of Infection by the Human Immunodeficiency Virus: The San Francisco Men's Health Study. *Journal of the American Medical Association* 257(3): 321–25.

Wooden, W. and Parker, J. (1982). *Men Behind Bars: Sexual Exploitation in Prison.* New York: Plenum Press.

Battered and Blue Crime Fighters
Myths and Misconceptions of Police Work

10

The public and media have had a long running fascination with police officers and their work. This fascination is reflected in books, newspaper and magazine accounts, as well as television documentaries. Depiction of the police and their work has been especially well represented by the media industry in television shows and movies. From the *Keystone Cops* of the early cinema to *RoboCop II*, many of us have grown up with media portrayals of policing. These images of policing usually carry with them certain recurrent themes that promote and shape our view of the nature of police work in American society. Two media characterizations of police work prevail: policing as an exciting yet dangerous profession and the stressful life of a police officer with its many negative side effects.

The danger and glamour of police work is revealed in movies like *Dirty Harry, Lethal Weapon I, II & III, Nighthawks, Silence of the*

Lambs, and *Die Hard with a Vengeance*. These movies and other television accounts of policing show the autonomous police officer, single-handedly or sometimes with a minor partner, fighting diabolical, sophisticated and well-armed criminals. These are not run-of-the-mill criminals like the drunk driver, the thief or the check forger. More often than not, police officers are pitted against psychosexual killers, serial murderers, and international terrorists. In almost every depiction of Hollywood policing, officers are shown shooting it out with armed criminal suspects while simultaneously being locked in conflict with the police department they work for — as well as the unenlightened criminal justice system that is unwilling to understand the unique demands of police work.

Movies like the *Blue Knight* and television serials such as *NYPD Blue* and *Homicide: Life on the Street* have painted portraits of police officers and their work as exciting but personally destructive. These more sophisticated presentations often focus on the effects of being a police officer — how policing destroys officers' personal lives. Media portrayals often chime the theme of mental distress because of a growing dissatisfaction and frustration with the criminal justice system's emphasis on criminal rather than victim rights. Stress is rampant among television cops and suicide is always a possibility. Each side effect is presented as commonplace for television cops. More recently, media fascination with policing has even extended to what police officers and policing might be like in centuries to come. Movies like *RoboCop* show policing in terms of its crime fighting role and allude to the almost superhuman qualities needed by modern law enforcement officers.

Media depiction of policing is, of course, not the only source from which we draw our images of policing and police work. The law enforcement community and political leaders alike reinforce media created perceptions of danger, glamour, and stress. America's "war against crime" and more recently the renewed "war on drugs" have helped reinforce an image of police officers locked in mortal combat with sophisticated high-tech international criminals and drug dealers who will use all means available to them to prevent detection and effect their escape. These arch criminals are shown as far more numerous and better armed than the police and willing to use deadly force in an instant.

In an attempt to become more open with the public, police executives have given the media access to police operations, allowing them to film drug raids, gang sweeps and other high profile operations. Television shows like *Cops* reinforce the notion that police work is dangerous and exciting; camera crews selectively move from call to call filming officers' unique activities. The image is projected that police officers—our most visible symbols of justice—are under siege by drug-dealing kingpins, youth gangs, occupational stress, and even their own police departments.

The allure to study the negative side of police work has not gone unnoticed by scholars. Virtually hundreds of articles have been written about dangers and stresses in police work, and almost every introductory text in criminal justice or policing contains a section devoted to these topics. One work on policing has even been entitled *The Custer Syndrome*, alluding to the way police are severely out-numbered by their criminal counterparts and the "belief that not losing ground [in the war against crime] can be counted as success" (Hernandez, 1989:2). How accurate are the depictions of American policing presented by the media and reinforced by the government and law enforcement community? How conclusive is the research on the dangers and stress of policing in America? This chapter will address a few of the common myths and misconceptions of crime fighting. We will conclude with a consideration of how the disjunc-ture between perceptions, expectations, and reality shapes the police as an occupational group as they live the myth of crime fighting.

Real Police Work

Despite the images and claims that police officers are outnumbered by their criminal counterparts and despite the political rhetoric of waging war on crime, police officers do considerably less "crime fighting" than one might imagine. When citizens reflect upon the role of the police, invariably they think in terms of law enforcement capacity. Whether they are being depicted in a police series on television or in a current movie, police officers are portrayed almost solely as crime fighters. Citizens spend hours of leisure time watching cops engage in such activities as high-speed pursuits of wanted felons, questioning persons suspected of having committed serious crimes, shooting it out with dangerous criminals, and in other law enforcement tasks requiring precision skills and often under threatening conditions.

Crime Fighting

Unfortunately, this media image is erroneous. It is a myth to believe that the police spend the majority of their time involved in crime-fighting activity. In fact, the average cop on television probably sees more action in a half-hour than most officers witness in an entire career. As a general rule, most police work is quite mundane. Police spend a considerable part of their time on such routine tasks as writing traffic citations, investigating automobile accidents, mediating disputes between neighbors and family members, directing traffic, and engaging in a variety of other service-related and order-maintaining activities. If television were to create a program that realistically depicted police work, it would soon go off the air due to poor ratings. It would offer little in the way of "action," and would quickly be tuned out by bored viewers.

Since the 1960s, a variety of research techniques have been employed to study police workloads (Greene and Klockars, 1991). Radio calls from dispatchers to patrol cars (Bercal, 1970), telephone calls by citizens to the police (Cumming et al., 1965), dispatch records (Reiss, 1971), observational data (Kelling et al., 1974), self-reports from police officers (O'Neill and Bloom, 1972) and telephone interviews of citizens (Mafstrofski, 1983) have all been utilized in an attempt to learn what the police actually do and how much time is spent on various activities. Despite the fact that these studies relied on different methodologies and were conducted in different communities and during different time periods, all determined that relatively little of an officer's day is taken up responding to crime-related activities. Although the proportions varied, only between 10 and 20 percent of the calls were of a law enforcement nature.

The findings from the various studies indicate that a substantial proportion of an officer's time does not involve any contact with the public. Police spend many hours engaged in preventive patrol, running errands, and performing a number of administrative tasks that consume a considerable part of their workday. In their 1991 study, Jack Greene and Carl Klockars excluded from their analysis time that was spent by the police in activities not involving direct contact with the citizenry. When officer workload is reconceptualized in this manner, the proportion of time that is classified as crime-related activity does increase. However, almost all this work involves taking crime reports from citizens. The authors conclude that the:

> findings in no way lend support to the headline news vision of police work as a violent running battle between police and criminals. It bears emphasis that our data show that the average police officer spent about one hour per week responding to reports of crimes in progress. When the officers arrive, they often

find that what was described as a crime in progress was, in fact, not a crime or that the perpetrator is gone (Greene and Klockars, 1991: 283).

Police Shootings

Both television and film frequently portray law enforcement officers as engaged in shoot-outs with dangerous criminals. Although this type of entertainment may produce high ratings for television programs and large profits for movie studios, how does this view of police work compare with reality? How often do police officers in real life fire their weapons at suspects? How many persons are shot and/or killed by the police each year in the United States?

Unfortunately, there are no national statistics published that address this issue. As a consequence, it is not a straightforward matter to determine how many people are killed and/or wounded by police bullets each year. Researchers have had to rely on data that have been collected for other purposes (*Vital Statistics of the United States*) and information that has voluntarily been supplied by police agencies to determine the annual number of killings attributable to police officers.

Vital Statistics records the birth and death records that are collected and published by the United States Public Health Service. Because they contain a category that notes deaths due to legal intervention, they have been useful to researchers who study killings of citizens by the police. According to *Vital Statistics*, there was an average of 360 deaths due to legal intervention in the United States each year between 1970 and 1975. Because judicially ordered executions did not take place during this period, it can be assumed that almost all these persons died at the hands of police officers. Unfortunately, Lawrence W. Sherman and Robert Langworthy (1979) note that *Vital Statistics* may underreport the number of police killings by as much as 51 percent. Therefore, there may have been as many as 735 killings by police each year during this period.

Sherman and Langworthy (1979) have concluded that data supplied by police departments is far more complete than the information on killings contained in *Vital Statistics*. Unfortunately, no national survey based on police records exists. The most comprehensive study to date was undertaken by Sherman and Ellen G. Cohn (1986) who utilized a variety of data sources, including information elicited from police departments, to examine the rate of police killings during a fifteen year (1970–84) period in the fifty largest cities of the United States. They report that in no year did the police in these cities kill more than 353 people (Sherman and Cohn, 1986).

Although these researchers report enormous variation in the rate at which police officers kill citizens, it is clear that these are relatively rare events. Even though Jacksonville (Florida) ranked at the top with respect to one measure of police homicide between 1980 and 1984, the average officer in that community would have to work 139 years before taking anyone's life. Honolulu, on the other hand, ranked at the bottom during this same period. A police officer in that community would kill a citizen, on average once every 7,692 years (Sherman and Cohn, 1986).

Not only are killings caused by police rare events, but the Sherman and Cohn (1986) study concludes that they are becoming even more infrequent. One of their major findings was that the number of persons killed by big city police officers declined from 353 in 1971 to 172 in 1984. In effect, law enforcement personnel were killing about half as many people in 1984 as they were in 1971. Despite a perception on the part of many citizens and by the media that the streets are becoming more dangerous, the number of citizens mortally wounded by the police has clearly declined.

There are several explanations for this phenomena (Sherman and Cohn, 1986). First, almost all police departments that serve large communities have adopted firearms policies that prohibit the use of deadly force against certain fleeing felons (Fyfe and Blumberg, 1985). Both James J. Fyfe (1979) and Sherman (1983) have reported that a change to a more restrictive policy is followed by a decline in the number of shootings by police officers. Second, training has been improved and the level of discipline has been tightened in many departments. Third, there has been an explosion of civil litigation. The net effect of this has been a substantial increase in the number of lawsuits that are filed as a result of police shootings by police. Municipalities now have a strong financial incentive to prevent unjustifiable incidents and thus avoid financial liability.

In order to gain an idea of how frequently police officers shoot citizens, nonfatal incidents must also be examined. Unfortunately, there is no national data that addresses this issue. However, Arnold Binder and Lorie Fridell (1984) have surveyed the various studies that have been conducted by researchers in individual departments. Based on this review, they conclude that approximately 30 percent of persons shot by the police will actually die. Based on this ratio of woundings to fatalities, a police officer in Jacksonville (the city with the highest rate of homicide by police officers) would have to work an average of forty-two years before shooting a citizen. In many other communities, the time period would be appreciably longer. Because a police career rarely lasts more than thirty-five years, the majority of police officers will go their entire career and never shoot anybody.

The Dangers of Police Work

One of the most pervasive myths about police work is that it is a dangerous occupation. Both film and television present portrayals of police officers being attacked and killed by criminals determined to commit crimes and escape punishment at any cost. This perception is reinforced by the occasional incident in which a police officer is gunned down. When such a tragic event occurs, the evening news will include footage of scenes taken at the deceased officer's funeral. This will vividly portray the hundreds of officers who have come from other departments to pay their last respects to the slain officer. Invariably, the story will include a commentary to the effect that police officers are on the frontline in the war against crime and that they face the possibility of death from a crazed assailant at any given moment.

Not only is policing portrayed as a dangerous occupation, but the message the public routinely receives is that it is becoming much more so. After all, our cities have become plagued with gangs, drugs, and automatic weapons. Police must deal with problems that did not even exist a decade ago, such as the epidemic of crack cocaine and the proliferation of high-powered weapons on the street. Obviously, being a cop today must be more dangerous than was the case in years past—or so we are told.

How accurate is this picture? Clearly, police officers are murdered by suspects. This is an undeniable fact, and each one of these killings is a terrible tragedy for the officer, the officer's survivors, the department, and the community. However, there are some questions that must be addressed: How pervasive is the danger that law enforcement officers face? Is policing really a dangerous occupation? Has it become more so in recent years?

Fortunately, these are relatively easy issues to resolve because the Uniform Crime Reports (UCR) publishes data each year with respect to the number of law enforcement officers who have been feloniously killed in the United States. It is believed that this is one of the most comprehensive and complete sections of the UCR (Vaughn and Kappeler, 1986; Konstantin, 1984). These data indicate that the killing of law enforcement officers is a rare event (Vaughn and Kappeler, 1986).

Not only are killings of police officers relatively rare events, but the data indicate that they have declined dramatically in recent years. From a high of 132 in 1974, police killings declined to 76 by 1994. In fact, when the period 1974–76 (Vaughn and Kappeler, 1986) is compared to the years 1986–94, the average annual number of killings drops from 124 to about 70. It is noteworthy that this risk associated with police work has declined despite the restrictions that have been placed on police use of firearms, the increase in the rate of violent crime, the proliferation of semi-automatic weapons on the streets of American cities, the war on drugs, and the increase in the level of gang-related violence that has occurred in many communities.

To some extent, these statistics on police killings mask the reduction in risk that has occurred because the number of law enforcement personnel has increased substantially during this period. Michael J. Hindelang, Michael R. Gottfredson, Christopher Dunn, and Nicolette Parisi (1977) report that there were 594,209 persons employed fulltime in law enforcement at all levels of government in 1974. By 1992, the number had risen to 841,099 (Flanagan and Maguire, 1990). Today it is estimated that over 850,000 people are employed in law enforcement. Because there were 132 killings of police officers in 1974, the aggregate risk per officer was approximately one chance in 4,501 that year. With 76 deaths in 1994, each officer stood one chance in 11,184 of being slain. Obviously, this is an aggregate rate of risk for all law enforcement personnel. Some officers patrol neighborhoods or perform assignments that place them in somewhat greater danger. Overall, the risk to law enforcement personnel has declined by more than 40 percent in twenty-one years.

Another way to examine the question of danger is to compare the fatality rate of police officers with that of persons working in other occupations and professions. Richard Holden (1991) has examined the mortality data published by the Bureau of Labor Statistics in an attempt to answer the question of whether policing is really more dangerous than other occupations. Comparative data for the years 1984–86 were reviewed. The analysis indicates that police officers consistently face a lower fatality rate than persons employed in mining, construction, transportation, and agriculture. However, the author cautions that a number of methodological problems make this comparison somewhat problematic. For example, the death rate for law enforcement personnel excludes officers who die as a result of traffic accidents unless they were in direct pursuit of a suspect. Therefore, this analysis must be considered somewhat tentative. Nonetheless, there is no support for the myth that policing is one of the most dangerous occupations.

The myth that policing is a dangerous occupation has a number of consequences for law enforcement. For one thing, this misperception is likely to result in an increased level of public support. Citizens who have an exaggerated sense of the danger that law enforcement personnel routinely confront are more likely to give the police the benefit of the doubt when it comes to various controversies involving the propriety of certain actions. Second, the public perception that the police are armed and ready to deal with danger twenty-four hours a day can be beneficial when it is time to engage in contract negotiations (Fyfe, 1982). Third, the belief that being a law enforcement officer is akin to the work of a soldier on the frontlines can have a deleterious effect on the officer's spouse (Niederhoffer and Niederhoffer, 1978). Finally, this pervasive sense that their mission is a dangerous one cannot help but affect the way that police officers deal with the public. One can only speculate about how many times officers use excessive force or are abrupt in their dealings with citizens because they perceive a world that is more dangerous than is actually the case.

Myth of Danger in Domestic Violence Incidents

There is perhaps no myth that is so widely ingrained in police folklore as the belief that the domestic violence call is the most dangerous for an officer. William K. Muir (1977) reported that it was the "unanimous sentiment" of the officers he studied that more police are killed in these situations than in any other type of call. Family violence researchers have also emphasized the danger that lurks for police in domestic violence encounters (Straus et al., 1980). However, the fact is that the risk of felonious death is far less in domestic violence situations than in many other types of assignments that the police handle.

This myth was seriously undermined by David Konstantin (1984) who analyzed the situational characteristics of all police killings that occurred in the United States between 1978 and 1980. He found that only 5.2 percent of these occurred in situations where officers had responded to domestic disturbances. This was substantially less than the proportion who died intervening in robbery situations, pursuing suspects, making traffic stops, investigating suspicious persons, or as a result of assaults (Konstantin, 1984).

Although this analysis suggests that domestic disturbance calls do not present a high level of risk, it is not definitive because it does not take into account the relative amounts of time that police officers spend performing various tasks. For example, domestic violence calls would be risky if they accounted for only one percent of total police calls for service but five percent of reported deaths. Fortunately, Joel Garner and Elizabeth Clemmer (1986) have utilized several existing measures of police activity to calculate the risk of death that officers face when they respond to a domestic violence complaint. These authors conclude that domestic violence consistently ranks below both robbery and burglary as a source of danger to police. A three-year study of domestic violence calls and police injuries concluded that "for the Charlotte Police Department, domestic disturbance calls are not a major source of assaults or injuries to the officers involved in relation to other types of calls" (Hirschel et al., 1994:99, 112). In fact, the calculations resulting from one activity measure actually result in domestic violence ranking at the bottom in terms of officer fatality and fifth out of ten types of calls for service "in the ratio of injuries to calls for service." Garner and Clemmer (1986:527) assert that "the available evidence strongly suggests that researchers and police managers abandon the notion that domestic disturbance calls result in a large number of police deaths."

How did the myth develop that many police officers die responding to domestic violence calls? Konstantin (1984) offers a number of possible explanations. The most likely explanation is that police officials and researchers misinterpreted the data that were provided by the FBI in its annual publication, *Law Enforcement Officers Killed* (LEOK). Prior to 1982, all officer deaths resulting from disturbances were lumped into one category regardless of whether they resulted from domestic violence calls or other types of disturbances (Garner and Clemmer, 1986). Many persons mistakenly assumed that all these incidents involved domestic disturbances; in fact, a substantial proportion were deaths that resulted from such calls as responding to bar fights, reports of a suspect with a weapon, and other types of disturbances that have nothing to do with family quarrels.

Konstantin gives other reasons why the level of danger in domestic violence calls may have been exaggerated. For one thing, responding to family quarrels can be a traumatic experience for a police officer. After all, it is the only situation where both the offender and the complainant may join forces against the officer. Second, it is possible that those who developed domestic crisis intervention training programs have overstated this danger in order to persuade police departments of the value of their programs. Finally, responding to family quarrels is likely to be perceived by police officers as "social work." Because these encounters take up so much of an officer's time, they may be viewed as demeaning to his/her image as a crime fighter. Therefore, in order to convince themselves that they are doing "real police work," the police may have exaggerated the danger from this type of assignment.

The myth that domestic violence calls represent a high level of danger results in a less effective response by police officers to these situations. Spokespersons for womens' rights organizations have often complained that the police do not take assaults perpetrated by husbands and boyfriends very seriously. As the police become educated to the true nature of the risk that this responsibility entails, it is hoped they will develop alternative strategies for dealing more effectively with this problem.

Myths of Police Stress

Stress is a neutral term but often carries a negative connotation. Stress can have both beneficial and adverse effects. Some people may perform at their best and be highly productive when enough stress is present to encourage or motivate high levels of performance. People undergoing mild forms of stress may experience an increased sense of awareness or alertness and will thus be capable of better performance in the workplace. Sometimes excessive work-related stressors can be debilitating and hinder performance and productivity. People undergoing excessive stress may begin to falter in their jobs and personal lives. Massive amounts of stress have been linked to impairment of the immune system and can have deleterious physical consequences.

Stress in police work has been examined for over a decade. Currently little more is known about police stress than when researchers began studying it more than a decade ago. While it is generally recognized that police stress exists, there is little agreement regarding its cause, effect or extent (Gaines and Van Tubergen, 1989; Mallory and Mays, 1984; Terry, 1983). While it is plausible to assert that police stress exists, little scientific research has been conducted that proves the cause behind the stress law enforcement officers experience. Instead scholars have developed several perspectives on the extent and sources of police stress.

Some researchers view stress as a personal adjustment problem. They have defined stress in terms of its negative aspects as a personal-environmental fit "problem" (Lofquist and Davis, 1969).

From this view of stress, police officers are seen as unable to cope with the demands made upon them by their profession. That is, certain police officers are not capable of performing under the strains of occupational demands. Stress affects officers differently, and since no two persons are the same, stress is thought to have differential effects on police officers. From this perspective, it is maintained that personal needs, values, abilities, and experiences all affect how individual police officers respond to the stress of their work environment.

An alternative and very different perspective views police stress as a structural problem that does not reside in any personal maladjustment but in the pathology of the police organization and the working environment. Scholars taking this perspective examine such factors as management style, role conflict, and other structural sources of stress. Scholars adopting this structural explanation feel that if officers are unable to perform, if they are hindered or having problems, the police organization and environment are at fault— not the individual officer.

Regardless of whether stress is a product of individual maladjustment or a structural deficiency in the police occupational environment, what are the effects of police stress and are they real? Do police officers experience higher levels of stress than bankers, lawyers or physicians? Are police suicides, drug abuse, divorce and mortality rates side effects of the stress inherent in the police profession?

The Myth of Police Suicide

One of the most superficial, yet appealing, arguments for the high levels of stress in police work has been based on the suicide rate found among police officers. Suicide attempts by police officers are often linked, at least in perception, to the stress associated with police work (see Alpert and Dunham, 1992). Some have argued that "An informal consensus appears to have arisen to the effect that the suicide rate among police is appreciably greater than for other occupational groups" (Bedian, 1982; cited in Josephson and Reiser, 1990:227).

While relatively few studies have been conducted to examine the actual cause of police suicide, early studies have focused on comparisons between the rates of suicide among police officers and the general population. With few exceptions early studies concluded that police officers suffer a higher rate of suicide than the general public (Lester, 1983; Labovitz and Hagedorn, 1971; Friedman,

1967). While the rate of suicide changes depending on the police population examined and the time periods covered by researchers, it has been a general contention that police officers experience suicide at higher rates than the general public. Urban police officers are said to experience the highest rate of suicide. Some studies have even suggested the rate of suicide among urban police might be six times higher than that experienced by the general public. Researchers studying the records of suicide in the city of Chicago found police officers were five times as likely to take their own lives as would ordinary citizens (Wagner and Brzeczek, 1983).

Additional research into police suicide has compared the rate of suicide across different occupations. In these studies, researchers have examined the suicide rates for numerous occupations and compared them to the police profession. One study of thirty-six occupations found that policing had the second highest rate of suicide (Labovitz and Hagedorn, 1971). Nonetheless, Lester's (1983) research into police suicide found the suicide rate was also high among the self-employed and people in manufacturing occupations. Uncritical readings of these findings are often offered as direct evidence of the stress inherent in police work.

Even though early research into police suicide has generally indicated a high rate of suicide among police officers, this myth of policing is beginning to change as researchers collect additional data and take a more critical look at the problem. A 1990 study of police officer suicide in the Los Angeles Police Department found the suicide rate of police officers remained lower than the suicide rate for other adults in the same geographic area (Josephson and Reiser, 1990:227). These scholars felt that "research done at the Los Angeles Police Department (LAPD) and the data available in the literature fail to provide support for the belief of an inordinately high suicide rate among police in general" (see also Dash and Reiser, 1978).

A 1994 study examined the National Mortality Detail Files to determine whether police officers had a higher rate of suicide than members of the public. The researchers concluded that when controls are added for differences in socio-economic variables like age, race, gender, and place of employment "being a police officer is not significantly associated with the odds of death by suicide" (Stack and Kelly, 1994:84). Other cautious researchers have offered alternative explanations other than stress for the seemingly high rate of police suicide. "First, police work is a male-dominated profession, and males have demonstrated a higher rate of successful suicide than females. Second, the use, availability and familiarity with firearms by police in their work provide them with a lethal weapon that affords the user little chance of surviving a serious suicide attempt" (Alpert and Dunham, 1992:160). The suicide rate for males is more than twice that of females yet females compose less than 12 percent of the police population. There is also evidence that suggests at least some suicides by police officers may be spawned from the uncovering of acts of corruption or deviance rather than the inherent stress of police work. In several cases, most recently the New York City Police Department's probe of the "Buddy Boys," a corrupt police ring, officers have taken their lives during the investigation of corruption. It is common for police officers to take their own lives following allegations of sexual assault or child molestation. While not all or even a majority of police suicides are a product of uncovering deviance and corruption, no research has been conducted regarding the relationship between corruption and suicide.

A review of the existing literature and arguments surrounding stress and police suicide indicates that conceptual and methodological problems associated with conducting this type of research makes it difficult to draw any firm conclusion. One can say with some confidence, however, that there is no available research that conclusively proves that the rate of suicide experienced by police officers is any greater than populations with similar background characteristics. Additionally, there is no conclusive evidence that work-related stress experienced by police officers is the cause of suicide. It is largely a myth that police kill themselves because of a level of stress greater than that experienced by members of other occupations.

Drug and Alcohol Abuse

Police officers are said to have high rates of alcoholism and drug abuse when compared to other occupations (Alpert and Dunham, 1992). Some have claimed that this is a product of police stress and a means by which police officers deal with the stress inherent in police work (Violanti et al., 1985). Researchers studying the correlation between police alcohol use and occupational stress have determined that "drinking problems among police officers are closely related to the perceived absence of alternative coping strategies" (Alpert and Dunham, 1992:159).

The first meaningful study of police misconduct specifically examining the use of alcohol by on-duty police officers was conducted by Albert Reiss in 1971. In researching infractions of departmental rules in three cities, Reiss found that drinking while on duty occurred in all cities examined and that the extent of on-duty use of alcohol ranged from 3.2 to 18.4 percent. A later study indicated that as many as 25 percent of police officers have serious problems with the use of alcohol (Kroes, 1976). Although these findings have been called into question (Lester, 1983), several studies of the use and abuse of alcohol and drugs support the finding that police use drugs and alcohol with much regularity.

Tom Barker (1983) found that of the forty-three officers responding to a self report survey, the "perceived" extent of drinking on the job was 8.05 percent. A 1988 study found that approximately 20 percent of police officers in a single agency used illegal drugs while on duty. Furthermore, these researchers found that the rate of on-duty alcohol use among veteran police officers reached nearly 20 percent (Kraska and Kappeler, 1988). Other researchers have drawn similar conclusions. More alarming, Van Raalte (1979) found that 67 percent of the officers studied admitted drinking alcohol while on duty. John Violanti, James Marshall and Barbara Howe (1985) as well as Peter Kraska and Victor Kappeler (1988) offered explanations for the conflicting claims among researchers regarding the degree of police drug and alcohol use. They suggest that the study of police deviance is difficult and that there is the distinct possibility of underreporting deviance by the police.

> Alcohol use among police is underestimated. Many officers, fearing departmental discipline, are unwilling to officially report their deviance. Police organizations appear ambivalent toward drinking problems, placing blame on the individual officer and not the police occupational structure (Kroes, 1976). Other departments may "hide" problem drinkers in positions where they will not adversely affect police operations (Violanti et al., 1985:106).

Current research on police drug use was prompted by the adoption of employment drug-testing practices by police departments. This research has generally indicated a small proportion of drug use by police officers. In 1986, the New Jersey State Police tested all 2,300 members of its force for drug use. Only five officers or .2 percent of the agency tested positive (Burden, 1986). Similar results were found for the City of New York Police Department. The conflict between earlier observational and self-report studies and the drug-testing results are more than likely a product of one or two factors. First, much media attention has been given to the issue of police drug use, possibly making officers more careful and fearful of detection. Second, these drug-screening tests are often administered to probationary employees with advance warning. Officers would therefore have time to modify their behavior before taking a drug test. Since many traces of illegal drugs leave the body rapidly, little advance warning is necessary for officers to modify their behavior.

While there is fairly strong evidence to support the extensive use of alcohol and drugs by police officers, there is less support of a direct causal relationship between drug use and police stress. An equally plausible explanation for the use of drugs and alcohol is that these substances are used for recreational purposes. In Kraska and Kappeler's (1988) study, they failed to uncover one police officer reporting current use of drugs who did not have a preemployment history of drug use. If police stress was a substantial cause of the abuse of these substances, one would expect to find officers without histories of drug use turning to these substances only after experiencing the stresses of police work. Similarly, the different proportions of officers using drugs and alcohol might suggest that officers have recreational drugs of choice. Veteran officers may be more likely to use alcohol and younger officers more likely to use other illicit drugs. Very little, if any, research has been done comparing cross-cultural/generational samples of police officers and drug use. There is a distinct possibility that the differences between the levels of alcohol and drug use is a product of police subcultural acceptance of one drug over the other. Alternatively, officers may engage in these behaviors out of boredom or peer pressure as much as from any stress inherent in crime fighting.

The Myth of Police Mortality

One myth prevalent among law enforcement officers is that they experience greater mortality rates from natural causes than do other citizens. This myth of policing can be viewed as the culmination of stress-related myths of policing. When one links the dangers, the suicide rate, and the stress myths, it is a natural inference that police officers must experience a greater rate of work-related mortality. This myth has been extended to the perception that police officers do not live long after retirement. If the stress and mortality myths were accurate, we would expect to find that officers who stayed in policing longer had shorter lives after retirement because of the toll exacted from crime fighters. Myths associated with police mortality have been given credence by misreadings of research and unsupported statements in the police literature.

Police officers are said to have higher rates of mortality from heart disease and diabetes. Other studies have found that police officers run a greater risk of developing colon and liver cancers. Danielle Hitz (1973) reported a higher rate of cirrhosis of the liver due to alcohol use by police officers. While there are conflicting claims on the extent to which police officers suffer from higher mortality rates due to these ailments, a study of 2,376 police officers in Buffalo, New York, found that while the overall mortality rate among police officers for a variety of ailments was comparable to the general United States population, police officers showed a significantly higher rate of mortality from certain forms of cancer. Officers were particularly susceptible to cancer of the digestive organs (Violanti et al., 1986). Stress, however, has never been demonstrated to cause cancer. Diet, smoking, and environmental factors are elements which would need to be analyzed before drawing any conclusions from the findings.

Despite these mixed findings, Richard Raub (1988) has pointed out that statements such as "The average police officer dies within five years after retirement and reportedly has a life expectancy of twelve years less than that of other people" (Dittmar, 1986, as cited in Raub) and "Police officers do not retire well" (Schwartz and Schwartz, 1975, as cited in Raub) are not supported by the data. These and similar statements combined with unfounded conclusions from the research literature reinforce the myth that police suffer an ill fate after retirement. While police stress has been linked to many problems including psychological, performance, and health issues (Terry, 1983; Kroes, 1976), Raub (1988) found that there was no empirical support for the myth that police officers have a shorter life expectancy after retirement than found in civilian populations. In his study of the life expectancies of retired officers from the Illinois, Kentucky, and Arizona state police agencies, he found that the length of time officers live after retirement matched mortality tables for general populations. This research also showed that officers who retired at older ages "enjoyed a longer life compared to those who are younger at retirement" (Raub, 1988:91–92). Thus, some police retirees may even live longer lives after retirement than other populations.

Several explanations can be advanced for the disjuncture between the myth of police mortality and the existing research. First, uncritical readings of stress-related research may be passed on to police officers in the training academy with little concern for the limitations of the research studies. Second, inferences on mortality may be drawn that were not originally supported in existing research. Third, as some researchers have pointed out, some problems experienced by officers may be in part an effect of stress but may also be related to officer lifestyle and diet (Violanti et al., 1986). There is little direct evidence that supports the myth that police experience higher rates of mortality because of the stress inherent in their work or that they experience shorter lives after retirement.

Police Divorces

Many authorities have commented on the high divorce rate that is believed to plague police marriages (Terry, 1981). Reports of this problem have come from a variety of sources. The media, police chaplains, departmental officials, the wives of police officers, and even some researchers have asserted that the stress inherent in law enforcement results in a very high level of divorce (Niederhoffer and Niederhoffer, 1978). Indeed, there are a number of features about police work that do place a strain on family life. For one thing, the schedule that many officers work may make it very difficult to have a normal social life. Because of rotating shifts, spouses must adjust to being left alone at night during certain periods of time. In addition, police officers may be required to work weekends and holidays. Second, the job presents many opportunities for marital infidelity. Spouses must take the officer's word that he/she really did have to work late or appear in court. Third, the trauma and pain that police witness as a routine part of their job can take an emotional toll on the officer and place an added strain on the relationship. Finally, police marriages are subject to all the same difficulties that trouble other couples (e.g., financial concerns, disagreements over child-rearing, etc.).

Because of the high level of interest in this topic, a great deal of empirical research has been conducted. However, the findings from various studies are contradictory. While some researchers report a high rate of police divorce (Durner et al., 1975), the majority conclude that the level of divorce is far lower than commonly assumed. Unfortunately, a number of methodological problems plague this body of research. The biggest drawback is that many studies do not distinguish between divorces that occurred prior to the time that the officer joined the department and those that occurred afterwards. Obviously, any stress inherent in law enforcement cannot account for a divorce that occurred before the individual joined the department.

It is noteworthy that the most comprehensive studies have concluded that police officers have a divorce rate that is no higher than the national average. James P. Lichtenberger (1968) examined data from the 1900 census and found that the rate of divorce for police was lower at that time than for most other occupations including doctors, lawyers, and college professors. Jack E. Whitehouse (1965) examined records from the 1960 census and observed that police and detectives had a divorce rate of 1.7 percent which compared favorably to the national average of 2.4 for males in the same age bracket. Nelson A. Watson and James W. Sterling (1969) undertook a massive study that brought responses from 246 police departments. They observed that not only was the police divorce rate lower than the national average for adult males, but that a far higher proportion of male officers were married. Finally, Arthur Niederhoffer and Elaine Niederhoffer (1978) came to a similar conclusion as a result of a questionnaire survey that elicited responses from 30 departments.

Despite all the anecdotal accounts and subjective reports detailing the horrors of police marriages, it is clear that these ideas are based on myth. The reality is that the overwhelming majority of police officers are family men who have stable marriages. As W. Clinton Terry, III (1981) reported after surveying the literature in this area, "the best evidence available supports the argument that police divorce rates are lower than the popular depiction of police family life would lead one to anticipate." In a similar vein, Niederhoffer and Niederhoffer (1978:170) conclude, "divorce, police style, may well be lower than divorce, American style."

Living the Crime Fighter Myth

Myths often become interpreted as reality for the people they affect. Behavior is often built around myth and perception rather than reality. Many of the myths of policing have contributed to the development of a group perspective among members of the police occupation. This cognitive group orientation and self-perception is often referred to as a culture. The term "culture" is used to describe differences between large social groups. Social groups differ in many aspects, and people from different cultures have varying beliefs, laws, morals, customs and other characteristics that set them apart from people of other cultures. These values and artifacts are unique to a given people and are transmitted from one generation to the next (Kappeler et al., 1994). Cultural distinctions are easy to see when one compares, for example, North American and Japanese cultures. Clearly, Americans have different traditions, laws, language, customs, religions, and art forms than do the Japanese.

There can also be cultural differences between people who form a single culture or social group. People who form a unique group within a given culture are called a subculture. The difference between a culture and a subculture is that members of a subculture, while sharing many values and beliefs of the larger dominant culture, have separate and distinct values. These differences make subcultural members unique as compared to the larger, more dominant culture. Clearly, police officers in America share the larger cultural heritage; they speak the same language; operate under the same laws; and share many of the same values. There are also certain myths and perceptions of the police subculture that make officers different from other members of society. Therefore, some scholars have maintained that the police are a unique occupational subculture.

The Dangerous World of Crime Fighting

Due in part to the police self-perception of danger and violence and the legal monopoly police have on the sanctioned use of violence (Reiss, 1971; Reiss and Bordua, 1967; Westley, 1956) and coercion (Bittner, 1970; Westley, 1970), police view themselves as a unique group in society. In effect, the police often set themselves apart from other members of society.

Because of their perception of police work—often based on myth—officers develop a unique worldview. Worldview is the manner in which a group sees the world and its own role and relationship to that world (Redfield, 1952). This means that various social groups, including the police, perceive the world, people, and situations differently from other social groups. By way of example, lawyers may view the world and events happening as a source of conflict and potential litigation. Physicians may view the world as a place of disease and illness needing healing. The police worldview categorizes the world into insiders and outsiders. "The police as a result of combined features of their social situation, tend to develop ways of looking at the world distinctive to themselves, cognitive lenses through which to see situations and events" (Skolnick, 1966:42). The way the police see the world can be described as a "we-they" or "us-them" orientation. Police officers tend to see the world as being composed of cops and others. Anyone who is not a police officer, is considered an outsider to be viewed with suspicion.

This we-they worldview is created for a variety of reasons, including the danger myth. The myth of danger is reinforced in the formal socialization processes. Police officers undergo formal socialization when they enter the academy. One author noted that in the police academy:

Group cohesiveness is encouraged by the instructors as well. The early roots of a separation between "the police" and "the public" is evident in many lectures and classroom discussions. In "war stories" and corridor anecdotes, it emerges as a full blown "us-them" mentality (Bahn, 1984:392).

Through these "war stories" in the course of field training and after graduation from the police academy, officers re–learn and experience the myths of crime fighting, particularly the potential for danger (Kappeler et al., 1994). Police officers often picture the world as dangerous. This view leads officers to see citizens as potential sources of violence or even as enemies. This crime fighting myth fosters the we-they police worldview. Where police officers see themselves as a close-knit distinct group and citizens as "outsiders" (Sherman, 1982; Westley, 1956).

The Spirit of Crime Fighting

The concept of ethos encompasses the fundamental spirit of a culture. Ethos is a subculture's sentiments, beliefs, customs and practices. Ethos often includes the things valued most by a sub-culture or occupational group. When this term is applied to the police subculture, some general observations arise. First, the police value bravery. Bravery is a central component of the social character of policing. As such, it is related to the perceived and actual dangers of law enforcement. The potential to become the victim of a violent encounter, the need for support by fellow officers during such encounters, and the legitimate use of violence to accomplish the police mandate all contribute to a subculture that stresses the virtue of bravery. Also, the military trapping of policing, organizational policies such as "never back down," and informal peer pressure all contribute to instilling a sense of bravery in the police subculture. It is not unusual for police training officers to wait until a recruit has been presented with a dangerous situation before recommending the recruit be given full status on the department. Until new officers have been tested on the street, they are usually not fully accepted by their peers.

Learning Myths of Crime Fighting

Myths often contain postulates or statements of belief held by a group which reflect their basic orientations. Myths, in a less formal sense than academy training, reinforce expressions of general truth or principle as they are perceived by a group. Myths act as an oral vehicle for the transmission of culture from one generation to the next and tend to serve as a reinforcer of the subcultural worldview. Myths are advanced in the police academy, by field training officers, and during informal gatherings of police officers. Stories are told and retold regarding the dangers of policing and the bravery of crime fighters. Through exposure to myth, the new generations of police officers combine their experiences and perceptions of the world viewed through a police officer's eyes with these "truths" and develop a belief system which dictates acceptable and unacceptable behavior. These myths serve as unconscious reinforcers of the dangers and stress of police work and act as part of the socialization process for new crime fighters.

While all occupational groups undergo a socialization process and while socialization into a profession is not necessarily negative, when that socialization is based on myth it can have negative consequences. People may be attracted to police work because of the myths of excitement and danger. When the reality of day-to-day police work is experienced, new officers may become disillusioned with their chosen career. If the myths of policing are internalized by a majority of a police force, very aggressive practices can result that have negative effects not only on individual officers and their departments but also on the community they serve. Much of the alienation of the police from their community is a product of socializing based on myth and misperception.

Sources

Alpert, G. and Dunham, R. (1992). *Policing Urban America*, 2nd ed. Prospect Heights, IL: Waveland Press.

Bahn, C. (1984). Police Socialization in the Eighties: Strains in the Forging of an Occupational Identity. *Journal of Police Science and Administration* 12(4): 390–94.

Barker, T. (1983). Rookie Police Officers' Perceptions of Police Occupational Deviance. *Police Studies* 6:30–37.

Bedian, A. (1982). Suicide and Occupation: A Review. *Journal of Vocational Behavior* 21:206–22.

Bennett, R. (1984). Becoming Blue: A Longitudinal Study of Police Recruit Occupational Socialization. *Journal of Police Science and Administration* 12(1): 47–57.

Bercal, T. (1970). Calls for Police Assistance. *American Behavioral Scientist* 13:681–91.

Berg, B., Gertz, M. and True, E. (1984). Police–Community Relations and Alienation. *Police Chief* 51(11): 20–23.

Binder, A. and Fridell, L. (1984). Lethal Force as Police Response. *Criminal Justice Abstracts* 16(2): 250–80.

Bittner, E. (1970). *The Functions of Police in Modern Society*. Chevy Chase, MD: National Clearinghouse for Mental Health.

Buder, L. (1985). Off-duty Abuse of Drugs Feared in Police Survey. *New York Times*, (July 5): 1, 4.

Burden, O. (1986). The Hidden Truths About Police Drug Use. *Law Enforcement News* (March 10): 5.

Cumming, E., Cumming, I. and Edell, L. (1965). Policeman as Philosopher, Friend and Guide. *Social Problems* 12:14–49.

Dash, J. and Reiser, M. (1978). Suicide Among Police in Urban Law Enforcement Agencies. *Journal of Police Science and Administration* 6(1): 18–21.

Durner, J., Kroeker, M., Miller, C. and Reynolds, C. (1975). Divorce — Another Occupational Hazard. *Police Chief* 62(11): 48–53.

Flanagan, T. and Maguire, K. (1990). *Sourcebook of Criminal Justice Statistics — 1989*. Albany, NY: The Hindelang Criminal Justice Research Center.

Friedman, P. (1967). Suicide Among Police. In *Essays in Self-destruction*, E. Scheidman (ed.). New York: Science House.

Fyfe, J. (ed.) (1982). In *Always Prepared: Police Off Duty Guns: Readings on Police Use of Deadly Force*. Washington, DC: Police Foundation.

_____. (1979). Administrative Interventions on Police Shooting Discretion: An Empirical Examination. *Journal of Criminal Justice* 7(4): 309–23.

Fyfe, J. and Blumberg, M. (1985). Response to Griswold: A More Valid Test of the Justifiability of Police Actions. *American Journal of Police* 4(2): 110–32.

Gaines, L. and Van Tubergen, N. (1989). Job Stress in Police Work: An Exploratory Analysis into Structural Causes. *American Journal of Criminal Justice* 13(3): 197–214.

Garner, J. and Clemmer, E. (1986). Danger to Police in Domestic Disturbances — A New Look. In *Critical Issues in Policing: Contemporary Readings*, 2nd ed., R. Dunham and G. Alpert (eds.). Prospect Heights, IL: Waveland Press.

Greene J. and Klockars, C. (1991). What Police Do. In *Thinking About Police: Contemporary Readings*, 2nd ed., C. Klockars and S. Mafstrofski (eds.). New York: McGraw-Hill.

Hernandez, J. (1989). *The Custer Syndrome*. Salem, WI: Sheffield Publishing.

Hindelang, M., Gottfredson, M., Dunn, C. and Parisi, N. (1977). *Sourcebook of Criminal Justice Statistics — 1976*. Albany, NY: Criminal Justice Research Center.

Hirschel, J., Dean, C. and Lumb, R. (1994). The Relative Contribution of Domestic Violence to Assault and Injury of Police Officers. *Justice Quarterly* 11(1): 99–117.

Hitz, D. (1973). Drunken Sailors and Others: Drinking Problem in Specific Occupation. *Quarterly Journal of Studies on Alcohol* 34:496–505.

Holden, R. (1991). Mortal Danger in Law Enforcement: A Statistical Comparison of Police Mortality with those of Other Occupations. Paper presented at the annual meeeting of the Academy of Criminal Justice Sciences, Nashville (March 6).

Josephson, R. and Reiser, M. (1990). Officer Suicide in the Los Angeles Police Department: A Twelve-Year Follow-up. *Journal of Police Science and Administration* 17(3): 227–29.

Kappeler, V., Sluder, R. and Alpert, G. (1994). *Forces of Deviance: Understanding the Dark Side of Policing.* Prospect Heights, IL: Waveland Press.

Kelling, G., Pate, T., Dieckman, D. and Brown, C. (1974). *The Kansas City Preventive Patrol Experiment: A Summary Report.* Washington, DC: Police Foundation.

Konstantin, D. (1984). Homicides of American Law Enforcement Officers, 1978–80. *Justice Quarterly* 1(1): 29–45.

Kraska, P. and Kappeler, V. (1988). A Theoretical and Descriptive Study of Police on Duty Drug Use. *American Journal of Police* 8(1): 1–36.

Kroes, W. (1976). *Society's Victim, the Policeman: An Analysis of Job Stress in Policing.* Springfield, IL: Charles C Thomas.

Labovitz, S. and Hagedorn, R. (1971). An Analysis of Job Suicide Rates Among Occupational Categories. *Sociological Inquiry* 41(1).

Lester, D. (1983). Stress in Police Officers: An American Perspective. *The Police Journal* 56(2): 184–93.

Lichtenberger, J. (1968). *Divorce: A Study in Social Causation.* New York: AMS Press.

Lofquist, L. and Davis, R. (1969). *Adjustment of Work.* New York: Appleton-Century-Crofts.

Mallory, T. and Mays, G. (1984). The Police Stress Hypothesis: A Critical Evaluation. *Criminal Justice and Behavior* 11(2): 197–224.

Manning, P. (1971). The Police: Mandate, Strategies and Appearances. In *Police and Society: Touchstone Readings,* V. Kappeler (ed.). Prospect Heights, IL: Waveland Press.

Mafstrofski, S. (1983). The Police and Non-Crime Services. In *Evaluating Performance of Criminal Justice Agencies,* G. Whitaker and C. Phillips (eds.). Beverly Hills: Sage.

Muir, W., Jr. (1977). *Police: Streetcorner Politicians.* Chicago: University of Chicago Press.

Niederhoffer, A. (1967). *Behind the Shield: The Police in Urban Society.* Garden City, NY: Doubleday.

Niederhoffer, A. and Niederhoffer, E. (1978). *The Police Family: From Station House to Ranch House.* Lexington, MA: Lexington Books.

O'Neill, M. and Bloom, C. (1972). The Field Officer: Is He Really Fighting Crime? *Police Chief* 39: 30–32.

Putti, J., Aryee, S. and Kang, T. (1988). Personal Values of Recruits and Officers in a Law Enforcement Agency: An Exploratory Study. *Journal of Police Science and Administration* 16(4): 249–45.

Raub, R. (1988). Death of Police Officers After Retirement. *American Journal of Police* 7(1): 91–102.

Redfield, R. (1952). The Primitive World View. *Proceedings of the American Philosophical Society* 96:30–36.

Reiss, A., Jr. (1971). *The Police and the Public.* New Haven: Yale University Press.

Reiss, A. and Bordua, D. (1967). Environment and Organization: A Perspective on the Police. In *The Police: Six Sociological Essays*, D. Bordua (ed.). New York: John Wiley and Sons.

Rubinstein, J. (1973). *City Police*. New York: Farrar, Straus and Giroux.

Sherman, L. (1983). Reducing Police Gun Use: Critical Events, Administrative Policy, and Organizational Change. In *Control in the Police Organization*, M. Punch (ed.). Cambridge: MIT Press.

_____ (1982). Learning Police Ethics. *Criminal Justice Ethics* 1(1): 10–19.

Sherman, L. and Cohn, E. with Garten, P., Hamilton, E. and Rogan, D. (1986). *Citizens Killed by Big City Police—1970–84*. Washington, DC: Crime Control Institute.

Sherman, L. and Langworthy, R. (1979). Measuring Homicide by Police Officers. *Journal of Criminal Law and Criminology* 70(4): 546–60.

Skolnick, J. (1966:). *Justice Without Trial: Law Enforcement In a Democratic Society*. New York: John Wiley and Sons.

Stack, S. and Kelley, T. (1994). Police Suicide: An Analysis. *American Journal of Police* 13(4): 73–90.

Stoddard, E. (1968). The Informal Code of Police Deviancy: A Group Approach to Blue-Collar Crime. In *Police and Society: Touchstone Readings*, V. Kappeler (ed.). Prospect Heights, IL: Waveland Press.

Straus, M., Gelles, R. and Steinmetz, S. (1980). *Behind Closed Doors: Violence in the American Family*. Garden City, NY: Anchor Books.

Terry, W., III (1983). Police Stress as an Individual and Administrative Problem: Some Conceptual and Theoretical Difficulties. *Journal of Police Science and Administration* 11(2): 156–65.

_____ (1981). Police Stress: The Empirical Evidence. *Journal of Police Science and Administration* 9(1): 61–75.

Van Raalte, R. (1979). Alcohol as a Problem Among Officers. *Police Chief* 44:38–40.

Vaughn, J. and Kappeler, V. (1986). A Descriptive Study of Law Enforcement Officers Killed, 1974–1984. Paper presented at the annual meeting of the Academy of Criminal Justice Sciences, Orlando, FL (March 18).

Violanti, J., Vena, J. and Marshall, J. (1986). Disease Risk and Mortality Among Police Officers: New Evidence and Contributing Factors. *Journal of Police Science and Administration* 14(1): 17–23.

Violanti, J., Marshall, J. and Howe, B. (1985). Stress, Coping, and Alcohol Use: The Police Connection. *Journal of Police Science and Administration* 13(2): 106–9.

Wagner, M. and Brzeczek, R. (1983). Alcoholism and Suicide: A Fatal Connection. *FBI Law Enforcement Bulletin* (August): 8–15.

Watson, N. and Sterling, J. (1969). *Police and Their Opinions*. Gaithersburg, MD: International Association of Chiefs of Police.

Westley, W. (1970). *Violence and the Police: A Sociological Study of Law Custom and Morality*. Cambridge: MIT Press.

_____ (1956). Secrecy and the Police. *Social Forces* 34(3): 254–57.

Whitehouse, J. (1965). A Preliminary Inquiry into the Occupational Disadvantages of Law Enforcement Officers. *Police* (May–June).

Wilson, J. (1968). *Varieties of Police Behavior: The Management of Law and Order in Eight Communities*. Cambridge: Harvard University Press.

Order in the Courts
The Myth of Equal Justice

11

Nor shall any State deprive any person of life, liberty, or property, without due process of law; nor deny to any person within its jurisdiction the equal protection of the laws. In all criminal prosecutions, the accused shall enjoy the right to a speedy and public trial, by an impartial jury . . .

Whether we recognize those excerpts as an Amendment to the Constitution or are only vaguely aware of the source, we often invoke the ideal they represent: equal justice for all determined by impartial judges and juries. Is the ideal a myth or reality? Is justice blind? Are cases decided on their merits, impervious to race, gender, and socioeconomic status? If justice itself were on trial, its guilt or innocence would probably vary depending upon what peers served on the jury. This chapter looks at some of the key principles and people in the judicial process—both the popular media-based trappings and the actual practice.

What images contribute to our perceptions of jurisprudence? The figure of justice symbolizes impartiality and usually appears as a blindfolded woman with a scale in one hand and a sword in the other. The Constitution and the Bill of Rights are echoes of the former; many segments of the public know only the latter. Language embodies the dual nature, as well. "With liberty and justice for all" implies fairness, equity, and what is right. "Is there no justice for that unspeakable crime" means punishment, atonement and redress. A third meaning is "lawful," but the other two reverberate more often in the collective conscience and contribute to mythical notions about how the judicial process functions.

Public images created by movies, television, novels, newspaper stories, and radio reports play up the adversarial nature of the system. Hushed spectators listen to brilliant orators arguing opposing positions in a point/counterpoint duet. The judge dressed in black robes referees the interaction from a bench elevated above the fray, gavel at hand to maintain order, fairness, and decorum. Oaths are sworn on a Bible; the language is formal and arcane: "Your Honor," "If it please the Court," "Hear ye, hear ye." The jury's attention is riveted first on testimony presented by the state—a sovereign power rather than a mere citizen—against the accused. The defense skillfully cross-examines and then presents its own version of the facts, employing all due process guarantees. Of course, these public, adversarial dramas do not bear any resemblance to the preponderance of cases disposed of bureaucratically. They do, however, offer images that creep into composite views of justice and contribute to the myth of equal justice under the law.

What is the relationship between law and society? The law, as the codified basis of the criminal justice system, serves as a banner to announce the values of society. It tells us where the boundaries of acceptable behavior lie and links those who violate the boundaries—criminals—with evil, pain, incarceration, and disgrace. Why are some behaviors illegal and not others? Are laws based on a culture's morality? Is every behavior considered deviant defined as illegal? As Erich Goode and Nachman Ben-Yehuda (1994:78) state, "Definitions of right and wrong do not drop from the skies, nor do they simply ineluctably percolate up from society's mainstream opinion; they are the result of disagreement, negotiation, conflict, and struggle. The passage of laws raises the issue of *who will criminalize whom*." By what process do crimes get defined, the criminal law created, and violators punished?

Society is composed of individuals struggling to defend their interests in interaction with others doing the same thing. According to George Vold (1958:208–9), "The whole political process of law making, law breaking, and law enforcement becomes a direct reflection of . . . fundamental conflicts between interest groups and their . . . struggles for the control of the police power of the state." The winners decide who is in violation of the law—that is, who is criminal. In Vold's description, the contact of groups is an endlessly changing kaleidoscope of force-ratios. Laws are the peace treaties intended to safeguard the prominence of the victors.

Goode and Ben-Yehuda (1994) point out that all groups in a society do not have equal access to the legal process. Some have more influence with the media, some with legislators, and some with the educational system. "Views of right and wrong do not triumph by becoming widely accepted in a society simply because they are objectively true or because they best preserve the social order or generate the greatest benefit for the greatest number of people" (Goode and Ben-Yehuda, 1994:78–79). In its most altruistic form, law is a consensus about how to safeguard everyone's interests—as understood by particular people at a particular time. The framers of the Constitution may have been engaged in unselfish efforts to construct an impartial rule of law, but women were not given the right to vote, and slavery was not illegal—constraints of the worldviews at that time.

The law, then, is not a natural, universal "truth." Law and legal institutions are a product of the society, culture and conflict. Even within a single culture, law varies (Black, 1976). The myth that police officers, prosecutors and judges are guided solely by law, rules, and regulations falls when confronted by the impossibility of full enforcement and the practice of selective enforcement. Discretion affects how much law is invoked in particular situations and occurs at every step of the process from arrest to sentencing. In actual practice, the law is much more frequently applied to visible street crimes. Lower socioeconomic groups are more likely to encounter the force of the law.

In addition, the amount of social diversity between offender and victim affects how the law is applied. Donald Black (1989:59) uses homicide to illustrate: "The amount of variation in the handling of homicide cases is spectacular, ranging from those that legal officials decide not even to investigate (as frequently occur when prisoners or skid-row vagrants kill each other) to those resulting in capital punishment (as may happen when a poor robber kills a prosperous stranger)." Impartial application of the laws is thus a myth in the case of homicide. As Michael Kramer (1994:32) notes, "Despite the many supposed safeguards, what matters most is who you are, who you kill, and who your lawyer is."

Some laws exist more to protect our mythical allegiance to what is right than to provide actual safeguards to those without power. For example, there may have been laws preventing cruelty to slaves, but if slaves could not testify in court, what use did the law serve (Williams and Murphy, 1995)? Legal rights are frequently insufficient. Citizens have the legal right to bring a lawsuit against someone who has wronged them, but the reality is that lawsuits require both time and money.

Laws prescribe and proscribe behavior; they are not philosophies. Despite the narrowness and limitations, the law often overpowers other forms of resolution. As soon as rules are written down, people suspend personal responsibility for acceptable behavior and rely on the written minimum. Social regard and concern are replaced with technical adherence to the "letter of the law." Have you ever heard someone mutter "There ought to be a law" in a situation where it would be easier to resort to some anonymous authority rather than personally devise a workable solution?

Such attitudes contribute to the myth that the law and the courts can solve all problems. Perhaps the most poignant examples come from cases involving adoptive versus biological parents. Jessica DeBoer was taken at age two and one-half from her adoptive home in Michigan and returned to her biological parents in Iowa. Baby Richard in Illinois was four years old and was removed from his adoptive home. The media seize these personal tragedies and broadcast the details incessantly; TV movies are made; books are written. The courts are criticized and judges vilified because the public refuses to recognize that the rule of law is limited. The courts do not dispense justice; at best, they administer and interpret the laws and rules as they were formulated.

A corollary of the myth that the law can solve all problems occurs when there are disparities between behavior and values. For instance, if drug use is increasing, yet society maintains a strong anti-drug value, laws can be written to punish suppliers. The original "criminals"—those who purchase the illegal drugs—can be replaced by much more evil villains, those who flaunt society's values by enticing and corrupting its youth. Society neatly resolves the discrepancy between professed values and behavior by redefining the "real" criminal. Rather than determining *why* values are rejected and redefining its laws, society shifts the blame through more laws.

The most frequent manifestation of criminal justice is repression. "Our criminal justice system—maybe every criminal justice system—includes an aspect that is downright oppressive. Criminal justice is, literally, state power. It is police, guns, prisons, the electric chair. Power corrupts; and power also has an itch to suppress. A strain of suppression runs through the whole of our story. The sufferers—burnt witches, whipped and brutalized slaves, helpless drunks thrown into fetid county jails, victims of lynch mobs—cry out to us across centuries" (Friedman, 1993:462). Once the myth that repressive laws will deter undesirable behavior takes hold, it is not easily abandoned. If two convictions were not enough to stop a criminal, "three strikes and you're out." The question about why the first two efforts at deterrence were unsuccessful is never addressed.

The media play an important role in shaping our perception of equal justice in the courts. Trials involving celebrities or spectacular crimes have an inherent attraction for the media. Even before the days of *Court TV*, the media have focused on such cases. In two instances in 1966, the media were cited by the Supreme Court in overturning convictions. Sam Sheppard's conviction for murdering his wife was overturned nine years later in part because of the "carnival" atmosphere in the courtroom. A popular television series and later a motion picture were based on the case. Jack Ruby's conviction for shooting Lee Harvey Oswald in front of television cameras was overturned after it was determined by an Appeals Court that ten of the twelve jurors had seen the shooting on television and believed he was guilty before the trial. In 1994, O.J. Simpson was accused of murdering his ex-wife and her friend; he was found not guilty in 1995. The case is instructive on a number of levels. It illustrates both the gulf between minority and majority attitudes toward the criminal justice system and the public's ambivalent attitude between enforcing the Constitution and "justice." It is also a prime example of the myth of equal justice.

After the arrest, the media engaged in endless polls about Simpson's guilt or innocence. Many more whites than African Americans believed he was guilty. Poll results probably had less to do with the evidence than with opinions about how African Americans are treated by the criminal justice system. An article in *Time* magazine described the pervasive perception among African Americans that the criminal justice system discriminates against them. Many African Americans "have begun to perceive Simpson as one more victim of the white power system. There is talk of a 'white-media conspiracy' to embarrass African Americans by toppling yet another black icon" (Smolowe, 1994:26). District of Columbia delegate Eleanor Holmes Norton expressed the opinion that "For many blacks, every black man is on trial. . . . the black man is increasingly seen as a criminal by virtue of his sex and color" (Smolowe, 1994:25–26).

The evidence gathered raised arguments over whether Simpson's rights were violated by unreasonable search and seizure. That, in turn, raises the recurring issue of how deeply the public believes in the rights of the defendant. The public desire to punish the guilty often outweighs the methods by which convictions are secured. The public is not alone in its waffling. Myron Orfield conducted a confidential survey of judges, prosecutors, and public defenders and found broad agreement that police frequently perjure themselves on 4th Amendment matters and that judges ignore the law to prevent evidence from being suppressed. Judges may be wary of antagonizing voters when the spotlight is on. One public defender said, "You bring a motion to quash in a heater case in the six months before a retention election and you should be cited for ineffective assistance of counsel" (Chapman, 1994:3).

Finally, the Simpson case has many of the trappings of the myth of equal justice. A "dream team" of fifteen defense attorneys worked on his case, at estimates of up to $60,000 per week. A hot line was established with a toll-free number and a $500,000 reward for tips leading to the arrest of the real killer. Simpson had no trouble finding a publisher for his book, *I Want to Tell You*, which will help pay for his defense and attempt to preserve his reputation. "While Simpson's fame and money alone will not garner him an acquittal, they will alter the balance of power that is traditionally skewed toward the state. Prosecutors, who can draw on big police departments, teams of investigators, and lawyers to prepare their cases, have success rates of more than 90 percent at trial in most jurisdictions. The typical murder defendant has little money and is represented by an underpaid, overworked public defender" (Streisand, 1994:63). Without the resources to combat the power of the state, most cases never reach the trial stage. Ninety percent of criminal cases are settled before trial. Albert Alschuler, law professor at the University of Chicago remarks: "Compare O.J. Simpson with the defendant who's represented by a public defender who has 500 cases a year and says 'You'd better plead guilty today because you'll get out sooner.' There's something obscene about the resources, both public and private, being devoted to this case" (Callahan, 1995:6).

"The Simpson case has demonstrated perhaps more starkly than ever before that in the American justice system, as in so much else in this country, money changes everything—and huge amounts of money change things almost beyond recognition" (Gleick, 1995:41). Paul Petterson, indigent defense coordinator for the National Association of Criminal Defense Lawyers stated, "There's a whole different system for poor people. It's in the same court-house—it's not separate—but it's not equal. If O.J. were a poor defendant from a county in rural Alabama represented by a public defender, the trial would be a two-day, open-and-shut case" (Gleick, 1995:41).

The one area over which there was some debate was whether Simpson would receive an impartial hearing. Most of the concern centered on the issue of race, as mentioned above. Questions of impartiality are not limited to race, gender, and socioeconomic bias, however. We have seen how laws reflect the culture of the society in which they are made and the interests of those who work to pass them. The judges elected to interpret the laws are equally subject to assorted influences, whether their own biases, public opinion, or unknown origins. In Maryland, voluntary manslaughter is an offense punishable by up to ten years, with recommended sentencing of three to eight years. Robert E. Cahill of the Baltimore County Circuit Court sentenced a man who pled guilty to voluntary manslaughter to eighteen months in jail, with work release. The truck driver defendant had come home, discovered his wife in bed with another man, used a loaded rifle to chase him from the house, began drinking heavily, and shot his wife in the head several hours later as she was lying on the couch. He called 911 and said he had shot his wife because she was sleeping around. During sentencing, the judge said "I cannot think of a circumstance whereby personal rage is [more] uncontrollable . . . I seriously wonder how many married men . . . would have the strength to walk away . . . without inflicting some corporal punishment" (Sjoerdsma, 1994:21). In Michigan, a Macomb County Circuit Court judge gave custody of a young child to her father (the parents had never married) because the mother had put the child in day care while she attended the University of Michigan (*Time*, 1994). Impartiality seemingly has so many hurdles that the very concept may be mythical.

The structure of equal justice in America rests on the premises of fairness and equality to legitimate the use of state power. Fairness and equality, however, are as ephemeral and mystical as the symbols of the court itself. The reality of justice in America is much harsher, and the reality of justice does violence to both fairness and equality.

The Bias of Arrest

Arrest, that point at which one is taken into official custody and charged with the commission of a crime, is in the truest sense the gateway to the criminal justice system. In a system guaranteeing equal protection under the law and equal justice to its citizens, an arrest should occur only after police and investigators have carefully gathered and sifted through the evidence of a crime. If probable cause exists, the suspect is taken into custody. The criteria for determining probable cause should be the same for everyone. This is the majesty of a criminal justice system that guarantees equal protection. It is also a myth.

The vast majority of people arrested and processed through the criminal justice system are poor, unemployed or underemployed, and undereducated (Eitzen and Zinn, 1992). Indeed, 19 percent of the individuals in our prisons had incomes of less than $3,000 prior to their arrests, 42.6 percent were not employed in full-time jobs, 60 percent had less than 12 years of education, and 50 percent made less than $10,000 a year in income (Reiman, 1995).

Research on the police clearly shows that suspects from lower socioeconomic groups and suspects who are members of minority groups are arrested more frequently, on weaker evidence, for more crimes than their white, affluent counterparts. A study by Joan Petersilia (1983) found that minority group members were arrested on weaker evidence than whites and as a result had their cases dismissed at a higher rate. In a study of the linkage between reported crimes and arrests, Liska and Chamlin (1984) found that arrest rates correlated not with reported crime, but with the degree of economic inequality in a community. "The simple fact is that for the same offense, a poor person is more likely to be arrested and, if arrested charged, than a middle- or upper-class person" (Reiman, 1990:87).

A study of police discretion in six southern cities (Powell, 1990) found a significant disparity in how police officers implement their discretionary decisions to arrest or not to arrest, with offender race strongly influencing the decision-making process. Police demonstrated a clear tendency to take more punitive actions against African-American offenders than white offenders, especially in the three most urban areas of the research sites. These findings were confirmed by recent research on case-processing in Nebraska (Johnson and Secret, 1990). In that study, race was found to be the major extralegal variable related to decisions of detention, referral to court, and sentencing. The only aspect of the justice system which seemed not to discriminate against African Americans was adjudication where whites were more likely than African Americans to be convicted. However, the researchers determined that this inconsistency was attributable not to "race-blind justice" but to the fact that African Americans are more likely to be charged and processed based on weaker evidence, as mentioned above.

There are many possible explanations for this bias in arrest (Reiman, 1990; Chambliss, 1984):

1. The living conditions, housing, and lifestyles of the poor do not provide the same level of privacy as the privileged enjoy. The wealthy have more opportunity to conceal what the poor do in public. Arrests for drugs, drinking violations, gambling, and sexual activity are more likely when warrants aren't required.

2. A middle-class or upper-class family can provide the arresting officer or prosecutor with an alternative to arrest. The son or daughter of a well-to-do family can always get "counseling," "drug treatment," "therapy," and other forms of professional help that might correct his or her aberrant behavior. The poor cannot make such overtures. The $5,000 or $10,000 needed to get a juvenile into drug treatment is not an option for the poor.

3. Police stereotyping, often learned in training, may direct attention to the disadvantaged and away from the advantaged.

4. Like all bureaucracies, policing seeks to avoid difficult problems and handles cases which are less troublesome. A middle-class or upper-class offender is more likely to take the case to trial, more likely to exercise political influence, more likely to afford a private attorney. The poor can offer no such resistance to the charges; therefore, arrests of the poor and disadvantaged are simply easier on the police bureaucracy.

Debates about the merits of these explanations obscure the basic fact that middle-class and upper-class offenders—participating in the same activities and engaging in a similar rate of criminality— are less likely to find their way into the criminal justice system.

The Bias of Trial

The police guard the entrance to the criminal justice system. As we have seen, the discretion granted officers often results in the poor, undereducated and underemployed being arrested most frequently. The criminal justice system ostensibly has safeguards to correct this injustice. The police may make arrests, but the courts will try the case.

The Participants

The judge, the prosecutor who will try the case, and the defense attorney who will represent the charged (but still innocent) defendant are all attorneys. Thus, a select group of people will try to determine the facts of the matter. Who are these select people? Judges, prosecutors, and defense attorneys are all members of their local, state and probably national bar associations. Prior to the 1920s, bar associations were exclusive social clubs, but they soon changed into professional associations of lawyers designed to restrict entrance to law as a career. The bar associations set strict educational standards, testing criteria and licensing requirements (Ladinsky, 1984). The argument for these standards, of course, was that the legal profession had a responsibility to ensure well-educated, high quality attorneys for the public. The reality, however, was that these standards virtually guaranteed that most attorneys come from segments of society whose families can afford the immense costs of a quality legal education (Chambliss and Seidman, 1986; Stone, 1915). The net result is that most attorneys come from the privileged strata of society. For example, while minorities make up about 20 percent of American society, they make up only 8.5 percent of the students in law schools (Bonsignore, et al., 1984). There is also a marked system of gender inequality in both law school admissions and in the practice of law. Most partners in law firms and most law school faculty members are still white males from middle- or upper-middle-class backgrounds. Few female lawyers have been promoted to partnership, and there are few members of racial minorities as partners in law firms (Spire, 1990). So, entrance to the legal profession is guarded not only by educational and licensing standards but by the reality of family income, gender, and ethnic background.

Once in the legal profession, this stratification process continues for most lawyers. The best lawyers, from the best schools, with the best experience are quickly absorbed into prestigious law firms practicing civil, and more particularly, corporate law. Those attorneys who find their way to the bar in the criminal courts are usually from less prestigious law schools, have less training, and come from lower socioeconomic backgrounds (Ladinsky, 1984). Greg Barak (1980) goes so far as to argue that corporate law as an institutionalized specialty acted to erode the quality of criminal defense attorneys, insuring that criminal lawyers are primarily those of poorer quality, experience, and training. Whether intended or not the outcome is the same.

Even those high-quality attorneys who choose to practice criminal law—whether out of feelings of social obligation, the eventual pursuit of a political career, or a desire for a challenge—are soon integrated into a system of mass-produced justice. While images of Perry Mason or Ben Matlock may motivate some attorneys, they soon find that the reality of practicing criminal law is far removed from the television glamour of being a defense attorney. They find themselves with heavy caseloads that preclude quality case preparation for all but the elite of the profession. They find themselves burdened with many cases, most of which are rather mundane—all of which are tried in a blur of assembly-line proceedings. Burnout among criminal lawyers is the rule, and it occurs early in their careers. Those who remain in the practice of criminal law often view a position on the bench as the next social step up and accordingly need the support of the local legal culture. Another route for practicing criminal law is to join the district attorney's office as a prosecutor. Many who aspire to future political office follow this path.

Those attorneys who come out of law school and join public defenders' offices are, for the most part, putting in their time and getting experience in order to move on to a law firm and eventually enter the more lucrative practice of civil and corporate law. Their priorities are clearly to avoid offending people in the system and to get through the public defender experience without incurring any black marks against their future acceptance into the upper strata of the practice of law (Platt and Pollack, 1975).

In *Gideon v. Wainwright* (1963), the Supreme Court ruled that indigent defendants must be supplied with counsel. They are either assigned a public defender or a private attorney appointed by the court. Neither necessarily serves the defendant well. The public defender is a public employee who is paid a salary and carries a heavy caseload. Public defenders often don't even have time to see their clients until fifteen minutes or so prior to trial, hardly time to prepare a quality defense:

> Most of the men spent very little time with their public defender. In the court in which they eventually pleaded guilty, they typically reported spending on the order of five to ten minutes with their public defender. These conversations usually took place in the bull-pen of the courthouse or in the hallway (Casper, 1972:239–240).

In addition, public defenders are employees of the court. Their professional lives depend on good working relations with prosecutors and judges. Rocking the boat will not enhance a public defender's professional life. Agreeing to a quick plea bargain that clears the court calendar and gives the prosecutor a "win," on the other hand, will (Blumberg, 1975; Casper, 1972; Skolnick, 1966). Court-assigned private attorneys are no more strongly motivated to represent their clients' interests. They are paid a set fee considerably lower than the fee they would be getting from their private clients for the same time and effort. Bringing a case to a rapid conclusion, preferably through a bargained guilty plea, is very much in their economic interest.

Abraham Blumberg's (1967) classic study of the Chicago criminal courts shows how the defense counsel impacts on the probability that the defendant will eventually go free. Blumberg (1975) found that in the majority of the cases he observed it was defense counsel who first suggested a guilty plea and then persuaded the defendant to accept the plea. Public defenders were almost twice as likely as privately retained counsel to argue for a guilty plea at the very first meeting with their client. In addition, as we might expect, privately retained counsel were twice as likely to get the charges against clients dismissed or gain a not guilty verdict than court-appointed attorneys or public defenders. Clearly the quality and commitment of the defense attorney affects the outcome of criminal cases. Equally as clearly, the ability of a defendant to successfully contest criminal charges depends on his or her ability to pay the cost of private representation. It would not stretch reality to suggest that justice is correlated with the ability to pay by the hour.

Judges sit at the apex of the judicial system. Their primary duty is the fair application of the law and the blind dispensing of individualized justice. Judges come from the highest strata of a highly stratified profession. Most are from families with considerable economic and political power—sufficient income to pay for the top law schools in the country and sufficient influence to gain admittance to those schools for their children (Chambliss and Seidman, 1986). The judiciary is a largely homogeneous group emanating from the upper-middle and upper classes of society. At the federal level this is even more pronounced. A requisite combination of an elite education, sufficient status to be appointed by the president, and a stature politically acceptable both to other lawyers and to powerful politicians ensures little social diversity on the federal bench (Chambliss and Seidman, 1986).

The underemployed, unemployed, and undereducated who make up the majority of criminal justice system clients find themselves in a legal system populated by people very unlike themselves, with little understanding of their backgrounds, their lives, or their needs. This is an obvious disadvantage, but it pales in the face of the disadvantageous position of the poor in the entire process from arrest to trial.

Pretrial Detention

After arrest, the next decision is whether to keep the defendant in jail awaiting trial, to set bond, or to release the defendant on his or her own recognizance. Bail itself is inherently discriminatory, since it requires the ability to pay. The process of arranging pretrial release is more discriminatory. Social class and race impact directly on how high bail is set (if at all) and on the probability of being released on personal recognizance (Farrell and Swigert, 1978; Carroll and Mondrick, 1976; Burke and Turk, 1975). Most of the poor brought to trial cannot pay even nominal bail, nor can they afford the services of a bailbondsman. In fact, about 42 percent of those individuals who populate our local jails are people who have been convicted of no crime at all; they are the presumed innocent awaiting their day in court (Reiman, 1990).

Beyond the obviously unpleasant fact that people who are presumed to be innocent are locked up in jails, the inability to make bail or gain release biases the entire criminal process from this point forward. First, the poor cannot afford to sit in jail. They have meager incomes from which they must support families. Unlike salaried professionals, they get no pay when they can't work—whether they are ill, in jail, or on vacation. The hardships for their families are serious and compelling. Second, they are unable to participate in preparing their own defense and seldom have the resources to hire those who could. Unlike the television image of Ben Matlock sending his trusty private detective side-kick out to track the truth, the poor are represented in court by court-appointed lawyers or public defenders, who have no investigative staff or budget. Getting statements from witnesses and gathering evidence falls on the defendant, who can do neither if he or she is behind bars. Private detectives, laboratory analyses, and expert witnesses are all expensive and well beyond the financial capabilities of almost all criminal defendants. All these factors create an irresistible pressure on the defendant to agree to a plea bargain.

Once again, contrary to our television images of trials and lawyers, very few cases actually go in front of a jury. In the rare instance that a case goes to trial, imagine the impression on the judge or jury of a defendant dressed in a jail uniform versus someone in a neatly pressed suit. Somewhere between 70 percent and 95 percent of all criminal cases are resolved by a plea bargain

(Reiman, 1995). The pressures on a poor defendant to plea bargain are enormous. A guilty plea usually means he or she will get out with time served (the time already spent in jail because bail or release were denied) or a small additional sentence. That means family support can resume and personal needs can be met. Even if the defendant believes that he or she is innocent, there is a powerful incentive working here to "cop a plea" to a lesser charge simply to end the ordeal begun by arrest. This powerful impetus toward a guilty plea, regardless of guilt or innocence, begins with the lack of quality legal representation compounded by the issue of pretrial detention.

The process of plea bargaining contributes to the bureaucracy of the court—and marks further divergence from the myth of justice through an adversarial system. Rather than a fair contest between evenly matched parties, the system becomes administrative screening: which cases are more likely to fit a profile of speedy prosecution and conviction? Plea bargaining is normally hidden from public view; discretion is more easily practiced without much scrutiny. Lawrence Friedman (1993) links the discovery process with this move toward administration. Although intended as beneficial to defendants, discovery was "also a symptom of the long-term secular shift in power away from the lay jury and the trial itself toward an administered, bureaucratic, professional system of justice. In this sense, discovery was, to a degree, a blood brother of plea bargaining . . ." (Friedman, 1993:387).

Most cases never reach the trial stage, as Friedman (1993:386) points out.

> Trial, especially trial by jury, is what all of us think of when we think of felony procedures. But, in fact, the trial is the residue of a residue: it is a mechanism for handling survivors of a long filtering process. Not all serious criminals are caught; not all those who are caught are arrested; not all those who are arrested are charged; and most of those who are charged never reach trial—their cases are dropped, or they plead guilty.

Despite the rarity of trial, it is interesting to contrast the mythical aspects of trials when they do occur with reality. Jury tampering is a common phrase that the public knows is illegal, but what precisely does the phrase mean? In highly publicized cases like the Simpson trial, both defense attorneys and prosecutors use the press to plant seeds in the public's—and potential jurors'—minds. Another perfectly legal resource—if clients can afford it—is the jury consultant. Clients pay up to six figures to hire experts who will attempt to predict how potential jurors will vote. They investigate the associations to which jurors belong, the cars they drive, where they live, how they maintain the lawn, and any other behavior which might give clues to predispositions or biases. Once the trial begins, consultants monitor jurors' responses (body language and other nonverbal indicators) to opening statements, cross-examination style, and objections. The jury itself is often composed of people who could not find an excuse not to serve. In today's increasingly disparate society, what precisely does a jury of one's peers constitute? Trials where juries are sequestered from their families for months at a time call into question the requirement of a unanimous vote. Will people continue to discuss the facts of the case endlessly, or will their patience be exhausted and they'll vote to be able to return home?

So, the poor are more likely to be arrested for crimes than the well-to-do, more likely to be denied their freedom awaiting an adjudication, and more likely to be convicted because they cannot afford high-quality legal representation. One distinguishing characteristic separates those who go free from those who do not—money. The same characteristic separates those who go to prison from those who do not.

The Bias of Sentencing

Once a defendant has been adjudicated as guilty it falls on the court to hand down a sentence appropriate to the crime and its circumstances. The doctrine of equality, fairness, and equal protection under the law dictates that this decision not be affected by extraneous factors, such as race, gender, or socioeconomic status. The reality is that such factors play a critical role in the sentencing decision.

The empirical research done by criminal justice scholars has demonstrated with remarkable regularity that minority group members (particularly African Americans) and the poor get longer sentences and have less chance of gaining parole or probation, even when the seriousness of the crime and the criminal record of the defendants are held constant (Bridges and Crutchfield, 1988; Myers, 1987; Walsh, 1987; Zatz, 1987). Without belaboring the point by discussing the dozens of studies which have demonstrated such bias in sentencing, a few illustrative examples will suffice in making the point.

A study by Chiricos and Bales (1991) of 1,970 defendants arrested in Florida found both race and class bias. They found that unemployed black defendants are most likely to be imprisoned.

They suggest that sentencing patterns demonstrate that in addition to using prison as a means of punishment they are also used as warehouses for surplus labor.

Even in rural areas such disparities are apparent. For example, a South Dakota study compared the severity of punishment meted out to whites and Native Americans. Race was the statistically significant variable which explained the differences in punishment severity (Feimer, Pommerstein, and Wise, 1990).

In a study of sentencing practices involving 8,414 Detroit-area defendants convicted of violent felonies, Spohn and Cederblom (1991) determined that the defendant's race had a direct effect on the decision to incarcerate and an indirect effect on sentence length. African-American defendants were significantly more likely than white defendants to be sentenced to prison.

Joan Petersilia (1983:28), studying sentencing patterns in California, Michigan, and Texas found:

> Controlling for the factors most likely to influence sentencing and parole decisions, the analysis still found that blacks and Hispanics are less likely to be given probation, more likely to receive prison sentences, more likely to receive longer prison sentences, and more likely to serve a greater proportion of their original time.

In looking at the death penalty, recent research has concluded that racial bias is both compelling and pervasive in capital cases. Keil and Vito (1992) found systematic discrimination in the application of capital punishment, with African Americans who kill white victims far more likely to receive capital punishment than whites who kill other whites. A Florida study by Radelet and Pierce (1991) found a strong correlation between both the defendant's race and the victim's race in the application of the death penalty. In cases with white victims the defendant was six times more likely to get the death penalty than in cases with African-American victims. Moreover, African-American defendants who killed white victims were more than twice as likely to receive the death penalty than were white defendants who killed white victims. Finally, African-American defendants who killed white victims were fifteen times more likely to be sentenced to death than were African-American defendants who killed African-American victims. Radelet and Pierce conclude that racial discrimination, both offender-based and victim-based, permeates the contemporary use of capital punishment.

The evidence of discrimination in sentencing based on socioeconomic status and race is compelling, but it is only part of the story. When we look at sentencing practices from the other side of the coin the disparity becomes even more marked. Consider this. If we look at crimes that only the affluent can commit—antitrust violations, embezzlement, income tax evasion, price-fixing—we find the courts "kinder and gentler." Rarely are these offenders sentenced to prison (Barnett, 1981). Despite the fact that these crimes of the affluent are indeed criminal offenses, the court is given— and exercises with regularity—other options for the more refined and sophisticated criminal. Rather than prison, these offenders usually face such punishments as fines, consent decrees, warnings, and cease and desist orders (Frank, 1985). Despite the fact that these crimes do infinitely more damage to society in terms of economic cost, death, and injury, the criminal justice system suddenly considers the "quality of mercy" in dealing with these offenders.

From the time of arrest, through pretrial detention, through the criminal trial and into prison, the key factor which determines the severity and harshness with which the criminal justice system treats its clients is money. Those who can commit sophisticated crimes, pay high-priced attorneys, and afford private treatment and counseling will find justice with a merciful and caring face. Those who cannot will find long sentences and prison to be their punishment for being poor.

Just as our concept of "criminal" extends far beyond "illegal," our concept of justice has become a mystical veil shielding us from the reality of unsolvable problems and a system that cannot live up to expectations. To improve the legal system, we apply the same failed formula—we pass more laws. We persist in the unfounded assumption that the legal code is similar to the cause-and-effect laws of nature. It is not. It is prescribed or proscribed behavior devised to protect and regulate interests. The law enables some interests and restricts others. It legitimates some behavior and punishes others. Behind every legal judgment is a social and political judgment. The shining ideal of justice is that it is blind; behind the ideal is the reality that the law is a social construction, not an unassailable truth.

This brings us to one additional definition of justice: justification. The reality of the legal system is not innocent until proven guilty beyond a reasonable doubt before a jury of peers. The reality is that who you are, where you live, whom you know, and the assets you have to defend yourself determine what kind of justice you will receive. Those most like "us" are presumed innocent—and often, for that reason, are never charged and never enter the process. Suspicions about "others" are usually cause for arrest—which in turn results in presumptions of guilt and justifies looking the other way when constitutional rights are violated or plea bargaining is accepted because someone cannot afford any other choice. Even the concept of applying the law equally is inherently inequitable, but we cling to the cherished notion of equality to justify the established system. The gap between standards and reality—the law in theory and the law in action—is much more than a philosophical discussion for those who must experience it.

Crime covers an extensive range of behavior. The only unifying theme is that the behavior has been defined as illegal. Again, the law only regulates behavior. It doesn't change attitudes, and it can't solve tangled political and social problems. Alcohol and abortion have been both legal and illegal. Attitudes about the two topics create problems which the law cannot solve, yet we continually turn to the system to accomplish a task for which it was not designed. Real solutions require rational thinking and hard choices by the public and elected officials, not tough-on-crime rhetoric mindlessly trumpeting the need for more laws and mandatory sentences.

Analyzing the myths about the legal system reveals a great deal about the values held by society. In the debate over freedom versus order, where does justice fit? Do we believe in defendants' rights, or does that depend on the defendant? Are protection of people and property more important than protection of constitutional rights?

Sources

Barak, G. (1980). *In Defense of Whom? A Critique of Criminal Justice Reform*. Cincinnati: Anderson.

Barnett, H. (1981). Corporate Capitalism, Corporate Crime. *Crime and Delinquency* 27(1): 4-23.

Black, D. (1989). *Sociological Justice*. New York: Oxford University Press.

——— (1976). *The Behavior of Law*. New York: Academic Press.

Blumberg, A. (1967). *Criminal Justice*. Chicago: Quadrangle.

——— (1975). The Practice of Law and a Confidence Game: Organizational Cooptation of a Profession. In *Criminal Law in Action*. W. Chambliss (ed.). Santa Barbara: Hamilton.

Bonsignore, J., Katsh, E., D'Errico, P. Pipkin, R., Arons, S. and Rifkin, J. (1984). *Before the Law: An Introduction to the Legal Process*. Dallas: Houghton-Mifflin.

Bridges, G. and Crutchfield, R. (1988). Law, Social Standing and Racial Disparities in Imprisonment. *Social Forces* 66(3): 699–724.

Burke, P. and Turk, A. (1975). Factors Affecting Post Arrest Disposition: A Model for Analysis. *Social Problems* 22:213–32.

Callahan, P. (1995). To O.J. or Not to O.J.: That is the Question at Law School. *Chicago Tribune*, (January 30), sec.1:6.

Carroll, L. and Mondrick, M. (1976). Racial Bias in the Decision to Grant Parole. *Law and Society Review* 11(1): 93–107.

Casper, J. (1972). Did You Have a Lawyer When You Went to Court? No, I Had a Public Defender. In *Criminal Justice: Law and Politics*, G. Cole, (ed.). Belmont, CA: Duxbury: 239–40.

Chambliss, W. (1984). *Criminal Law in Action*, 2nd ed. New York: John Wiley.

Chambliss, W. and Seidman, R. (1986). *Law, Order, and Power*, 2nd ed. Reading, MA: Addison-Wesley.

Chapman, S. (1994). The Simpson Case and the Problem of the Constitution. *Chicago Tribune*, (July 10): 3.

Chiricos, T. and Bales, W. (1991). Unemployment and Punishment: An Empirical Assessment. *Criminology* 29(4): 701–24.

Eitzen, D. and Zinn, M. (1992). *Social Problems*. Needham Heights, MA: Allyn and Bacon.

Farrell, R. and Swigert, V. (1978). Prior Offense Record as a Self-Fulfilling Prophecy. *Law and Society Review* 12:437–53.

Feimer, S., Pommerstein, F. and Wise, S. (1990). Marking Time: Does Race Make a Difference? A Study of Disparate Sentencing in South Dakota. *Journal of Crime and Justice* 13(1): 86–102.

Frank, N. (1985). *Crimes Against Health and Safety*. Albany, NY: Harrow and Heston.

Friedman, L. (1993). *Crime and Punishment in American History*. New York: Basic Books.

Gideon v. Wainwright, 372 U.S. 335 (1963).

Gleick, E. (1995). Rich Justice, Poor Justice. *Time*, (June 19):41.

Goode, E., and Ben-Yehuda, N. (1994). *Moral Panics: The Social Construction of Deviance*. Cambridge, MA: Blackwell.

Johnson, J. and Secret, P. (1990). Race and Juvenile Court Decision Making Revisited. *Criminal Justice Policy Review* 4(2): 159–87.

Keil, T. and Vito, G. (1992). Effects of the *Furman* and *Gregg* Decisions on Black-White Execution Ratios in the South. *Journal of Criminal Justice* 20(3): 217–26.

Kramer, M. (1994). Frying Them Isn't the Answer. *Time*, (March 14): 32.

Ladinsky, J. (1984). The Impact of Social Background of Lawyers in Legal Practice and the Law. In *Before the Law*, Bonsignore et al., (eds.) Boston, MA: Houghton-Mifflin.

Liska, A. and Chamlin, M. (1984). Social Structure and Crime Control among Macrosocial Units. *American Journal of Sociology* 90(2): 383–95.

Milovanovic, D. (1988). *Weberian and Marxian Perspectives on Law*. Aldershot, Hampshire: Gower.

Myers, M. (1987). Economic Inequality and Discrimination in Sentencing. *Social Forces* 65(3): 376.

Petersilia, J. (1983). *Racial Disparities in the Criminal Justice System*. Santa Monica, CA: The Rand Corporation.

Platt, A. and Pollack, R. (1975). Changing Lawyers: The Careers of Public Defenders. *Issues in Criminology* 9.

Powell, D. (1990). Study of Police Discretion in Six Southern Cities. *Journal of Police Science and Administration* 17(1): 1–7.

Radelet, M. and Pierce, G. (1991). Choosing Those Who Will Die: Race and the Death Penalty in Florida. *Florida Law Review* 43(1): 1034.

Reiman, J. (1995). *The Rich Get Richer and the Poor Get Prison*, 4th ed. Boston: Allyn & Bacon.

_____ (1990). *The Rich Get Richer and the Poor Get Prison*, 3rd ed. New York: Macmillan.

Sjoerdsma, A. (1994). Justice: Eighteen Months for a Wife's Life. *Chicago Tribune*, (November 14): 21.

Skolnick, J. (1966). *Justice Without Trial: Law Enforcement in a Democratic Society*. New York: John Wiley and Sons.

Smolowe, J. (1994). Race and the O.J. Case. *Time*, (August 1): 25–26.

Spire, R. (1990). Breaking Up the Old Boy Network. *Trial* 26(2): 57–58.

Spohn, C. and Cederblom, J. (1991). Race and Disparities in Sentencing: A Test of the Liberation Hypothesis. *Justice Quarterly* 8(3): 305–27.

Stone, H. (1915). Legal Education and Democratic Principle. *American Bar Journal*, 639–46.

Streisand, B. (1994). Can He Get a Fair Trial? *U.S. News & World Report*, (October 3): 61–63.

Time (1994). Day Careless. (August 8): 28.

Vold, G. (1958). *Theoretical Criminology*. New York: Oxford University Press.

Walsh, A. (1987). The Sexual Stratification Hypothesis and Sexual Assaults in Light of the Changing Conception of Race. *Criminology* 25(1): 153–74.

Williams, J. and Gold, M. (1972). From Delinquent Behavior to Official Delinquency. *Social Problems* 20(2): 209–29.

Williams, H. and Murphy, P. (1995). The Evolving Strategy of Police: A Minority View. In *The Police and Society: Touchstone Readings*, V. Kappeler (ed.). Prospect Heights, IL: Waveland.

Zatz, M. (1987). The Changing Forms of Racial Ethnic Bias in Sentencing. *Journal of Research in Crime and Delinquency* 24(1): 69–92.

Cons and Country Clubs
The Mythical Utility of Punishment

12

In the previous chapter, the myth of equal justice was dissected. We learned that who you are and who your lawyer is often determine whether you are presumed innocent or assumed guilty. Now we turn to the corrections system which oversees the results of the efforts of the police and the courts. If a verdict of guilty is returned, is the playing field finally levelled? The comforting myth tells us that fairness and equity determine punishment. But does it?

In 1995 a jury returned a guilty verdict for an unspeakable crime. In this instance, the jury chose life imprisonment for Susan Smith for drowning her two young sons. For nine days in the fall of 1994, Smith told her neighbors in Union, South Carolina—and the nation—that a black man in a knit cap had carjacked her vehicle and abducted her sons at gunpoint. Richard Lacayo (1994:46) described it as reaching for the "available nightmare" to excuse her own deadly impulses by "recasting them in the features of some unnerving outsider." Despite the rage generated when the deception was revealed, ten months later the jury chose not to invoke the death penalty. The trial had revealed a tragic childhood of sexual abuse and suicide attempts. The question is would the mythical carjacker have received the same sympathy? Was the jury influenced by the fact that Susan Smith was "one of them"—not an unknown stranger, no matter how reprehensible her crime. Do we focus on the offense when it is committed by those who are not "like us" and on the offender if we "know" them?

Equity of punishment for similar crimes is one fertile area for myths about corrections. In the preceding chapters, we have looked at myths which have been invented to explain otherwise incomprehensible crimes and at myths devised to make us feel good about ourselves or about the system—idealized versions of much more gritty reality. The corrections system is interesting in that the media play a reduced role in contributing to and promoting myths. The occasional article will report the latest statistics released by government sources about the number of people in the system, and the prison film is sometimes revisited. For the most part, the public simply isn't interested in corrections, unless a sensational event occurs such as a riot or the murder of Jeffrey Dahmer. The death penalty is the only topic that receives consistent news coverage— or programs for which officials are seeking approval (and funding) such as boot camps, shock incarceration or electronic monitoring. The assumptions which helped construct the system also assume the problem is solved once this phase is reached.

What are the assumptions which helped create the system? Lawrence Friedman points to the universality of punishment as a solution to undesirable behavior. Parents punish children by taking away privileges. The punishment is often characterized as "teaching a lesson." Teachers discipline students who don't follow the rules; managers penalize unproductive employees. In Friedman's (1993:10) terms, punishment raises the price of undesirable behavior and attempts to control certain actions by making them more costly.

Punishment is thus a cornerstone of corrections. Beyond the concept of punishment, what is expected of the corrections system? As one group of researchers (Crouch et al., 1995:65) put it, "In spite of our extensive use of prisons, we do not have a unified and widely accepted prison policy. Our failure to develop a consistent prison policy results from the many conflicting definitions of what prison can or should accomplish. For example, we expect prisons to keep honest citizens honest (general deterrence), deter offenders from additional law-breaking behavior (specific deterrence), isolate criminals from the community (incapacitation), inflict a just measure of suffering on them (retribution), and yet somehow 'cure' them of their anti-social attitudes and behavior (rehabilitation)." As these researchers ask, are these rationales for incarceration reasonable, compatible, and/or achievable? Is the system grounded on mythical, incompatible premises masquerading as rationales?

The public appetite for more punitive sanctions including "three strikes" and "truth in sentencing" laws has taken a harsh toll on the criminal justice system. In California, for example, defendants charged with a third felony (25 years to life imprisonment, as dictated by the law) refuse to plea bargain which previously settled 90 percent of all felony cases (Smolowe, 1994b:63). The result is overcrowded jails, courts which cannot handle the cases, and endless delays. Each month, Los Angeles County's jail releases 4,200 inmates ahead of schedule because of third-strike felons awaiting a jury trial (Brandon, 1995) Compounding the problem is the fact that California's law does not distinguish between violent and nonviolent felons for the third strike. One judge reported, "In practice, it nets in a huge number of lightweight offenders" (Smolowe, 1994b:63). In April 1995, Steven White, a drug addict who stole to support his drug habit but never committed a violent crime, was charged with his third strike—stealing a VCR. He committed suicide before going to trial. His public defender in San Diego County stated, " It's a morally irresponsible law. Even from the most benign light, it's financially irresponsible. Do you want to pay $20,000 to $40,000 a year to house people who are essentially a public nuisance, or do you want to focus on individuals who are murderers and rapists?" Despite its thirty prisons and four more under construction, California will need more by the end of the century if the incarceration rate continues unabated.

As Lawrence Friedman writes, "We throw people into prison at an astonishing rate. There has never been anything like it in American history. Penology is overwhelmed by the sheer pressure of bodies. The general public is not interested in rehabilitation, not interested in what happens inside the prisons, not interested in reform or alternatives. It wants only to get these creatures off the streets." According to Friedman, society does not randomly choose methods of punishment. Ideas about the causes and cures of crime "rattle about in the heads of good citizens. How afraid are people of crime? How high on the agenda is crime and punishment?" (Friedman, 1993:315–16). Erich Goode and Nachman Ben-Yehuda point out that during times of stress, "punitive policies reflect the public's desire for scapegoats who are seen as responsible for society's problems, against whom anger, resentment, and anxiety can be directed. During times of stress, such policies 'express a collective yearning' for retribution" (Goode and Ben-Yehuda, 1994:130, citations omitted).

Also contributing to the unparalleled growth in inmates is the war on drugs. As the warden at Stateville Correctional Center in Illinois, Tony Godinez, puts it, "No one foresaw the magnitude of the drug problem. An absolute explosion. It's possible, however, that we have exacerbated the problem by making the laws as strict as they are. You put a dealer away, you make an opportunity for someone else to step in and take his job. Yesterday you had one criminal. Today you've got one criminal and one inmate. Are you safer? No. Does it cost you more? Yes" (Lindeman, 1995:19).

While there have been periods when rehabilitation was considered an appropriate response to deviant behavior, the often revisited attitude has been that criminals deserve whatever they get—punishment is supposed to be painful. Much of the history of prisons in this country was one of abominable living conditions. Joseph Fishman visited a number of jails early in the twentieth century and described them as "human dumping grounds" where inmates were left "to wallow in a putrid mire demoralizing to body, mind, and soul" (Friedman, 1993:310). The Oklahoma Commissioner of Charities and Corrections, Kate Barnard, visited the Kansas Penitentiary in 1908 and found massive brutality, floggings, water torture, and "minor" operations to the genitals of sodomists (Friedman, 1993).

Current charges that prisons coddle prisoners are not new. They repeat a well-established myth. "The underlying problem of prisons, of course, was political and social: the men and women locked up were the lumpenproletariat; many of them were black; and the general public neither knew nor cared what happened to them. Indeed, people *wanted* prisoners to be treated harshly. Anything halfway decent was sneered at as a 'country club.' Governor Haskell's reaction to Kate Barnard's charges were typical 'Kate would like to see the prisoners kept in rooms and fed and treated as if they were guests at the Waldorf Astoria'" (Friedman, 1993:312, citations omitted).

Theoretically, prisoner's rights had always been protected by the Eighth Amendment which prohibits cruel and unusual punishment, but during the first half of this century, courts refused to respond to complaints. Federal judges felt that they should not interfere in prison operations even if prisoners complained that their rights were violated by abuse and overcrowding (Crouch et al,

1995). The classic prison institution was viewed as a zone of power in which inmates were essentially slaves. The prison was "a model of discipline; the prisoner was silent, isolated, cut off from the world, helpless but not hopeless—raw matter, which the prison tried to mold. The prison controlled every aspect of the prisoner's life: food eaten, clothes worn, type of haircut, books read, mail written, when to get up, and what time lights went out" (Friedman, 1993:314).

Eventually, the courts ruled against some practices—sometimes against entire state systems—as violating standards of decency, being disproportionate to the offense, and as unnecessary and wanton infliction of pain. However, "court intervention to improve prison conditions and limit crowding was on a collision course with trends promoting a more punitive attitude toward offenders and greater degrees of incarceration" (Crouch et al, 1995:73).

The attitude of the 1950s and 1960s that offenders were sometimes as much victims of society as the reverse lost ground. "While researchers have at various times declared offenders to be biologically deficient, mentally defective, poorly trained, or lacking social controls, to most citizens they are simply evil. The public wants criminals to be dealt with in a way that not only controls their behavior but symbolizes society's anger and desire to exclude, hurt, or eliminate law violators" (Crouch et al, 1995:68). The thorny issue of prisoner's rights which the public perceived as an oxymoron spurred an emphasis on victim's rights. The public reacted against a system that was perceived as caring more for the rights of criminals than the rights of the innocent—which granted the undeserving far more than was deserved. "In an age of paralyzing fear, the middle class gives off as it were a great shout: 'We don't care who these people are, and what excuses they give, or what their backgrounds are. We want them caught, convicted, and put away!' " (Friedman, 1993:306).

Despite some rulings protecting prisoners from cruel and unusual punishment, the courts have also supported the belief that prison should be unpleasant. As Robert Johnson and Hans Toch (1982:13) tell us, this concept

> has been sanctioned (one is tempted to say "sanctified") by the courts. The Supreme Court held that "to the extent that (prison) conditions are restrictive and even harsh, they are part of the penalty that criminal offenders must pay for their offenses against society" (Rhodes v. Chapman, 1981:2392, 2400). The Court's majority not only concluded that "the Constitution does not mandate comfortable prisons," but that "prisons . . . which house persons convicted of serious crimes, cannot be free of discomfort."

Another assumption of the correctional system is that prison serves as a deterrent both for committing crime and for keeping criminals away from committing more crime. After all, if the promised punishment is severe enough, people will think twice about committing a crime.

> Stiffen the backbone of the system, make it more certain that criminals pay for their crimes, and pay hard; surely crime will dwindle as a consequence. Deterrence—that is the key. Moreover, a burglar in jail can hardly break into your house. This effect is called "incapacitation." It, too, seems like plain common sense. If the crooks are all behind bars, they cannot rape and loot and pillage. The death penalty, of course, is the ultimate incapacitator.

> Never mind soft-headed worry about causes of crime; forget poverty, unemployment, racism, and slums; forget personality and culture. Use the steel rod of criminal justice to stamp out crime, or to reduce it to an acceptable level. Get rid of sentimentality; take the rusty sword down from the wall; let deterrence and incapacitation do their job. (Friedman, 1993:456, citations omitted.).

Unfortunately, the theory is flawed. Wilbert Rideau, an inmate in the Louisiana State Penitentiary, responded to a question about whether tougher sentences were a restraining influence.

> Not at all. The length of a prison sentence has nothing to do with deterring crime. That theory is a crock. I mean, I've lived with criminals for 31 years. I know these guys, and myself. That's not the way it works. When the average guy commits a crime, he's either at the point where he doesn't care what happens to him, or more likely he feels he is going to get away with it. Punishment never factors into the equation. He just goes ahead because he feels he won't get caught (Woodbury, 1993:33).

A Milwaukee gang member had the same reaction when asked about Wisconsin's third strike law. "The law don't make no difference to me because I ain't gonna get caught. I mean, if I really thought I was gonna get caught, I wouldn't commit a crime in the first place, now would I?" (Smolowe, 1994b:63).

So we have a number of assumptions and attitudes contributing to views of the correctional system. The public sees prisons as a place to send prisoners to punish them and to get them off the streets; judges assume they are responsibly discharging their duties to distribute punishment fairly, without the emotional vengeance of the public; the police and prosecutors hope deterrence will keep others from committing similar crimes. Finally, there are the prison administrators who must store, feed, clothe, supply medical care, and protect the inmates with the help of corrections officers—within the limits of the budget provided. So what is life in prison like now that the courts have provided rudimentary guarantees of sanitary conditions? The second part of this chapter will look specifically at losses suffered as a result of incarceration, but first we'll briefly look at some "inside views."

Behind Bars

Prison Life is a magazine for inmates which was resurrected in 1994. Its editor-in-chief is Richard Stratton, who spent eight years in a penitentiary before having his sentence commuted. He believes that inmates need a voice and the public needs to be set straight. "I'm not going to pull any punches. Prison is a profane place. It's a place with gritty, harsh realities and that's what I want the magazine to reflect." The magazine takes issue with the Drug war, mandatory sentencing, abusive correctional officers, inhumane prison conditions and the perception that inmates are worthless animals who deserve to rot behind bars (Marx, 1995b:2.).

Wilbert Rideau answered a question about the effect of the get-tough mood on prisons.

> Since the 1970s, they have increasingly become just giant warehouses where you pack convicts to suffer. Look around me in this place. It's a graveyard, a human wasteland of old men— most of them just sitting around waiting to die. Of the 5,200 inmates here, 3,800 are lifers or serving sentences so long they will never get out. America has embraced vengeance as its criminal-justice philosophy. People don't want solutions to crime, they only want to feel good. That is what politicians are doing, they're making people feel secure. They offer them a platter of vindictiveness (Woodbury, 1993:33).

A corrections officer at Cook County Jail's Division 1 maximum-security facility in Chicago asked: "You ever had a dream where there is a huge ball of fire and you're entering hell? Well, this is it. This is worse than hell" (Marx, 1995a:2). The reporter who interviewed Warden Godinez described Stateville like this:

> It's a factory with only one product: detention, keeping these people away from you. Almost two out of three inmates are

double-celled, meaning they live with another inmate in a 6-by-9 room built for one person. Two bunks and a toilet. It's like living in your bathroom with a roommate. . . . When the place is locked down, the inmates leave their cells—escorted—only for visits or medical emergencies. They eat in their cells. On the eighth day they get a shower (Lindeman, 1995:19).

Contrary to these portrayals, many citizens believe that our prisons do not punish offenders severely enough. Institutions are perceived as places where individuals leisurely pass their time watching color TV, oblivious to the responsibilities that persons on the outside are forced to meet. After all, inmates are provided with three meals a day and have a roof over their heads. The only problem with this view is that it is largely a myth. As Robert B. Levinson (1982:242) writes, "the idea of a country club correctional center is about as viable a notion as the existence of the Loch Ness monster—many people believe in it but nobody has ever seen one." In reality, prison is the harsh and painful experience described above that provides inmates with few amenities.

Most research has concentrated on inmates in male medium and maximum security institutions. As a result, much of the discussion in this chapter is restricted to male prisoners. This is not for reasons of exclusion but rather a recognition that crime is predominately a male pastime.

In 1994, the 64,403 women incarcerated represented 6.1 percent of the total number (1,053,738) of persons incarcerated (BJS, 1995). Until more research is available on female prisoners, views of the system are primarily confined to discoveries made in male prisons.

After discussing general deprivations in prison, we take a look at how contrary to popular myth, prison has become a more painful experience in recent decades and how several recent innovations in punishment make incarceration even more unpleasant. Next, we explore some of the problems that inmates must overcome after release if they are to adjust to life in the community. Finally, to gain some insight regarding the question of whether American inmates are actually being "coddled," we compare their experience with that of persons incarcerated in Scandinavian prisons.

The Pains of Imprisonment

Many years ago, Gresham Sykes (1958) noted that inmates in maximum security prisons face a number of significant deprivations. In addition to losing their liberty, inmates are deprived of heterosexual relationships, goods and services, autonomy, and security. According to Robert Johnson and Hans Toch (1982:17), "Much of Sykes's work applies to today's prisons. Deprivations remain basic and painful, some convicts play stylized subcultural roles, and [correctional officers] sometimes compromise principles to maintain order. Prisons still explode in senseless violence."

They point out that inmates often face manipulation, exploitation and violence. Crowded prisons are not only uncomfortable, they are volatile. Riots often represent organizational failures, yet the public commonly views them as certifying established attitudes as legitimate: prisoners are incorrigible and unworthy of the rights enjoyed by the rest of us.

> Living in prison has never been easy, and this holds true whether we are talking about the ostensibly hardened convict or the tender novice. The task of adjustment is made more difficult by the fact that simple survival or endurance is not enough. Prisoners must cope with prison life in *competent* and *socially constructive* ways if the experience of imprisonment is not to add to recurring problems of alienation and marginality. . . . The prisoner is confronted by a hostile or indifferent prison environment in which denial of personal problems and manipulation of others are primary ingredients of interpersonal life. The result is that the prison's survivors become tougher, more pugnacious, and less able to feel for themselves or others, while its nonsurvivors become weaker, more susceptible, and less able to control their lives (Johnson and Toch, 1982:19).

The discussion below provides a generic overview of the losses inmates confront in prison. Of course, each of the 1.5 million inmates incarcerated today will react differently to the losses, depending on their individual ability to adapt.

Clearly, the loss of liberty is central to the prison experience. Inmates are cut off from the outside world, and their personal space shrinks almost to extinction. Christopher A. Innes (1986) reports that about one-third of prison inmates in 1984 were held in single-cells that averaged 68 square feet of living space per individual. Almost twenty-five percent were housed with another inmate in cells originally designed for one person—thus reducing living area to 34 square feet per individual.

Movement within the institution is controlled. For some prisoners, their movement is almost entirely constricted. John Irwin and James Austin (1994) note that a number of states are constructing so-called "maxi-maxi" facilities to house recalcitrant inmates. These facilities are modelled on the federal prison at Marion, Illinois, where inmates remain in lock-down almost around the clock. For example, California has constructed a segregated housing unit at Pelican Bay where prisoners spend 22.5 hours each day in windowless cells built of stainless steel and solid blocks of concrete (Irwin and Austin, 1994).

The loss of liberty includes separation from family members and friends. Although inmates are allowed to receive mail and have approved visitors, it is often difficult to maintain relationships. Many institutions are located in remote rural areas—far from the urban centers where most inmates and their families reside. Frequently, these facilities are not accessible by public transportation. If visitors do not have access to a dependable automobile, the funds to operate it, and time off from jobs, traveling to the institution on a regular basis can be difficult and time-consuming, if not impossible.

Enforced separation places an enormous psychological strain on the bond between inmate and family. Prisoners may become concerned about the sexual fidelity of their partner; inmates with children worry about their well-being. Many individuals become anxious that their status in the family will diminish or that they will be abandoned by their spouse.

Deprivation of heterosexual relationships is a significant pain of imprisonment that often has serious social and psychological impacts on the prisoner. Relatively few jurisdictions in the United States allow inmates to have conjugal visits. This absence contributes to the high level of sexual tension that pervades institutions.

Another pain that prisoners must confront is the loss of goods and services. The basic survival needs are met; inmates do not go hungry or die from exposure to the elements. In addition, inmates generally receive adequate health care and are provided with an opportunity to exercise. However, prisoners are confined to the bare minimum, with enormously restricted opportunity to seek higher levels of satisfaction. Their environment is stark and forbidding. Although the food meets basic nutritional standards, it is generally boring and plain. There are only a few pieces of basic furniture and inmates are allowed few personal effects with which to express their individuality. Having been reared in a society that measures the worth of an individual largely in terms of material possessions, this deprivation results in an enormous amount of psychological distress and questioning of one's self-worth.

Loss of autonomy is another pain that inmates must confront. Persons incarcerated in correctional institutions are told when they may eat, sleep, shower, leave their cells or engage in other activities. One of the characteristics of adulthood is the ability to make decisions about things that affect one's life. Because inmates are denied any opportunity to make these basic decisions, they are in effect being reduced "to the weak, helpless, dependent status of childhood" (Sykes, 1958). This problem is compounded because the prison administration generally does not give prisoners any rationale for decisions. As Sykes (1958) notes, "providing explanations carries an implication that those who are ruled have a right to know."

The most significant pain of imprisonment is the loss of security. As an inmate at the New Jersey State Prison told Sykes (1958:77), "the worst thing about prison is you have to live with other prisoners." Lee H. Bowker (Bowker, 1982; 1980) notes that prison victimization may be either psychological, economic, social or physical. There are numerous negative effects for inmates: withdrawing from prison activities, "feelings of helplessness and depression, economic hardship, physical injury, disruption of social relationships, damaged self-image" (1982:69).

Psychological victimization is extremely common in prisons. It may involve verbal manipulation designed to trick inmates into performing sex or giving up certain material goods without a fight (Bowker, 1982). In other cases, inmates may be psychologically damaged by rumors circulated by other prisoners or correctional officers specifically to inflict emotional distress and to damage reputations. Claims that an inmate is homosexual or an informer and rumors alleging infidelity on the part of a prisoner's spouse are examples of psychological victimization with a variety of unpleasant consequences for the recipient (Bowker, 1982).

Economic victimization is prevalent in many American prisons. Because material goods and services are relatively scarce, a sub-rosa economic system has developed in most institutions to provide inmates with a variety of items which are in demand. Howard Abadinsky and L. Thomas Winfree, Jr. (1992:523) note that "in any high volume illegal business, there is a great deal of cash, which is itself the object of theft, extortion, robbery and blackmail; prisons are no exception." In effect, inmates may be victimized twice. In many cases, they not only pay a high price for illicit goods and services, but they may subsequently lose them to the predatory activity of other prisoners (Abadinsky and Winfree, 1992). Eight different types of economic victimization within prisons have been identified: 1) loansharking, 2) gambling frauds, 3) pricing violations, 4) theft, 5) robbery, 6) protection rackets, 7) deliberate misrepresentation of products and, 8) nondelivery of products (Bowker, 1982).

Social victimization occurs when inmates are targeted because of their membership in an identifiable social category or group.

Bowker (1980) reports that individuals may become vulnerable as a result of their race, ethnicity, religion, ideology or type of offense (e.g., child molestation). In recent decades, membership in a particular gang has become an important factor contributing to this form of victimization. Individuals have been assaulted or murdered in American prisons because they were associated with a rival gang (Bowker, 1982).

Physical victimization is often the greatest fear—whether in the form of homicide, assault or rape. Many prison systems have experienced a significant rise in the level of violence among inmates in recent decades. Although most jurisdictions still report no homicides, some institutions have rates that are 15 times greater than that for the nation as a whole (Klofas, 1992). The frequency of assaults is more difficult to measure since prisons do not report comprehensive statistics regarding this problem (Abadinsky and Winfree, 1992). Nonetheless, the available data are quite disturbing with some researchers estimating that there are 20 times more assaults per capita in prisons than on the outside (Klofas, 1992).

Several factors account for the high level of violence in American institutions. First, there are a substantial number of incarcerated individuals who are prone to violence. Robert Johnson (1987) notes the presence in many facilities of "state-raised" convicts (individuals who have grown up in orphanages, detention centers, training schools and youth prisons). Second, a number of factors in the prison environment contribute to the cycle of violence: "1) inadequate supervision by staff members, 2) architectural designs that promote rather than inhibit victimization, 3) the easy availability of deadly weapons, 4) the housing of violence-prone prisoners in close proximity to relatively defenseless victims, and 5) a generally high level of tension produced by the close quarters and multiple, crosscutting conflicts among both individuals and groups of prisoners" (Bowker, 1982:64). Finally, violence is facilitated by aspects of the social climate of the prison, including the high degree of social distance between inmates and correctional officers and the taboo that prevents inmates from reporting altercations to the staff (Toch, 1985).

Sexual Victimization

The issue of sexual victimization within institutions is complex. Stan Stojkovic and Rick Lovell (1992) and Daniel Lockwood (1985) report that there are several commonly accepted myths associated with this topic. Among these are the notion that rape is the most common type of sexual activity that takes place in prison and that this type of assault is a frequent occurrence (Davis, 1968). It is ironic that many people believe rape is endemic in institutions yet hold the view that these facilities are "country clubs."

Researchers who have examined the frequency of sexual assault in prison generally conclude that this type of victimization is a rare event (Tewksbury, 1989; Nacci and Kane, 1983; and Lockwood, 1980). Richard Tewksbury (1989) questioned 150 individuals at a correctional facility in Ohio and did not uncover a single case. Likewise, only one prisoner out of a sample of 330 (0.3 percent) reported that he had been raped or sodomized in a federal facility (Nacci and Kane, 1983). Finally, Lockwood (1980) conducted extensive interviews with inmates in two facilities in New York State and could find only one case of actual sexual assault. Based on information that was provided by inmates and staff, it was estimated that between one and two incidents occur each year among the 2,000 prisoners incarcerated in the adult facility. However, this type of assault was somewhat more common in the youth prison that was examined (Lockwood, 1980).

Although relatively few inmates actually experience coerced sex, a substantial number are threatened, insulted, propositioned, fondled, and sometimes even physically attacked. In some cases, the harassment continues for a considerable length of time. Both Nacci and Kane (1983) and Lockwood (1980) report that sexual aggression is a much more common occurrence than actual assault. Nacci and Kane (1983) note that 29 percent of the inmates in their sample had been propositioned in their current institution. Nine percent reported that someone had attempted to force them to perform sex against their will in a prison. Lockwood (1980) determined that 28 percent of the inmates in his sample had been the targets of sexual aggression. For younger white males, the risks were considerably greater. Not surprisingly, this type of conduct has a number of deleterious consequences for both the victim and the social climate within the institution (Lockwood, 1985). The most significant impact is fear. Inmates who have been targets of sexual aggression remain concerned long after the incident has occurred that they may be sexually assaulted or even killed. Victims sometimes experience other effects as well including anxiety, anger, isolation and stress. In extreme cases, these individuals may respond violently or have suicidal thoughts.

Social relations among inmates suffer if inmates become so concerned about sexual assaults that they become withdrawn and reluctant to form friendships. More serious consequences are also possible including fights between prisoners and even murder. Nacci and Kane (1983) note that 5 of 8 homicides reported over a 26-month period at the United States Penitentiary at Lewisburg had a sexual motivation and that "a quarter of the major assaults were linked to inmate homosexual activity."

The Modern Prison

Clearly, incarceration is not a pleasant experience. Furthermore, conditions in many institutions have deteriorated in recent decades due to: 1) changes in both the demographic composition and the size of the prison population; 2) the unintended consequences of judicial interventions designed to "humanize" the prison environment; 3) the demise of the rehabilitative model of corrections; and 4) the increased tendency to use prison incarceration as a response to the social problems created by a growing underclass of socially disadvantaged individuals.

Earlier in this century, the "Big House" was the prevalent type of penal institution in the United States. Although the environment in these prisons was extremely regimented and harsh forms of discipline were often utilized by the staff, violence on the part of inmates was a relatively infrequent occurrence. Prisoners were generally guided by a code of conduct which "could be translated into three rules: Do not inform, do not openly interact or cooperate with the guards or the administration, and do your own time" (Johnson, 1987:77). The inmate with the highest status was the so-called "right-guy." This was an individual who stoically accepted the pains of imprisonment, did not betray the interests of other inmates and avoided causing trouble. Although there were occasional eruptions of violence in the "Big House," it was not something that inmates and staff were forced to confront on a continual basis.

Since the 1960s, a number of changes have taken place which have dramatically altered the nature of these prisons. In many cases, "what was once a repressive but comparably safe Big House is now often an unstable and violent social jungle" (Johnson, 1987:74) where inmates and staff no longer feel secure. Problems that were formerly quite rare have become commonplace in many American prisons. These include gangs, attacks by prisoners on correctional officers and violence by inmates directed against other inmates. The "right guy" has been replaced by the "convict" or "hog" as the most respected individual. This role has been described by Irwin (1980:195): "the convict or hog—stands ready to kill to protect himself, maintains strong loyalties to some small group of other convicts (invariably of his own race), and will rob and attack or at least tolerate his friends' robbing and attacking other weak independents or their foes."

Demographic changes in the composition of the inmate population have contributed to the institutional climate that currently exists in many facilities. Until recent decades, most southern states maintained a segregated prison system. It was common for institutions to house black and white inmates in separate units (Irwin and Austin, 1994). These practices ended as the drive to integrate American society gained momentum in the 1950s. However, prison integration was followed by a dramatic rise in the proportion of minority inmates. Andrew Hacker (1992) notes that between 1950 and 1986, the proportion of Blacks increased from 29.7 to 45.3 percent. By 1994 the incarceration rate among adult males was seven times greater for blacks than for whites; blacks comprised 54.2 percent of the prison population (Bureau of Justice Statistics, 1995). In some states, there has also been a growing concentration of Hispanic inmates.

There have been several consequences of the greater heterogeneity found among prison populations (Irwin, 1980). Racial tension and racial polarization have increased among inmates in many institutions. In addition, prison gangs have formed along racial and ethnic lines, or have continued associations formed prior to incarceration, in many facilities in the large industrial states. Gang members have often been involved in assaults, robberies and murders directed at rival gangs and independents. Members have also shown little reluctance to attack correctional officers. As Warden Godinez at Stateville puts it, "Gangs are nothing more than a replacement for the family structure. We should not be shocked at how young men and women gravitate to a subcultural family if they don't get recognition and emotional support at home and in the community. All the images, all the impressions, all the lessons they get—or don't get—in those early years, how am I going to overturn all that when they get here?" (Lindeman, 1995:22).

Another factor that has contributed to the development of the modern violent prison is the rapid growth in the size of the inmate population that has taken place since the 1970s. With more and more persons being incarcerated, institutions in most states have become seriously overcrowded. Although the findings from research studies which have examined the impact of prison overcrowding are mixed (Innes, 1986; Farrington and Nuttall, 1985), some deleterious effects are unavoidable when institutions operate far beyond their designed capacity.

Double-celling is one consequence of overcrowding. Richard Sluder (1995) reports that double celling and overcrowding are associated with a number of problems. These include: 1) a deterioration of sanitary conditions within the facility; 2) more rapid transmission of contagious diseases; 3) an increase in concerns regarding security; 4) difficulties in providing inmates with basic necessities; 5) a decrease in access to programs and services; and 6) feelings of helplessness and loss of privacy among the inmates. Despite these problems, double-celling continues to be utilized by many jurisdictions as a means of housing an expanding prison population.

The intervention of the courts has also had a significant impact on the prison environment. In the "Big Houses" of earlier years, discipline was sternly enforced (Johnson, 1987). It was common for administrators to place severe restrictions on inmate associations and expression and to ensure compliance with prison regulations through the use of corporal punishment by correctional officers. Many of these measures were declared unconstitutional in the 1960s and 1970s, as courts gradually abandoned their reticence to monitor prison procedures.

While the judicial efforts attempted to correct violations of prisoners' rights, nothing replaced the old system of control that had been dismantled. Inmates were not given a "constructive role in shaping the conditions of their confinement" (Johnson, 1987:82), and no one came up with alternative means of guaranteeing cooperative behavior. Increasingly, "order yielded to disorder, violence and fear fed upon one another, producing a climate of terror" (Johnson, 1987:84). Correctional officers often became demoralized because of a perception that their authority had been undermined. The net result was that more inmates sought out protection in protective custody, many correctional officers became reluctant to enforce the rules and eventually, "the prison was given over to the most predatory convicts" (Johnson, 1987:84).

Finally, the demise of the rehabilitative model of corrections had an adverse impact on the quality of life within prisons. Since the late 1960s, there has been agreement among both liberals and conservatives that the rehabilitative model is flawed and should be abandoned (Cullen and Gilbert, 1982). A consensus had developed across the political spectrum that release from institutions should not be contingent on inmate participation in a treatment program.

Instead, prisoners should be required to serve a fixed amount of time under the new "justice" model of corrections. The consensus, according to Lawrence Friedman (1993) had both ambiguous roots and equivocal results. Some had supported the move to determinate sentences as a way to curb possible discriminatory practices and to make punishment uniformly consistent for like crimes. The actual results of the change from indeterminate to determinate sentencing played into the increasingly punitive tendencies discussed earlier. Alan Dershowitz, the Harvard law professor handling the appeal of Heidi Fleiss convicted of three counts of pandering and given a mandatory sentence of three years, said about mandatory sentencing, "It reflects the worst sense of priorities of our criminal justice system. The idea that a jail cell will be taken up by Heidi Fleiss is outrageous." The case against Fleiss also points to the myth that mandatory sentencing is fair. None of the men listed in Fleiss' directory of clients were charged (Smolowe, 1994a:59).

The justice model also provided correctional authorities with an ideological justification for reducing the level of services provided to inmates (Cullen and Gilbert, 1982). After all, why should money be spent to improve the quality of life for prisoners if they have been incarcerated solely for the purpose of punishment? Proponents of the "justice" model do not believe that rehabilitative efforts have been effective. As a consequence, many jurisdictions that shifted to this approach have reduced their level of funding for various programs, including educational and vocational training, designed to assist inmates (Irwin and Austin, 1994). The political and popular thinking about prisoners today has no regard for concepts such as incentives. The pervasive "get tough" mentality gives lawmakers an excuse to avoid addressing the complex problems of a huge prison population.

Dora Schriro, director of the Missouri Department of Corrections, believes prisons need support for education and job training. "I do not want to rehabilitate inmates, which means return them to what they were. I want to *habilitate* them. My focus is on mandatory education that results in high school equivalency, and mandatory industry work to have a vocation. I want them to have the basic tools for citizenship—literacy, employability, sobriety" (Gavzer, 1995). Another source also emphasized the benefits of providing opportunities, "Prison officials say higher-education courses significantly reduce an inmate's likelihood of returning to prison after he has been released. And the classes make the prison population easier to manage by helping keep inmates out of prison gangs and providing incentives for good behavior" (Editorial, 1995a:20). Yet increasingly, inmates are warehoused in institutions that provide few activities to channel their time productively. Even if research were to contradict beneficial results of such programs in prison, the question would remain whether the programs themselves were intrinsically flawed or whether prisons are not viable rehabilitative centers.

The "justice" model has also weakened the link between institutional behavior and release. In the past, parole authorities had tremendous discretion under indeterminate sentencing statutes to hold individuals who did not conform to prison regulations or to release them for good behavior. In jurisdictions that have adopted fixed sentences, the authority to parole obedient inmates no longer exists. Because sentences have tended to become longer under this approach (Cullen and Gilbert, 1982), many prisons now contain a substantial number of inmates serving long sentences with little incentive to cooperate with authorities.

Recent Innovations in Punishment

Despite the harsh conditions that already exist in many American prisons, recent years have witnessed the rise of correctional practices designed to be even more punitive in nature. These include the development of the so-called "maxi-maxi" prison, the return of the chain gang and the move to create military-style boot camps in many jurisdictions.

Super-maximum prisons and "maxi-maxi" units within prisons have been constructed in several jurisdictions to house inmates who have engaged in disruptive or violent behavior within the institution (Irwin and Austin, 1994). AdminMax, nicknamed Alcatraz of the Rockies, was constructed in 1994 and cost $60 million. It was designed to hold 484 high-risk inmates. These institutions are generally designed with "state of the art" technology that restricts inmate interaction and allows prisoners to receive essential services including meals without leaving their cells. In many cases, these facilities have a central control center which houses heavily armed guards who maintain constant surveillance on the units. The inmates are required to spend almost all their time in cells which have fully sealed front doors (Irwin and Austin, 1994). Visitors are not permitted to have physical contact with these individuals, they must communicate by telephone with prisoners who can be seen behind double layers of glass (Territo et al., 1992).

Another practice designed to address the concern that inmates are not sufficiently punished is the return of the "chain-gang," a feature of American corrections that had disappeared in recent decades. Alabama and Arizona have reinstated the use of "chain gangs" (*Criminal Justice Newsletter*, 1995a). Typically, these inmates clear brush, cut weeds and perform similar tasks along state highways. Alabama locks inmates to each other in groups of five. In Arizona, each prisoner works 10 hours per day, four days per week and has his own separate chain to prevent an escape. He is compensated for his efforts at the rate of 10 cents per hour (*Criminal Justice Newsletter*, 1995a). These "chain-gangs" have proven to be extremely popular with the public and several other states are planning to institute similar programs.

The most commonly adopted recent innovation is the creation of military-style boot camps. The first boot camps were opened by the states of Georgia and Oklahoma in 1983. One decade later, there were 60 facilities with a capacity of over 9,000 inmates operated by 30 states and the federal government (Dickey, 1994). These institutions attempt to create an environment for offenders that is similar to military basic training. Although there is a great deal of variation among boot camps, these facilities generally subject participants to strenuous physical exercise, hard work and stringent discipline. In addition, many also provide education, counseling and drug treatment (Mackenzie, 1995). Offenders typically spend 90 to 180 days in the boot camp as an alternative to a lengthy prison sentence (Dickey, 1994). Initially, these institutions were designed for young nonviolent male offenders. However, the programs have been extended to include females as well as some violent offenders (*Criminal Justice Newsletter*, 1994).

Boot camps are extremely popular with the public. Televised visual images of offenders being marched around in military formation are appealing to many citizens (Dickey, 1994) who believe that institutions have coddled criminals for too long. Boot camps, it is believed, will instill discipline and respect for authority in individuals who lack these values. In fact, the claims made on behalf of the long-term effects of boot camps have reminded some of the unfulfilled promises that accompanied the development of earlier programs such as "Scared Straight" (Sechrest, 1991). This was an effort to deter juveniles from a life of crime through conversations with verbally abusive, institutionalized convicts who make threats and describe their prison experience in the most graphic terms.

Correctional administrators have often seen boot camps as a means of reducing prison crowding and conserving scarce resources. This can occur if these facilities are used as an alternative to incarceration in a more traditional prison. Because offenders placed in boot camps also serve much shorter sentences, it is hoped that the creation of these facilities will alleviate some of the pressures that institutions currently face.

Recently, Doris Layton Mackenzie (1995) reported the findings from an evaluation study of these programs in eight states. The data indicated that boot camps could reduce overcrowding if these facilities were used as an alternative to prison and not as an alternative to probation. However, there was no reduction in recidivism rates in most jurisdictions (Criminal Justice Newsletter, 1994). Ironically, the only impact on recidivism was noted in states that provide boot camp inmates with treatment programs and intensive supervision upon release (Mackenzie, 1995). Facilities that rely solely on military-style discipline to effect change do no better than regular prisons. Nonetheless, the punitive nature of this sanction has provided policymakers in some jurisdictions with the necessary political cover to increase spending on the types of programs and services that may turn some offenders around.

Post-Institutional Adjustment

Irwin and Austin (1994) discuss many of the problems that do not end with release from the institution. For most inmates, incarceration only increases the number of obstacles that must be surmounted if one is to make a satisfactory adjustment to life on the outside. Indeed, the vast majority of prisoners were seriously disadvantaged before they entered the institution. In many cases, their lives were impaired by a history of alcohol or drug abuse, strained personal relationships, a poor education and few job skills with which to compete in a modern technological economy. With the demise of the rehabilitative model of corrections, institutions are now less likely to provide education or vocational training than was the case in past years. As a consequence, inmates leave prison with all their previous disadvantages as well as the additional stigma of a felony conviction. The latter not only bars former offenders from certain occupations, it also makes it difficult to obtain employment of any kind. Furthermore, should a parolee fail to disclose his status to a potential employer, this may constitute grounds for revocation and return to the institution. Given these facts, it is not surprising that only 21 percent of the parolees in the state of California were employed full-time in 1991 (Irwin and Austin, 1994).

In addition to finding a job, the individual must locate a place to live. Prisoners released from custody rarely have more than the few hundred dollars that they may have earned in the institution. Financing an apartment is only part of the problem. The former inmate may not be able to supply potential landlords with satisfactory references. Routine questions about previous addresses and requests for credit bureau reports become insurmountable hurdles for many former inmates.

Relationships with friends and family are often strained (Irwin and Austin, 1994). The stigma of incarceration creates situations in which friends or family members question whether this individual can be trusted.

There are psychological adjustments that must be made as well. Irwin and Austin (1994:125) discuss the "reentry" difficulties that ex-inmates face passing "suddenly from a highly routinized, controlled, reduced and slow-paced prison life into the complex, fast-moving impersonal world of the streets." In effect, the former prisoner leaves a regimented existence that offered little opportunity to exercise autonomy for an environment where stressful interactions with many people in a variety of unfamiliar settings occur at a frenetic pace. Whether it is shopping for groceries, taking the subway, crossing the street during rush hour or performing other routine tasks that most citizens take for granted, these are activities that are alien after a prolonged period of incarceration.

Former prisoners frequently confront legal difficulties. These individuals are often subjected to police attention. When a crime occurs in the community that is similar to the one for which they were incarcerated, it is not uncommon for the police to "round up the usual suspects" for questioning. Even if the period of detention is brief, this can be a very unnerving experience for an individual who is trying to readjust to life in the community.

This problem is compounded for convicted sex offenders because 38 states have enacted statutes which require these individuals to register their address with the police (*Criminal Justice Newsletter*, 1995b). Some jurisdictions even allow this information to be released to the media or to private citizens. An editorial warned that efforts to protect citizens should be equally careful not to abrogate the rights of those who are presumed to have paid their debt to society. "Feelings run high, understandably, on the issue of notification—particularly in cases where children have been victimized.

The New Jersey law was passed quickly last year in the wake of Megan Kanka's murder. But no measure with such serious potential ramifications ought to be swept into law on a wave of charged emotions" (Editorial, 1995b:22). Public disclosure is likely to lead to harassment or even violence as illustrated by recent events reported by Fred Cohen (1995:155) in which "a father and son vigilante team, acting on information gained from the application of 'Megan's Law,' broke into a Phillipsburg, New Jersey home and began beating a man they mistook for a recently released sex offender." Civil libertarians warn about just such vigilante attacks. They fear that the instinct to protect will hurt innocent people. They also warn that some statutes "allow a state to continue incarcerating sex offenders after their sentences are complete—even for the rest of their lives—if a state panel deems them likely to commit further crimes. . . . [Seattle University School of Law Professor, John La Fond] If this year we do it for sex offenders, next month it could be gang members and the next month spouse abusers. Where do you draw the line?" (Popkin 1994:72). We should also keep in mind that members of these panels are political appointees.

Finally, there is "the rising tide of parole failures" (Irwin and Austin, 1994:121). Between 1980 and 1989, the rate of parole violations increased in the United States by 324 percent. By the end of the decade, only 39 percent of the parolees discharged from supervision were classified as "successful" (Irwin and Austin, 1994). The others had been returned to prison either for committing a new crime or because of a technical violation (i.e., they had violated one of the conditions of their parole supervision). As Irwin and Austin explain (1994:122), the reason for this dismal trend is that the nature of parole supervision has changed in recent years: "Instead of a system designed to help prisoners readjust to a rapidly changing and more competitive economic system, the parole system has been designed to catch and punish inmates for petty and nuisance-type behaviors that do not in themselves draw a prison term."

Basically, parole supervision has become more intrusive. Increasingly, surveillance is taking the form of electronic monitoring, intensive parole supervision, and drug testing to monitor the behavior of persons released into the community (Irwin and Austin, 1994). As a consequence, officers can more easily detect situations where a violation of parole conditions has occurred. This has led to a vast increase in the number of inmates returned to prison for technical violations.

Given all these difficulties, it should not come as a surprise that many individuals who are released from prison are not successful on the outside. In fact, Irwin and Austin (1994) report that a U.S. Department of Justice follow-up study of 108,580 inmates released from prison to parole in 11 states in 1983 found that 63 percent of these individuals were arrested again within three years on either a felony or serious misdemeanor charge. [Ironically, the public does not view this as evidence of the myth of deterrence; again, it simply impugns the character of the inmate rather than seeing the faults of the system.] However, they also point out that even those who "stay out of prison do not live successful or gratifying lives. . . . They remain dependent on others or the state, drift back and forth between petty crime to subsistence, menial, dependent living, or gravitate to the new urban underclass—the homeless. Many die relatively young" (Irwin and Austin, 1994:139).

Scandinavian Prisons

The harsh nature of many prisons in the United States can also be illustrated by a brief examination of penal institutions in Scandinavia. Although these types of cross-cultural comparisons are often fraught with difficulty, it may be useful to point out some of the features that distinguish secure facilities in those societies from their American counterparts.

John R. Snortum and Kare Bodal (1992) have surveyed the conditions of confinement that exist within secure prisons across Scandinavia (Norway, Sweden and Finland) and in the state of California. They report that "California's two maximum security prisons projected a particularly oppressive picture of prison life, including overcrowding, lack of privacy, lack of space, lack of cell amenities, lack of safety, long hours of confinement, prison labor at slave wages, sexual deprivation, and visiting conditions that were, for the most part, chaotic and demeaning" (Snortum and Bodal, 1992:56).

Scandinavian institutions lack the racial polarization, the ever-present threat of violence, and the serious overcrowding that characterizes many American facilities. "The contrast with U.S. prisons was dramatized in 1979 when Sweden's Supreme Court refused to extradite a convicted American sex offender because conditions of confinement in U.S prisons were judged to be inhumane and the 59-year sentence was considered to be excessive" (Snortum and Bodal, 1992). To some extent, these differences are due to the nature of Scandinavian societies which are: 1) much more racially and ethnically homogeneous than the U.S.; 2) have far lower rates of violent crime; and 3) contain very few economically disadvantaged individuals.

Nevertheless, certain distinctive features of Scandinavian prisons are the result of deliberate policy choices. There is no double-celling of prisoners. All inmates in Sweden and Norway are provided with a private cell that includes both a desk and a chair as well as a bed. Instead of bars, each cell has a solid door which can be closed to insure privacy. In both countries "systems have generous provisions for home leaves and both allow easy access to unsupervised privacy with prison visitors" (Snortum and Bodal, 1992:55). In the words of a Swedish administrator, "sexual activity is regarded as a private matter for every person, including prisoners" (Snortum and Bodal, 1992:52). As a consequence, the sexual tension that pervades many American institutions is lacking. Prison sentences are much shorter, with more than one-half of the inmates in Sweden serving two months or less (Snortum and Bodal, 1992). Finally, a number of programs have been instituted in Sweden which allow inmates to leave the facility for a substantial period of time in order to participate in drug treatment, vocational training or military service (Snortum and Bodal, 1992).

Conclusion

Prison in our society has always been and remains a harsh and painful experience. In recent decades, these institutions have become even more unpleasant. Nonetheless, legislators and the public continue to seek ways to further increase the level of discomfort. Whether this entails reinstating "chain-gangs" or placing offenders in boot camps, the motivation is similar: incarceration is punishment for breaking society's rules. Many citizens focus on retribution and find any amenities that detract from the goal of punishment to be inappropriate "coddling" of inmates. They do not recognize what most correctional authorities and inmates have long understood: doing time in America's prisons is not now and never has been easy. The notion of a "country-club" prison is a myth.

The anger and frustration that lead to the "lock 'em up mentality" wants to pretend that we can "throw away the key." The fact is that most inmates will return to the "mean streets." In 1994, $22 billion dollars ($10 billion higher than five years earlier) was spent operating the nation's prisons. Stateville Warden Godinez explains the problem:

> I'll tell you this. Prisons are not the answer. Incarceration should be the final, final resort. We've got a million people locked up today, more than ever. But ask yourself this: "Do I feel any safer?" When you get robbed, you're a victim twice. First, when they take whatever they take. Second, when they're caught and you're paying $18,000 a year for them to stay here.
>
> What's the answer? As a society, we need to decide if this [prison] is going to be our answer. If it is, then we need to get the police, the justice system and corrections all on the same page. Decide we're going to convict and incarcerate. Send me all of 'em, but get ready to pay like you've never paid before (Lindeman, 1995:22).
>
> You want to vote against paying an extra thousand dollars per kid to improve education, and then you turn around and give me $18,000 per inmate to watch 'em for the rest of their lives. . . .
>
> Don't get me wrong. I'm no liberal. If someone does a crime and is convicted, they deserve to do their time. I'm just saying, if you treat the symptoms and do nothing about the causes, this is what you get. You build forty more prisons thinking that's going to solve your problem, and I guarantee you you'll fill the prisons (Lindeman, 1995:19).

Wilbert Rideau (the Louisiana inmate) had similar comments about how to address the problem and how to pay for it.

> Crime is a social problem, and education is the only real deterrent. Look at all of us in prison: we were all truants and dropouts, a failure of the education system. Look at your truancy problem, and you're looking at your future prisoners. Put the money there.
>
> [Pay for education programs] by shortening sentences. Sure, that's a hot button, but the public must come to realize that it can't enjoy its full measure of vengeance and expect at the same time to reduce bulging inmate populations. The citizenry must determine the minimum amount of punishment that it is willing to settle for, and then channel the millions it has saved into schools and preventive programs (Woodbury, 1993:33).

So the myths about the corrections system that need debunking are many: punishment does not always fit the crime, deterrence is not a rationale for prisons, prisons are not country clubs, and perhaps most importantly, the more than four million people in the corrections system are not all equally reprehensible predators. Some are innocent, some are old and harmless, some are unfortunate, and some are, in fact, incorrigible. Anyone who has ever driven after drinking more than the legal limit, shoplifted, used illegal drugs, or taken something of value from work could all find themselves in our correctional system. Rather than ignoring (or denying) possible similarities between "us" and "them" by segregating the offenders in prisons and increasing their distance from us, perhaps we should take another look at what we want the correctional system to accomplish. The more we understand the behavior that offends and attempt to look at the offender rather than resorting to predetermined stereotypes, the better the chances of reaching rational alternatives to prisons which offer no programs, no opportunities, and no hope.

This requires hard choices and rational thinking rather than "feel good" rhetoric. When public policy relies on baseball for its slogans, we're in serious trouble. As Ellen Goodman (1994:13) explains:

> Life is more complicated than baseball and so is crime. Not every felon warrants the same punishment. Some first crimes deserve much harsher sentences than they get. Some third crimes deserve lighter sentences than these laws would mandate. . . . To be rational about criminals is not to be soft on crime. Violent criminals—first- as well as third-timers—should indeed be punished harshly. They should be punished by the quality of their crimes, not just the quantity. I'm afraid it's going to take a whole league of brave legislators to step up to that plate and question the utility of punishment.

Sources

Abadinsky, H. and Winfree, L., Jr. (1992). *Crime and Justice: An Introduction*, 2nd ed. Chicago: Nelson-Hall Publishers.

Allen, H. and Simonsen, C. (1995). *Corrections in America: An Introduction*, 7th ed. Englewood Cliffs, NJ: Prentice Hall.

Bowker, L. (1982). Victimizers and Victims in American Correctional Institutions. In *The Pains of Imprisonment*, R. Johnson and H. Toch (eds.), pp. 63–76. Prospect Heights, IL: Waveland Press.

Bowker, L. (1980). *Prison Victimization*. New York: Elsevier.

Brandon, K. (1995). "Three-Strike Law Taxing California Prisons," *Chicago Tribune*, (July 7, 1995), sec. 1:3.

Bureau of Justice Statistics (1995). *Prisoners in 1994*. Washington, DC: U.S. Department of Justice.

Cohen, F. (1995). From the Editor: Sex Offender Registration Laws; Constitutional and Policy Issues. *Criminal Law Bulletin* 31(2): 151–56.

Criminal Justice Newsletter (1995a). Chain Gangs Return to Prisons in Alabama and Arizona, 26(10, May 15): 1–3.

_____ (1995b). Justice Department Announces Plans for Sex Offender Notification, 26(8, April 17): 3–4.

_____ (1994). Boot Camps Do not Reduce Inmate Recidivism, Study Finds, 25(23, Dec. 1): 1–3.

Crouch, B., Alpert, A., Marquart, J. and Haas, K. (1995). The American Prison Crisis: Clashing Philosophies of Punishment and Crowded Cellblocks. In *The Dilemmas of Corrections*, 3rd ed., K. Haas and G. Alpert (eds). Prospect Heights, IL: Waveland Press.

Cullen, F. and Gilbert, K. (1982). *Reaffirming Rehabilitation*. Cincinnati: Anderson.

Davis, A. (1968). Sexual Assaults in the Philadelphia Prison System and Sheriff's Vans. *Trans-Action* 6: 8–16.

Dickey, W. (1994). *Evaluating Boot Camp Prisons*. March. Washington, DC: Campaign for an Effective Crime Policy.

Editorial Staff (1995). *Chicago Tribune*, (June 21), sec. 1:20.

Editorial Staff (1995). *Chicago Tribune*, (January 14), sec. 1:22.

Farrington, D. and Nuttall, C. (1995). Prison Size, Overcrowding, Prison Violence and Recidivism. In *Prison Violence in America*, M. Braswell, S. Dillingham, and R. Montgomery, Jr. (eds.), pp. 113–31. Cincinnati: Anderson.

Friedman, L. (1993). *Crime and Punishment in American History*. New York: Basic Books.

Gavzer, B. (1995). Life Behind Bars. *Chicago Tribune*, (August 13), Parade: 4–7.

Goode, E. and Ben-Yehuda, N. (1994). *Moral Panics: The Social Construction of Deviance*. Cambridge, MA: Blackwell.

Goodman, E. (1994). Our Problem with Strangers. *Chicago Tribune*, (March 28), sec. 1:13.

Hacker, A. (1992). *Two Nations: Black and White, Separate, Hostile, Unequal.* New York: Ballantine Books.

Innes, C. (1986). *Population Density in State Prisons.* December. Washington, DC: Bureau of Justice Statistics.

Irwin, J. (1980). *Prisons in Turmoil.* Boston: Little, Brown.

Irwin, J. and Austin, J. (1994). *It's about Time: America's Imprisonment Binge.* Belmont, CA: Wadsworth.

Johnson R. (1987). *Hard Time: Understanding and Reforming the Prison.* Pacific Grove, CA: Brooks/Cole.

Johnson, R. and Toch, H. (1982). *The Pains of Imprisonment.* Prospect Heights, IL: Waveland Press.

Klofas, J. (1992). The Effects of Incarceration. In *Corrections: An Introduction,* S. Stojkovic and R. Lovell (eds.), pp. 295–327. Cincinnati: Anderson.

Levinson, R. (1982). Try Softer. In *The Pains of Imprisonment,* R. Johnson and H. Toch (eds.), pp. 241–55. Prospect Heights, IL: Waveland Press.

Lindeman, L. (1995). Between Bars: Wondering How the War on Crime is Going? *Chicago Tribune,* (January 22): 19–22.

Lockwood, D. (1985). Issues in Prison Sexual Violence. In *Prison Violence in America,* M. Braswell, S. Dillingham and R. Montgomery, Jr. (eds.), pp. 89–96. Cincinnati: Anderson.

Lockwood, D. (1980). *Prison Sexual Violence.* New York: Elsevier Books.

Mackenzie, D. (1995). Boot Camp Prisons: Examining their Growth and Effectiveness. In *The Dilemmas of Corrections: Contemporary Readings,* 3rd ed., K. Haas and G. Alpert (eds.), pp. 396–405. Prospect Heights, IL: Waveland Press.

Marx, G. (1995). *Chicago Tribune,* (May 12), sec. 5:2.

_____ (1995). Swift Justice. *Chicago Tribune,* (April 27) sec. 5:1–2.

Nacci, P. and Kane, T. (1983). The Incidence of Sex and Sexual Aggression in Federal Prisons. *Federal Probation* 47(4, December): 31–36.

Popkin, J. (1994). Natural Born Killers. *U.S. News & World Report,* (September 19): 65–72.

Sechrest, D. (1991). Prison "Boot Camps" Do not Measure Up. In *The Dilemmas of Corrections: Contemporary Readings,* 2nd ed., K. Haas and G. Alpert (eds.), pp. 345–56. Prospect Heights, IL: Waveland Press.

Sluder, R. (1995). Double Celling. In *Encyclopedia of American Prisons,* M. McShane and F. Williams (eds.). New York: Garland.

Smolowe, J. (1994a). "A High Price to Pay." *Time,* (December 19): 59.

_____ (1994b) "Going Soft on Crime" *Time,* (November 14): 63.

Snortum, J. and Bodal, K. (1992). Conditions of Confinement Within Security Prisons: Scandinavia and California. In *Prisons Around the World,* M. Carlie and K. Minor (eds.), pp. 38–60. Dubuque, IA: William C. Brown.

Stojkovic, S. and Lovell, R. (1992). *Corrections: An Introduction.* Cincinnati: Anderson.

Sykes G. (1958). *The Society of Captives: A Study of a Maximum Security Prison.* Princeton: Princeton University Press.

Territo L., Halsted, J. and Bromley, M. (1992). *Crime and Justice in America: A Human Perspective*, 3rd ed. St. Paul, MN: West.

Tewksbury, R. (1989). Fear of Sexual Assault in Prison Inmates. *The Prison Journal* (Spring/Summer): 62–71.

Toch, H. (1985). Social Climate and Prison Violence. In *Prison Violence in America*, M. Braswell, S. Dillingham, and R. Montgomery, Jr. (eds.). Cincinnati: Anderson.

Woodbury, R. (1993). "A Convict's View: People Don't Want Solutions." *Time*, (August 23): 33.

Wooden, W. and Parker, J. (1982). *Men Behind Bars: Sexual Exploitation in Prison*. New York: Plenum.

The Myth of a Lenient Criminal Justice System

13

The evidence is overwhelming that the United States has the highest rate of violent crime among Western industrial societies. Homicide, rape and robbery are four to nine times more frequent in the United States than they are in Europe, and burglary, theft and auto theft are also more frequent, but not to the same degree. The homicide rate offers a good illustration of the differences that exist with respect to violent crime between the United States and other Western democracies. In 1984, there were 7.9 homicides in the United States per 100,000 people. This contrasts with a rate of 2.7 for Canada, 1.1 for England and Wales, 2.1 for Italy, 1.7 for New Zealand and 1.4 for Sweden (Kalish, 1988). In other words, if the United States had the same homicide rate as Canada, there would not have been 18,690 murders in 1984 (Flanagan and McGarrell, 1986) but 6,388 instead. Likewise, if the rate had been 1.1 as in England and Wales, the total number of killings reported that year would have been 2,602. The same pattern is true with respect to other violent crimes (Kalish, 1988).

The homicide data for young males are even more disturbing. The *Journal of the American Medical Association* has examined the rate at which men 15 through 24 years old were killed in various industrial democracies during 1986 and 1987 (Rosenthal, 1990). The analysis indicates that the United States is far ahead of these other nations with 21.9 murders per 100,000. Scotland is next with a rate of 5.0 killings. In fact, it is noteworthy that in 13 nations including England, France and Ireland, there were fewer than 2 young males murdered per 100,000. Austria had the lowest rate of homicide (0.3). In other words, a young man living in the United States was 73 times more likely to be the victim of a homicide than a similarly situated individual residing in the Republic of Austria. As Steven F., Messner and Richard Rosenfeld (1994:22) remark, "When it comes to lethal violence, America remains the undisputed leader of the modern world.

Why does the United States have such a high rate of violent crime compared to other Western societies? One explanation often advanced is that the courts are too lenient with offenders. Various politicians, most police officers, and a majority of the citizenry all decry the fact that criminals do not receive the severe punishments they deserve. If judges would impose tougher sentences, then we would be able to reduce the crime rate, or so it is often suggested. According to a Gallup survey, 83 percent of the respondents subscribe to the view that their local courts do not deal harshly enough with criminals (Maguire and Flanagan, 1991).

This chapter examines both cross-national and longitudinal data with respect to punishment. In the first section, correctional practices in the United States are compared with those of other Western democracies. The analysis utilizes two indicators of leniency: incarceration rates and practices with respect to the use of capital punishment. In both cases, it is clear that the United States is not more lenient than other comparable societies.

The second section of this chapter addresses the myth that the justice system is becoming more lenient and coddling criminals in a country-club atmosphere. This conclusion is based on an examination of the data regarding various correctional populations. Included in this analysis are statistics with respect to the number of jail inmates, sentenced federal and state prisoners, probationers and parolees. When the underlying trend is examined in each of these populations, it is difficult to make the case that our system of justice has become lenient in recent years.

International Comparison

Incarceration Rates

In an attempt to determine whether the high rates of violent crime in the United States are the result of lenient criminal justice practices, it is necessary to examine correctional policies that are currently followed in other Western nations. Because these societies share our democratic political tradition and have economies that are quite similar to ours, a strong case exists for comparing correctional practices in the United States to those of Canada, Great Britain, Australia, and the other industrialized nations of Western Europe.

Table 1 examines the incarceration rates for various Western democracies. It is clear from inspection of these data that the United States incarceration rate is far higher than that of any other Western nation. In 1992/93, the United States imprisoned 529 persons for every 100,000 residents in the population. This is a rate more than 5.6 times greater than that of England, six times greater than the rates of France and Germany, around 7.6 times greater than Sweden, and more than ten times the rate for the Netherlands. Northern Ireland has the highest incarceration rate among the nations of Western Europe—four times lower than in the United States, despite the fact that a civil war has been taking place.

When we examine Western nations that lie outside Europe, the picture does not change. Canada, our neighbor to the north and a society that is remarkably similar to the United States, has an incarceration rate of around 116 persons for every 100,000 residents in the population. Australia and New Zealand, two other nations with which we share not only a common language but also the same legal tradition, incarcerate only 91 and 135, respectively.

The United States not only has the highest rate of incarceration among Western nations, it is second highest in the entire world (Mauer, 1994). Only Russia with a rate of 558 per 100,000 imprisons more people per capita than the United States. It is ironic that our nation should share the lead in this area with its former cold war rival. Clearly this review of cross-national incarceration rates does not lend any support to the myth that the United States is lenient with offenders.

Table 1

**Incarceration Rates for the United States
and other Western Democracies, 1992–93**

Nation	Rate*
United States**	519
Australia	91
Austria	88
Canada	116
Denmark	66
England/Wales	93
France	84
Germany	80
Greece	60
Italy	80
Netherlands	49
New Zealand	135
Northern Ireland	126
Portugal	93
Spain	90
Sweden	69
Switzerland	85

*Per 100,000 population.
**Includes both prison and jail populations

Sources: *American Behind Bars: The International Use of Incarceration, 1992–1993,*
by Marc Mauer, The Sentencing Project, Washington, DC (September 1994);
Bureau of Justice Statistics, (1995). *Prisoners in 1994.* Washington, DC: U.S.
Department of Justice.

Capital Punishment

When we inquire whether the United States is lenient with convicted criminals, it is also helpful to look at practices with respect to the death penalty. Here "the pattern is so simple, it is stunning. Every Western industrial nation has stopped executing criminals, except the United States" (Zimring and Hawkins, 1986:3). Canada, Great Britain, Australia, New Zealand, and all the nations of Western Europe have halted this practice. In the United States, however, capital punishment statutes remain on the books in 38 states, and over 250 executions have taken place since 1977.

The abolition of capital punishment is not a recent development in many societies. The last execution for a civil crime took place as far back as 1860 in the Netherlands, 1863 in Belgium, and 1892 in Denmark. Norway has not imposed the death penalty for a civil offense since 1875 and Italy since 1876 (Zimring and Hawkins, 1986). Of course, in other cases, abolition is of more recent origin. Great Britain did not have its last execution until 1964. Canada did not abolish the death penalty for civilian offenses until 1976. Spain and France were among the last Western European societies to do away with capital punishment, in 1978 and 1981 respectively.

Most jurisdictions in the United States have not followed suit. Although no executions took place between 1968 and 1976, the trend in recent years has been lenient in the opposite direction. Not only are the number of persons sentenced to death increasing, but executions are becoming increasingly more frequent. It appears that the United States is not ready to join the rest of the Western world which has seen fit to abolish capital punishment.

The United States is not merely the only Western society that retains the death penalty, it is one of the few societies in the world that permits the execution of persons for crimes committed as juveniles. More than three-quarters of the nations have set 18 as the minimum age for execution (Streib, 1987). This policy has won the support of the United Nations as well as the Geneva Convention which prohibits, even in wartime, the execution of civilians for crimes committed under the age of 18. Although it is not common for juveniles to be put to death in the United States, this sentence is permitted under the statutes that have been enacted in approximately half the states. More recently, the Supreme Court has paved the way to allowing states to execute mentally retarded offenders. Clearly, with respect to capital punishment, there is no evidence that the United States is lenient with offenders.

Why is the United States far more punitive in its treatment of offenders than other Western democracies? Part of the explanation obviously lies in the fact that the United States has a substantially higher crime rate than most other societies (Bureau of Justice Statistics, 1987). James P. Lynch (1988) has argued that when overall crime rates are considered, United States courts do not incarcerate a greater proportion of offenders. However, rising crime rates do not explain the tremendous increase in correctional populations that have occurred in recent years. Nor does the myth of leniency with offenders explain the high crime rate. The United States is the only Western democracy that still uses the death penalty and is among a small minority of nations where juveniles can be executed for crimes. Despite a system of justice that is far more harsh in its treatment of offenders, the United States continues to have far higher rates of violent crime than any other Western nation.

The Trend Toward Greater Punitiveness in the United States

As indicated above, not only is the American system of justice more punitive than systems in other democracies, but there is also strong evidence that the United States has become even more severe in its treatment of offenders in recent years. It should be noted that the trend toward increased incarceration is not a universal phenomenon. Both Denmark (Brydensholt, 1992) and England (Mauer, 1992) have developed policies that are designed to reduce the number of prison inmates. The United States is moving in the opposite direction. In this section, four sources of data are examined which highlight the trend toward more persons under the control of the criminal justice system. These include statistics regarding the number of offenders incarcerated in prison, incarcerated in jail, under supervision in the community on probation and parole, and under judicial sentence of death.

Prison Incarceration

Table 2 indicates that the number of sentenced prisoners in state and federal institutions increased fivefold during the 22-year period between 1972 and 1994. In 1972, there were 196,092 prison inmates in the United States. During this period, the number increased by 857,646 to an all-time record of 1,053,738. Data that go back to 1925 are available regarding the number of sentenced prisoners (see Maguire and Flanagan, 1991). They indicate that such an increase is unprecedented in American history.

In order to determine whether population changes account for this increase, Table 2 presents data regarding the rate of prison incarceration per 100,000 residents during this period. Between 1972 and 1994, this rate increased over fourfold—from 93 to 387. Although the United States population increased somewhat during these years, the population increase accounted for a very small proportion of the growth in prison incarceration. In addition, there has been a decline in the number of persons in the most "crime prone" age group of 15–24 (Steffensmeier and Harer: 1991).

Table 2
Number and Rate of Sentenced Prisoners
in State and Federal Institutions 1972—1994*

Year	Total	Rate*
1972	196,092	93
1974	218,466	102
1976	262,833	120
1978	294,396	132
1980	329,821	139
1982	413,806	170
1984	462,002	187
1986	544,972	216
1988	627,600	244
1990	773,919	292
1992	883,656	344
1994	1,053,738	387

*Rate per 100,000 population on December 31; includes only prisoners sentenced to 1 year or more.

Sources: U.S. Department of Justice, *Record Number of Prisoners Reached Again Last Year*, Press Release (June 1, 1994); U.S. Department of Justice, *Prisoners in 1993*, Bureau of Justice Statistics, Washington, DC; *Sourcebook of Criminal Justice Statistics–1993*. The Hindelang Criminal Justice Research Center, Albany, NY; Bureau of Justice Statistics (1995). *Prisoners in 1994*. Washington, DC: U.S. Department of Justice.

The rise in the number of inmates has been so dramatic that overcrowding has become the major problem in American prisons. In many states, the situation is so critical that courts have ruled that this condition constitutes "cruel and unusual punishment" and is in violation of the constitution. As a consequence, correctional administrators have been ordered to reduce the number of persons in these institutions. By the end of 1994, the problem had become so serious that 22 jurisdictions reported a total of 48,949 state prisoners held in local jails or other facilities because of overcrowding in state facilities (BJS, 1995). Given this level of overcrowding, it would be very difficult to argue that the prison environment has become less harsh than in previous years.

Jail Incarceration

Generally speaking, prisons hold inmates who have been convicted of a felony and have been sentenced to serve more than one year in custody. Jails, on the other hand, house persons who are awaiting trial or have been convicted of a misdemeanor. However, Table 3 indicates that the situation with respect to both prisons and jails is quite similar. In 1978, the average daily population of local jails was 157,930. By 1994, there had been an increase of approximately 320,000 to 479,757. In a span of sixteen years, the jail population has more than tripled.

The increase in the number of jail inmates cannot be explained by population growth in the United States. In 1978, there were 76 inmates in local jails per 100,000 residents; this proportion increased to 96 by 1983 and grew to 188 per 100,000 by 1994 (Perkins et al., 1995). During this period, the rate of jail incarceration more than doubled. Had the total population of the United States remained unchanged during this time span, there would have been at least twice as many people in the nation's jails in 1994 compared to 1978. In short, demographics cannot account for the rising tide of jail inmates.

As the number of jail inmates has skyrocketed, many jails are facing some of the same problems with respect to overcrowding as prisons. In 1990, 28 percent of the jurisdictions in the United States were under court order to limit population in at least one jail under their control; in addition, over 150 jail jurisdictions were operating under court directive to improve one of a number of specific conditions of confinement (Stephan and Jankowski, 1991). Clearly, it cannot be argued that jail is a more pleasant environment than in previous years.

The enormity of the rise in institutional populations is even more striking when the numbers of inmates in both jails and prisons are combined. In 1978, there were a total of 452,326 persons in America's penal institutions. Sixteen years later, this number had surpassed the million mark, growing to a grand total of 1,325,545 persons. The combined rate of prison and jail incarceration also skyrocketed during this period, from 208 per 100,000 in 1978 to 519 in 1992. Based on these statistics, the view that the United States has become lenient with criminal offenders is clearly a myth.

Probation and Parole Populations

Not only have institutional populations increased dramatically in recent times, the number of persons under community supervision

---

Table 3
Average Daily Population of Jail Inmates

Year	Average Daily Population
1978	157,930
1983	227,541
1984	230,641
1985	265,010
1986	265,517
1987	290,300
1988	336,017
1989	386,845
1990	408,075
1991	426,479
1992	441,889
1993	459,804
1994	479,757

Sources: *Sourcebook of Criminal Justice Statistics–1993*, The Hindelang Criminal Justice Research Center, Albany, NY; *Jail Inmates, 1987–1990*, U.S. Department of Justice, Bureau of Justice Statistics, Washington, DC; *Jails and Jail Inmates, 1993–94*, U.S. Department of Justice, Bureau of Justice Statistics, Washington, DC.

has risen quite rapidly as well. Table 4 indicates that in 1980, there were 1,118,097 adult probationers and 220,438 adult parolees in the United States. Thirteen years later, these populations had risen to 2,843,445 and 671,470 respectively. Not only has the number of probationers and parolees more than doubled in this time period; the total now exceeds one percent of the United States population.

If jail and prison populations had declined during this period, a strong argument could be made that the greater number of probationers and parolees was indicative of a trend toward greater reliance on community alternatives to institutionalization. However, this is not the case. The data indicate that not only are more individuals being placed in institutions but that this is occurring at a pace which is unprecedented in American history.

In order to get an even better picture of the changes that have taken place in the criminal justice system in recent years, it is

Table 4
Number of Adults On Probation and Parole in the United States 1989–1994*

Year	Probation	Parole
1980	1,118,097	220,438
1982	1,357,264	224,604
1984	1,740,948	266,992
1986	2,114,621	325,638
1988	2,356,483	407,977
1990	2,670,234	531,407
1992	2,811,611	658,601
1994	2,962,166	690,159

*All counts reflect the total at the end of the year.

Sources: *Nation's Correctional Population Tops Five Million*. (1995). U.S. Department of Justice, Bureau of Justice Statistics, Washington, DC; *Prisoners in 1994*. (1995). U.S. Department of Justice, Bureau of Justice Statistics, Washington, DC; *Probation and Parole Populations Reach New Highs*, U.S. Department of Justice, Press Release on September 11, 1994; *Probation and Parole (1981–1990)*, U.S. Department of Justice, Bureau of Justice Statistics, Washington, DC.

helpful to examine the data with respect to the total number of persons under correctional supervision. This includes not only inmates in the nation's jails and prisons but also persons who have been placed under probation or parole supervision. According to the National Council on Crime and Delinquency (Austin, 1990), there were 1,832,350 individuals under the control of the correctional system in 1980. Fourteen years later, this total had increased to an estimated 5,100,000 persons, approximately 2.7 percent of the adult population (Bureau of Justice Statistics, 1995a).

The data reported indicate that the United States punishes a substantial number of its citizens, a proportion far greater than any other Western democracy. For young African-American males, the situation is even more bleak. Mauer (1990:3) noted that "almost one in four (23 percent) black men in the age group 20–29 is either in prison, jail, on probation, or parole on any given day." In fact, "the number of young black men under the control of the criminal justice system—609,690—is greater than the total number of black men of all ages enrolled in college—436,000 as of 1986." In 1993 the incarceration rate of African-American males was seven times that of whites (Bureau of Justice Statistics, 1995a). Furthermore, African-American males in the United States have a rate of incarceration that is four times greater than that of black males in South Africa (Mauer, 1991). It would be quite difficult to make a case that this pattern is indicative of a criminal justice system that is soft on crime.

Persons Under Sentence of Death

Two decades ago, the United States Supreme Court ruled in *Furman v. Georgia* (1972) that the death penalty was unconstitutional because of the selective and arbitrary manner in which it was being applied. As a consequence, all the statutes authorizing capital punishment were stricken from the books. The United States seemed ready to join the other Western democracies which had halted the practice of executing citizens for crimes committed in peacetime.

The Supreme Court in its 1972 Furman decision did not, however, address the question of whether executions in themselves were cruel and unusual punishment. Instead, the court merely stated that the manner in which the death penalty had previously been administered violated the constitution. The door was therefore left open for states to draft new statutes with respect to capital punishment. Within four years, approximately thirty-five states had done so. By the time the United States Supreme Court finally addressed the question of whether executions were constitutional (*Gregg v. Georgia*, 1976), the composition of the court had changed in a more conservative direction. In addition, public opinion had also shifted, with many more Americans voicing support for the death penalty. Thus, it was not very surprising when the Supreme Court ruled that capital punishment in and of itself does not violate the constitution.

Between 1968 and 1976, no one was executed in the United States. However, in *Gregg v. Georgia* (1976), the United States Supreme Court ruled that the death penalty may be imposed as long as certain procedural standards are followed. As a consequence, executions resumed in 1977. At first, the pace was quite slow. The late 1970s saw only a handful of individuals put to death. As time passed, the numbers increased substantially. By the mid-1980s, executions had become relatively routine events which generated little public attention and little media publicity in most cases. Between 1977 and 1993, 226 prisoners were executed in the United

States (Stephan and Brien, 1994). By 1990, there were, on average, two executions per month (Bureau of Justice Statistics, 1992).

The number of persons actually executed is only part of this picture. Following the *Gregg* decision, the number of convicts under sentence of death also increased rather substantially. Table 5 indicates that there were only 423 persons on death row in 1977, the year after the United States Supreme Court gave its constitutional approval to the continued use of the death penalty. Six years later, there were almost three times as many persons under sentence of death (1,209). By 1993, the total had grown to 2,716. Because defendants were being sentenced to death at a pace which outstripped the ability of the courts to dispose of the various appeals, the number of individuals on death row was more than five times greater in 1993 than had been the case in 1977.

Table 5
Persons Under Sentence of Death, 1973–1993

Year	Number
1973	134
1977	423
1979	593
1981	856
1983	1209
1985	1591
1987	1984
1989	2250
1991	2482
1993	2716

Source: *Sourcebook of Criminal Justice Statistics, 1990–1993*, The Hindelang Criminal Justice Research Center, Albany, NY; *Capital Punishment, 1993*. U.S. Department of Justice, Bureau of Justice Statistics, Washington, DC.

The Crime Rate in the United States

What factors account for the more punitive criminal justice practices that have evolved in recent years? It has already been noted that population changes do not account for the increased number of individuals under correctional supervision. Another possibility is that these changes in the jail, prison, probation, and parole populations merely reflect changes in the crime rate that have occurred during this period. If there was a dramatic rise in crime, we would expect more offenders to be incarcerated and/or released into the community under the supervision of the courts.

Despite the fact that the crime rate has declined, the number of adults arrested rose somewhat (34 percent—from 6.1 to 8.2 million). However, this increase was dwarfed by the dramatic rise in various correctional populations during the 1980s. Between 1980 and 1990, the number of jail inmates rose 146 percent, the number of prisoners rose 134 percent, the number of probationers increased by 139 percent, and the number of parolees increased 141 percent (Irwin and Austin, 1994). Clearly, these data suggest that the huge rise in the number of persons under correctional supervision in the United States has not been in response to an increased crime rate.

If increased crime rates do not explain the dramatic rises in various correctional populations that have occurred in recent years, what factors do account for this trend? There are several explanations. The "war on drugs" has contributed to a substantial part of the increase (Austin and McVey, 1989). In the federal prison system, the number of persons serving time for drug offenses has more than doubled since 1981 and now accounts for 53 percent of the inmate population (Mauer, 1992). The Bureau of Justice Statistics (1988a) notes that a greater proportion of drug violators are being incarcerated than in previous years and that sentence lengths for this crime have increased. On the state and local level, the impact of the war on drugs is also evident. In recent years, the proportion of offenders sentenced to prison for drug violations has increased dramatically (Austin and McVey, 1989). In addition, the increased emphasis on drug testing has contributed to a higher failure rate among parolees. The United States Department of Justice reports that there was "a 284 percent increase in the number of parole violators returned to prison between 1977 and 1987" (Austin and McVey, 1989: 5). The fact that nearly 46 percent of the rise in the state prison population between 1980 and 1992 was the result of an increase in the number of inmates convicted for drug offenses should not be overlooked (Gilliard and Beck, 1994).

Secondly, sentencing practices have become more punitive as many states and the federal government have enacted mandatory sentence statutes that apply to various offenses (Mauer, 1992). These laws *require* judges to sentence offenders to a period of incarceration, often for a specified period of time. There is no possibility of the defendant receiving probation or a suspended prison sentence. Forty-six states now have mandatory sentence statutes (Bureau of Justice Statistics, 1988b). An analysis by the United States Sentencing Commission concluded that mandatory sentences have been a contributing factor in the dramatic rise of the federal prison population (Mauer, 1992).

In addition, the federal government and at least a dozen states have enacted so-called "Three Strikes and You're Out" statutes which mandate life imprisonment without parole for certain offenders upon the conviction of a third felony (Mauer, 1994). These laws are likely to exacerbate the trend toward increased incarceration. In California, the Department of Corrections projects that over the next 5 years, this provision will cause the prison population to grow by almost 70 percent and force the state to spend an additional $4.5 billion on new prison construction (Claiborne, 1995). The impact is likely to be similar in other states that pass these types of overreaching statutes.

Finally, a conservative ideology has developed which asserts that society can solve its crime problem by taking a hard-line approach (Marenin, 1991). One result of this philosophical shift has been a narrowing of defendants' rights. Although the impact of such changes in criminal procedure is mostly symbolic (Gordon, 1990), this attitude has encouraged politicians to offer the public other simplistic "get tough" measures for dealing with offenders instead of rational policies that seek to alleviate the root causes of crime and violence. In fact, Richard Thornburgh, the former attorney general of the United States, opened a "crime summit" several years ago by telling law enforcement officials to leave consideration of the causes of crime to ivory-tower types (Fyfe, 1991). Increasingly, candidates for political office appear unwilling to propose solutions that could make a difference. Instead, policymakers continue to call for more prisons, longer sentences, and the death penalty for more offenses. Proposals to spend money on prevention programs are derided by opponents as "pork." It is not surprising that these policies resurged during a decade that also witnessed declining public interest in the problems of the disadvantaged and greater income disparity between rich and poor (Phillips, 1990).

If the get-tough approach had significantly reduced the level of crime and violence in America, a strong case could be made that it was worth the human and financial costs. However, what is striking is how little impact these policies have had on the crime problem. Not only is this approach to crime control ineffective, it is also expensive. State and local government spending on correctional institutions totaled over fifteen billion dollars in 1988 (Maguire and Flanagan, 1991). In fact, during the 1980s, spending by state governments for corrections was increasing at a substantial pace while expenditures for other needs, such as education and hospitals, lagged behind (Austin, 1990). Not only is the money spent on jails and prisons producing little in the way of tangible results, it is also diverting funds from programs that could have a positive impact on the lives of citizens. As Elliott Currie (1985:12) has written, the time has come to view the get-tough approach to crime as a conservative social experiment which failed:

> It is difficult to think of any social experiment in recent years whose central ideas have been so thoroughly and consistently carried out. The number of people we have put behind bars, for ever-longer terms, is unprecedented in American history. And unlike most such experiments which are usually undertaken with minimal funding and on a limited scale, this one has been both massively financed and carried out on a grand scale in nearly every state of the union. If it has failed to work in the way its promoters expected, they have fewer excuses than most applied social theorists.

Conclusion

Despite the data, the myth persists that we are lenient with offenders. Public opinion surveys indicate that the proportion of Americans who believe the courts do not deal harshly enough with criminals is identical to the number who expressed this sentiment in 1980 (Maguire and Flanagan, 1991). How can one account for this disparity between the attitudes of citizens and the reality of our justice system?

To some extent, this public perception is shaped by the fact that some offenders are treated more leniently than is appropriate. Because citizens receive much of their information regarding the operation of the criminal justice system from accounts that are presented in the media, anecdotes that discuss how a serious offender escaped punishment probably play an important role in shaping perceptions about the system. Unfortunately, citizens often do not appreciate the fact that such accounts receive so much press attention precisely because they are atypical. Thus, events that are relatively rare (for example, a murder suspect who escapes punishment as a result of a legal technicality) come to be viewed as everyday occurrences. The reality of the situation is that most serious offenders are not treated leniently by the courts.

Another factor that may account for the false perception that the system is lenient is the perceived level of crime and violence in our society. Citizens, especially those residing in urban areas, hear and read reports in the media of murders, robberies, and rapes which seem to occur on a continuing basis. Despite the increased probability during the 1980s that a convicted offender would go to prison (Cohen, 1991), there are still a large number of crimes that do not result in an arrest. For this reason, citizens see society as inundated with crime and assume that the criminal justice system must not be doing its job. Often, the complaint is that "the courts must be soft, why else would there be so much crime?" Unfortunately, what most citizens fail to appreciate is that this is a problem which the criminal justice system cannot solve by itself and that harsh sentences do not necessarily deter crime. Without basic social reforms, there is little that the police, the courts, and the corrections system can do. Proponents of the "get tough" approach should try to explain why other democracies can achieve a far lower rate of violent crimes without incarcerating so many of their citizens.

The most harmful consequence for society of the leniency myth is that it continues to divert public attention and resources away from policies that could really make a difference in the fight against crime. As Marenin (1991:17) has noted, "conservatism politicized and ideologized a difficult social problem and made it harder to seek solutions which might work but which cannot be reduced to a thirty-second commercial." As a consequence, decision makers have been forced to pursue policies which focus on increasing the severity of criminal penalties and locking up more offenders. Programs which could have a real impact on crime (such as expanding job training, increasing access to drug treatment, or providing more economic opportunities for members of the underclass) are dismissed as too "soft" or as "political pork." However, these measures are likely to be far more effective and less costly in the long run than a continuation of the present "get tough" approach.

Sources

Austin, J. (1990). *America's Growing Correctional-Industrial Complex* (December). San Francisco: National Council on Crime and Delinquency.

Austin, J. and McVey, A. (1989). *The 1989 NCCD Prison Population Forecast: The Impact of the War on Drugs* (December). San Francisco: National Council on Crime and Delinquency.

Brydensholt, H. (1992). Crime Policy in Denmark: How We Managed to Reduce the Prison Population. In *Prisons Around the World*, M. Carlie and K. Minor, (eds.). Dubuque, IA: Wm. C. Brown.

Bureau of Justice Statistics (1995a). *Nation's Correctional Population Tops Five Million*. Washington, DC: U.S. Department of Justice.

———— (1995b). *Prisoners in 1994*. Washington, DC: U.S. Department of Justice.

———— (1992). *National Update*. 1 (3, January) Washington, DC: U.S. Department of Justice.

———— (1991). *National Update*. 1 (1, July) Washington, DC: U.S. Department of Justice.

———— (1990). *Census of Local Jails 1988* (February). Washington, DC: U.S. Department of Justice.

———— (1988a). *Drug Law Violators, 1980-86* (June). Washington, DC: U.S. Department of Justice.

———— (1988b). *Report to the Nation on Crime and Justice,* 2nd ed. (March). Washington, DC: U.S. Department of Justice.

———— (1987). *Imprisonment in Four Countries* (February). Special Report. Washington, DC: U.S. Department of Justice.

———— (1984). *The 1983 Jail Census* (November). Washington, DC: U.S. Department of Justice.

Claiborne, W. (1995). Three Strikes and You're Out of Wiggle Room. *Washington Post* (National Weekly Edition), (March 20–26).

Cohen, R. (1991). *Prisoners in 1990* (May). Washington, DC: Bureau of Justice Statistics.

Currie, E. (1985). *Confronting Crime: An American Challenge*. New York: Pantheon Books.

Flanagan, T. and McGarrell, E. (1986). *Sourcebook of Criminal Justice Statistics–1985*. Albany, NY: The Hindelang Criminal Justice Research Center.

Furman vs. Georgia, 408 U.S. 238 (1972).

Fyfe, J. (1991). Why Won't Crime Stop? Because We Cling to Our Favorite Social Myths. *Washington Post,* (March 17): D1.

Gilliard, D. and Beck, A. (1994). *Prisoners in 1993,* (June). Washington, DC: Bureau of Justice Statistics.

Gordon, D. (1990). *The Justice Juggernaut*. New Brunswick, NJ: Rutgers University Press.

Gregg v. Georgia, 428 U.S. 158 (1976).

Irwin, J. and Austin, J. (1994). *It's About Time: America's Imprisonment Binge*. Belmont, CA: Wadsworth.

Kalish, C. (1988). *International Crime Rates* (May). Washington, DC: Bureau of Justice Statistics.

Lynch, J. (1988). A Comparison of Prison Use in England, Canada, West Germany, and the United States: A Limited Test of the Punitive Hypothesis. *Journal of Criminal Law and Criminology* (79)1.

Maguire, K. and Flanagan, T. (1991). *Sourcebook of Criminal Justice Statistics–1990*. Albany, NY: The Hindelang Criminal Justice Research Center.

Maguire, K. and Pastore, A. (1994). *Sourcebook of Criminal Justice Statistics–1993*. Albany, NY: The Hindelang Criminal Justice Research Center.

Marenin, O. (1991). Making A Tough Job Tougher: The Legacy of Conservatism. *ACJS Today* 10 (2, September/October).

Mauer, M. (1994). *Americans Behind Bars: The International Use of Incarceration, 1992–1993*. Washington, DC: The Sentencing Project.

_____ (1992). *Americans Behind Bars: One Year Later* (February). Washington, DC: The Sentencing Project.

_____ (1991). *Americans Behind Bars: A Comparison of International Rates of Incarceration* (January). Washington, DC: The Sentencing Project.

_____ (1990). *Young Black Men and the Criminal Justice System: A Growing National Problem* (February). Washington, DC: The Sentencing Project.

Messner, S. and Rosenfeld, R. (1994). *Crime and the American Dream*. Belmont, CA: Wadsworth.

Perkins, C., Stephan, J. and Beck, A. (1995). Jail and Jail Inmates 1993–94. (April) U.S. Department of Justice, Bureau of Justice Statistics.

Phillips, K. (1990). *The Politics of Rich and Poor: Wealth and the American Electorate in the Reagan Aftermath*. New York: HarperCollins.

Rosenthal, E. (1990). U.S. Is by Far the Homicide Capital of the Industrialized Nations. *New York Times*, (June 20).

Steffensmeier, D. and Harer, M. (1991). Did Crime Rise or Fall During the Reagan Presidency?: The Effects of an 'Aging' United States Population on the Nation's Crime Rate. *Journal of Research in Crime and Delinquency* 28 (3, August).

Stephan, J. and Brien, P. (1994). *Capital Punishment 1993* (December). Washington, DC: Bureau of Justice Statistics.

Stephan, J. and Jankowski, L. (1991). *Jail Inmates, 1990* (June). Washington, DC: Bureau of Justice Statistics.

Streib, V. (1987). *Death Penalty for Juveniles*. Bloomington: Indiana University Press.

U.S. Department of Justice (1994a). *Record Number of Prisoners Reached Last Year.* Press Release (June 1).

U.S. Department of Justice (1994b). *Probation and Parole Populations Reach New Highs.* Press Release (September 11).

Zimring, F. and Hawkins, G. (1986). *Capital Punishment and the American Agenda.* Cambridge: Cambridge University Press.

Debunking the Death Penalty
Myths of Crime Control and Capital Punishment

14

Capital punishment is an issue that has generated intense public interest over the centuries. Criminologists have written volumes on this subject; appellate courts have devoted considerable time to deciding death penalty cases, and politicians have used it as an effective campaign issue. Capital punishment has even played a role in presidential elections. For example, it is widely believed that the response of Michael Dukakis during the second presidential debate to a question posed regarding the death penalty contributed to his landslide defeat by George Bush in the 1988 election. The Democratic nominee had been asked by a journalist if he would favor this sanction if his wife were raped and murdered. He replied that he would not.

As the Democrats learned to their chagrin, the question of capital punishment has taken on a large symbolic meaning in recent years. Increasingly, crime and many other policy questions are discussed

307

in a simplistic manner that focuses more on symbols than on solutions to complex social problems. Politicians have found that it is easier to reaffirm their support for the death penalty during a political campaign by using a thirty-second sound bite than to offer a meaningful program that seriously addresses the crime problem in America. As a consequence, support for capital punishment has become a litmus test of how tough one is willing to be on crime. At the same time, policymakers and citizens place an importance on this sanction that is disproportionate to its actual role in the criminal justice system.

Although the question of capital punishment is often debated more passionately than any other public policy question in the area of corrections, there is good reason to believe that the public is not well informed on this subject. Various opinion polls suggest that sizeable segments of the public believe that the death penalty acts as a deterrent to murder or that it is necessary to protect society (Jamieson and Flanagan, 1989). Citizens also sometimes question whether society should be forced to bear the cost of incarcerating convicted murderers for life, thereby implying that it would be less expensive to execute these individuals. In addition, it is routinely asserted that any vigorous attack on our tremendous crime problem must include capital punishment if it is to be successful. Yet all these beliefs are based on myth. There is no empirical support in the research literature on capital punishment for any of these positions.

This chapter debunks a number of common myths regarding the death penalty. These include: 1) the myth that the death penalty is a more effective deterrent to murder than life imprisonment; 2) the myth that the death penalty is less expensive to impose than life imprisonment; 3) the myth that the death penalty is necessary to protect society from convicted killers who are likely to repeat their offense; and 4) the myth that capital punishment is necessary in order to fight crime.

The Myth of General Deterrence

In a Gallup Poll taken in 1986, 67 percent of Americans expressed the view that the death penalty is a deterrent to murder (Jamieson and Flanagan, 1989). This belief is probably due to the strong confidence that most Americans place in the ability of punishment to alter behavior. It is often reasoned that if parents are able to modify their children's actions with very mild sanctions, then the threat of execution (a very serious penalty) should deter people from committing murder (a very serious crime). However, a review of the literature indicates that this confidence in the efficacy of capital punishment is misplaced. The overwhelming majority of studies report finding no deterrent effect. Below, the methodology and the findings from the various research reports are examined.

Probably no other question has received as much attention as the issue of whether the death penalty is a more effective deterrent to murder than a lengthy prison sentence. From a scientific perspective, the ideal way to address this question would be to use a lottery drawing to assign persons at birth to either life imprisonment or the death sentence should they eventually be convicted of capital murder (Zeisel, 1977). It would then be possible to ascertain whether persons who were at risk of receiving the death penalty were less likely to commit those types of murder that could land one on death row. For moral and legal reasons that require little explanation, this kind of experiment is unthinkable in a democratic society. As a consequence, scholars have been forced to rely on research designs that utilize "naturally grown" data in an attempt to approximate this impossible experiment.

Exploring the question of whether the death penalty is a better deterrent, researchers have employed a variety of strategies. This chapter examines nine approaches that have been utilized to address this issue: 1) an examination of homicide statistics in other Western democracies; 2) a comparative analysis of homicide rates in contiguous states where one jurisdiction exercises capital punishment and another does not; 3) an examination of the change in the homicide rate after the death penalty has been abolished or reinstated in a particular state; 4) the impact of an execution on the homicide rate in a specific jurisdiction where the sentence was recently carried out; 5) a comparative examination of the rate at which police officers are murdered in states that do and do not have capital punishment; 6) an examination of whether prison inmates are more likely to kill in states that have abolished capital punishment; 7) an analysis of the same question regarding the behavior of murderers who are eventually released on parole; 8) the impact of the death penalty on the level of noncapital felonies that are committed; and 9) various statistical models that have attempted to determine whether the death penalty is a more effective deterrent to murder than imprisonment.

Other Western Democracies

Very little research on the question of deterrence has compared homicides rates across various societies. Nonetheless, as noted earlier, the United States is the only Western democracy that retains captial punishment. At the same time, the United States has the highest homicide rate in the industrialized world. Although our high homicide rate results from many factors that have nothing to do with the death penalty, the relationship between these variables certainly does not support the notion of general deterrence. If this punishment was indeed a deterrent, why would the only Western nation that still employs it also have the highest rate of homicide?

Contiguous States

Some of the earliest work on the question of deterrence involved a comparative examination of the homicide rates in contiguous states where one jurisdiction had abolished capital punishment and the other(s) retained this penalty. The rationale underlying the use of contiguous states is that they are likely to be similar in other ways that could affect their homicide rate. If these jurisdictions share various economic, demographic, and social characteristics, any difference observed with respect to their murder rate should be attributable to the fact that they differ in the imposition of the death penalty. The classic studies utilizing this approach were conducted by Thorsten Sellin (1980). He compared Kansas (an abolitionist state) with Missouri and Colorado (retentionist states) as well as Maine (an abolitionist state) with the retentionist states of Massachusetts and New Hampshire. Sellin observed that the homicide rates in the abolitionist states were not higher (in some cases they were actually lower) than those reported in the retentionist states. Based on a number of comparisons of this type, Sellin (1980) was able to conclude that there is no evidence of a greater deterrent effect when a jurisdiction retains the death penalty.

Abolition/Retention of the Death Penalty

Another approach that was used by Sellin (1980) to study this issue was to examine jurisdictions that have either abolished or reinstated the death penalty. During the nineteenth and twentieth centuries, a number of states changed their statutes regarding this sanction.

The early studies only looked at the before and after homicide rate in jurisdictions that had revised their death penalty statute. However, later studies also examined the trend in contiguous states that had not made a change (Zeisel, 1977). This research found no evidence of an increased deterrent effect in jurisdictions that retained or reintroduced the death penalty. In general, the homicide rate closely followed the trend in contiguous states (Sellin, 1980). Whether capital punishment was abolished or reinstated did not seem to matter.

Impact of an Execution

The fourth approach employed is to examine the impact of an execution on the murder rate in the specific jurisdiction where the sentence was recently carried out. The first such study was conducted by Robert Dann (1935) during a period when executions were quite common in the United States. He examined the impact of five executions in Philadelphia which had not been followed by another execution for a sixty-day period. The rationale underlying this approach was that if capital punishment indeed deterred murder, all the publicity that surrounded an execution should cause the homicide rate to decline in the days and weeks subsequent to the execution. However, Dann observed that the murder rate actually increased somewhat in the sixty-day period that followed this punishment.

In California, a similar study was conducted by William Graves (1956). He examined the homicide records of Los Angeles, San Francisco, and Alameda counties in order to determine whether there were fewer murders in the days following an execution than was the case in the days leading up to this event. As a comparative measure, he examined the same days of the week for those periods in which an execution did not occur. Graves (1956) reported that compared with weeks when no death sentences were carried out, the number of murders actually increased the day prior to an execution and on the day of the execution. However, they declined in the two-day period that followed the execution. The result was that the slight deterrent effect was almost entirely cancelled out by the earlier brutalization effect. This finding led Graves (1956:137) to speculate that persons contemplating homicide may be "stimulated by the state's taking of life to act sooner." What Graves did not note because of the manner in which his data had been classified was "that homicides were higher in the weeks after than in the weeks before executions" (Bowers et al., 1984:284).

More recently, Steven Stack (1987) has conducted an analysis of publicized executions that took place in the United States between 1950 and 1980. This researcher does report a small deterrent impact for those executions which received national publicity. However, the number of executions in this category is quite small. No deterrent impact was observed in the overwhelming number of cases that did not generate national publicity. The author notes that "as executions become more common, the amount of press coverage tends to decline" (Stack, 1987:538). As a consequence, the death penalty soon loses even the marginal deterrent impact that was observed in this study.

Killings of Police Officers

Under our legal system, not all homicides are eligible for the death penalty. As a general rule, in order to be convicted of first degree murder, one must either act with premeditation or take a life during the commission of a felony. For this reason, killers of police officers would appear to be excellent candidates for this sanction in jurisdictions that retain capital punishment. Unlike many homicides that are so-called "passion crimes," these killings generally meet the necessary legal criteria to qualify as capital offenses. In addition, the apprehension rate is very high. Persons who murder police officers can expect to be both arrested and convicted. Therefore, if the death penalty is a more effective deterrent than incarceration, criminals should be less likely to kill police officers in those states that have retained this penalty.

There have been several studies that have addressed this question (Bailey and Peterson, 1987; Bailey, 1982; Sellin, 1980; Cardarelli, 1968). Despite the fact that these were conducted by different researchers, who utilized different methodologies and examined various time periods, the results have been remarkably similar. The homicide rate among law enforcement officers is no higher in states that have abandoned capital punishment. Nor does the severity of sanctions influence the rate of assaults on police officers (Hunter and Wood, 1994). The job of a police officer is not made more hazardous by the abolition of the death penalty.

Homicides Committed by Prisoners

Another approach employed to assess the deterrent impact of the death penalty is to compare the homicidal behavior of prisoners incarcerated in retentionist and abolitionist jurisdictions. In a study undertaken by Sellin (1980), it was reported that over 90 percent of these killings occurred in states that retained capital punishment. Furthermore, Wolfson (1982:167) has concluded that "the percentage of imprisoned murderers who recidivate is approximately the same in retentionist and abolitionist jurisdictions." She criticizes as seriously flawed an assumption of the deterrence argument that these individuals can be deterred by the same legal threat that was ineffective in preventing them from killing before they arrived in prison.

Homicides Committed by Parolees

In the United States, a substantial proportion of inmates serving a life sentence are eventually released on parole. Because even in retentionist jurisdictions, the overwhelming majority of persons convicted of homicide receive a prison sentence, many persons convicted of murder will eventually be released from custody. Researchers have asked whether these parolees are less likely to kill again in jurisdictions that retain the death penalty. Although the data to address this issue are scarce, the tentative conclusion is encouraging. Hugh Adam Bedau (1982:180) observed that murderers rarely kill again: "Both with regard to the commission of felonies generally and the crime of homicide, no other class of offenders has such a low rate of recidivism." In addition, the post-release conduct of murderers in abolitionist states was actually somewhat better than the conduct of those released in jurisdictions that still retained capital punishment. We will return to this issue later in the chapter.

Deterrence of Noncapital Felonies

Almost all research has focused on the impact that the death penalty has on the murder rate. The only exception is a study conducted by William Bailey (1991) who attempted to ascertain whether executions deter persons from committing noncapital felonies. Drawing upon arguments offered by Johannes Andenaes (1974), Marlene Lehtinen (1977), Ernest van den Haag (1978), and Walter Berns (1979), Bailey suggests three conceivable ways that the death sentence acts as a deterrent for other types of offenses. The first is that as a form of punishment the death penalty serves to educate people regarding the importance of obeying the law. The second is that the death penalty deters those crimes where a killing is not intended but could result nonetheless. Armed robbery is an example of this type of offense because there is always the possibility that the victim will resist and thus be killed (whether intentionally or inadvertently). Finally, the third hypothesis is that the death penalty conserves scarce criminal justice resources which could be used to investigate and prosecute other types of crime if capital punishment had the effect of actually lowering the homicide rate.

The analysis undertaken by Bailey (1991) offers no support to the deterrence argument. Despite the fact that this study measured the death penalty in a number of ways (e.g., the number of executions during the year, the ratio of the number of executions to the number of homicides reported during the same year, etc.), there was no observed relationship between the use of capital punishment and the index felony rate. The author notes that "this pattern holds for the traditional targeted offense of murder, the person crimes (sic) of negligent manslaughter, rape, assault, and robbery, as well as the property crimes of burglary, grand larceny, and vehicle theft. In other words, there is no evidence . . . that residents of death penalty jurisdictions are afforded an added measure of protection against serious crimes by executions" (Bailey, 1991:35).

Multiple Regression Analysis

All the previous methodologies refute the myth that the death penalty is a more effective deterrent than incarceration for the crime of murder. Therefore, it was quite a shock when Isaac Ehrlich (1975) reported that his statistical model indicated that each execution saved the lives of seven to eight innocent victims. He had used a complex statistical technique known as multiple regression analysis to examine the impact of various factors on the homicide rate in the United States between 1933 and 1969. Multiple regression is a procedure that allows researchers to examine many variables simultaneously in order to determine the independent impact that each has on the murder rate. Theoretically at least, it should be possible to separate the impact on the homicide rate of the death penalty from other factors that also may contribute to homicide (such as the unemployment rate, the age distribution of the population, the proportion of citizens who own handguns, etc.). In practice, however, multiple regression models may give conflicting results depending on what variables are included in the analysis, how they are measured, and what period of observation is employed (Shin, 1978).

Ehrlich's study received widespread notice both in the popular media and among policymakers. Not surprisingly, it was the only study on deterrence cited by the Solicitor General (Robert Bork) in a brief before the United States Supreme Court that purported to show that executions deter homicide (Ellsworth, 1988). The work of Ehrlich also stimulated a great deal of research by other scholars who employed the same methodology. There were many attempts to replicate his findings. Invariably, these were unsuccessful because subsequent analysis revealed a number of critical flaws in the design of the Ehrlich study. Unfortunately, it is only possible to provide a brief overview in this chapter of these methodological shortcomings. Persons who wish to examine this issue in greater detail should consult additional sources (Bowers, 1988; Wilson, 1983; Klein et al., 1978; Zeisel, 1977; Passell and Taylor, 1976; and Bowers and Pierce, 1975).

Peter Passell and John Taylor (1976) have recognized one serious problem with Ehrlich's analysis. They report that when the 1960s are omitted from Ehrlich's data, the deterrent effect disappears. The 1960s were a period when executions were becoming relatively uncommon in the United States. Therefore, one is left to ponder the implausible conclusion that executions were not a deterrent during the 1930s and the 1940s when they were relatively routine but that they served as a deterrent during the entire time span studied by Ehrlich.

Another major criticism is that Ehrlich conducted a national analysis which did not distinguish between jurisdictions that did and those that did not execute citizens (Zeisel, 1977). Others have noted that the study failed to incorporate important variables in the data analysis (Wilson, 1983). Most importantly, the overwhelming majority of scholars who have utilized this methodology (and even the same data) have not reached the same conclusion (Passell and Taylor, 1976). Although a few studies have reported evidence of deterrence (Layson, 1985; Yunker, 1976), the overwhelming evidence on this issue points in the opposite direction (Bowers, 1988).

None of the studies that examine the deterrence question can reach the level of design that would be provided by our impossible experiment discussed earlier. Much of the research in this area contains shortcomings that have been noted by various authors (Wilson, 1983). First, the use of contiguous states may mask important differences between jurisdictions that can impact their homicide rate. Second, researchers may classify a state as retentionist because the death penalty remains on the books, even though no executions have been carried out in many years. Third, many studies utilize the total homicide rate to measure deterrence. However, not all homicides are capital crimes. A more appropriate measure would include only homicides which qualify for the death penalty. Unfortunately, these data generally do not exist.

Despite these shortcomings, what is striking is that studies utilizing a wide array of different methodologies have almost always come to the same conclusion: the belief that capital punishment is a more effective deterrent to murder than imprisonment is a myth. In fact, there are a number of research reports that suggest the death penalty may actually have a brutalizing impact on individuals (Bowers, 1988). In other words, the state does not deter homicide but in fact does the opposite when it executes a criminal. It sets a bad example, and thereby its citizens also commit murder. If this turns out to be correct, the use of capital punishment may actually be counterproductive to the goals that many supporters believe it can accomplish.

Why is the death penalty not a more effective deterrent? First, the majority of homicides occur between people who are acquainted with each other. Most of these are killings that do not involve any kind of rational calculation. Instead, the offender commits the crime in a moment of rage or passion without giving any thought whatsoever to the future consequences of this behavior. Second, in those cases that do involve premeditation, the offender generally does not expect to be apprehended. Regardless of the potential sanction, it cannot serve as a deterrent if the perpetrator does not believe that it will be applied. Finally, the death penalty does not deter more effectively than life imprisonment because these are both very harsh sentences. Douglas Heckathorn (1985) notes that no difference can be expected with respect to the general deterrent impact of two sanctions if both are perceived as severe, even if one is somewhat harsher than the other. In other words, an upper threshold is reached with respect to severity beyond which no additional deterrence occurs. For most persons, there is little meaningful difference between being put to death and spending a good part of the rest of their lives in prison. Both are very unattractive options.

The Cost of the Death Penalty

It is commonly believed that it is cheaper to execute a criminal than to keep him/her in prison for life. In fact, the authors have often been asked by students, "why should society pay to keep convicted killers housed, clothed and fed for the rest of their lives when they could be executed?" Implicit in this question is the belief that the death penalty can reduce the financial burden on the corrections system. However, this is not the case.

Intuitively, one would think that executions should be cheaper than supporting an offender in the penitentiary for many years. Indeed, a system of justice that executed suspected murderers on the spot would be less expensive than maintaining those individuals in prison for life. However, this is not the way that capital punishment is carried out in a democratic society. Because our justice system places a very high premium on protecting the lives of innocent persons, an extensive number of procedural burdens must be met before a defendant can be executed. These protections are extremely costly, but they are necessary to insure that only guilty persons receive the death penalty. Although there is some question as to whether these safeguards are always effective in accomplishing this goal, their presence insures that any system of capital punishment devised by our society will be much more expensive than life imprisonment.

There are several factors that contribute to the high cost of capital punishment. First, capital cases almost always go to trial. As we learned in chapter 11, the overwhelming majority of other felony cases are resolved through plea bargaining. This option is virtually never applied in capital cases. Because the prosecutor is asking for the death penalty, the state has nothing to offer that can induce the defendant to enter a guilty plea. Very few defendants are likely to consent to a death sentence. In a few unique cases, defendants have requested that a death sentence be carried out. These requests, however, are seldom made before adjudication. Therefore, a criminal trial becomes inevitable.

Obviously, trials take considerably more time and are more expensive than simply accepting a guilty plea from the defendant at arraignment. However, capital trials are even more time consuming and involve far greater expense than do noncapital cases. The Supreme Court has stated on several occasions that death as a punishment is qualitatively different and that defendants in such cases are entitled to a higher standard of due process. This makes every aspect of a capital trial more complex and more time consuming for the parties involved.

When the state seeks to impose the death penalty, the costs begin to accumulate even before the case is heard by the court. In a noncapital trial, prosecutors and defense attorneys routinely scrutinize prospective jurors in an attempt to gain maximum advantage at trial. However, in capital cases, the *voir dire* process becomes considerably more time consuming and requires that a greater number of prospective jurors be interviewed. To some extent, this results from the fact that the United States Supreme Court allows prosecutors in capital cases to exclude opponents of capital punishment from serving as jurors if they are unable to vote for a death sentence (*Wainwright v. Witt*, 1985). As a consequence, each prospective juror must be questioned at length regarding their views on capital punishment.

There are other reasons as well why the *voir dire* process takes longer in a capital case. Each side may be allowed a greater number of peremptory challenges than in a noncapital trial. More importantly, because there is a high degree of public interest in a capital case, a great amount of pretrial publicity may have been generated. Therefore, the defense attorney may be required to spend a substantial period of time questioning prospective jurors to insure that they have not formed an opinion prejudicial to the defendant. The cumulative effect of all these factors is that the *voir dire* process takes 5.3 times longer than in noncapital trials (Spangenberg and Walsh, 1989).

The extensive *voir dire* is not the only additional cost in a capital trial. Several other factors also come into play. Not only are defendants likely to raise a greater number of pretrial motions in these cases, these motions also tend to be more lengthy, more complex and to involve issues unique to cases where the death sentence is a potential outcome (Spangenberg and Walsh, 1989). In addition, there is generally greater use of expert witnesses in capital cases. If the defendant raises the insanity defense (which is more likely in a capital case), psychiatric testimony will be presented by experts on behalf of both the defense and the prosecution. Because many defendants are indigent, the state will be obligated to pay the psychiatric witnesses from both sides, unlike noncapital cases.

There is one final cost that must be considered when analyzing the trial stage of a capital case. In almost every jurisdiction in the United States, capital trials are bifurcated. This means that the issue of sentence (execution or imprisonment) is determined in a separate hearing that follows the verdict. In essence, there are two phases to the trial: conviction and punishment. Both of these allow for the introduction of evidence and the presentation of witnesses before the jury. As a consequence, both the prosecutor and the defense attorney may be forced to incur some of the same expenses twice. In the process, court time is also utilized in a manner that would not occur in noncapital trials.

The trial is not the only added financial burden in a capital case. There is also an appeals process that is more drawn out than in other criminal cases. Obviously, if the state is seeking the death penalty, the courts seek assurance that a grievous error has not been committed. For this reason, most states with capital punishment provide for an automatic review of death sentences by a state appellate court. In addition, there are other appeals by the defendant to both state and federal courts. Because appellate courts often give somewhat greater scrutiny to death penalty cases than to other appeals, prejudicial errors are more likely to be uncovered (Nakell, 1982). The result is that capital cases result not just in more trials but in more retrials as well.

The appeals process adds greatly to the cost of processing capital defendants. Both judges and prosecutors are forced to spend a considerable amount of time (both in court and out) dealing with issues that are raised by the defendant. This is a burden on defense attorneys as well. Robert Spangenberg and Elizabeth Walsh (1989) note that on average a capital appeal requires between five hundred and one thousand hours of defense attorney time. In some cases, the entire defense cost is paid by the state.

The final cost consideration is that capital defendants require special accommodations within the correctional system. They are not treated like other inmates. Instead, they are placed in a maximum security setting in jail upon arrest. This is followed by a move to death row after their sentence is handed down. The level of security on death row is far more elaborate than in other sections of the prison. This entails substantially greater cost in terms of staff time than would be needed to house other inmates. In addition, the stay is not brief. For persons executed during 1989, the average time spent under a sentence of death was seven years and eleven months (Bureau of Justice Statistics, 1990).

When all these extra costs are considered, it is not surprising that a number of empirical studies have found that a criminal justice system that includes the death penalty is more expensive than one without this sanction. For example, Duke University professors Philip Cook and Donna Slawson studied North Carolina's experience with the death penalty and found that it costs taxpayers an additional $2.2 million to execute a killer as opposed to a sentence of 20 years to life. As Franklin Zimring of the University of California explains, "It's always more expensive to have and use the death penalty than it is not to have it, for the simple reason that lawyers are more expensive than prison guards" (Chapman, 1995:25).

Similar findings have been reported for other states as well (Tabak and Lane, 1989). In Florida, each execution cost that jurisdiction over $3 million, or approximately six times the amount that would be spent to incarcerate these individuals for life. The cost of executing one person in New Jersey was estimated to be approximately $7.3 million. In California, it has been reported that the taxpayers could save $90 million per year by abolishing the death penalty (Tabak and Lane, 1989). Finally, the enormous costs associated with capital cases were a factor in the reluctance of the Kansas legislature to reinstate the death penalty during the 1980s (Spangenberg and Walsh, 1989). However, they did do so in 1994 (Dvorak, 1994).

Having observed that capital punishment is more expensive than life imprisonment, the question arises: how much weight should financial considerations carry in the debate over the death penalty? Proponents of the death penalty would argue that if justice demands this sanction for certain offenders, cost should not be a factor in the decision-making process. However, this rationale overlooks the fact that only a finite amount of resources are available to the criminal justice system. Therefore, the proper context in which to consider cost is to compare the benefits of capital punishment versus other policy options. For example, is society better protected by executing a small number of persons, or could these dollars be utilized more effectively by permanently incarcerating three times as many offenders? Perhaps it would be wiser to allocate this money for more police officers. These are the kinds of public policy alternatives that could be addressed once it is understood that the death penalty is more expensive than life imprisonment.

Incapacitation

Another myth surrounding the death penalty is the belief that this punishment is necessary to protect both society and prison inmates from persons who are likely to kill again. Indeed, correctional administrators often express concern that if convicted capital offenders are not put to death, they will cause mayhem in the institution and place the lives of other inmates in jeopardy. Whether this concern is warranted is a question that has received some attention in the research literature.

Clearly, persons who receive the death penalty cannot commit future murders. However, the question that must be addressed is whether capital punishment performs this incapacitative function more effectively than life imprisonment. In other words, what is the marginal benefit of the death penalty in terms of protecting society from persons who have already demonstrated that they have the capacity to take human life? This is a question that has been examined from a number of perspectives.

Persons serving time for murder may have the opportunity to kill again under one of two circumstances: they may commit another homicide while in prison or in the community if released on parole. The most massive study of recidivism by parolees who had been convicted of murder was undertaken by Sellin (1980). He reported on the post-release behavior of 6,835 male convicts serving sentences for willful homicide who were released on parole from state institutions between 1969 and 1973. This study concluded that in the three-year period following their release, 310 (4.5 percent) of these individuals were returned to prison for committing a new crime. However, only 21 (0.31 percent of the total group) returned because they had committed another willful homicide (Sellin, 1980). In fact, these individuals were less likely to commit murder while on parole than persons who originally had been sentenced for armed robbery, forcible rape or aggravated assault (Sellin, 1980).

Unfortunately, the Sellin study is not an examination of the behavior of persons who had been sentenced for capital murder. Many of the individuals in his study had been convicted of second degree murder or voluntary manslaughter. Thus, it may not be possible to infer from this research how persons convicted of capital murder would behave if released from prison. However, an event occurred in 1972 that made such analysis possible. The United States Supreme Court ruled in *Furman v. Georgia* that the death penalty as it had been administered up to that time was cruel and unusual punishment in violation of the Eighth and Fourteenth Amendments to the constitution. As a consequence, all persons who were awaiting execution in the United States had their sentences commuted to life imprisonment.

At the time of the *Furman* decision, there were over 600 inmates on death row. This ruling by the Court therefore provided an opportunity to conduct a natural experiment. Researchers have been able to follow up on the activities of these commuted inmates and observe how they behave when released into the general prison population. In addition, because many of these prisoners have eventually been placed on parole, it has been possible to examine their behavior upon release into the community.

To date, several researchers have tracked the behavior of inmates whose sentences were commuted as a result of the *Furman* decision. James Marquart and Jonathan Sorensen (1988) looked at 47 persons in Texas who were taken off death row by this decision. They compared these convicts to a control group of 156 inmates who had been sentenced to life imprisonment for either murder or rape (the same offenses for which the *Furman* inmates had been sentenced to death). Comparisons were drawn between the behavior of these inmates both in prison and following release on parole.

The study reported that despite the fact that both groups spent an average of approximately one decade in prison, 75 percent of the *Furman*-commuted inmates and 70 percent of the comparison group did not commit a serious violation of institutional rules (Marquart and Sorensen, 1988). Most significantly, no inmate in either group was implicated in a prison homicide. The authors conclude that "the *Furman* inmates, as compared with the life sentence cohort, were not unusually disruptive or rebellious, nor did they pose a disproportionate threat to other inmates and staff, as had been previously predicted by clinicians and administrators" (Marquart and Sorensen, 1988:686).

These researchers also analyzed the parole behavior of inmates who had been released into the community. Overall, only 14 percent of the *Furman*-commuted inmates committed a new felony upon release. Although this is a somewhat higher figure than the percentage for the life sentence cohort (6 percent), the authors attribute this finding to the somewhat longer period that the former group had spent in the community (Marquart and Sorensen, 1988). There was little actual difference upon release between the behavior of convicts who had originally been sentenced to death and those who had been given life imprisonment. Furthermore, only one of the parolees who had spent time on death row committed another homicide after being released from the institution. Clearly, fears that these individuals would be a menace to society if released turned out to be unfounded.

Gennaro Vito, Pat Koester and Deborah Wilson (1991) have undertaken additional analysis of *Furman*-commuted inmates. Although their focus is similar to that of Marquart and Sorensen, the cohort they examined includes all persons still living in 1987 who were removed from death row in twenty-six states by the *Furman* decision in 1972 (N = 457). These authors report that 177 of these inmates were eventually paroled and that eight (4.5 percent) committed another violent crime after release. This included three parolees who committed a new murder. Consequently, the repeat homicide rate for this group was 1.6 percent. Based on these findings, the authors conclude "that societal protection from convicted capital murderers is not greatly enhanced by the death penalty" (Vito et al., 1991:96).

Although various studies found a few convicted murderers who killed again. Sellin (1980) observed that murderers on parole are less likely to kill than convicts paroled after being convicted of other violent offenses. Marquart and Sorensen (1988) noted that persons who originally were placed on death row in Texas were no more dangerous either in prison or upon release into the community than inmates sentenced to life imprisonment. In fact, many of the convicts who had their sentence commuted by *Furman* became model prisoners.

Therefore, it must be concluded that the death penalty offers little additional protection to society over that which can be achieved through life imprisonment. It is a myth to believe that the safety of citizens, inmates or prison staff depends in any way on the imposition of capital punishment.

Fighting Crime

Another myth regarding the death penalty is that it is an effective tool in the battle against crime. It is true that the United States is plagued with an inordinate amount of violent crime compared to other Western nations. However, whether or not we continue to execute offenders is irrelevant in society's attempt to control crime. Despite the rhetoric that is often generated by candidates for public office, much of the discussion regarding capital punishment that takes place in political campaigns is a diversion from the real issues that must be confronted if we are to reduce the level of crime in America.

The United States Supreme Court ruled in *Coker v. Georgia* (1977) that the death penalty may not be imposed for the crime of raping an adult woman. Although the court did not explicitly rule out the use of capital punishment for other offenses that do not include the death of the victim, the rationale of this decision would seem to preclude this possibility. The holding was that rape is a very serious crime, but it does not involve the taking of a human life. Consequently, to execute an offender for the rape of an adult woman would constitute cruel and unusual punishment in violation of the Eighth Amendment. This decision would seem to rule out the use of capital punishment for other serious crimes that did not cause death, such as armed robbery and air piracy.

As a result of the *Coker* decision, the death penalty is a possibility only in cases where the defendant is charged with murder. In fact, in those jurisdictions that retain this sanction, it is authorized only for certain types of murder. Not only must the crime meet the requisite legal criteria to be classified as capital murder, the prosecutor must also demonstrate to the jury that certain aggravating circumstances were present. As a consequence, only a small proportion of persons charged with murder can be sentenced to death. Even fewer are actually sentenced and executed.

In order to understand how infrequently capital punishment is actually carried out, it is necessary to present a few facts. Between 1980 and 1989, there were 206,710 murders reported to the police (Maguire and Pastore, 1994). However, during the same period (1980–1989), only 117 executions were actually carried out (Bureau of Justice Statistics, 1994). This translates into approximately one execution for every 1,767 murders committed during this time frame. "The United States has nearly 3,000 people on death row, but last year [1994], it executed only 31, Meanwhile, it has some 24,000 homicides a year. A killer has only a slightly greater chance of dying in the electric chair than of being struck by lightning" (Chapman, 1995:25). Clearly, the death penalty is a rare event and cannot be considered a serious crime control strategy.

Capital punishment is applied in only a tiny fraction of murder cases. However, murder is only part of the crime problem in the United States. In most cases, citizens are not afraid to walk the streets of our cities because they fear being murdered. Most killings occur between persons who are acquainted with each other. What makes citizens fearful for their safety are concerns related to muggings, rapes, and assaults. These are the offenses that occur with great frequency and that diminish the quality of life in many communities. During 1992, there were 672,480 robberies, 1,126,970 aggravated assaults, and 109,060 rapes reported to the police in the United States (Maguire and Pastore, 1994). The death penalty is totally irrelevant in these cases.

Therefore, it must be concluded that the notion that the death penalty is a solution to the crime problem is a myth. Legally, it may only be imposed for certain types of murder; even under those circumstances, it is rarely used. It is totally irrelevant to the question of how to make our streets safe from the reported 1.9 million or so other violent felonies that occur each year. Perhaps the most unfortunate aspect of the debate regarding capital punishment is that it diverts attention away from legitimate solutions to the crime problem. It is far easier for a politician to flaunt his or her support for the death penalty (especially when opinion polls indicate that this is a popular position) than to offer meaningful proposals for reducing the level of street crime.

William Rentschler (1994:19) notes: "The death penalty is so widely accepted largely because it provides a measure of seeming certainty to a society greatly frustrated by its inability to solve its most vexatious problems. But it is a simplistic answer, akin to the primitive law of the jungle. It is evidence of a society unwilling and incapable of coming to grips rationally with hard challenges. Capital punishment makes a mockery of such noble legal canons as equal justice under law. . . . The death penalty is reserved exclusively for society's little people, its powerless, its rabble, its dregs. This alone makes capital punishment wrong in a just society." He points to the Simpson case as an example of the fact that wealth, fame and community standing prove a Russian proverb: "No one is hanged who has money in his pocket." Another commentator rephrased the concept in the vernacular of the streets "If you've got the capital, you don't get the punishment" (Page, 1995:15). As Robert Bohm has noted (1989:192) "capital punishment offers a simplistic and believable solution to a complex phenomenon of which the public is frightened and of which it is generally uninformed." A more educated public can serve as a catalyst to raise the level of discourse in this area.

Conclusion

This chapter has attempted to debunk a number of myths regarding the death penalty. The discussion began with a broad overview of the vast literature on the question of general deterrence. It was noted that, despite a wide range of methodologies that have been employed to address this issue, there is no evidence that capital punishment is more effective as a deterrent to murder than incarceration. This was followed by a discussion of the costs that capital cases entail. Contrary to what many persons believe, it was noted that a system of justice which includes the death sentence is actually more expensive than one without this sanction.

Other myths were examined as well. Proponents of capital punishment often assert that executions are necessary to protect citizens from convicted killers who are likely to repeat their crimes. However, evidence was presented that suggests rather clearly that capital offenders do not present an inordinate risk to other inmates, correctional staff, or to persons in the general community. Finally, the discussion explored whether the death penalty is necessary to fight crime. It was concluded that capital punishment is largely irrelevant to the war on crime.

Having observed that the death penalty is not a more effective general deterrent to murder, that it is more costly than life imprisonment, that it is not necessary to protect society or to fight crime, the question remains: is there any rational basis for supporting retention of capital punishment? Clearly, this sanction can only be defended on grounds of retribution. In William Rentschler's (1994:19) words:

> Many want to rid society permanently of the slavering brutes they perceive as perpetrators of violence. A sizable majority of citizens would give the state virtual carte blanche to exterminate these beasts.

> But wait. The "slavering brute" image embraces only a fraction of those who murder, maim and commit hideous, heinous crimes. . . . homicides are committed in greater numbers by family members, including parents and children, friends, neighbors and business associates, than by prowling, predatory strangers.

The death penalty is "a punishment of perfect exactness administered by a justice system filled with imperfect human beings who often have inexact knowledge. Imprisonment leaves us moral room to make the inevitable errors and arbitrary applications; killing does not" (Zorn, 1995:1). It is disproportionately applied to the poor, illiterate, African-Americans and Hispanics. Proponents should consider a number of questions before embracing the mythical aspects of the death penalty. For example, why have all other Western nations abandoned this practice (Zimring and Hawkins, 1986)? Are innocent persons occasionally executed (Bedau and Radelet, 1987)? Is the death penalty carried out in a racially discriminatory manner (Paternoster and Kazyaka, 1988)? Whether the public will remain supportive of capital punishment if executions become routine events is uncertain (Wallace, 1989). What is certain is that aspects of these myths cling tenaciously in the public conscious and politicians exploit public fear to gain favor. If public policy is based on myth, areas that should be analyzed will be ignored.

Sources

Andenaes, J. (1974). *Punishment and Deterrence*. Ann Arbor: University of Michigan Press.

Bailey, W. (1991). The General Prevention Effect of Capital Punishment for Non-Capital Felonies. In *The Death Penalty in America: Current Research*, R. Bohm (ed.). Cincinnati, OH: Anderson and Academy of Criminal Justice Sciences.

———— (1982). Capital Punishment and Lethal Assaults Against Police. *Criminology* 19:608–25.

Bailey, W. and Peterson, R. (1987). Police Killings and Capital Punishment: The Post-Furman Period. *Criminology* 25(1): 1–25.

Bedau, H. (ed.) (1982). *The Death Penalty in America*, 3rd ed. Oxford: Oxford University Press.

Bedau, H. and Radelet, M. (1987). Miscarriages of Justice in Potentially Capital Cases. *Stanford Law Review* 40:21–179.

Berns, W. (1979). *For Capital Punishment*. New York: Basic Books.

Bohm, R. (1989). Humanism and the Death Penalty, with Special Emphasis on the Post-*Furman* Experience. *Justice Quarterly* 6:173–95.

Bowers, W. (1988). The Effect of Executions is Brutalization, Not Deterrence. In *Challenging Capital Punishment: Legal and Social Science Approaches*, K. Haas and J. Inciardi (eds.). Newbury Park, CA: Sage Publications.

Bowers, W. and Pierce, G. (1975). The Illusion of Deterrence in Isaac Ehrlich's Research on Capital Punishment. *Yale Law Journal* 85:187–208.

Bowers, W., Pierce, G. and McDevitt, J. (1984). *Legal Homicide: Death as Punishment in America, 1864–1982*. Boston: Northeastern University Press.

Bureau of Justice Statistics (1994). *Capital Punishment 1993*, Washington, DC: U.S. Department of Justice.

———— (1990). *Capital Punishment 1989*. Washington, DC: U.S. Department of Justice.

———— (1987). *Sentencing Outcomes in Twenty-Eight Felony Courts 1985*. Washington, DC: U.S. Department of Justice.

Cardarelli, A. (1968). An Analysis of Police Killed in Criminal Action: 1961–1963. *Journal of Criminal Law, Criminology and Police Science* 59:447–53.

Chapman, S. (1995). Dead Reckoning. *Chicago Tribune*, (March 2): 25.

Coker v. Georgia, 433 U.S. 584 (1977).

Dann, R. (1935). The Deterrent Effect of Capital Punishment. *Friends Social Service Series* 29.

Dvorak, J. (1994). Kansas Passes Death Penalty. *Kansas City Star*, (April 9): A1.

Ehrlich, I. (1975). The Deterrent Effect of Capital Punishment: A Question of Life and Death. *American Economic Review* 65:397–417.

Ellsworth, P. (1988). Unpleasant Facts: The Supreme Court's Response to Empirical Research on Capital Punishment. In *Challenging Capital Punishment: Legal and Social Science Approaches*, K. Haas and J. Inciardi (eds.). Newbury Park, CA: Sage Publications.

Flanagan, T. and Maguire, K. (1990). *Sourcebook of Criminal Justice Statistics 1989*. Albany, NY: The Hindelang Criminal Justice Research Center.

Furman v. Georgia, 408 U.S. 238 (1972).

Graves, W. (1956). A Doctor Looks at Capital Punishment. *Medical Arts and Sciences, Journal of the Loma Linda University School of Medicine* 10(4): 137–41.

Heckathorn, D. (1985). Why Punishment Does Not Deter. In *The Ambivalent Force: Perspectives on the Police*, 3rd ed., A. Blumberg and E. Niederhoffer (eds.). New York: Holt, Rinehart and Winston.

Hunter, R. and Wood, R. (1994). Impact of Felony Sanctions: An Analysis of Weaponless Assaults upon Police. *American Journal of Police* 13(1): 65–89.

Jamieson, K. and Flanagan, T. (1989). *Sourcebook of Criminal Justice Statistics 1988*. Albany, NY: The Hindelang Criminal Justice Research Center.

Klein, L., Forst, B. and Filatov, V. (1978). The Deterrent Effect of Capital Punishment: An Assessment of the Estimates. In *Deterrence and Incapacitation: Estimating the Effects of Criminal Sanctions on Crime Rates*, A. Blumstein, J. Cohen and D. Nagin (eds.). Washington, DC: National Academy of Sciences.

Layson, S. (1985). Homicide and Deterrence: A Reexamination of the United States Time-Series Evidence. *Southern Economic Journal* 52:68–89.

Lehtinen, M. (1977). The Voice of Life: An Argument for the Death Penalty. *Crime & Delinquency* 23:237–52.

Maguire, K. and Pastore, A. (1994). *Sourcebook of Criminal Justice Statistics 1993*. Albany, NY: The Hindelang Criminal Justice Research Center.

Marquart, J. and Sorensen, J. (1988). Institutional and Postrelease Behavior of *Furman*-Commuted Inmates in Texas. *Criminology* 26:677–93.

Nakell, B. (1982). The Cost of the Death Penalty. In *The Death Penalty in America*, 3rd ed., H. Bedau (ed.). Oxford: Oxford University Press.

Page, C. (1995). The Murky Line Between Who Gets Life or Death. *Chicago Tribune*, (August 2), sec. 1:15.

Passell, P. and Taylor, J. (1976). The Deterrent Controversy: A Reconsideration of the Time Series Evidence. In *Capital Punishment in the United States*, H. Bedau and C. Pierce (eds.). New York: AMS Press.

Paternoster, R. and Kazyaka, A. (1988). Racial Considerations in Capital Punishment: The Failure of Evenhanded Justice. In *Challenging Capital Punishment: Legal and Social Science Approaches*, K. Haas and J. Inciardi (eds.). Newbury Park, CA: Sage Publications.

Rentschler, W. (1994). The Death Penalty—A Pivotal Issue. *Chicago Tribune*, (November 29): 19.

Sellin, T. (1980). *The Penalty of Death.* Beverly Hills: Sage Publications.

Shin, K. (1978). *Death Penalty and Crime.* Fairfax, VA: Center for Economic Analysis.

Spangenberg, R. and Walsh, E. (1989). Capital Punishment or Life Imprisonment?: Some Cost Considerations. *Loyola of Los Angeles Law Review* 23:45–58.

Stack, S. (1987). Publicized Executions and Homicide, 1950–1980. *American Sociological Review* 52:532–40.

Tabak, R. and Lane, J. (1989). The Execution of Injustice: A Cost and Lack-of-Benefit Analysis of the Death Penalty. *Loyola of Los Angeles Law Review* 23:136.

van den Haag, E. (1978). In Defense of the Death Penalty: A Legal-Practical-Moral Analysis. *Criminal Law Bulletin* 14:51–68.

Vito, G., Koester, P. and Wilson, D. (1991). Return of the Dead: An Update on the Status of Furman-Commuted Death Row Inmates. In *The Death Penalty in America: Current Research*, R. Bohm (ed.). Cincinnati, OH: Anderson and Academy of Criminal Justice Sciences.

Wainwright v. Witt, 105 S. Ct. 844 (1985).

Wallace, D. (1989). Bloodbath and Brutalization: Public Opinion and the Death Penalty. *Journal of Crime and Justice* 12:51–77.

Wilson, J. (1983). *Thinking About Crime*, rev. ed. New York: Basic Books.

Wolfson, W. (1982). The Deterrent Effect of the Death Penalty upon Prison Murder. In *The Death Penalty in America*, 3rd ed., H. Bedau (ed.). Oxford: Oxford University Press.

Yunker, J. (1976). Is the Death Penalty a Deterrent to Homicide? Some Time Series Evidence. *Journal of Behavioral Economics*, 5:1–32.

Zeisel, H. (1977). The Deterrent Effect of the Death Penalty: Facts v. Faith. In *The Supreme Court Review 1976*, P. Kurland (ed.). Chicago: University of Chicago Press.

Zimring, F. and Hawkins, G. (1986). *Capital Punishment and the American Agenda.* Cambridge: Cambridge University Press.

Zorn, E. (1995). Davis' Execution may Reveal Folly of Eye for an Eye. *Chicago Tribune*, (May 18). sec. 2:1.

Merging Myths and Misconceptions of Crime and Justice

15

E ventually, public focus on a particular crime wanes allowing the mythical characteristics to settle into social reality. New social problems will then emerge or old myths will be dredged up to remind us of who the criminals are and how to go about solving crime problems. After the initial fear and panic surrounding a crime myth subsides, the conceptual residue becomes a frame of reference for determining our future views of social problems. Crime myths become mental filters through which social issues are sifted. Although crime myths fade, their effect on our conception of crime and justice linger. Once a myth becomes entrenched in thought, it takes only an occasional incident to fan the smoldering embers of the latent myth into another flame of public attention. This process of interpreting problems to fit our myth-based notions of crime and justice is enhanced if mythmakers construct new problems or events within the framework of previously constructed myths. Such characterizations and historical frames of reference insure that mythical conceptions of crime never truly die. One of the powers of crime myth is that past conceptions blend with present events to create future conceptions of crime. In this sense, crime myths lend historical and conceptual continuity to our perceptions of crime and its control.

It is too early to speculate on the specific effects contemporary crime myths will have on our future conceptions of crime and justice, but it is not too early to heed the admonishment that our picture of violent crime in America results from a composition of panics promoted by the mythmakers of society. Moreover, these panics tend to fold into one another, supporting the idea that society is somehow under siege by crime (Jenkins and Katkin, 1988). As crime myths fold into one another, they begin a recycling process that can form a single, unified, and very popular conception of the reality of crime in America. Conceptual bits and pieces of the myths of stranger child abduction, serial murderers, stalkers, organized crime and predatory street criminals may merge to form an enveloping mythology of violent crime. Similarly, myths of the dangers of police work, the equity of the judicial process and misconceptions of punitive justice may fuse to create a single ideology of the proper social response to crime. Once a unified conception of crime and its control becomes a part of popular thought and governmental policy, the empirical reality of crime will mirror and support our mythology.

Under our mythology of crime, the police role will be limited to vigorously tracking stereotyped criminals—unfettered by constitutional restraint. Social service aspects of policing will be reduced to rhetoric that merely masks the core function, and crime fighting will truly become the police response to social problems. The role of the judiciary will be similar to an assembly line with judges moving through their dockets at great speed, unhindered by the niceties of due process. We will fill our newly built prisons with those who are "different" (the poor, uneducated, minority members, organized criminals, and drug offenders), and we will continue to search for new technologies that enable the justice system to widen its net of social control. The death penalty, the ultimate and most final solution to crime, will be carried out with greater swiftness and frequency without constraints and delays.

The empirical reality of crime (which results from the focus we choose) will be offered as evidence of our mythical conceptions. Stalkers kill—especially if we only study stalkers who have killed. A neat tautology but dangerously unenlightening. Consider the rise in reported child abuse. Few issues raise more concern, fear, and the impulse to protect than child abuse. In 1973, Congress passed the Child Abuse Prevention and Treatment Act (CAPTA) which provides federal matching funds to states that comply with strict federal guidelines for child-abuse detection, prosecution, and prevention programs. From 1976 to 1993, the yearly number of child abuse reports grew from 669,000 to more than 2.9 million (Brott, 1995). In 1995, there were proposals to dismantle CAPTA and to return child abuse policy to the states. Opinions are sharply divided over whether the law should be changed. It has focused attention on terrible harm, but that focus has sometimes been skewed. Under CAPTA, states must pass laws requiring people in contact with children (such as doctors, therapists and teachers) to report all incidents of suspected abuse. If they do not, they may be fined or imprisoned; if they do, they are granted immunity from prosecution for causing false prosecutions. According to Richard Gardner, professor of child psychiatry at Columbia Medical School, "The mandated reporting and immunity provisions have created a child-abuse establishment—a network of social workers, psychologists and law-enforcement officials who actually encourage charges of child abuse, whether they're reasonable or not" (Brott, 1995:10). Gardner cites figures indicating that unsubstantiated reports of abuse increased from 35 percent in 1973 to 66 percent in 1993. Therapists in San Diego testified before a grand jury that they fear removal from an approved list of mental health professionals if they oppose the recommendations of child protection agencies. Critics of the law claim that people falsely accused or even imprisoned have little or no recourse. While the act was passed for defensible purposes, its mandates have created unforeseen difficulties and, in many cases, have "manufactured" criminals. Not only have the lives of persons unjustly accused been irrevocably changed, but the process of demonization creates more anxiety as the public unconsciously assimilates a distorted view of a world out of control.

In all myths, there resides a kernel of truth. How that kernel germinates and proliferates and the intended and unintended consequences attached to proposed solutions determine its potency. We cannot look only at reported crime, police records, court dockets, the composition of prison populations, and who is put to death to determine the characteristics of criminals or to determine if society is more dangerous today. Rather, we must examine all facets of the system and the social context in which the system operates to determine if our definitions and the processes we endorse are the problem.

Solutions to Mythical Crimes

Will political leaders, government officials and the media continue to promote mythical solutions to crime? One of the most obvious effects of crime myths is political. Calls for stiffer penalties for the unpopular group and further protections of innocents are the two most prominent political actions requested. The emotional furor and fear generated by myth production create a context for political grandstanding. This grandstanding often takes the form of proposing new crimes and classes of criminals. It is common for political leaders to advocate the use of the most severe criminal sanctions, such as the death penalty, at the pinnacle of sensationalism over a particular issue. Although few of these calls are ever transformed into formal social control, they do promote current beliefs that existing solutions to crime are acceptable and viable options for reducing both crime and the related social problems. What is certain is that while there has been a marked downturn in crime for the last twenty years, there has also been an accompanying increase in punitiveness. Starting in the 1970s and extending to today, there has been a trend in the United States toward becoming one of the harshest nations in the world in dealing with crime. Despite the myth that criminal justice is "soft" on crime, the facts are simple: we lock up more people, for longer sentences, for more offenses than any nation on the face of the earth. Not only is this incongruous in a country with a declining crime problem—and inherently brutal—but the policy is self-defeating. Mythical definitions are making the situation worse and creating more crime—the very situation the mythical solutions set out to correct.

Longer sentences for repeat offenders continue to be a political panacea for crime. It is an easy solution to sell because it seems logical. According to popular folk wisdom, severe punishment and the certainty of prison will deter crime. That may be commonsense logic, but it is wrong. The simple fact is that prison does not deter crime, and severe sanctions probably increase the amount of crime in society. If prison terms deterred further criminality, we would expect that people who go to prison would be among those least likely to be there again. However, the fact is that about 60 percent of everyone in prison has been there previously (Greenfield, 1985). Most prisoners eventually released from correctional institutions are rearrested, and about two out of five end up back in prison (Beck and Shipley, 1987). Does length of time spent in prison affect future criminality? Research studies have clearly demonstrated that there is no connection between time served in a correctional institution and the likelihood that a prisoner will commit further crimes (Cook, 1980, cited in Livingston, 1992). Research shows that individuals paroled before the end of their sentences are no more likely to commit additional crimes than prisoners who serve their full sentences (Greenberg, 1975, cited in Livingston, 1992). In fact, several studies have shown that the more severe the sanctions and the more frequent their administration, the greater the probability of additional criminality (Livingston, 1992; Shannon, 1982; Gottfredson, et al. 1973). As discussed earlier, the same lack of deterrence is clearly demonstrated for the death penalty, which not only fails to deter homicide but may well stimulate additional homicides through a "brutalization effect."

So the commonsense logic of deterrence is neither logical nor sensible. It is based on a fundamental misunderstanding of both criminals and crime. For deterrence to work, the offender must be a logical actor who understands the consequences of criminal behavior, knows the penalties and weighs the costs of crime against the benefits of crime. Logic and calm reflection are simply not parts of the crime equation. In addition, a sizable number of offenders are people without hope, living in desperate circumstances. They are the poor, the unemployed and underemployed, the uneducated, and the socially alienated. Fear of prison is a relatively minor consideration when stacked up against the dismal hopelessness of their day-to-day existence. Yet, police and politicians continue to pledge eradication of mythical crime problems through more law and order and more punishment.

An inevitable part of fighting mythical crime is a call for more police power. The mythmakers argue that if the police are unable to solve our crime problems it is only because we have failed to employ enough law enforcement officers or because we have not allowed them to be aggressive enough in fighting crime. Myths of the dangers of police work and the growing dangerousness of criminals merged to form federal legislation. In 1988, a New York police officer named Eddie Byrne was killed while investigating a drug-related crime. This incident, in part, led Congress to enact a federal death penalty clause that allows the sentence of capital punishment to be imposed for "a defendant who kills or counsels to kill a law enforcement officer, while attempting to avoid apprehension, punishment, or sentencing for a drug violation . . ." (Williams, 1991:394). The legislative history of the act indicated that "the murder of New York City police officer, Eddie Byrne, was one of the motivations for applying the death penalty section to those who kill law enforcement officers over drug-related offenses" (Williams, 1991:394). While the killing of any law enforcement officer is a tragedy that should not go unnoticed by society, it is a rare event. Law enforcement officers and their families, as well as the general public, may feel that this legislation is a necessary step to protect police officers. As noted earlier, however, the number of police officers killed in the line of duty has been declining for over two decades. Very few officers are killed under circumstances that would allow for the use of the federal drug death penalty clause. It is ironic that the federal government created a federal death penalty law when the state in which the incident occurred did not deem such a law necessary. Another factor that makes the Congressional action noteworthy is that the government has helped to promote linkage between the myths of the dangers of police work, the evils of drug use, and the viability of the death penalty. Congress took no similar action against Miami police officers who killed drug traffickers in order to steal and later sell their drug cargo, and there are far more incidents of police drug corruption than there are cases of police officers killed by drug trafficking criminals. Nor were there calls from the citizens of New York for the death penalty for corrupt police officers like Michael Dowd. The drugs reach the same market whether sold by "criminals" or corrupt police officers. In the New Orleans Police Department corruption extended to the murder of an officer by his partner, yet there were no calls for the death penalty.

The myth that the death penalty will reduce crime is gaining more support everyday. In 1993 New Jersey legislators sought to allow prosecutors to seek the death penalty even in cases where the accused had no intent to injure or kill the victim. In 1994, Iowa's Governor announced that he would introduce a bill that mirrored the federal death penalty clause for drug-related homicides, despite the fact that Iowa abolished the death penalty in 1965. In 1995, legislators were taking another look at re-enacting the death penalty. Also in 1995, Governor George Pataki signed legislation to make New York the thirty-eighth state with a death penalty—an act all previous governors of that state had refused.

Two explanations exist for the enactment of the federal death penalty clause and New York's second look at using death. Either Congress was drawn into the myths of policing, drug crime and the death penalty, or the motivations were purely political. What better way for politicians to promote myths than to create a law that gives the impression of being tough on crime but which has little or no potential for use. Such a symbolic law does, however, reinforce myths of drug crime and police work while forging a symbolic link to the death penalty as the final solution to our crime problems. In President Clinton's State of the Union address in 1995, he proudly stated that the death penalty could be used in over sixty federal crimes. He also was careful to protect the recently passed Brady Bill by vowing not to allow automatic weapons back on to the streets so that law enforcement officers would no longer have to confront a "hail of bullets."

In the aftermath of the 1995 bombing of the federal building in Oklahoma City, the political reaction was swift, certain—and redundant. Political leaders called for the hiring of an additional 1,000 federal law enforcement officers, the passage of sweeping legal reform to grant greater powers to law enforcement officials to invade citizens' privacy, and the more frequent use of the death penalty. Law enforcement officials also added their voice to the chorus calling for the creation of a national center for tracking and monitoring "dangerous" groups. Political leaders, law enforcement officials and the media gave scant attention to the fact that law enforcement's quick capture of a suspect was not the work of brilliant criminalists, not a product of elaborate profiling, nor was it made possible by a newly surrendered civil right, but rather it was the product of a chance encounter with a state trooper enforcing a traffic violation. Government officials, law enforcement officers, political leaders and the media were silent as to the fact that the government's own research indicates that terrorist acts in the United States and its territories have declined dramatically over the past decade. Consider Robert Wright's (1995:86) observations on the bombing:

> In a sense, it is natural that we worry irrationally—that we are terrified by images of Americans "just like us" dying violently. The human mind evolved to assess and address risk on the basis of such images. But that's because during human evolution, before television, such images did reflect risk—local risk. Further galvanizing us is the fact that bombings are intentional; aspiring bombers are out there somewhere, to be stopped. Death by traffic mishap, in contrast, has no plan, no perpetrator. It seems the inexorable working of fate or chance, and we accept each year's statistics, if we notice them at all, with resignation.
>
> Sounds rational, but it isn't. Whereas heading off the next bomber is a chancy business at best, we could, if we chose, adjust highway death downward with nearly the precision of a volume control knob. We could better enforce speed limits, say, or close all bars at dusk. Implicitly, society chooses not to save lives this way. Drivers and drinkers would bridle at the

inconvenience. Indeed, most states have raised the speed limit to 65 m.p.h. since 1987, adding an estimated 400 to 500 deaths a year nationwide.

That's defensible. Life is full of tough trade-offs between ease and safety, and we have to draw the lines somewhere. But do these trade-offs of convenience really warrant more reverence than trade-offs of civil liberty? If saving a few hundred lives— including children's lives—wouldn't justify a loss in highway efficiency, does it really justify growth of the government's power to eavesdrop and otherwise intrude on our lives?

There are very real consequences to supporting the hard-line law and order approach to crime control, flooding our streets with law enforcement officers and surrendering civil rights because of fear. One of these consequences is allowing the "troops" in the crime war to develop their own means for dealing with crime and criminals. In March of 1991 an amateur video camera enthusiast captured footage of Los Angeles Police Department (LAPD) officers beating a young African-American man following a traffic stop. California Highway Patrol officers had detected Rodney King speeding in an automobile. Following a brief chase, the unarmed King exited his vehicle. He was shocked with a 50,000 volt stun-gun and struck savagely at least fifty times as he lay upon the ground. Over twenty police officers from several different departments stood watching or participated in the beating. King's injuries included a fractured skull, a broken cheek bone and ankle, various internal injuries, burns, and brain damage.

As disturbing as the beating was, the investigation of the incident by officials was even more shocking. Tests of vehicles similar to that driven by King found that even a newer version of his car could not travel at the speeds the California Highway Patrol officers had reported. "California Highway Patrol records confirmed that during the car chase that preceded the beating, King was never going more than 65 mph, not 115 mph as police reported earlier" (Baker, 1991:19). Also, the LAPD officers' official arrest report claimed that King was under the influence of PCP—a strong hallucinogenic. According to blood tests, however, no PCP was detected.

LAPD officers apparently had learned their myths well—they were waging a war in society which called for drastic and often brutal measures, but characterizing suspects as drug users and "enemies" defying authority would shield officers from the consequences of misconduct. To characterize King as a PCP user justified an aggressive police response, since the public knows that persons under the influence of drugs are violent. Would the incident have received any attention at all if there had been no video detailing the severity of the beating? Would King have been characterized as a drug user and therefore just another casualty in the war against mythical crime? We should note that there was no legislative frenzy to create a new crime category targeting police officers who savagely torture motorists—only explanations: the police have a hard time fighting the war against crime; the LAPD is understaffed; police have to be aggressive; and remember, King had a criminal record.

Incidents like this beg for increased expenditures for law enforcement—not for the development of national centers to track down mythical criminals or tactical forces with "no-knock" latitude to invade our homes—but to train law enforcement officers on the realities of social problems like murder, domestic violence and child abuse, as well as reasonable police responses. Through our growing panic and concern over serial murder, missing children, stalkers, street crime and terrorist activities, we have enhanced law enforcement resources, developed task forces, implemented national programs, and created vast bureaucracies to deal with crime myths. Once created, bureaucratic machines are seldom dismantled even when their need is called into question. They take on a life of their own and have a vested interest in creating and continuing the very crime myths they were designed to eliminate.

Consider Otwin Marenin's (1991:17) reflections on the legacy of the law and order conservatism sweeping America:

> As rights were denounced, so were procedures which protect them. A false solution was created—if only some rights were stripped away we will succeed in fighting the scourge of lawlessness; if only the Police had a few more powers they might not have to beat on people who look as if they might insist on their rights; if only Judges were denied control of cases and evidence then guilty people could not avoid being found guilty; if prisoners could be housed four to a cell and death-row inmates killed off speedily all criminals could be taken off the street. In practice, as all who work in the system know, these changes would be minor and have little systematic impact on crime or the effectiveness of criminal justice policies. For the public which knows how the system works from anecdotal cases and stereotyped cop-shows, such imagery hits the right note. Yet the promise made—crime will decrease and you will be safer— cannot be delivered. . . .

Masking Social Problems with Myth

Crime control bureaucracies consume an ever expanding amount of social resources as they widen their sphere of influence and modify their missions to fit organizational and political goals. Such enforcement policies serve to burden an already overtaxed criminal justice system and mask other social problems. We have noted that fear develops based on the notion of victimization by strangers or persons different from ourselves. Children are abducted by strangers. Criminals prowl our city streets. Organized crime is controlled and operated by foreign-born nationals having little allegiance to our way of life. Homosexuals and drug users carry with them the AIDS virus and threaten criminal justice personnel with infection. Serial murderers prowl looking for innocent victims to slay, and police officers are under assault from criminals. Such characterizations of crime, criminals and the criminal justice system, as we have seen, have little basis in the reality of crime and justice in modern American society, but they are real to the public.

People fear walking the streets; car doors are locked as we enter dangerous parts of the city; we avoid contact with strangers and generally withdraw from society. Fear of victimization and social isolation begins a downward spiral that can produce more crime, more victimization, and more myth. As we remove ourselves from the street and isolate ourselves from the concerns of others in our communities, we abandon society and its real problems. We are no longer willing to become involved in our communities, much less in real crime prevention and the workings of the criminal justice system. We leave matters of justice to the mythmakers.

Government officials are free to spawn myths of crime and justice and to waste valuable resources on ineffective crime control practices that expand the crime control industry. One of the latest attempts to expand law enforcement and government control involves computers. FBI agents arrested 20-year-old Jake Baker at the University of Michigan for posting a fictitious story on the Internet entitled, "Pamela's Ordeal." The story described the gruesome torture, rape and murder of a woman by two men. Because he used the name of a student in one of his classes and because he used interstate communication to transmit the story, Baker spent a month in a federal prison cell. Baker was indicted for violating Section 875(c) of the U.S. Criminal Code: "Whoever transmits in interstate or foreign commerce any communication containing any threat to kidnap any person or any threat to injure the person of another shall be fined not more than $1,000 or imprisoned not more than 5 years, or both." Bond was originally denied because the judge had a "gut feeling that he wouldn't want his daughter out on the streets if Baker were set free" (Lowenstein, 1995:1). Although Baker was charged with an existing statute, the Internet offers fertile ground for mythmakers. It is an unknown territory, and "people typically react to new communication technologies by trying to reign them in" (Lowenstein, 1995:1). Sen. James Exon (D-Neb.) has introduced a bill to regulate obscenity and indecency on computer communication networks that would hold providers of network services criminally liable for transmission of indecent messages. The FBI is currently lobbying Congress for unrestricted access to the information superhighway.

When crime control policy is developed based on myth or misconception, it has the effect of diverting resources and attention from real social problems. It is far easier to report issues like child abduction or stalkings than to present threats of an infinitely larger potential but decidedly more technical nature. Child abductions, stalkings, and child abuse can be immediately condensed into a personal, dramatic package which touches on universally held values. It is excruciatingly painful to read the details of a young mother killed by her ex-husband despite asking the police for help. There is immediate identification with her tragedy and an intense desire to have prevented the harm. Yet despite our emotions, to varying extents, each of the crime myths we have considered in this book blinds us to social problems of greater magnitude and consequence. When vast social resources are expended to hunt down mythical criminals, prevent stranger abductions of children or investigate foreign-born organized crime figures, resources are consumed that could be used to study and to control real social problems. While we have diverted and are continuing to divert enormous sums of public money to law enforcement and corrections, we are failing to deal with basic problems that impact directly on crime in American society. Consider Sam Walker's (1994:8–9) remarks on the plight of urban America:

> neighborhoods suffered a complete economic disaster in the 1980s. The number of manufacturing jobs in the cities—the traditional route out of poverty for older immigrant groups—declined drastically. New York City lost 520,000 manufacturing jobs between 1967 and 1987; Chicago lost 326,000 manufacturing jobs in the same period. On top of this social services were cut. Aid to Families with Dependent Children (AFDC) programs reached fewer families, and the average payment fell steadily below the government's own poverty line.

> Federal aid for low-income housing fell by 67 percent in the 1980s, helping to create a new crisis in homelessness. Federal revenue-sharing funds for cities disappeared completely, as did urban development action grants. Employment and training funds declined 70 percent.

Not only have we been irresponsibly throwing public dollars at crime-control solutions that have no chance of working, but we have, in the process, increased the amount of social misery and desperation in the country enormously.

> We know that poverty, slums and unemployment are sources of street crime. We do not know if (or how) they cause crimes, because we know that many, if not most, poor unemployed slum-dwellers do not engage in street crime. Yet to say that this means we do not know that such conditions increase the likelihood of an individual resorting to violent crime is like saying that we do not know that a bullet in the head is deadly because some people survive . . . (Reiman, 1990:23–24).

Professor Reiman points us in the right direction;, we know that social inequality and social disorganization is a stimulant to street crime. Unlike the alchemy of those suggesting more police and stiffer punishment combined with those suggesting biological, psychological, or moral weakness as causes of crime, the evidence is compelling and overwhelming that the root of crime is to be found in the soil of social and economic desperation that are masked by crime mythology. Consider the following:

- More than 50 million Americans live in poverty (Wilson, 1991).

- The criminological research demonstrates that inequity, poverty, feelings of alienation, and community social disorganization explain inner-city crimes rates (Bursik, 1988; Rainwater, 1970).

- The percentage of people living in poverty and the percentage of families no longer intact is strongly correlated to neighborhood crime rates (Messner and Tardiff, 1986).

- A study of gang homicide in Chicago demonstrated that delinquency and homicide rates correlated with the percentage of the neighborhood living below the poverty line, the lack of mortgage investment in the neighborhood, and the unemployment rate (Curry and Spergel, 1988).

- Violent crime has been linked to neighborhood employment levels (Menard and Elliott, 1990; McGahey, 1986).

- Crime rates and particularly violent crime rates are directly connected to income inequality, particularly in communities where the very poor live in close proximity to the comfortable (Blau and Blau, 1982; Block, 1979).

- Income inequality is highly correlated with crime rates (Rosenfeld, 1985).

The preponderance of the evidence is clear: economic inequality, poverty, unemployment and underemployment and relative deprivation are stimulants to crime in American society. They are also the most neglected and masked aspects of crime control policy. Without belaboring the argument further, it should be amply clear that our priorities are in the wrong place and our punitive response to mythical crime is a social disaster.

Because of crime myths we overlook other broader, underlying social problems like teenage runaways, children abused at the hands of their relatives, and the crime "organized" in corporate board rooms and governmental offices across the country. We wage wars against inanimate objects such as drugs and pornography as if they have a life of their own—without considering the supply- and-demand equation and the spin-off crimes caused by waging crime wars and criminalizing behavior. Consider just a few of the questions and problems that are masked when we focus on mythical crime.

- What is the real extent of crime in America?
- Why do children run away from their parents?
- Why is law enforcement unable to deal with crime?
- What is the magnitude and cost of corporate crime?
- How many deaths are associated with drugs like alcohol and tobacco?
- What spin-off crimes are caused by the drug war?
- Can we reduce AIDS by implementing drug education programs?
- Are injuries caused by the government's drug crop eradication programs?
- How much corruption of governmental officials results from drug criminalization?
- Is there true equity in our courts?
- What percentage of the public demands vice-related services and products?

- Is there a symbiotic relationship between government and corporate crime?
- Who pays the $231 billion dollar price tag of corporate and white collar crime?
- What are the vested interests of the criminal justice industry?

For the past century, social scientists have researched and argued the "causes" of crime. The debate has ranged from the sublime to the ridiculous, from the slope of one's forehead and the spacing of one's eyes to the alleged moral inferiority of some of the residents of our inner-cities. No one has isolated a cause of crime. This is, of course, not surprising. Crime is a socially constructed event created by many social processes interacting over time and space. Unfortunately, crime myths also serve to undermine the scientific study and treatment of crime. Crime myths change our perception and understanding of crime and criminal behavior by offering up simplistic solutions to complex problems. Crime myths are often "quests for evil." They sometimes use simplistic and even supernatural explanations for crime to the detriment of scientific understanding. This is especially the case in crimes that have been characterized as predatory. When crime is characterized as evil, rehabilitation is rejected in favor of harsh punishment including death. Less sensational, but equal in effect, is the characterization of criminal behavior as a product of freely chosen behavior. When the causal and social bases of crime are rejected, punishment becomes the logical social response. Legal prescriptions are used to treat the symptoms of social problems and science is relegated to crime detection and criminal profiling rather than understanding crime and its social causes. Offenders are stereotyped as pathological and violent, and their behavior is analyzed from a simplistic prey-predator paradigm. Challenges to the scientific study of crime often alter the empirical reality of crime. The restructured study of crime begins to mirror our mythical conceptions of crime by providing more "evidence" that is tainted by a detection, apprehension, and control paradigm of criminology.

Unfortunately, myths of crime and justice are not put to rest with the same vigor with which they are created. Debunking myths does not have the same attraction as does their construction. After clear definitions of criminal behavior have been developed and the actual frequency of the crime has been determined, there are few newspaper accounts, television documentaries, commercials, or calls by political leaders to demystify our images of crime. Often, all that exists in the aftermath of a crime myth are criminal law, more cops, harsher punishments, misplaced social resources, a feeling of moral superiority, and growing intolerance for human diversity.

We hope this text has challenged you to view crime myths with a critical eye—to think about the origin of issues and to watch for patterns of myth construction. Myths can only be challenged by critically processing information. Critical thinking must develop alternative filters through which to sift myths—questions must be posed, stories must be challenged and simple solutions must be questioned. We must begin to ask: Who is the mythmaker? What is the mythmaker's motivation? What group is being targeted by the myth? What behavior is being targeted for control and why? Most importantly we must ask: What are the consequences of waging war against mythical crime?

Sources

Baker, J. (1991). Los Angeles Aftershocks. *Newsweek*, (April 1): 18–19.

Beck, A. (1992). Murderous Obsession. *Newsweek*, (July 13): 60.

Beck, A. and Shipley, R. (1987). Recidivism of Young Parolees. *Bureau of Justice Statistics Special Report*. Washington, DC: U.S. Government Printing Office.

Blau, J. and Blau, P. (1982). The Cost of Inequality: Metropolitan Structure and Violent Crime. *American Sociological Review* 147:114–29.

Block, R. (1979). Community Environment and Violent Crime. *Criminology* 17:647–73.

Brott, A. (1995). Major Reworking of Child Abuse Law. *Chicago Tribune*, (February 1): 10.

Bursik, R. (1988). Social Disorganization and Theories of Crime and Delinquency: Problems and Prospects. Criminology 26:521–39.

Cook, P. (1980). Research in Criminal Deterrence: Laying the Groundwork for a Second Decade. In *Crime and Justice: An Annual Review of Research*, vol. 2, N. Morris and M. Tonry, M. (eds.). Chicago: University of Chicago Press, 211–68.

Curry, G. and Spergel, I. (1988). Gang Homicide, Delinquency and the Community. *Criminology* 26:381–407.

Dawsey, D. and Malnic, E. (1989). Actress Rebecca Schaeffer Fatally Shot at Apartment. *LA Times*, (July 19): 1.

Gottfredson, D., Neithercutt, M., Nuffield, J., and O'Leary, V. (1973). Four Thousand Lifetimes: A Study of Time Served and Parole Outcomes. *Law and Contemporary Problems* 41.

Greenberg, D. (1975). The Incapacitative Effects of Imprisonment: Some Estimates. *Law and Society Review* 9:541–80.

Greenfield, L. (1985). Examining Recidivism. *Bureau of Justice Statistics Special Report*. Washington, DC: U.S. Government Printing Office.

Jenkins, P. and Katkin, D. (1988). Protecting Victims of Child Sexual Abuse: A Case for Caution. *Prison Journal* 58(2): 25–35.

Leavitt, P. (1993). Tennis Coach Was Stalking Suspect. *USA Today*, (April 28): 3A.

Livingston, J. (1992). *Crime and Criminology*. Englewood Cliffs, NJ: Prentice-Hall.

Lowenstein, J. (1995). How Free Is Speech in Cyberspace? *Chicago Tribune*, (March 12), sec. 4:1

Marenin, O. (1991). Making a Tough Job Tougher: The Legacy of Conservatism. *ACJS Today* 10(2): 1, 17, 19.

McGahey, R. (1986). Economic Conditions, Organization, and Urban Crime. In *Communities and Crime*, A. Reiss and M. Tonry (eds.). Chicago: University of Chicago Press: 231–70.

Menard, S. and Elliott, D. (1990). Self-Reported Offending, Maturational Reform, and the Easterlin Hypothesis. *Journal of Quantitative Criminology* 6:237–68.

Messner, S. and Tardiff, K. (1986). Economic Inequality and Levels of Homicide: An Analysis of Urban Neighborhoods. *Criminology* 24:297–317.

National Criminal Justice Association (1993). *Project to Develop a Model Anti-Stalking Code for States*. Washington, DC: National Institute of Justice.

New York Times New Service (1995). Wanted Poster: Texan Offer $5,000 Bounty for Killing Criminals. *Chicago Tribune*, (February 12): 26

Puente, D. (1992). Legislators Tackling the Terror of Stalking. *USA Today*, (January 21): 9A.

Rainwater, L. (1970). *Behind Ghetto Walls: Black Families in a Federal Slum*. Chicago: Aldine.

Reiman, J. (1995). *The Rich Get Richer and the Poor Get Prison*, 4th ed. Boston: Allyn and Bacon.

_____ (1990) *The Rich Get Richer and the Poor Get Prison*, 3rd ed. Boston: Allyn and Bacon.

Rosenfeld, R. (1985). Urban Crime Rates: Effects of Inequality, Welfare Dependency, Region and Race. In *The Social Ecology of Crime*, J. Bryne and R. Sampson (eds.), pp. 975–91. New York: Springer Verlag.

Shannon, L. (1982). Reassessing the Relationship of Adult Criminal Careers to Juvenile Careers: A Summary. *Report for the U.S. Department of Justice*. Washington, DC.

Sohn, E. (1994). Antistalking Statutes: Do They Actually Protect Victims? *Criminal Law Bulletin* 13: 203–41.

Thomas, K. (1993). How to Stop the Stalker: State Antistalking Laws. *Criminal Law Bulletin* 12:124–36.

Walker, S. (1994). *Sense and Nonsense About Crime and Drugs*, 3rd ed. Belmont, CA: Wadsworth.

Williams, C. (1991). The Federal Death Penalty for Drug-Related Killings. *Criminal Law Bulletin* 27(5): 387–415.

Wilson, W. (1991). Studying Inner-City Social Dislocations: The Challenge of Public Agenda Research. *American Sociological Review* 56:1–14.
Wright, R. (1995). What Do 167 Deaths Justify? *Time*, (May 15): 86.

Index